Shawnee Pottery

THE FULL ENCYCLOPEDIA

With
Value Guide

Pamela Duvall Curran

77 Lower Valley Road, Atglen, PA 19310

Dedication

This book is dedicated to Bob Heckman, a skilled craftsman, and a true friend.
and
To my best friends, my family: George, Karen, Lynda, Mom, and Dad.

Library of Congress Cataloging-in-Publication Data

Curran, Pamela Duvall.
Shawnee pottery: the full encyclopedia with value guide
Pamela Duvall Curran.
p. cm.
Includes bibliographical references and index.
ISBN 0-88740-845-1 (hard)
1. Shawnee Pottery Company--Catalogs.
2. Pottery--20th century--Ohio--Zanesville--Catalogs. I. Title.
NK4210.S52A4 1995
738.3'09771'91--dc20 95-20256
CIP

Printed in China
ISBN: 0-88740-845-1

We are interested in hearing from authors with book ideas on related topics.

Published by Schiffer Publishing Ltd.
77 Lower Valley Road
Atglen, PA 19310
Please write for a free catalog.
This book may be purchased from the publisher.
Please include $2.95 postage.
Try your bookstore first.

CONTENTS

ACKNOWLEDGMENTS

Jody Kay Adam
Randy & Stephanie Adrian
Don & De Anderson
Louise Elizabeth Bauer
Terry & Sandra Bauer
Arthur & Rita Bee
Robert Bettinger
Sue Blodgett
John F. Bonistall
Katherine Braly
Ron Brown
Tom & Kathy Bulmer
Donna Buster
Robert & Kathy Chema
Patricia Claar
Lillian Cole
Joe & Florence Cristiano
Toni Crittenden
George W. Curran
Joseph Devine
Mercedes DiRenzo
Terry Donnelly
Harvey Duke
Robert & Lois Duvall
Sharon Figura
Melvin & Jean Gibson
Donna Gilbert
Robert & Linda Giles
Richard & Linda Guffey
Ryan Guffey
Tom & Debbie Hartwig
Robert & Pauline Heckman
Michael & Sharon Helmke
Myrt Holland
Burnita Illing
Lanny & Shawn Jones
Pat & Elaine Jones
Tyler Jones
Tim & Sandy Kightlinger
Juan Klinehoffer
Barbara Knoblauch
Shirley Legum
Hughy & Chris Mahloch
Elizabeth McConnell
James & Vivian McDuffie
Linda McPherson
Ralph Meranto
Ray & Robin Morrisey
Marvin Mulligan
Linda M. Nelson
James Novonglosky
Nita Parentice
Dolores Rains
Linda Romberg
Karen Lynn Schaffer
Lynda Marie Schaffer
Norris Schneider
Paul & Joy Schneider
Jerry Schueller
Richard S. Schweiker
Tony & Evadne Serra
Paul & Linda Spenst
Carl Stickland
Mark & Ellen Supnick
Joyce Swanson
Jessie A. Turbayne
Bernard Twiggs
Eleanor Twiggs
Francis & Judy VanHooser
Art Voorhees
Dennis & Patricia Walsh
Lea West
George L. Williams
Robert & Betty Winning

My greatest fear is to forget to publicly thank somebody who helped in some way with the compilation of this book. If I do so, it is inadvertent and sincerely regretted.

This book was a massive team effort, with contributions coming in from Shawnee collectors and former employees in virtually every corner of the United States. My sincere gratitude is extended to those who wrapped and shipped small fortunes in pottery; those who spent countless dollars and hours cleaning, rearranging, and photographing pottery; those who patiently re-photographed pottery; those who rushed to send pictures of a new find, so that it could be included in this book; those, like Joe, who kept turning up the wonderful new finds so that I could photograph them; and those who worked at Shawnee Pottery so many years ago and have shared their knowledge and experiences with us.

A very special thank you ... and I mean special .... goes to Robert and Pauline Heckman, who opened up a whole new vision of Shawnee Pottery to me. This book would not be what it is without their extraordinary commitment and participation. More than anything else, Bob and Pauline wanted to bring recognition to many of the truly talented and dedicated people whose efforts made Shawnee Pottery a respected leader in the pottery field.

Thank you to John F. Bonistall, George L. Williams, Bernard E. Twiggs, Louise Elizabeth Bauer, Mrs. Siegfried W. Illing, Mrs. Jess Parentice, Mrs. Mack Holland, Robert and Kathy Chema, and Richard S. Schweiker. All of you, or your loved ones, were there so many years ago. I appreciate, and will always cherish, the personal memories you have shared with us.

Several of the finest Shawnee collections in this country were photographed for this book, and collectors everywhere should appreciate what the owners went through. I will always treasure the wonderful hospitality and friendship of Richard and Linda Guffey, Paul and Joy Schneider, and Melvin and Jean Gibson. For days, all semblance of their normal daily life came to a virtual standstill, while pottery was moved, looked for, pulled out, unpacked, compared with, carried downstairs, carried upstairs, carried outdoors, carried indoors, photographed, and then put away. If retakes were needed, the whole process began again, with each move increasing the chances for damage to some very valuable and irreplaceable pottery. Thank you all for some memorable experiences, and for sharing your wonderful collections with all of us!

Several other collections are well-represented in this book also, and my sincere gratitude is extended to Sharon & Michael Helmke, Linda Romberg, Terry & Sandra Bauer, Linda Spenst, and Marvin Mulligan. You all responded above and beyond the call of duty, and I am grateful for your help.

Special thank you to Rich and Linda Guffey and family, whose friendship I will always treasure. You are true collectors who love the pottery, and have a remarkable eye and feel for Shawnee, and you have provided me with some of my most cherished Shawnee. Right up to the very last minute, you were taking pictures of new discoveries and finds for inclusion in this book. Thank you from the bottom of my heart.

Thank you Peter Schiffer for your confidence in my abilities, and your patience with my schedules.

Thank you to Jessie Turbayne, whose one telephone call managed to increase my workload and stress, and decrease my sleep time, for the next two years. It was worth it, and I truly appreciate your friendship.

Thank you to Mark Supnick, for your friendship and support, especially during those early years. I counted on you, and you were always there for me, and for Shawnee collectors everywhere.

Thank you to Joyce Roerig, for your friendship and encouragement. Like you and Fred, I want to give the best that can be given to collectors.

Thank you Harvey Duke, for your friendship and honest guidance. You have taught me that the word "assume" has no place in a writer's vocabulary.

Thank you to my father and mother, Robert and Lois Duvall, who soon joined me in my love for Shawnee pottery. After all, it was a childhood Smiley Pig pitcher in our home that prompted me to fall in love with Shawnee. Going "back home" to visit is all the more wonderful, with your home full of smiling Shawnee faces, and your willingness to head out in search for more. I am deeply grateful for the help you have given me in making this book a reality.

Thank you to my two daughters, Karen Schaffer and Lynda Schaffer, who have spent countless hours helping me with this book. Preparing patent reports, cross-referencing photo and position numbers, proofreading text, and labeling negatives until our eyesight blurred is hardly the way you envisioned your days off from regular work schedules. I sincerely appreciate the love and support you have both given me, and yes, I am thrilled when a favorite piece of Shawnee pottery ends up in your homes.

Thank you to my husband, George, who has always been a willing helper and companion, and has encouraged me to pursue my dreams. Long ago, you resigned yourself to living with a serious collector, understanding my need to search for yet more Shawnee, while wondering where in the world I'd put it! My work on this book or my newsletter, often finds you getting up in the morning and discovering me at my computer, right where I was when you said "Good Night".

So my very special thanks are reserved for those I love most; George, Karen, Lynda, Mom, and Dad. You have all, at one time or another, helped me prepare the Shawnee newsletter for mailing, helped me in some special way with this book, admired my pottery, traveled with me to search far and wide for another piece for my collection, and just understood what the Shawnee excitement was all about. I love you!

Preface

My first introduction to Shawnee Pottery was a *Smiley Pig* pitcher that was a part of my childhood memories. Our Smiley Pig had a red neckerchief and a beautiful embossed clover blossom on his fat little rump, and we poured summertime lemonade out of his open mouth. His eyes were closed, he had a contented smile on his face, and he seemed happy to be at the dinner table with us. During the winter Smiley disappeared onto the top shelf of a high cupboard (or so it seemed to a small child), waiting for the summer months of serving ice cold lemonade.

As a baby boomer growing up in a typical '40s and '50s household in a quiet New Hampshire city, I loved going to my grandparents farm, just a short walk down the road from home. My country roots where there were pigs, cows, horses, chickens, roosters, cats, and dogs, had a significant influence on my eventual love for Shawnee Pottery.

Once I became aware of Shawnee Pottery as a collectible, and had purchased my first book on the subject (Mark Supnick's *Collecting Shawnee Pottery* of course), I soon realized that I needed to know more. I wanted to know WHO made these adorable pieces of pottery, WHEN exactly were they made, WHAT did they cost when brand new, and most important of all .... HOW MANY other collectors were wandering around out there looking for Shawnee too.

My curiosity soon sent me down a road I would never have envisioned only a few short years ago. I found myself placing ads in newspapers and magazines actually seeking people who wanted to join me in a collectors' club to learn more about Shawnee Pottery! My astonishment at the response I received soon turned into a realization that I was in this for keeps.

Because of a lifelong hearing impairment, the written word has always been extremely important to me. Reading was a passion for me: books, magazines, newspapers, billboards, street signs, etc. If it was there, I read it for fear of missing something. There is a tendency to believe that what is written is truth. It came as a total shock to me, therefore, that so much of what had been written about the history of the Shawnee Pottery Company has turned out to be incorrect. Therefore, when you read the text about the history of the company, it may occur to many of you that I have in fact *rewritten* the history of Shawnee Pottery. I have checked, cross-checked, referenced, cross-referenced, talked to, written to, begged, cajoled, borrowed, bought, and listened ..... in order to bring together the people, catalogs, and information needed, to make this the most accurate and comprehensive book that you could possibly have in your library of Shawnee references.

For five years before the publication of this book, I have published (and continue to publish) a newsletter about the products and the people of the Shawnee Pottery Company. My greatest thrill was when someone would say to me, "Oh, I know someone who worked at Shawnee!". A name or telephone number would often lead me on an incredible journey back a half a century to the time when Shawnee was in production. Slowly, a whole new picture was developing about the history of the pottery, its' products, and its' personnel.

Never before have so many people who played key roles in Shawnee's history come together to provide so much accurate and previously unpublished information for one book. I am proud to be a part of one more chapter in the history of Shawnee; one in which we give recognition to the many talented and innovative employees at Shawnee Pottery!

SECTION I

INTRODUCTION

The Shawnee Pottery Company was a large corporation controlled by shareholders whose main concerns were to make their investment profitable. Very little information about the operation and products of the company was preserved with one individual or group, unlike some family-owned American potteries where information has been kept in the family domain. Making contact with key personnel spanning each of the decades in which Shawnee operated, was crucial to the research of Shawnee. Recording the events and changes at Shawnee was like putting together a huge puzzle, with pieces slowly falling into place.

As you read this book and admire the pottery, you will begin to understand that Shawnee's production methods could be broken down into three distinctive eras.

The first era was the pre-and-early World War II years. During this time Shawnee mainly produced kitchenware, utilitarian items, console sets, teapots, coffeepots, planters, figurines, flower bowl inserts, jardinieres, other miscellaneous, and Valencia dinnerware. Almost without exception, this early ware was produced in solid colors. Often, the only added decoration was cold paint applied to eyes, ears, noses, etc. on items such as figural planters and figurines. In time, most of this cold paint wore or washed off, leaving these pieces looking somewhat plain.

The second era included the later World War II years of limited production, yet improved methods of decorating, and lasting into the mid 1950s. Shawnee produced today's most collectible lines during this time: notably, their figural cookie jars, teapots, pitchers, creamers, salt & pepper shakers, and the highly collectible Corn King dinnerware line. The popularity of Disney influenced many of the planters and figurines made at this time. Decoration was done either by hand painting or spray painting the item, or a combination of the two, then glazing and firing it. This underglaze decoration did not wear off with the passing of time or the cleaning of the item.

The final era from late 1954 to 1961 saw Shawnee making needed changes in order to survive in a competitive market. Figural pieces requiring hand and spray decorating were too expensive to produce. Mr. John F. Bonistall became President and General Manager, and changed over most production to the Corn Queen dinnerware line and floral ware. Typical of this era are the non-figural planters, vases, and window boxes, as well as ashtrays, bathroom accessories, clocks, and more. The floral ware lines were very successful, as they utilized the techniques and textures that had made Shawnee famous.

My goal is to give you a renewed respect and admiration for the pottery and the people who made it. Shawnee Pottery was a leader in their field, and they constantly strived to improve and perfect their products. They were considered innovators, by developing newer more modern techniques, by developing unique textures and finishes unknown in the manufacture of mass-produced pottery at that time, by employing successful and innovative marketing techniques, by using automation more than any of their competitors, and by hiring the best key personnel available. Designers, ceramic engineers, mold and die makers, sales and marketing reps, and company officers were all regarded as the most promising in their fields. Factory workers were time studied and given the opportunity to earn bonus pay for increased piece work, a first in the pottery industry at that time. Wages, supplemented by piece work pay, greatly reduced employee turnover. It was no accident that Shawnee produced the highest quality product in their price range.

A fair number of items in this book, positively identified as having been made at Shawnee pottery, have appeared in books on other potteries. Great pains were taken to verify everything pictured in this book, though I soon realized that was an impossible task. Not every item produced by Shawnee has been so well-documented as to have appeared in their catalogs; that would have made a tough job too easy. However, if I doubted the validity of an item, I chose not to picture it until further research erased all doubts, though I have come to the realization that we will probably never be able to positively catalog all of the Shawnee pottery out there.

Shawnee pottery has arrived, and will continue to delight collectors for many years. One of the best features of collecting Shawnee is that if you can't afford to buy the higher priced items such as cookie jars, you can still find many lower priced pieces that can tickle your fancy. Miniature vases and jugs, animal figurines, vases, figural planters, salt & pepper shakers, Corn dinnerware, and the 1950s floral ware are some specific areas of collecting that entice the Shawnee collector today.

Condition and Value

Prices listed in this guide have been compiled using a variety of methods and information, taking into account that geographic location and collector density in an area often determine quoted and paid prices. It's the simple rule of supply and demand .... if there is a large collector population in a given area, then higher prices will prevail. Areas where there are fewer collectors, therefore lower demand, will often see prices in the low range.

Prices are a necessary evil in books such as this, and are the single most-scrutinized feature. We always worry that we paid too much for a piece of pottery .... OR .... that we passed on what was a deal of a lifetime because we thought a price was too high. The next couple of guidelines should be memorized:

No price should *ever* be considered as a hard-and-fast rule....only as a guideline to help you decide whether to buy or not buy an item.

All prices are based upon the item represented being in excellent condition, with no chips, hairlines, cracks, staining, or crazing. Another factor is coloration: whether a piece is neatly, not carelessly, decorated; whether the colors are bright, not faded; whether the original cold paint is still present on the piece, not worn off.

Completely intact, not partial, original labels often indicate that an item has not been used, and generally, collectors are willing to pay a slightly higher price for a labeled item.

Gold trim and floral decals add a value of 50% to 100% to an item, depending upon the item. Cookie jars are typical of the 100% category, while small planters typically are in the 50% category.

Ironically, most gold trim and decal decorations were added to the original Shawnee products that did not meet Shawnee's strict quality control standards. These 'seconds' were often sold in quantity to outside decorators who covered flaws in the pottery with gold trim, fired-on decals, hand-painted flowers, bugs, bees, butterflies, hair, patches, etc., and then sold them to higher priced gift shops and stores.

Professional repair to pottery is another controversial issue. Some collectors prefer to have higher-value pottery repaired so that it looks nice on display. Other collectors despise any kind of repair, and love their pottery despite the "battle scars". I prefer to think of repaired pottery as still damaged, but with a higher investment. Personally, I like to see exactly what I am buying, with no cover-up repairs that may wash away later (this has been known to happen). If pottery has been repaired, it should always be represented as repaired when you are selling it....no exceptions!

One final note in regard to prices: they are intended only as a guideline. No matter what the collectible, there will always be those exorbitant prices paid in the heat of auction bidding, or when money is burning a hole in your pocket. The threat of going home empty-handed can prompt even the most astute collector to overspend on occasion. Hopefully, the scales are balanced with an occasional yard sale or flea market bargain. Part of the fun of collecting is the challenge of keeping that price scale balanced!

Is it Shawnee?

One of the decisions that Shawnee Pottery collectors must make individually is whether to collect lines of pottery that may have been produced in the plant, but marketed by specific customers. Two examples come to mind.

The most important are the designs produced for George Rumrill, a jobber, of Little Rock, Arkansas. Mr. Rumrill approached Shawnee Pottery around April of 1938 and engaged them to produce art ware for him to his design specifications. There is evidence that designer Louise Elizabeth Bauer also created designs while at Shawnee, which were then incorporated into Rumrill's lines, and marketed under the RumRill label.

The difficult question is how do we know exactly which pieces were made at Shawnee for Rumrill? He had many other potteries produce for him, one of which was Red Wing Pottery of Minnesota. In addition, certain designs, shapes, and sizes of pieces that appear in the RumRill catalogs, have also turned up in the Shawnee Pottery catalogs of the same era. So, once the original labels, if any were affixed, have been washed off, how do we know if that item was marketed as Shawnee or RumRill? Or made at Shawnee or Red Wing, or anywhere else? So the question is whether Shawnee collectors can first identify, and then want to categorize, this pottery as Shawnee, and ultimately invest money in it.

The second example is drawing the line on items produced for the Great Northern Company of Merchandise Mart in Chicago, Illinois. Indications are that Great Northern was a large distributor of "private label" lines, which they then marketed under their own name. Shawnee obviously created the Dutch Boy and Dutch Girl cookie jars, with design changes, for Great Northern to market under their name. We also feel that the Sugar Bucket marked Great Northern was produced by Shawnee, along with Dutch Boy & Girl salt and pepper shakers. But not all items found marked with the Great Northern name should be assumed to have been produced by Shawnee. I feel that considerably more research into this area is needed before decisions are made to attribute more Great Northern pieces to manufacture by Shawnee.

Continuing the Search

Shawnee Pottery collectors are invited to submit photographs or related information to the author for evaluation and possible inclusion in future updates of this publication.

Information and examples of additional colors and decorations of any known piece of Shawnee Pottery are welcome. Inquiries about pottery that might possibly have been made at Shawnee are also encouraged, for how else would we learn about new discoveries!

Any reproductions and/or tampered-with Shawnee Pottery found by collectors should be photographed and reported, in order to keep the public informed.

Please address all inquiries, photographs, or information to the author. A business size self-addressed stamped envelope is requested for any expected replies and return of photographs.

Pamela D. Curran
P. O. Box 713
New Smyrna Beach, FL 32170-0713

Section II: History

Chapter 1: Shawnee Pottery History & Photographs

The Shawnee Pottery Company was incorporated in the State of Delaware on December 9, 1936, listing an address of 100 West Tenth Street, Wilmington, Delaware.

Two days later, December 11, 1936, Shawnee Pottery Company signed an agreement with the Ohio Encaustic Company to lease the former American Encaustic Tile plant at 2200 Linden Avenue, Zanesville, Ohio.

The Shawnee Prospectus declared that the annual meetings would be held on the third Wednesday of March of each year, at the Wilmington, Delaware address. Fiscal year is the calendar year.

A mid-1930s aerial view of the American Encaustic Tile buildings in Zanesville, Ohio, situated between Linden Avenue and the Muskingum River. When the Shawnee Pottery Company purchased this property, they removed some of the dilapidated buildings, and twenty-two of the twenty-five periodic kilns. The periodic kilns were the cone-like extensions seen above the roofs of various buildings.

Before Shawnee .... There Was A. E. Tile

A. E. Tile had begun in 1874 on Hughes Street in Zanesville, but moved to a second facility in 1879 on the Marietta Road. By 1890 there was need for a larger plant, and A. E. was considering moving all operations to their New Jersey plant. Zanesville residents did not want to face the impending unemployment, so the city held a special election on March 9, 1890, and approved a bond issue to meet special demands that would keep A. E. Tile in Zanesville.

The city gave A. E. Tile thirty-five (35) acres of land outside the city limits; $10,000 for developing natural gas; free water and gas mains; and adequate railroad facilities.

Completed at a cost of nearly a million dollars, American Encaustic Tiling Co. Ltd. held the official grand opening of their new 2200 Linden Avenue plant on April 19, 1892. Ohio Governor William McKinley delivered the main address to an estimated twenty thousand people who had arrived for the dedication. A beautiful four-inch square blue souvenir Dedication Tile was presented to attendees.

A. E. Tile Works Dedication Tile.

Essentially a self-sufficient operation, A. E. Tile consisted of fifty-seven (57) detached buildings, built mainly of brick, ranging from one to three stories high. The office building housed general offices, executive offices, consulting rooms, ventilated fireproof vaults, dining room, kitchen, showroom, and supply rooms.

Other buildings on the property housed: raw clays; clay processing area; drying kilns; press room; seggar making room; tile drying rooms; bisque kilns; sorting rooms; glazing rooms and kilns; glaze grinding mills; ware sorting rooms; decorating, packing, shipping, designing, and drafting departments; cooperage; machine shop; blacksmith; and carpentry, painting, tinsmithing, plumbing, and steam-fitting shops; also a power plant, hospital, and a post office branch.

In the late 1920s, over one thousand people worked in this plant; by 1935 it sat vacant and idle in the midst of the Great Depression.

The Schweiker's of Pennsylvania

Frontrunners in the organization of the Shawnee Pottery Company were two brothers named Malcolm A. Schweiker and Roy W. Schweiker. Graduates of the eminent Williamson Trade School in Media, Pennsylvania, both men were in the building trades in the 1920s, when they were faced with difficulty in obtaining ceramic tiles. Malcolm Schweiker had worked for a year or two as superintendent in a floor and wall tile company, and the brothers concluded that they could produce ceramic tile as well as anyone else. They amassed a working capital of $55,000 and founded the Franklin Tile Company in October of 1923, in Lansdale, Pennsylvania. Malcolm was a natural-born engineer, and he personally designed the kiln and other equipment for straight-line production at Franklin, as well as managed the business end of things. Roy's talents lay with carpentry, the production, and marketing of the company's products.

Malcolm A. Schweiker.
February 27, 1895 - June 12, 1982.
1973 photo

A. E. Tile....A Company In Trouble

During the Great Depression, A. E. Tile had suffered tremendous operating losses due to the drop in building construction. A. E. Tile had sold off three of their plants in order to meet financial obligations, leaving two plants operating: one in Perth Amboy, New Jersey, and one at 2200 Linden Avenue, Zanesville, Ohio. By 1935, A. E. Tile was forced to close the Zanesville plant, leaving Perth Amboy as their only operating establishment. A. E. Tile was perilously close to failing completely, when the Reconstruction Finance Corporation stepped in and reorganized the company in federal courts, renaming it the American Encaustic Tiling Company, Inc. At the time of the reorganization in 1936 in New York, the R.F.C. invited Malcolm Schweiker of Franklin Tile to step in and help turn the company around, as Franklin Tile was growing and prospering during the depression. With Malcolm and Roy Schweiker holding about 75% of the stock, Franklin Tile acquired interest in A. E. Tiling Co., Inc., along with about 1500 stockholders who had been issued new stock. Franklin Tile then renovated the A. E. Tile plant in Perth Amboy, New Jersey, and were operating there by fall of 1936. In addition, when American Encaustic Tiling Co., Inc. was reorganized, Malcolm A. Schweiker resigned as the President of Franklin Tile (though he retained his seat on the board) and became the President of the new A. E. Tile. Roy W. Schweiker, who had been Executive Vice President of Franklin Tile, moved up to become president after his brother resigned.

Ohio Encaustic Company was formed as a wholly owned subsidiary of the new American Encaustic Tiling Co., Inc., with its' only asset being the now-closed plant at 2200 Linden Avenue in Zanesville, Ohio.

Shawnee's Financing and Production Plans

On December 11, 1936, the Shawnee Pottery Company signed a five-year lease with Ohio Encaustic for the property at 2200 Linden Avenue, Zanesville, Ohio. This was sealed with an initial $1,000 payment. Included was an agreement that Shawnee Pottery had rights to purchase the property on or before June 15, 1937, with certain terms and conditions to be met. Application was made for Shawnee, a Delaware corporation, to have authority to do business in Ohio.

An important restrictive covenant between Ohio Encaustic and A. E. Tiling with Shawnee Pottery Company, was that Shawnee would not engage in the manufacture or sale of floor or wall tile at any time during their operation on this property, effective for a period of 25 years. This was to prevent any competition with Franklin Tile's primary production.

The aggregate price to Shawnee Pottery Company for the property at 2200 Linden Avenue was $185,000, with the breakdown as follows: $50,000 down payment at closing; $100,000 first mortgage on the buildings, which would mature on or before December 31, 1941; $35,000 to purchase machinery and equipment. The interest rate was 5% per annum on the unpaid principal balance, with two payments due per year, on June 30 and December 31. Engineering services provided by A. E. Tile would also cost an additional $15,000 to Shawnee. A. E. Tile would assist Shawnee in planning and altering their plant for straight flow pottery production. Improvements and alterations to the property would cost another estimated $15,000.

Early photo of the Shawnee Pottery property, taken from the south end, looking northward on Linden Avenue.

This property consisted of most, if not all, of the original fifty-seven buildings built on thirty-five acres with nine-tenths of a mile frontage on Linden Ave. The rear of the property abutted the right of way to the Wheeling and Lake Erie Railroad. The buildings had floor space of approximately 650,000 sq. ft. (15 acres) with a two-story brick office building, and fireproof construction throughout including two large concrete record vaults. There were 25 periodic kilns, 22 of which would be removed as they served no purpose for Shawnee; three large Harrop car tunnel kilns (one 350' long, one 275' long); decorating kilns; and test kilns.

The arrangement of the three Harrop Car tunnel kilns made it possible for Shawnee to set up three complete manufacturing units, operable either separately or simultaneously. The tunnel kilns would operate continuously day and night, seven days per week, with shut-downs only for needed repairs. It was contemplated that manufacture would begin by operating only one unit initially, with the second and third units placed into production as sales increased.

The First Officers And Management

The first President, Chief Executive Officer, and General Manager at Shawnee Pottery was Addis Emmet Hull, Jr. of Zanesville, Ohio. Hull's five-year contract with Shawnee was signed in December of 1936, and was to terminate December 31, 1941. Hull was to resign as president and general manager of Hull Pottery of Crooksville, Ohio, no later than March 15, 1937. Because of his position at Hull Pottery, Addis Hull had devoted only part of his time and attention to the affairs of Shawnee since its incorporation in December of 1936. Addis Hull, Jr. had a degree in Ceramic Engineering from Ohio State University, and had been at the helm of Hull Pottery since the death of his father in 1930. Shawnee paid Mr. Hull an annual salary of $6,000 plus 5% of the net profits.

The first Vice-President and Treasurer (Chief Financial and Accounting Officer) was Robert C. Shilling of Zanesville, Ohio. Formerly, Mr. Shilling had been in full charge of manufacturing operations for the old A. E. Tile Co. Shilling drew a $4,000 annual salary.

The first Secretary for Shawnee was Ernest B. Graham of Zanesville, Ohio. Graham, a member of the Zanesville law firm of Graham & Graham, drew a $500 annual salary. Graham held this position throughout Shawnee's history.

The first Assistant Secretary (General Sales Manager) was J. Brannon Hull of Zanesville, Ohio. Brannon Hull was a brother of Addis E. Hull, Jr., and drew an annual salary of $3,600.

Directors listed for the new company were Addis E. Hull, Jr., W. Herbert Keller, and Robert C. Shilling. Persons who were to become directors were listed as Maurice Iserman of New York City, and Malcolm A. Schweiker of Montgomery County, Pennsylvania. Iserman was an attorney and friend of Malcolm Schweiker; Keller was a business partner of Schweiker's who produced red clay flower pots.

Employees Are Hired And Production Begins

On June 4, 1937, the Shawnee Pottery Company acquired the Linden Avenue property. The reopening of the old A. E. Tile plant in 1937 was welcomed by the people of Zanesville and surrounding area, many of whom had lost jobs during those bleak years of the Great Depression. Laborers were hired for the renovations and equipment set-up needed on the property before the manufacture of pottery could begin. Some dilapidated buildings, as well as twenty-two unneeded periodic kilns, were torn down. George C. Earle was the first plant superintendent, but only remained until production began. Then George Frauenfelter was brought in as superintendent, and he stayed on until around 1949.

One of the employees hired before the pottery opened was Siegfried W. Illing. Sieg was a young man who eventually worked his way up in the company, remaining there until it closed in 1961. Gertrude Trittipo, who had worked at A. E. Tile, became the Office Manager for the new company.

Siegfried W. Illing wearing white clothing and overalls at Shawnee Pottery. *1939± photo*

The first in-house designer hired at Shawnee was Louise Elizabeth Bauer, whose talents had caught the attention of Addis E. Hull. After four years of formal training, two of which were at the Columbus School of Art and Design, Louise had been doing design and modeling work for her father at the family-owned Bauer Studios in Zanesville, Ohio. Many of the early designs of teapots, vases, planters, and miniatures were the work of this talented woman.

Louise Elizabeth Bauer.
Birthdate: July 29, 1915.
1993 photo

Another early employee was Bernard E. Twiggs, who initially worked as a Block and Caser for six months. Bernard went on to become the Supervisor of the Mold and Die Room, remaining with Shawnee until they closed. Bernard's uncle, Clifford Twiggs, was also a long-time employee at Shawnee.

Bernard E. Twiggs, born September 5, 1904, remained at Shawnee as the Foreman of the Mold & Die Dept. until they closed.
1994 photo

Around July of 1937, with a full management and production team assembled, and with extensive renovations well underway, Shawnee released the following information and Letter of Introduction to the trade:

SHAWNEE POTTERY COMPANY

ZANESVILLE, OHIO

●

Works and Offices

LOCATION: One mile North of U. S. Routes 22 and 40 on Linden Avenue, Zanesville, Ohio.

FLOOR SPACE IN BUILDINGS: 650,000 sq. ft., or 15 acres.

KILN CAPACITY: Three large Harrop Car Tunnel Kilns, Periodic and Decorating Kilns.

PRODUCTIVE CAPACITY: 100,000 articles each working day.

SHIPPING FACILITIES: Wheeling and Lake Erie, Pennsylvania, Baltimore & Ohio, and New York Central Railroads. Numerous motor transportation companies operating to all parts of the United States.

SHAWNEE POTTERY COMPANY has been formed for the creation, the manufacture and the distribution of Earthenware products.

On June 4th the Company acquired the Zanesville, Ohio, plant of the American Encaustic Tiling Company, Inc. Among the assets purchased were the various formulae, research data and practical knowledge in Ceramic Art gained during many years of experience.

Since that time, new machinery and equipment have been purchased or constructed and are now being installed in the factory which is undergoing the alterations necessary to transform it into one of the most mechanically efficient and largest producers of Earthenware in the industry.

Ceramic engineers and designers have been engaged in research to produce the bodies, glazes, shapes and decorations that will be used. Unusual progress has been made in this work which is nearing completion. The body and glazes being developed will withstand extreme temperature changes. Resistance to heat and cold shock will extend beyond present standards for earthenware bodies and glazes. Glazes of varying texture will be produced in shades and tones of bright and pastel colors. Underglaze and overglaze decorations will be done by entirely new methods. The product will be light in weight and yet quite strong enough to meet all the requirements of hard usage in the home.

The policy of the company will be to develop a large volume of sales through broad consumer acceptance by creating and producing earthenware articles in a wide range of shapes and sizes, designed and styled in the modern mode, possessed of high quality and unusual durability, and sold at popular prices. The range of products to be manufactured will include useful Art Pottery; Bright Colored Dinnerware and Kitchenware; Lamp Bases; a large variety of specialties for ornamental purposes; specially designed products for packaging foods, chemicals and chemical combinations, and for premium requirements. A department will be maintained for the development of specialties to meet unusual needs.

The name and trademark of the Company were selected because the Shawnee tribe of American Indians once made the land adjoining the west bank of the Muskingum River their home and hunting ground. The site on which the factory is located is believed to have been a Shawnee village. These Indians were probably the first master craftsmen west of the Muskingum River in Ohio, and undoubtedly produced pottery from Zanesville clays long before white men settled the territory. The arrowhead in the trade mark is a duplicate of one found in the vicinity. It is an example of the craft of the Shawnee. The name is easily pronounced and associated with the trade mark will be remembered by the consumer from seeing their combination upon the product and in consumer advertising.

Operations will commence during August. About the same time, representatives of the company will begin calling on the trade and any courtesy extended them will be appreciated. Suggestions or advice relating to sizes and shapes of items, the decoration, treatment and styling, or any other matter of mutual interest will be gratefully received. The company hopes it will be favored with your patronage, and that a mutually satisfactory relationship will result.

You are extended a cordial invitation to visit the office and works at Zanesville after the 15th of September so you may see the facilities for manufacturing, the products, and the methods by which they are produced.

SHAWNEE POTTERY COMPANY

Works and Offices, Zanesville, Ohio :: SHAWNEE POTTERY COMPANY

Decorative Art Pottery

- Aquarium Ornaments
- Animal Ornaments
- Ash Trays
- Berry Dishes
- Bilikins
- Bird Bath Ornaments
- Book Ends
- Boudoir Sets
- Bridge Sets
- Bulb Bowls
- Candelabra
- Candle Holders
- Cereal Dishes
- Clock Cases
- Coasters
- Coffee Sets
- Compartment Plates
- Cream Pitchers
- Cups and Saucers
- Decanters
- Door Stops
- Egg Dishes
- Figurines
- Flower Blocks and Inserts
- Flower Pots and Saucers
- Fruit Bowls
- Glazed Pots and Saucers
- Hanging Baskets
- Honey Jars
- Humidors
- Incense Burners
- Ivy Balls and Jars
- Jardiniers
- Lamp Bases
- Liqueur Sets
- Novelties
- Nut Sets
- Oatmeals
- Ornaments and What-Nots
- Paper Weights
- Plaques
- Platters
- Rose Bowls
- Salad Dishes
- Service Plates
- Statues
- Statuettes
- Strawberry Jars
- Sugar Jars
- Tea Sets
- Tobacco Jars and Covers
- Trays
- Vases
- Wall Pockets

Works and Offices, Zanesville, Ohio :: SHAWNEE POTTERY COMPANY

Kitchen and Pantry Ware

- Baked Apple Dishes
- Baking Dishes
- Beating Jars
- Beverage Sets
- Bottle Service Jars
- Bowls (All sizes)
- Butter Jars
- Cake Plates
- Cake Servers
- Carafes
- Casseroles
- Cereal and Spice Sets
- Cheese Plates
- Chop Plates
- Coasters
- Coffee Pots and Drips
- Compartment Plates
- Comports
- Cookie Jars
- Cracker Jars
- Cups
- Custard Cups
- Egg Beaters
- Egg Cups
- Flour and Sugar Shakers
- Grease and Rouge Jars
- Hors d'ouvre Plates
- Ice Tubs, Pots, Jars, Pitchers
- Lipped Bowls
- Marmalade Jars
- Match Holders
- Mugs
- Mustards
- Nappies
- Pie Plates
- Pitchers
- Pretzel Jars and Plates
- Pudding Dishes
- Ramekins
- Refrigerator Jars
- Relish Trays
- Salad Bowls
- Salt Boxes
- Salad Forks
- Salad Spoons
- Salt and Pepper Shakers
- Saucers
- Skillets
- Steins
- Tankards
- Tea Pots
- Tom and Jerry Bowls and Mugs
- Tumblers
- Utility Trays
- Whipping Jars

As part of its sales policy, the company offers its customers a complete design and style service. Special articles will be made for special purposes and the designing department will be pleased to offer suggestions and advice relating to sizes and shapes of items, the decoration, treatment and style.

SHAWNEE POTTERY COMPANY :: Works and Offices, Zanesville, Ohio

Dinner Ware

- Bakers and Nappies (All sizes)
- Bowls (All sizes)
- Butters
- Cake Plates
- Casseroles
- Coffees
- Cups and Saucers
- Covered Dishes
- Creams
- Cream Soups
- Desserts
- Dishes (All sizes)
- Egg Cups
- Fruits
- Jugs and Covers
- Oatmeals
- Onion Soups
- Pickles
- Plates (All sizes)
- Sugars
- Teas
- Tea Pots

Names and Trademarks

The Indian arrowhead found by Malcolm Schweiker while inspecting the grounds of the A. E. Tile property in 1936, inspired the name given to the new company when it was incorporated in December of that year.

However, it was not until designer Louise Elizabeth Bauer had been hired at Shawnee Pottery in 1937, that a formal trademark was designed. Louise had found an arrowhead in her own back yard in Zanesville, and created a profile of a Shawnee Indians' head, centering it within a drawing of the arrowhead. This easily recognized logo and trademark was used by Shawnee throughout the history of the company on such items as letterheads, envelopes, pottery labels, and the covers of Annual Reports.

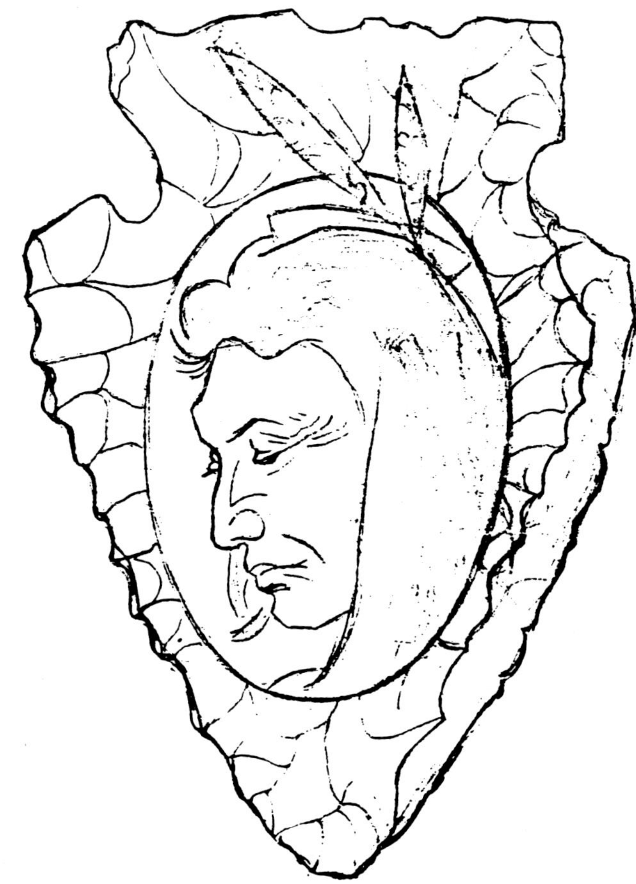

Original sketch of Shawnee Indian Arrowhead logo.

Operations Were Under Way

Malcolm A. Schweiker kept a close eye on the operation of Shawnee Pottery. While his brother, Roy Schweiker, concentrated on the operation of Franklin Tile, Malcolm divided his time between Franklin Tile and Shawnee Pottery. Spending an average of three days a week at Shawnee, Malcolm Schweiker's proficiency in engineering prompted him to constantly strive for better and more efficient methods of production. The straight-line production implemented at Shawnee Pottery was the same concept he had designed at his Franklin Tile plant in 1929. Malcolm was respected and well-liked by his employees, and he encouraged them to continue their formal education so that they could better themselves.

Siegfried W. Illing, initially hired as a laborer, moved to a new job of brushing the ware once the pottery began operating. This was a short-lived position, and Sieg soon moved on to become supervisor of the Glaze Department. Following Schweiker's advice, he took a course in Foremanship, and by 1938 Sieg began another new job as the General Foreman of the plant.

Sieg Illing (from back), Baker (hidden), Dupler, and Wilkins on lunch break in pre-WWII Shawnee Pottery.

Shawnee employees Mossman, Bowen, and Miller, making out times for pieces. *Pre-WWII photo*

The Shawnee Pottery plant was a light, airy, clean, well-kept, and well-run operation. Considerable expense was made in maintaining a huge dust removal system, which eliminated much of the dust created from processing the clay. Employees were required to wear white clothing to work, giving the appearance of cleanliness and uniformity. If employees needed to go into a particularly dirty area, they had to don white overalls in order to keep their basic white clothing clean. This strict dress code was a carryover from Franklin Tile, but was eventually relaxed, and then eliminated completely sometime around World War II.

The products that Shawnee manufactured were marketed to a wide variety of buyers, among them Butler Brothers, Sears Roebuck and Co., Montgomery Ward, Procter & Gamble, and Great Northern Company. Butler Brothers were national distributors of general merchandise, with offices located in New York, Chicago, St. Louis, Baltimore, Minneapolis, Dallas, and San Francisco. Department and chain stores such as Ben Franklin, S. S. Kresge, J. J. Newberry, McCrory, F. W. Woolworth, G. C. Murphy, and S. H. Kress carried the Shawnee Pottery lines.

In 1937, representatives from Sears Roebuck, and Co. approached President Addis Hull, and asked for sketches of a new dinnerware line that would compete with the Fiesta dinnerware line that the Homer Laughlin Company had introduced in 1936. Sears sent Jane Miller, housewares stylist, F. R. Henniger, division merchandise manager, and James Butler, pottery buyer, to help Shawnee with ideas for the design. Louise Bauer came up with the winning design, creating *Valencia,* the first dinnerware line to be produced at Shawnee.

Though designers like Louise E. Bauer and Jim Davis were kept busy coming up with new products, some of the early wares made at Shawnee were designs provided by the customers themselves. Among these, were lamp bases made for a company out of New York; and designs provided by T. K. Kirkpatrick of S. S. Kresge; H. W. Smith of S. H. Kress; H. H. Lindquist of F. W. Woolworth; and W. W. Dixon of McCrory. George Schwerber modeled these pieces, and Clifford Twiggs made the dies and cases.

Contracts for individual lines for large companies such as Sears Roebuck, Butler Brothers, and Procter & Gamble helped get the new company off to a start. Sears, in particular, always wanted products that were made exclusively for them.

A very successful venture for Shawnee was when Procter & Gamble, their largest account for premiums, contracted to have them produce a 5-inch cereal bowl in bright deep colors of blue, yellow, green and tangerine. These bowls were placed in boxes of Oxydol soap powder as a premium. Shawnee had to construct a special jigger machine for this operation, but it proved to be a most successful endeavor for both the pottery and Procter & Gamble, and they sold several millions of these bowls.

During these early years, nearly all of the ware was of solid color, with either embossed designs or cold paint on the pieces for decoration. Some kitchenware lines of this era were Snowflake, Fern Leaf, and Flower & Fern; and of course the Valencia dinnerware.

The Rumrill Connection

George Rumrill, of the RumRill Pottery Company of Little Rock, Arkansas, approached Shawnee Pottery in April of 1938 to have them produce pottery for him. Rumrill had abruptly left the Red Wing Pottery Company of Minnesota, which had been manufacturing his art pottery for many years. Shawnee agreed to work with Mr. Rumrill, with Rumrill providing most of his own designs. George Schwerber and Bernard Twiggs, provided the modeling, blocks and casing. However, Louise E. Bauer did create some designs which Rumrill incorporated into his line, and which Shawnee produced. The association between Rumrill and Shawnee was ended less than a year later, when Rumrill moved his operation to Mt. Gilead, Ohio.

Updating The Changes

Growth of the Shawnee Pottery Company had been steady since its' incorporation, with the pottery growing into one of the largest of its' kind in the country. Shawnee remained the sole occupant of this huge complex of buildings, though they certainly did not utilize all of it; and they had a pre-war work force of around six hundred (600) employees.

Leadership changed when Malcolm A. Schweiker became the President of Shawnee Pottery, while Addis E. Hull, Jr. became a Vice President and retained a seat on the Board of Directors. Around 1938, Rudy Ganz had been hired to head the Design Department, while Louise Elizabeth Bauer had departed after a few years at Shawnee. Louise became a freelance designer, with her most famous design being the *Little Red Riding Hood* line of kitchenware that was patented by Hull Pottery of Crooksville, Ohio. Eventually, Louise became a full-time Hull designer.

The Japanese bombing of Pearl Harbor on December 7, 1941, was a turning point in the lives of many Americans. The United States, which had declared a National Emergency on May 27, 1941, was now drawn into the war in Europe.

Figural Cookie Jars Make Their Debut

Though the war had begun, Shawnee Pottery was able to continue operations, producing the whimsical and popular designs created by the design department under the direction of Rudolph V. Ganz.

Rudy Ganz, chief designer for Shawnee, is shown here with the child's picture coloring book where he obtained the inspiration for his widely popular "Smiling Pig" cookie jars.
Courtesy of The Sunday Times-Signal, Zanesville, OH, copyright 1942

Smiley Pig cookie jar heads are being cold paint decorated by Elizabeth Richardson.
Courtesy of The Sunday Times-Signal, Zanesville, OH, copyright 1942

The original Smiley Pig salt & pepper shakers are lined up on a circular table, patiently waiting to be decorated by Clarkie Gatewood.
Courtesy of The Sunday Times-Signal, Zanesville, OH, copyright 1942

Rudy Ganz was a German who had arrived in America in February of 1929. During high school, Rudy learned modeling at a pottery in his home town in Germany. Then in college he specialized in all forms of art, particularly carving and sculpturing. Ganz finished his college education at the University of Indiana. Newspaper accounts indicate that Ganz had worked at Frankoma Pottery in Oklahoma, though this has not'been confirmed. Prior to joining Shawnee, he did work for Niloak Pottery Company of Benton, Arkansas, and for the Daly Monument Works in Fort Smith, Arkansas.

Rudy Ganz, along with modeler Ed Hazel, was responsible for the first figural cookie jars that were designed and produced by Shawnee Pottery. The inspiration for Smiley Pig came from a child's picture coloring book that Rudy had. It was April of 1942 when Smiley Pig cookie jars first made their appearance, and they were an immediate hit. Butler Brothers had contracted to buy every cookie jar, as well as the matching Pig salt & pepper shakers, and Shawnee had difficulty keeping up with production. Along with Smiley Pig, there were four other figural cookie jars: Sailor Boy, Jack, Jill, and Sitting Elephant. These early jars were all produced with cold paint decoration applied over the glaze.

The U.S. Government Takes Over

In October of 1942, nearly a year after Pearl Harbor, Shawnee Pottery was one of the first Zanesville plants to be awarded a war contract. Several employees were hired to operate a new department using the patented Formrite process for making molds for airplane propellers.

Formrite was a process where a powder and liquid were mixed under a vacuum for 45 minutes to produce a creamy substance which was poured into molds to produce duplicates of a part. Used in the automotive and aviation industries, the product consisted of jigs, dies, molds, patterns and fixtures. The use of this Formrite process was discontinued in early 1943.

Machinist William Mohler and Fred Brown, machine shop foreman, with Formrite molds for airplane propellers made during WWII.
Courtesy of The Times Recorder, Zanesville, OH, copyright 1960

Effective April 27, 1943, Shawnee Pottery leased the major portion of their buildings to the United States Government. The initial lease agreement was for the period from May 1, 1943 to June 30, 1944, and from year to year thereafter. The terms of the lease agreement provided for the government to make certain improvements to the Shawnee property, of which the most important to Shawnee involved conversion of the entire electrical power and light system from direct current to alternating current. Effective November 1, 1943, the fixed lease amount to be paid by the government was $6,000 per month, with one-third withheld to compensate for Shawnee's share of the improvements.

Entrance to the headquarters of the 833rd Army Air Force Specialized Depot during WWII.
Courtesy of The Times Recorder, Zanesville, OH, copyright 1960

The War Years

When the government came in on May 1, 1943, they took over approximately 500,000 square feet of floor space from Shawnee, leaving the company with about 50,000 square feet. The original 650,000 square footage of the property had been reduced during Shawnee's early renovations.

The 833rd Army Air Force, under the command of Major George J. Klein, leased most of the property "to receive, store, maintain, modify, and ship A.A.F. materials throughout the world". One of the materials stored was raw rubber that was being shipped into the states from the islands, before Japan captured our source of supply. The A.A.F. Depot stocked approximately 8,000 items ranging from small parts to a three-ton lathe, for shipment to distant parts of the world.

Shawnee Pottery was carrying on operations in the 50,000 square feet left to them at the northern end of the property. The manufacturing unit was very compactly organized and equipped, and the volume of sales was unusually large for the small manufacturing space. By 1943, key employees such as Sieg Illing, who had been appointed as the Night Superintendent of the plant in 1940, were being called into the armed services. Sieg had gone to work in the A.A.F. Depot, and was shortly thereafter inducted into the service and sent overseas. By early 1944, the work force at Shawnee was around 200 employees, with the War Manpower Commission decreasing that ceiling amount later that year. About equal numbers of men and women worked at Shawnee at that time.

Still under the able leadership of Malcolm Schweiker, Shawnee survived the war years by confining its' production to about twenty-five products, such as cookie jars, teapots, pitchers, and food containers. All products manufactured were made available only to good customers who had been with Shawnee before the war. The lack of raw materials was making it difficult for Shawnee, as well as other potteries, to operate, and there was a substantial backlog of orders on file. The old customers who were still being supplied by Shawnee were willing to accept frequent shipments, thereby eliminating the necessity of maintaining warehouses and large inventories of finished goods. This was crucial to Shawnee, considering their confined operating space.

It was during these war years that Shawnee improved some of their glazing and decorating techniques, and created exciting designs in anticipation of full production at the wars' end. New patents were filed for such items as Winnie Pig, Puss 'n Boots, Muggsy, and Winking Owl cookie jars; Granny Ann teapots; and BoPeep pitchers. These designs were produced using the newly-perfected underglaze decorating techniques. In addition, three of the five original jars patented in 1942 were now being produced with underglaze decoration. Smiley had tulips, shamrocks, and chrysanthemums added to him; and Jack and Jill had stripes and tulips added to their clothing.

Post-War Rebuilding

As the war in Europe drew to a close in 1945, Shawnee was preparing for an expected post-war manufacturing boom. Formal application had been filed on October 28, 1945 for the U.S. government to turn over all of its' occupied property to the company.

The war was not without its' casualties. The oldest son of Malcolm A. Schweiker, Malcolm Jr., was killed in the 1945 invasion of Okinawa. By March of 1945, it was known that at least four former employees of Shawnee Pottery had also "paid the supreme sacrifice in various theatres of the war."

Sieg Illing did return to Shawnee when the war ended, and was assigned to be Project Supervisor to assist Plant Manager Albert P. Braid. Braid had been brought in by Mr. Schweiker from his New Jersey plant to oversee renovations of the buildings the government had turned back over to Shawnee on June 30, 1946. The government agreed to pay Shawnee $30,000 to cover the cost of repairs needed for damage done during the wartime occupation, and Shawnee agreed to do the work.

By now, Rudy Ganz, as well as Ed Hazel, had departed Shawnee. Hazel left in 1944 to help form the Cordelia China Company located in Dalton, Ohio.

It is here that employees begin to refer to the "Old Pottery" and the "New Pottery" when talking about Shawnee. It was decided that manufacturing would be moved from the old section in the north end of the property, into a renovated area in the central part of the property. This new manufacturing unit was scheduled to begin operating around July 1, 1947, but delays set manufacturing back to the middle of 1948.

Aerial view of the Shawnee Pottery Company as pictured in a 1941 catalog, and again in a 1944 Annual Report. Dilapidated buildings in the far upper left corner and along the railroad tracks behind the pottery, as well as the cone-like periodic kilns, had been removed by the time this photo was taken.

In the meantime, Shawnee leased approximately 260,000 square feet in the southern part of the property to General Electric Company. Effective on October 1, 1946, General Electric took possession, using the leased area for warehousing replacement parts or supplies. Plans were for hiring less than 100 employees.

Once Shawnee had vacated the buildings in the northern section of the property (approximately 60,000 square feet), they were leased to the Timken Roller Bearing Company in 1948 for light manufacturing and assembly. Timken had come to Zanesville in 1943, and moving into the Shawnee plant allowed them to consolidate their three factories into one unit.

A New Team Is Assembled

With the wars' end, 1945 saw a new management team being formed, and some bustling activity setting up a new manufacturing unit. Production was maintained as efficiently as possible in the "Old Pottery" while building of the "New Pottery" was making demands on the time and talents of the personnel.

George L. Williams was recruited from U. S. Steel in 1945 to serve as Treasurer, in charge of accounting, finance, purchasing, cost analysis of production, and related functions. Williams had an Administrative Engineering degree from Lafayette College, and a Master of Science degree in Business and Engineering Administration from Massachusetts Institute of Technology.

George L. Williams.
Birthdate: February 22, 1914.
1964 photo

Every pottery seems to have one "Designer Extraordinaire." One whose work later became extremely recognized, loved, and collected. One whose designs were consistently placed into production. One whose experiments led to a unique variety of textures and finishes not previously produced. One who could hear of an idea, and immediately envision and produce exactly what was being described.

Shawnee Potterys' "Designer Extraordinaire" was Robert Heckman. He created Corn King, Pennsylvania Dutch, Sunflower, cookie jars such as Drum Major, Little Chef, Clown & Seal, and countless planters, vases, and shakers. Heckman had studied under well-known potter Chester Nicodemus, at the Columbus School of Art and Design. Nicodemus had a great influence on Bob's life; creating his interest in ceramics, and arranging for scholarships for art school. Heckman went on to Ohio State University to get his degree. Professor Arthur Baggs, a well-known ceramist, was head of the O.S.U. Ceramic Department. Shawnee Vice President Addis Hull asked Prof. Baggs to recommend someone to design for them, and Prof. Baggs introduced Robert Heckman to Hull. During the 1945 holiday season Heckman began working at Shawnee on a part-time basis, and by the Spring of 1946 when he graduated, he began working full-time.

Robert Heckman.
Birthdate: October 9, 1919.
1994 photo

Rolf John Falk was already a member of the team as Vice President in charge of Merchandising and Sales. Falk was trying to create a backlog of design ideas, and as Heckman had a tendency to work fast in clay, he was expected to produce one design a day. Heckman later worked with Ceramic Engineer A. E. "Ned" Lepper, of the Body and Glaze Department, devising a new glaze treatment using a wax from the Sunoco Oil Co. This treatment was later used on the first Kenwood lines and in floral lines such as Chantilly. Besides the many figural designs and the vastly improved color palette contributed by Bob Heckman, he was responsible for many innovative textures and glaze treatments that Shawnee introduced to the industry.

Another Shawnee designer was Martha Holmes Breithaupt, who had been in school with Bob Heckman. Graduating just after Bob, Martha then joined Shawnee, and stayed on for several years until her marriage.

The Labor Boss at Shawnee during this time was James White. Working for White was Paul Chema, Sr., whose son Robert Chema was hired at Shawnee after a three-year military stint. Bob Chema worked for a short time for White, then moved to the Mold and Die Shop where he spent the next five years working for Bernard E. Twiggs. Some fellow workers in this department with Chema were Bill Deaton, Conrad Burkhart, Dewey Lee, Jim Baldwin, and Cecil Corwin.

In January of 1947, President Malcolm A. Schweiker welcomed Jess L. Parentice to Shawnee. Jess, who had been in the employ of Butler Brothers and working out of their San Francisco office, was already familiar with the products of Shawnee. Parentice was hired to be Sales Manager and Assistant to Vice President Rolf John Falk. When John Falk was forced to leave the company due to health problems, Parentice headed up the Sales Division, and would prove to be a driving force in merchandising the wares of Shawnee Pottery. It was Jess who traveled to southern California each year in search of new ideas; sometimes with Bob Heckman accompanying him. Jess attended the china and glass trade shows, promoting the latest Shawnee lines. Jess came up with the idea of merchandising the corn ware in attractive display boxes, to stimulate sales of multiple pieces at one time.

Sieg Illing became an assistant to Jess Parentice, with duties such as helping to take care of in-plant sales and to service their customers. Often, they made sales trips together, covering the Eastern, Western, and Southern territories. Jess and Sieg often attended the Trade Shows that were held in New York, Chicago, Pittsburgh, and Atlantic City, promoting Shawnee's new lines.

Jess L. Parentice.
December 13, 1908 - September 17, 1992.

Siegfried W. Illing.
August 29, 1914 - September 4, 1989.

The 1949 Annual Report shows this aerial view of the "New" Shawnee Pottery as it was renovated after WWII. The north end of the property (top left corner of photo) was leased to Timken Roller Bearing Company; Shawnee Pottery occupied the central buildings; and General Electric leased the southern end of the property.

The New Pottery And Labor Unions

Shawnee had completed only part of the New Pottery in the central section in 1947. By early 1948, renovations were completed, but production was not on a substantial and stabilized basis until mid-1948. Shawnee lost ground with the delays, and consumers had unexpectedly slowed purchasing by 1948. This created a buyers' market, with art pottery and kitchen ware falling to a new low in retail prices.

In renovating the New Pottery, Shawnee again set up a straight-line production, whereby every department is set up so that the raw clay comes in one end, and is processed through each department in sequence. The finished product efficiently ends up in the packing and shipping area, with minimal handling. Shawnee also boasted the only overhead bisque kiln in the world, which saved considerable floor space, as employees could walk under the kiln instead of having to walk around it.

It is during this late-1940s era that Shawnee first implemented the cost-effective method of spray decorating their ware. Spray guns were used to airbrush colors onto the larger part of a piece such as a skirt of a Dutch Girl shaker; then smaller features such as eyes are painted with a brush. Most of the figural ware produced from this time on, was decorated using both spray and brush decorating methods.

Malcolm A. Schweiker resigned as President in 1948, focusing his attention on the operations of Franklin Tile, which had now been renamed American Encaustic Tiling Company, Inc. Still a major stockholder of Shawnee, Schweiker remained on the Board of Directors.

Albert P. Braid was promoted to President of Shawnee in 1948, succeeding Schweiker. In an information booklet given to the "associates" (employees), Braid emphasized that "operating employees, management employees, and stockholders, do not represent classes of people, but are equally important in the affairs of the company. Trying to prove which is more important is like trying to prove which leg of a three-legged stool is more important."

Braid's booklet for associates was dated the same day, April 29, 1948, that factory employees would begin being represented by the National Brotherhood of Operative Potters. The union had negotiated a wage increase effective November 1948 ..... 10 cents per hour for men; 8 cents per hour for women. Though the union had been voted in, it was hardly more than a representation, because Shawnee employees were already receiving the best wages and piece work pay in the industry at that time, with working conditions far superior to other potteries in the area. In addition, Shawnee provided the opportunity for any employee who had been sick, to come in on Saturday to make up lost wages.

In January of 1949, Shawnee's new low-priced lines were placed on the market, creating a large backlog of orders that the company hadn't experienced in years. Volume production and stability of prices were the key to making these lower priced lines profitable for the company. The outlook was optimistic.

Volume of sales was up in 1949, showing a small profit for the company, the first in several years. The company employed 252 workers, producing mainly kitchen ware, novelties, art pottery, and lamp bases; being sold to chain stores, wholesalers, and lamp manufacturers.

Also in 1949, the Board of Directors elected George L. Williams, to a new post as Vice President and Treasurer. More changes were in the making.

A New Decade

On January 16, 1950, investment bankers Lilley and Company of Philadelphia made an offer to purchase the stock of the approximately 1090 stockholders of the company. This offer was on behalf of Director Albert J. Grosser, whose intent was to purchase all stock offered to him by February 28, 1950.

During February, Grosser bought the stock of Malcolm A. Schweiker, Roy W. Schweiker, and Mrs. Maurice Iserman, prompting the resignation of three founding directors of the company: Malcolm A. Schweiker, W. Herbert Keller, and Maurice

Iserman. Malcolm Schweiker, having been so instrumental in the development and success of Shawnee, had now stepped down.

As 1950 continued, three more directors resigned: Albert J. Grosser, the Chairman; Albert P. Braid, President; and Addis E. Hull, Jr., Vice President. This enabled Braid to return to the Perth Amboy, New Jersey plant, in the employ of Malcolm Schweiker. Addis Hull was hired as President of Monmouth-Western Stoneware Company in Monmouth, Illinois, on July 18, 1950, and remained there until August 31, 1963.

George L. Williams was elected the new President of Shawnee, becoming a member of the Board of Directors, and Adolph Hirsch of New York became the new Chairman of the Board of Directors. Jess L. Parentice was elected Vice President in Charge of Sales. The new Plant Superintendent was Fred Brown.

Despite the total transition to a new top management and directorial team in 1950, increased sales to old customers brought about a significant profit increase over 1949. The year 1950 closed out with a total of 242 employees.

Dedicated personnel and teamwork in the early 1950s contributed to the success of Shawnee. When he was president, George Williams would walk around the plant, even on the third shift, getting feedback directly from the employees. Morale was high at Shawnee, and teamwork resulted in production of a high quality product that was well-priced for the mass market. Problems arising at the pottery were met by the competent leadership of Williams and Parentice. Friction between departments, common in manufacturing organizations, had all but been eliminated at Shawnee since department heads had gotten to know one another better through organized social events. These social events were often in the form of picnics or barbecues, with all department heads and their families attending.

Fred Brown, Plant Superintendent, George L. Williams, President, and Jess L. Parentice, Vice President, shown in a 1951 photo.

When a Time Study position became available, Jess Parentice offered it to Robert Chema, who was still working for Bernard Twiggs. In his new job, Chema had to prepare cost estimates on all items that Shawnee made, and keep them on file. The busy time was generally when a new line came out, sometimes involving ten to fifteen new items. After the cost was complete, time studies in all the piece work departments were entered in piece rate books, so employees could see what the rates were on each item. Each employee was assigned a number, which was stamped on the bottom of some pieces they worked on. This number was used as identification of whom to charge back bonus pay to for unsatisfactory work. Piece work earnings were posted daily in each department, so employees could see how much bonus was being made. Bonus amounts averaging $20 to $30 a week were welcomed. Bob Chema stayed with this job until the plant closed.

Kenwood Ceramics Division

Jess Parentice organized the Kenwood Ceramics Division in 1953 for a separate line of high-class gift ware items to be distributed to department stores, gift and floral shops. This was felt to be a necessary measure because of a shrinking sales volume of domestic pottery in the chain stores; the imports were again hurting the American pottery industry. The name Shawnee had the stigma of being five-and-dime-store merchandise, so a new Kenwood logo was designed by Bob Heckman, and Jess recruited a sales force from Royal China to handle the Kenwood line. It was a good relationship, as the Royal China line did not compete with Kenwood, yet sold in the same stores.

The Kenwood lines were sold at higher prices, so Shawnee was able to make them with a little more care and expense. The finishing was a little better to improve the quality, such as smoother seams, a little more expensive decorating finishes were used, and sometimes felt was applied to the bases to protect fine furniture. In both Kenwood and Shawnee lines, two pieces of pottery were often fired together, such as the Kitten and Basket planter, to look more expensive.

In May of 1953, George L. Williams resigned as President. Announcement was made that a new President, Arthur K. Grindley, 46, would join Shawnee on July 1, 1953. Formerly associated in an executive capacity with Grindley Artware Company of Sebring, Ohio, Grindley had 22 years experience in the family's artware business. Grindley brought to Shawnee the Lobster Ware line which had originated at Grindley Artware.

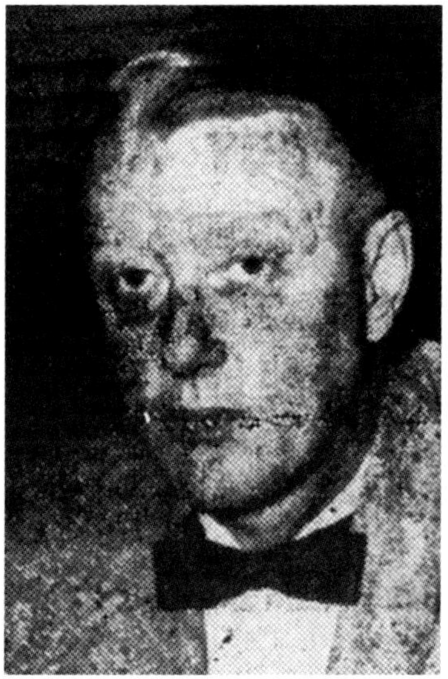

Arthur K. Grindley.
1907 - September 18, 1967.
Courtesy of The Times Recorder, Zanesville, OH, copyright 1953

Art Grindley met problems on October 3, 1953, when he saw the walkout of nearly 160 employees who were members of the Federation of Glass, Ceramic, and Silica Sand Workers, CIO. This CIO union had been representing the workers since an election in November 1952. Despite the strike, more than 75% of the employees returned to work, and operation at the plant remained virtually unaffected. The union filed a suit claiming that Shawnee had refused to negotiate, but dropped that charge four months later.

Arthur K. Grindley's tenure as President ended with his resignation effective January 11, 1954. This left Jess L. Parentice alone at the helm of Shawnee Pottery, until a new President could be hired.

John F. Bonistall.
September 20, 1914 - April 24, 1994.
1950s photo

In early August 1954, announcement was made that John F. Bonistall of Pittsburgh, Pennsylvania, would become Executive Vice President and General Manager of Shawnee Pottery effective September 1, 1954. Bonistall had attended the University of Pittsburgh, and served as an infantry officer in Europe during World War II. Prior to coming to Shawnee, Bonistall had been at Moore Enameling and Manufacturing Company at West Lafayette, Ohio, as general sales manager for three years.

By December 17, 1954 it was announced that John F. Bonistall had been elected President and General Manager of Shawnee, becoming a member of the Board of Directors at the same time.

On December 26, 1954, Jess L. Parentice tendered his resignation to President John Bonistall, effective February 1, 1955. Parentice had agreed to remain with Shawnee through the Pittsburgh China and Glass Show, and the Housewares Show in Chicago which ended on January 21, 1955, in order to introduce the new Kenwood line. Jess was moving on to become Sales Manager of the Moe Light Division in Fort Atkinson, Wisconsin, a subsidiary of Thomas Industries Inc.

Early 1955 saw the resignation of Robert Heckman. With nearly ten years at Shawnee, Bob was reluctantly leaving a company where so many of his designs and ideas had been met with success. Heckman was also to join Thomas Industries Inc. in Wisconsin, where his work would consist mainly of designing lighting fixtures. Eventually, Bob became self-employed, doing design and consulting work for an assortment of companies.

Joining Shawnee in 1955 was Jean C. Shaw, who had worked with John Bonistall at Moore Enameling and Manufacturing Company. Bonistall's policy was to hire executive and sales personnel who had no prior experience in the manufacture of pottery. By January of 1956, Shaw had been elected Vice President by the Board of Directors. The Treasurer since 1950 was Frank K. Ralston, a public accountant in Philadelphia, who did not participate in the daily management of the pottery.

Products To Fit The Times

Net operating profits of $55,000 were recorded for 1953, while 1954 showed a serious operating loss of $18,000. The industry was still experiencing a downward trend in sales of domestic pottery, and Shawnee's work force was approximately 165 employees at the close of 1954. Bonistall was preparing to implement production changes that he hoped would turn the company around.

After studying the Japanese import situation, Bonistall determined which products Shawnee couldn't compete with them in, and which types of outlets the Japanese had overlooked. As a result, three divisions would be maintained by Shawnee, with new designs developed in each that would be competitive.

The three divisions and their markets would be:

1) Shawnee Division, which would sell to variety chains such as Woolworth, Newberry, Kresge, Murphy, etc.; plus variety merchandise distributors, drug chains, supermarkets, rack jobbers, exporters, and premium users. Shawnee also sold lamp bases to assemblers.

2) Kenwood Division, which sold separately styled lines to giftware and housewares distributors, stamp plans, party plans, mail order, and department stores.

3) Architectural Ceramics Division, set up in an attempt to take Shawnee outside the pottery industry. It marketed ceramic bathroom accessories to the floor and wall covering trade, plus sales to ceramic tile manufacturers under their trademarks, and building specialties for sales to contractors through architects.

Gladys Robinson and Betty Dickerson spray decorating Petit-Point floral ware.
Courtesy of The Times Recorder, Zanesville, OH, copyright 1960

Bonistall's most revolutionary change was to phase out production of figural pottery, which had been a fundamental product of Shawnee's kilns since 1937. Even the new Kenwood lines that had been figural, were being changed over to Kenwood lines of ashtrays and floral ware such as flower pots, jardinieres, and planting dishes.

Mack Holland, an Ohio native and graduate of the Cleveland School of Art, had joined Shawnee as a designer after an 18-year teaching career at the Hadley Technical High School in St. Louis, Missouri. Holland, who had been hired by Jess Parentice, began work on the new products and changes that John Bonistall wanted to implement. Sales of Corn King had fallen off, so it was renamed Corn Queen in 1955, with the husks changed to a darker green, and the kernels changed to a lighter transparent yellow glaze. Corn Queen was met with some renewed interest from the buying public and was marketed right up until Shawnee closed, but it never attained the popularity of Corn King.

Mack Holland.
May 10, 1909 - April 19, 1974.

By 1956, John Bonistall introduced Touché, his first line of floral ware, and it was extremely successful. This type of product would sustain Shawnee for the rest of the decade, enabling it to grow and prosper.

Consistent sales efforts, with substantial advertising and promotional programs, resulted in a net profit of over $40,000 in 1956 for Shawnee. By 1957, net profits fell to just over $19,000, with Shawnee employing approximately 185 people. Shawnee was distributing two lines of merchandise, under the Shawnee and Kenwood names, but the planned Architectural Division never seemed to get off the ground. This was most likely due to the restrictive covenant Shawnee signed in 1936 with Ohio Encaustic and A. E. Tile, agreeing never to manufacture tiles at the plant.

When John Bonistall became President, there was an outstanding first mortgage of $200,000 on the property, the balance of which had been extended time and again since 1950. Refinancing had taken place in 1950 when Albert Grosser bought up the stock of the Schweiker's and other founders. During the presidency of George Williams, payments of $30,000 and $60,000 had been made against the debt; plus a $50,000 payment made in late 1953. The years of 1954, 1955, 1956, and 1957, saw payments of $50,000 per year made under the direction of Bonistall. With all principal and interest payments paid in full, the first mortgage was discharged in 1957.

Shawnee Pottery Closes Forever

As Shawnee Pottery entered yet another decade, the 1960s, steady progress had been made under the management of John Bonistall. Profits had been consistently realized, and long-term debts had been met. Still, there were underlying reasons to liquidate the Shawnee Pottery Company.

The Board of Directors had decided to sell this huge parcel of land and buildings, now listed as 30 acres with 500,000 square feet of manufacturing space. Shawnee occupied approximately 180,000 sq. ft. for their manufacturing. Timken Roller Bearing Company had vacated the property in 1958, moving to Canton, Ohio. General Electric Company would be vacating their leased area by April 30, 1961, as they were moving to a new facility in New Concord, Ohio. This would leave Shawnee to take over the taxes, insurance, maintenance, and other costs that had formerly been covered by the lessees.

The Shawnee Pottery Company office entrance, taken in September 1960, just four months before the pottery would close forever.
Courtesy of The Times Recorder, Zanesville, OH, copyright 1960

The directors believed that it was unlikely that any purchaser of the property would be interested in absorbing the pottery, so the decision was made to liquidate. This would make the property easier to sell, as strictly a real estate dealing. Closing Shawnee would put about two hundred employees out of work, some of whom had been at the pottery since its inception.

On January 3, 1961, the Board of Directors of the Shawnee Pottery Company held their stockholders meeting in New York, voting to sell the assets of the company and liquidate the plant's holdings. At this same meeting, John F. Bonistall tendered his resignation as President, effective immediately, and this was accepted by the Board of Directors.

The Shawnee Pottery Co., Inc. had ceased operations immediately. Adolph Hirsch, Chairman of the Board of Directors, was named President of Shawnee Pottery once it became inactive. Liquidation of Shawnee Pottery was completed on June 20, 1963.

Author's Note: Built more than a century ago, the former Shawnee Pottery property at 2200 Linden Avenue, Zanesville, OH remains standing today, and is occupied by the United Technologies Automotive Group.

Shawnee Pottery Company, Zanesville, Ohio.
Management, Supervisory, and Office Personnel, August 22, 1958.
Seated, left to right:
Harris Perkins, Glaze Technician - A. E. "Ned" Lepper, Ceramic Engineer - Robert Chema, Industrial Engineer - Jean C. Shaw, Vice President and Production Manager - John F. Bonistall, President and General Manager - P. T. Beutell, Office and Credit Manager - James Van Sant, Controller - Gerald Root, Maintenance Engineer - T. H. Abbot, Plant Superintendent.
Standing, left to right:
Bill Smith, Glaze Technician - Kelly Davis, Foreman, Packing Dept. - Ted Holsky, Foreman, Decorating Dept. - Helen Keller, Payroll Clerk - Helen Tracy - Margaret Saad, Secretary - Irene Everly, Receptionist and Clerk - Jeanette Shuey, Clerk - Emily Walker, Clerk - Pauline Clark, Purchasing Clerk - Sylvia Burkhart, Inventory Clerk - Maude Carpenter, Supervisor, Finishing Dept. - Thelma Fulton, Shipping Clerk - Gertrude Trittipo, Manager, Purchasing Dept. - Roy Mohr, Foreman, Casting Dept. - Bernard E. Twiggs, Foreman, Mold and Die Dept.
Not Present: James White, Labor Foreman - Russell Murray, Foreman, Gloss Kiln - Albert Stemm - Robert Wilson - George Lewis, Foreman, Decorating.

Chapter 2: Shawnee Plant Tour

We would like to take you on a tour of the Shawnee Pottery plant, compliments of designer Robert Heckman. Bob provided the drawing of the floor plan layout, and much of the text describing the process.

When Shawnee renovated their property after World War II, the "New Pottery" was set up in straight-line production, shown here, similar to what they had before the war. Straight-line production provides for the raw clay to begin its process at one end of the plant, with the finished item ending up at the other end of the plant, ready to be shipped. Every department at Shawnee did an inspection before an item was sent to the next department.

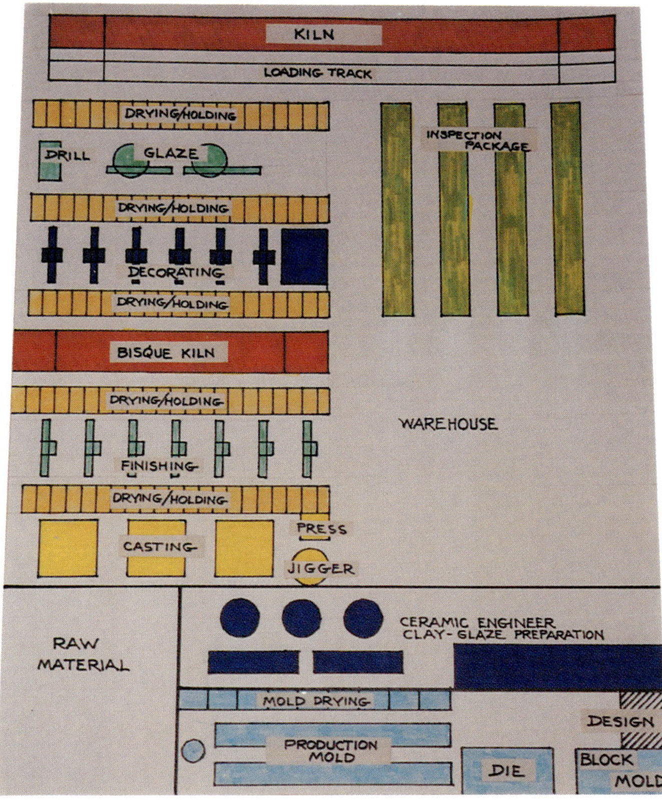

Shawnee Pottery Post-WWII Floor Plan.
Courtesy of Robert Heckman

Ceramic Engineering was a separate department that essentially worked for all other departments except Shipping. Ceramic Engineering prepared the clay for Casting, Jiggering, and Ram Press; made and mixed underglazes for Decorating; and mixed and checked glazes throughout the day to keep the viscosity even. Of necessity, Ceramic Engineering was located near the raw materials, where an overhead tramway with buckets moved the clay into bins and vats. Preparing the clay meant washing it to remove lignite, a mineral which would burn out in the kiln and leave holes or pitting in the ware. When dry, most clays were passed under heavy muller wheels and plows to blend the materials with a water spray mixed into them, to achieve the desired slip consistency. Some clay was prepared by pulverizing it and adding water until it became slip; then was dried in a filter press and made into a cake.

Design was generally the first step in producing any item, with the Design department working very closely with the sales and merchandising departments. The merchandising department spelled out what was needed, e.g., figural planters of a certain size in a certain price range.

Once an idea was formed by Design, the item was made in clay, plaster, or whatever necessary, in a larger size than the finished product because of clay shrinkage in manufacturing. All Shawnee items were shipped in air cell cartons of certain dimensions, so design also had to make sure that the finished sizes would fit these air cells. This was a big design limitation at Shawnee.

In making a design, some thought also had to be given to the color, decorating, and mold line (seams). If an idea was for something new or different, consultation was required with the Ceramic Engineer so they could be developing their ideas at the same time Design was working on their project.

When design had completed the new item, they turned it over to the **Block Mold** department. Block Mold made a plaster mold and cast a few samples for experimentation with colors and decorating. From these samples, an item was either chosen, changed, or dropped. Those chosen were temporarily set aside for the new line being developed.

The block mold for a chosen item was turned over to the **Die** department. The dies were made mostly of Hydrocal which is a little like cement, though some highly detailed items were made in rubber. Markings such as order numbers and U.S.A. were added to the bottoms of the dies.

From the die, plaster **Production Molds** were made. At Shawnee, a unique system was used in mixing the plaster. A full 100-lb bag of plaster was mixed under a slight vacuum. This helped keep air bubbles out of the plaster, and made the mold last longer in production. A soap separator was used to keep the plaster from sticking to the die. This soap built up on the die, which in time looked like it had been varnished, and could cut down on detail. The plaster production molds were dried in dryers, and sent on to Casting.

Casting is where Casting, Jiggering, and Ram Press were all done, sort of a form-shaping department, with casting by far the largest part. Casting molds at Shawnee were unique, as they were in four sections, making straps or bands unnecessary for holding them together. The casting machine had a ferris-wheel-type table drop from the heat/dryer area and stop, where molds were then filled with slip. More than one mold was filled at a time, the number depending upon how many molds were across the table. After the desired thickness of wall was obtained, the molds were emptied of the remaining liquid slip, which was then reused. This table would then move to another station and be replaced by a table from the heat/dryer area. The almost-leather-hard ware would be emptied from the molds at one of the three remaining stations, before being lifted back up into the heat/drying area. This casting/drying machine increased production by drying the molds faster.

Jiggering was done by mostly semi-automatic machines. In this process, a wet ball of clay is dropped into a mold, and a templet is used to squeeze the wet clay against the turning mold.

The Ram Press was introduced to Shawnee by Bob Heckman. While he was attending Ohio State University, this new machine was being developed in research. Ram Press molds were made of plaster, with a porous hose imbedded in the mold when the mold is made. This hose allows the ware to be released by applying air pressure. This is the basis behind the Ram Press development. The Ram Press was used for all flatware, bowls, and dishes, and was limited to items 4-inches in height or under. From casting, the item was sent into a Drying / Holding area.

Finishing was the next step, where seams were removed and sponged. Then on to another Drying / Holding area, waiting to be loaded into the Bisque Kiln.

Shawnee had an elevated **Bisque Kiln** with an elevator at each end, leaving an open area through the plant. This saved space, since loading was done under the kiln. Temperature of the kiln was about 1000· F, producing what is known as greenware that is stronger and easier to handle by decorators and glazers.

Another Drying / Holding area was reached before the greenware goes on to **Decorating**. Underglaze decorating was accomplished in the post WWII era by either hand brushing, spraying with an air gun, stamp and wipe off (as in the Antique Brown pieces), or any combination of these. This was where a supervisor would stamp an operators' number on the bottom of an item to charge back bonus pay if work was not satisfactory. The piece was sent to Drying / Holding again.

Next was the **Glaze** department, where items were hand dipped in glaze. Before being dipped, the foot of each item was pressed into a hot paraffin pad. This made it easier to wipe off the excess glaze, and kept the item from sticking when being fired in the kiln. You will notice that the foot of most items had a vent cut through; this kept air from being trapped under the foot and made for a cleaner wax line. Ware again went into a holding area, except for the salt and pepper shakers. The shakers went from glazing to have the holes drilled, then went to holding.

From the holding area, items were loaded onto a shelf of a kiln car and fired in the **Tunnel Kiln** at a little over 2000· F. The complete trip through the kiln took about 12-14 hours. When ware was cooled, it went in one of two directions. Finished ware was placed in air cell inserts and sent to **Inspection.** Items needing further painting (such as the red lobster on the Lobster line), gold trim and/or decals, went on for more decorating and were fired a third time at temperatures of 1200-1500· F, then placed in air cell inserts.

The finished ware in air cell inserts that passed inspection, were then sent to **Packaging,** where the inserts were placed in master cartons and sent to the warehouse. From the warehouse, shipment was made by freight, express, parcel post, or truck, to points all over the United States, Canada, and Latin America.

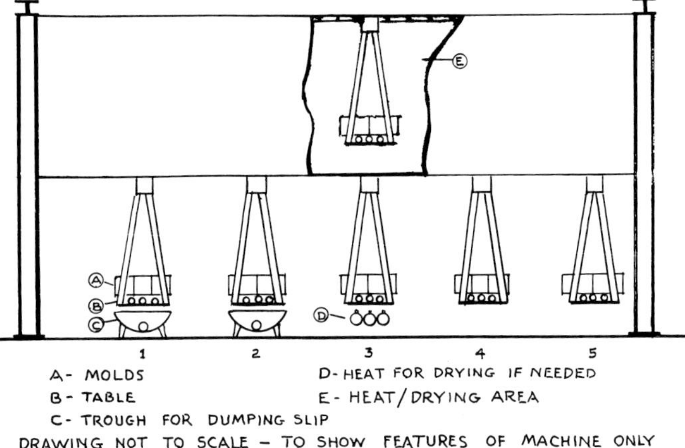

Casting Machine layout and workings.
Slip was poured into molds at Station #1. Slip was dumped from molds at Station #1 or #2. Ware was removed from molds at Station #3, #4, or #5. On large items, extra drying may be needed at Station #3.
Drawing Courtesy of Robert Heckman

Ram Press dies used at Shawnee. *Courtesy of Bernard Twiggs*

Chapter 3: Management and Personnel

Information provided through Shawnee Pottery Prospectus, Annual Reports, and the Zanesville Time Recorder. Whenever possible, actual dates are provided in parenthesis.

1936
(At time of incorporation December 9, 1936)

President (chief Executive Officer)
Addis E. Hull, Jr.
1426 Maple Ave., Zanesville, OH

Vice President and Treasurer (Chief Financial and Accounting Officer)
Robert C. Shilling
526 Thurman St., Zanesville, OH

Secretary
Ernest B. Graham
1170 Culbertson Ave., Zanesville, OH

Assistant Secretary (General Sales Manager)
J. Brannon Hull
2379 Dresden Rd., Zanesville, OH

Present Directors
Addis E. Hull, Jr., Zanesville, OH
W. Herbert Keller, Norristown, PA
Robert C. Shilling, Zanesville, OH

Persons Who Will Become Directors
Maurice Iserman
60 East 42nd St., New York City, NY
Malcolm A. Schweiker
Worcester, Montgomery County, PA

1944

President	Malcolm A. Schweiker
Executive V.P.	Albert P. Braid
Vice President	Rolf J. Falk
Vice President	Addis E. Hull
Secretary	Ernest B. Graham
Treasurer	Leo J. Decker
Directors	Albert P. Braid Ernest B. Graham Addis E. Hull Maurice Iserman W. Herbert Keller Malcolm A. Schweiker

1946

President	Malcolm A. Schweiker
Executive V.P.	Albert P. Braid
Vice President	R.J. Falk
Vice President	Addis E. Hull
Secretary	Ernest B. Graham
Treasurer	George L. Williams
Directors	Albert P. Braid Ernest B. Graham Addis E. Hull Maurice Iserman W. Herbert Keller Malcolm A. Schweiker

1947

President	Malcolm A. Schweiker
Executive V.P.	Albert P. Braid
Vice President In Charge of Sales	R.J. Falk
Secretary	Ernest B. Graham
Treasurer	George L. Williams
Sales Manager	Jess L. Parentice

1948

President	Albert P. Braid
Vice President	Addis E. Hull
Secretary	Ernest B. Graham
Treasurer	George L. Williams
Directors	Albert P. Braid Ernest B. Graham Addis E. Hull Maurice Iserman W. Herbert Keller Malcolm A. Schweiker

1949

President	Albert P. Braid
Vice President	Addis E. Hull
Secretary	Ernest B. Graham
Vice President & Treasurer	George L. Williams
Directors	Albert P. Braid Ernest B. Graham Albert J. Grosser John Hemphill Addis E. Hull Frank K. Ralston

1950

President	George L. Williams
Vice President In Charge of Sales	Jess L. Parentice
Secretary	Ernest B. Graham
Treasurer	Frank K. Ralston
Directors	Adolph Hirsch, Chairman Ernest B. Graham John Hemphill Frank K. Ralston George L. Williams

1951

President	George L. Williams
Vice President In Charge of Sales	Jess L. Parentice
Secretary	Ernest B. Graham
Directors	Adolph Hirsch, Chairman Ernest B. Graham John Hemphill Frank K. Ralston George L. Williams

1952

President	George L. Williams
Vice President In Charge of Sales	Jess L.Parentice
Secretary	Ernest B. Graham

1953

President	George L. Williams (Resigned May 1953)
President	Arthur K. Grindley (July 1, 1953)
Vice President In Charge of Sales	Jess L. Parentice
Secretary	Ernest B. Graham

1954

President	Arthur K. Grindley (Resigned January 11, 1954)
President & General Manager	John F. Bonistall (September 1, 1954)
Vice President In Charge of Sales	Jess L. Parentice
Secretary	Ernest B. Graham
Treasurer	Frank K. Ralston
Directors	Adolph Hirsch, Chairman John F. Bonistall Ernest B. Graham Frank K. Ralston George L. Williams

1955

President	John F. Bonistall
Secretary	Ernest B. Graham

1956

President	John F. Bonistall
Vice President	Jean C. Shaw
Secretary	Ernest B. Graham
Treasurer	Frank K. Ralston
Directors	Aldoph Hirsch, Chairman John F. Bonistall Ernest B. Graham T. R. Murphy Frank K. Ralston

1958

President	John F. Bonistall
Secretary	Ernest B. Graham

1959

President	John F. Bonistall
Secretary	Ernest B. Graham

1960

President	John F. Bonistall
Secretary	Ernest B. Graham

1961

President	John F. Bonistall (Resigned January 3, 1961)
President	Adolph Hirsch (apparently was named President during the liquidation process)

Shawnee Pottery Personnel

List Of Known Employees Spanning The Years 1936 Through 1961

T. H. Abbot, Plant Superintendent
Robert Adams
Eva Arnold
Ruth Axline
Baker
Guy Ball
Icel Ball
James Baldwin, Mold & Die Department
Barlow
Eleanor Bash, Decorator
Louise Elizabeth Bauer, Designer
P. T. Beutell, Office & Credit Manager
John F. Bonistall, President & General Manager
Bowen
Albert P. Braid, President & General Manager
Martha Holmes Breithaupt, Designer
Margaret Brokaw
Robert Brokaw
Fred Brown, Plant Superintendent
Conrad Burkhart, Glaze Department
Sylvia Burkhart, Inventory Clerk
Maude Carpenter, Supervisor, Finishing Department
Kathy Chema, Packing Department
Paul Chema, Sr.
Robert Chema, Time Study
Pauline Clark, Purchasing Clerk
Mildred Combs, Secretary to Jess Parentice
Cecil Corwin, Mold & Die Department
Hubert Coulson, Ceramic Engineer
Ruth Cover, Head Bookkeeper
Helen Craig
Eddie Dantz, Bisque Kiln
Alicia "Lish" Daugherty
Jim Davis, Designer
Kelly Davis, Packing & Shipping Foreman
Bill Deaton, Casting Department
Leo J. Decker, Treasurer
Betty Dickerson, Decorator
Edith Dozer, Decorator
Cecil Dunhauer
Dupler
Mary Elizabeth Duvall, Office
Grace Dye
George C. Earle, Plant Superintendent
Ebersbach
Irene Everly, Receptionist & Clerk

Rolf John Falk, Vice President, Sales
George Fraunfelter, Plant Superintendent
Thelma Fulton, Shipping Clerk
Rudolph V. Ganz, Designer
Howard Gibeau
Ernie Gibson, Glaze Department
Josephine Gorby
Frances Grable, Decorator
Ernest B. Graham, Secretary
Arthur K. Grindley, President
Ruth Hay
Edward Hazel, Die Maker
Robert Heckman, Designer
Mary Hepler, Decorator
Edna Holdren
Mack Holland, Designer
Ted Holsky, Foreman, Decorating Department
Avery Horner, Time Study
Addis E. Hull, Jr., President
J. Brannon Hull, General Sales Manager
Siegfried W. Illing, General Foreman to Sales Assistant
John Johnson
Mildred Johnson
Helen Keller, Payroll Clerk
Inez Kendall
Dewey Lee, Casting Department
A. E. "Ned" Lepper, Ceramic Engineer
Charlie Lewellen, Casting Department
Ralph Lewellen, Casting Department
Ann Lewis
Ethel Lewis
George Lewis, Foreman, Decorating Department
Mary Ludwig
Eloise McCann
Miller
William Mohler, Machinist
Roy Mohr, Foreman, Casting Department
Mossman
Russell Murray, Foreman, Gloss Kiln
Margaret Neff, Office
Elinor Osborne
Jess L. Parentice, Vice President, Sales
Harris Perkins, Glaze Technician
George Popp, Shipping
Clifford Potts, Die Maker
Frank K. Ralston, Treasurer
Elizabeth Richardson, Decorator
Marjorie Ringer, Office
Tommy Rivers, Foreman
Gladys Robinson, Decorator
Gerald Root, Maintenance Engineer
Margaret Saad, Secretary
Malcolm A. Schweiker, President and Founder
Roy W. Schweiker, Founder
George Schwerber, Modeler
Jean C. Shaw, Vice President & Production Manager
Robert C. Shilling, Vice President & Treasurer
Jeanette Shuey, Clerk
Bernard Sims
Kenneth Smith, Casting Department Foreman
Robert Smith
William Smith, Glaze Technician
Lulu Sneed
Lowell Soliday, Glaze Lab
Mary Louise Steil
Albert Stemm
Martha Rose Thomas, Secretary to Malcolm Schweiker
William Thorpe
Helen Tracy
Gertrude Trittipo, Office Manager, Purchasing Department
Bernard E. Twiggs, Mold & Die Supervisor
Clifford Twiggs
James Van Sant, Controller
Mildred Vasco, Assembly Line
Art Wagner, Decorator
Emily Walker, Clerk
Carolyn Walters
J. R. Westbrook, Plant Engineer
Bonnie Wetzel
Floyd Wetzel, Industrial Engineer
Frank White
James White, Labor Foreman
William White, Glaze Department
Wilkens
George L. Williams, President
Robert Wilson

Chapter 4: Labels and Marks

Labels and marks found on various pieces of Shawnee Pottery are pictured here; the figural labels are first.

Darn-Aide label, found on lady darning aide.
Courtesy of Dolores Rains

Valencia dinnerware label.
Courtesy of Pat & Elaine Jones

Corn King dinnerware label, Crown.

Painter's Palette, found on gold trim decorated items.

Accent Ashtray label.

Liäna label.

Cameo Ware label.

Essex China label.

Petit-Point label.

Chantilly label.
Courtesy of Marvin Mulligan

Shawnee China Underglaze Hand Decorated Indian Arrowhead label.

Kashäni label.
Courtesy of Melvin & Jean Gibson

Fairy Wood label.
Courtesy of Sue Blodgett

Kenwood label.
Designed by Robert Heckman

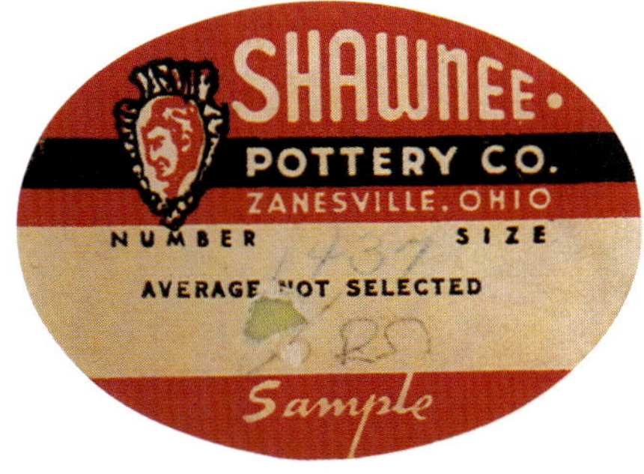

Shawnee Sample Label, red, black, white paper label, with Indian Arrowhead.

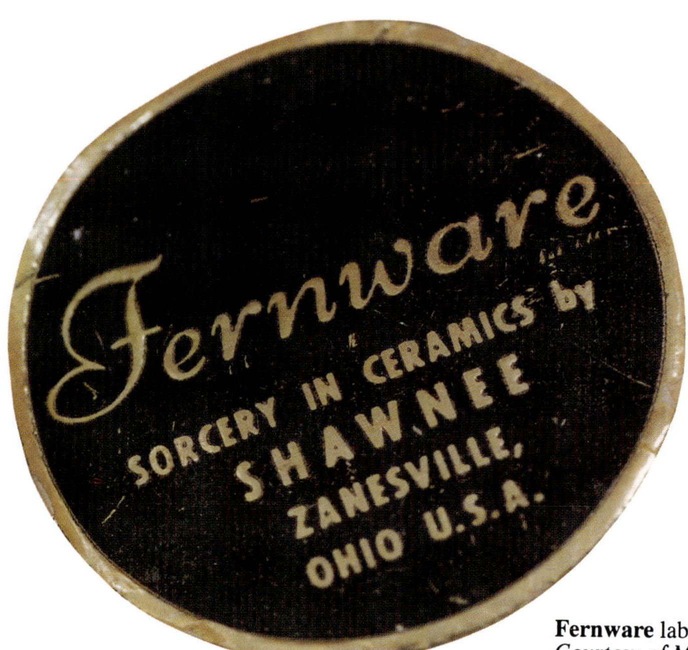

Shawnee Sample Label, green & white paper label.

For African Violets and all House Plants label.

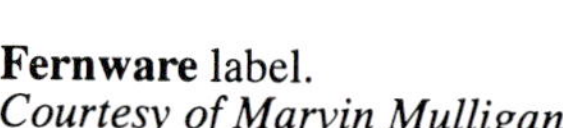

Fernware label.
Courtesy of Marvin Mulligan

Stardust label.
Courtesy of Paul & Linda Spenst

Shawnee Zanesville, Ohio banner label.
Courtesy of Shawn Jones

Tiara label.

Missing are two labels: **Cherie** and **Elegance**. Both are black triangle labels identical to Fairy Wood, Liäna, and Petit-Point labels.

Shawnee U.S.A.
Embossed mark typical of post-WWII era. The number 47 appears on the later version of the airbrushed red Bo Peep pitcher.

Touché label.

Patented Smiley U.S.A.
Impressed mark found on cookie jar.

Patented Puss 'n Boots U.S.A.
Impressed mark found on cookie jar.

Patented Winnie U.S.A.
Impressed mark found on cookie jar.

Patented Chanticleer U.S.A.
Impressed mark found on pitcher.

Patented Muggsy U.S.A.
Impressed mark found on cookie jar.

Tom The Piper's Son Patented U.S.A.
Impressed mark found on teapot. Number 44 appears on the later version with airbrushed colors.
Granny Ann teapots found marked with **U.S.A.** or **Patented Granny Ann U.S.A.**

Patented Bo Peep U.S.A.
Impressed mark found on earlier white hand decorated Bo Peep pitchers.

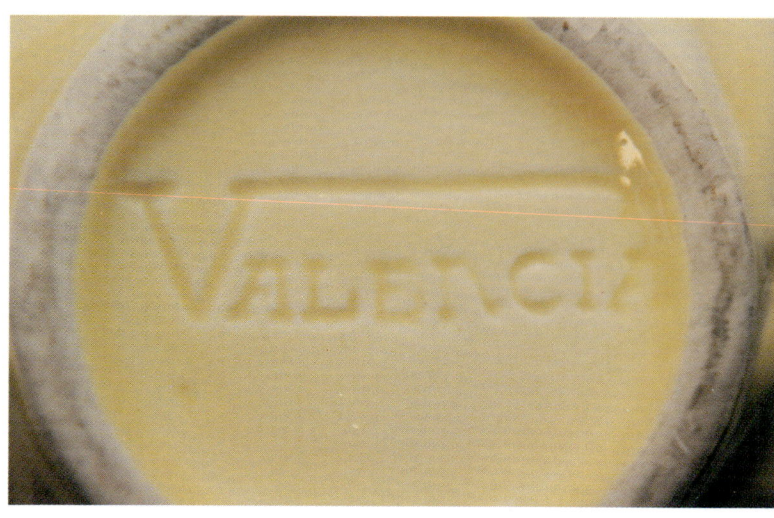

Valencia
Impressed mark found on Valencia dinnerware.

Mark found on Smiley Bank Head Cookie Jar.

Kenwood U.S.A.
Kenwood and U.S.A. are embossed, while number is incised. Found on Colt planter.

Mark found on Winnie Bank Head Cookie Jar.

Kenwood U.S.A.
Kenwood is embossed, while U.S.A. and number is impressed. Found on Confetti planter.

U.S.A.
Impressed mark found on most earlier pre-WWII items.

U.S.A. 616
Incised marks found on post-war items, with three-or-four-digit number being the reorder number. Note the ink stamped decorator's number 11 under the glaze; found on Colonial Lady planter.

727 U.S.A.
Embossed marks found on post-war items, with three-or-four-digit number being the reorder number. Found on High Chair planter.

Le Mieux China Hand Decorated 24 Karat Gold
Stamp found on gold goblet.

Le Mieux China Hand Decorated Platinum
Stamp found on platinum Smiley pitcher.

Le Mieux China Hand Decorated Platinum
Stamp found on platinum Sunflower teapot.

Section III: Kitchenware

Chapter 5: Cookie Jars

Additional cookie jars may be seen in the following chapters or sections: **Clover Blossom, Cottage, Fern, Fruit and Basket,** and **Snowflake.**

Smiley Pig

Design Patent 134,513 applied for October 9, 1942

Smiley Pig was the most popular of the five original figural cookie jars that Shawnee began producing in 1942. He was white, with cold painted red or blue neckerchief, brown hooves and eyelashes, and pink ears, nose, and tongue. As with all cold painted items, some paint wear is normal.

Smiley Pig with cold painted red neckerchief and brown hooves, 11-1/4 inches. Marked: U.S.A.

Smiley Pig with repainted blue neckerchief and brown hooves. Smiley's customized hand painted strawberries, his overall straps, and his facial features were added in later years, perhaps to coordinate him with the home in which he lived, 11-3/4 inches. Marked: U.S.A.

Smiley Pig with blue china paint neckerchief and black hooves, 11-1/4 inches. Marked: U.S.A.

All **Smiley Pig** cookie jars from this point on were underglaze decorated and fired, unless otherwise specified.

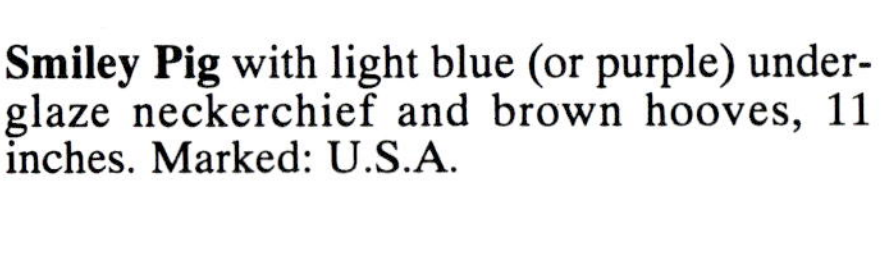

Smiley Pig with light blue (or purple) underglaze neckerchief and brown hooves, 11 inches. Marked: U.S.A.

Smiley Pig with blue neckerchief, black hooves, buttons, and eyelashes, 11-3/4 inches. Marked: U.S.A.

Tulip Smiley Pig, decorated with hand painted red and yellow tulips.
Both jars 11-1/4 inches. Marked: U.S.A.
Left: plain Tulip Smiley.
Right: gold trim Tulip Smiley.

Smiley Pig with red neckerchief, brown hooves, buttons, and eyelashes, 11-1/4 inches. Marked: U.S.A.

Shamrock Smiley Pig, decorated with hand painted green shamrocks.
Both jars 11-1/4 inches. Marked: U.S.A.
Left: plain Shamrock Smiley.
Right: gold trim Shamrock Smiley.

Chrysanthemum Smiley Pig, decorated with hand painted red chrysanthemums. Both jars 11-1/4 inches. Marked: U.S.A.
Left: plain Chrysanthemum Smiley.
Right: gold trim Chrysanthemum Smiley.

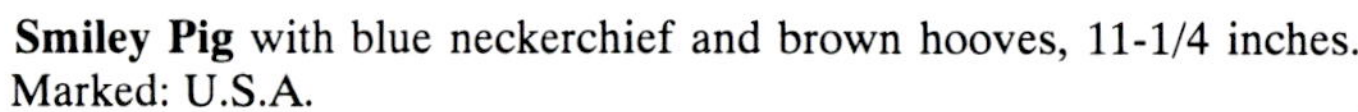

Smiley Pig with blue neckerchief and brown hooves, 11-1/4 inches. Marked: U.S.A.
Left: plain Smiley.
Right: Smiley with gold trim and flower decals.

Roses Smiley Pig, decorated with gold trim, and rose decals. Both jars 11-1/4 inches. Marked: U.S.A. Note that the green neckerchief Smiley does not have his name decal on the front of his overalls.
Left: Roses Smiley with green neckerchief.
Right: Roses Smiley with red neckerchief.

Smiley Pig with yellow neckerchief, gold trim, and flower decals.
Both jars 11-1/4 inches. Marked: U.S.A.
Left: yellow Smiley with red feet.
Right: yellow Smiley with white feet.

Smiley Pig with blue neckerchief. Both jars have gold trim, including on his overall buttons, flower decals, and are Marked: U.S.A.
Left: blue Smiley with black hooves.
Right: blue Smiley with brown hooves.

Daisy Smiley Pig with gold trim and pink daisy decals with yellow centers and green leaves, and a deep pink neckerchief, 11-1/4 inches. Marked: U.S.A. *Rare jar!*
From The Collection of Rich and Linda Guffey

Smiley Pig with yellow neckerchief, gold trim, flower decals, and brown feet, 11-1/4 inches. Marked: U.S.A.

Left: **Smiley Pig** with yellow neckerchief, gold trim and decals, and reddish-brown feet. Note the height of the blue on his sleeves. Marked: U.S.A.
Right: **Smiley Pig** with blue neckerchief, gold trim and decals, and brown hooves. Note that his overall buttons are brown, not gold trimmed. Marked: U.S.A.

Smiley Pig with yellow neckerchief, gold trim, flower decals, and reddish- brown feet. Note that Smiley's name decal is block-printed, not the usual script name decal. Marked: U.S.A.

Smiley Pig with hair, yellow neckerchief, gold trim, flower decals, original Painter's Palette label, 11-1/4 inches. Marked: U.S.A.

Smiley Pig with hair and bug, center-part hair, yellow neckerchief, gold trim and flower decals, 11-1/4 inches. Marked: U.S.A.

Smiley Pig with hair, yellow neckerchief, gold trim, flower decals, and hand painted green and rust flowers in the crooks of his arms.
From The Collection Of Linda Romberg

Chrysanthemum Smiley Pig with auburn hair, green neckerchief, and gold trim. Marked: U.S.A. *Rare Jar!*
From The Collection Of Hughy & Chris Mahloch

Top view of auburn haired Chrysanthemum Smiley.

Smiley Pig with hair, gold trim and decals.
From The Collection Of Katherine Braly

Smiley Pig has blue airbrushed neckerchief with hand painted flowers, gold trim, and flower decals. Marked: U.S.A.
From The Collection Of Hughy & Chris Mahloch

Smiley Pig with 2 bees on head, and patch on left shoulder. Marked: U.S.A. *From The Collection of Paul and Joy Schneider*

Back view of blue airbrushed Smiley Pig showing hand painted flowers on neckerchief bow.

Smiley Pig with blue airbrushed neckerchief, gold trim, flower decals, and black hooves, 11-1/4 inches. Marked: U.S.A.

Top view of center-part hair on Smiley.

Top view of Smiley's hair and bee.

Top view of Lee Boy's head.

Smiley Pig with center-part hair, gold trim and flower decals. Marked: U.S.A.

Smiley Pig with hair and bee on nose, gold trim and flower decals. Marked: U.S.A.

Smiley Pig, also known as Lee Boy, with hair, gold trim, flower decals; note red lines around mouth area. Marked: U.S.A. *From The Collection Of Paul and Joy Schneider*

Shamrock Smiley Pig with butterfly. Smiley has gold trim and a hand painted butterfly on his head, 11-1/4 inches. Marked: U.S.A. *From The Collection Of Arthur & Rita Bee*

Top view of Shamrock Smiley's butterfly.

Shamrock Smiley Pig with gold trim and hand painted bug on his head. Marked: U.S.A. *From The Collection Of Hughy & Chris Mahloch*

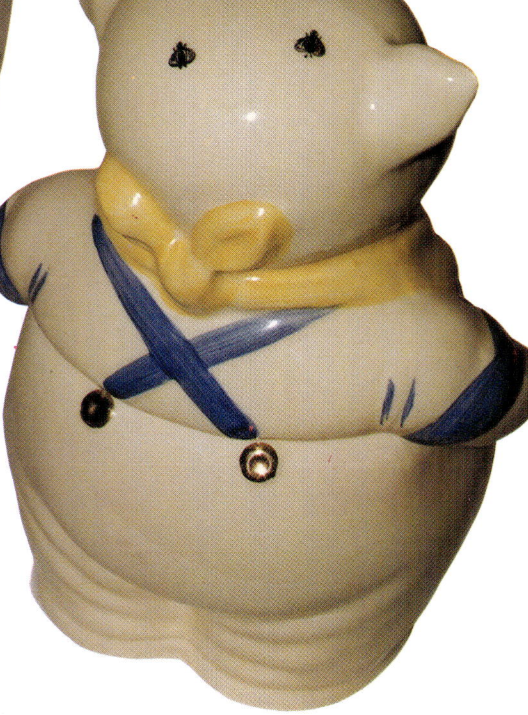

Back view of Smiley's head with three hand painted flies.

Smiley Pig with Shamrock bottom and blue neckerchief lid with gold trim, 11 inches, Marked: U.S.A. *From The Collection Of Elizabeth McConnell*

Note: First impressions are that this jar is mismatched. However, inquiries have turned up two of these jars, one of which comes with a special history, confirming that it was bought from the store matched like this.

Smiley Pig with gold trim, flower decals, a partial label, two hand painted flowers on overalls, and three hand painted flies on his head. Marked: U.S.A. *From The Collection Of Hughy & Chris Mahloch*

Smiley Pig with open eyes. Blue neckerchief, gold trim, flower decals, and unusual open eyes painted under the glaze. You can still see the embossed eyelashes that were never painted. Marked: U.S.A.
From The Collection of Dennis & Patricia Walsh.

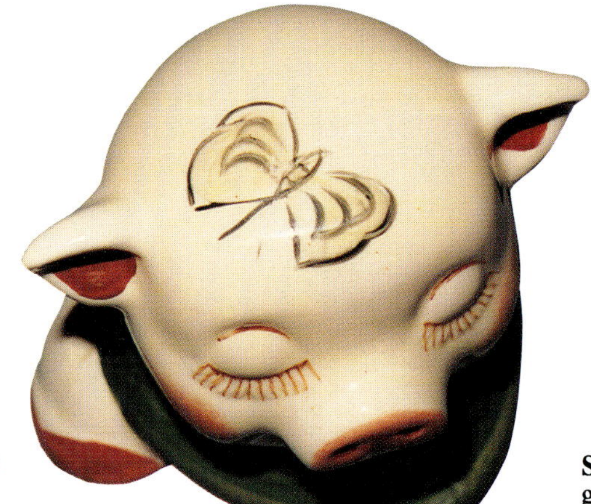

Shamrock Smiley Pig with butterfly on head, gold trim. Marked: U.S.A.

Butterfly on Shamrock Smiley.

Smiley Pig with black patch on back of overalls, gold trim, flower decals. Marked: U.S.A.

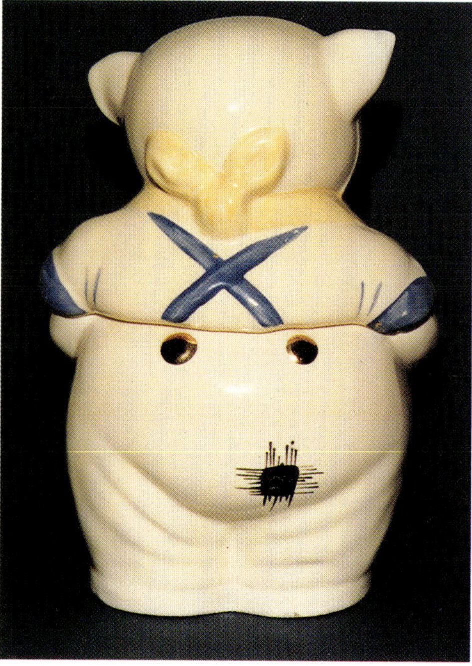

Smiley Pig with gold trim and hand painted flowers on overalls, red feet. Marked: U.S.A.

Smiley Pig with hair and hand painted flower on arms, gold trim and flower decals. Marked: U.S.A. *From The Collection of Melvin and Jean Gibson*

Black patch covering very rough blemish on Smiley's overalls.

Smiley Pig with two bugs, gold trim and flower decals, block-printed Smiley name decal on front. Marked: U.S.A. *From The Collection of Melvin and Jean Gibson*

Smiley Pig with red neckerchief, gold trim and flower decals. Marked: U.S.A.

Smiley Pig with green neckerchief, gold trim and flower decals, 11 inches. Marked: U.S.A.

Smiley Pig with pink poppy flower decals, gray leaves and stems on poppy, and gold trim. Note that the decals point to the sides as well as upward. Marked: U.S.A.
Note: This poppy decal with a stem and poppy bud extending beyond the large open poppy, has also appeared on a Smiley Pig cookie jar.

Smiley Pig with poppies. Poppy decals, in pink and gray, are pointed upward. Gold trim. Marked: U.S.A.

Smiley Pig with solid gold decoration. This gorgeous jar picks up the reflections of everything around him, 11-1/4 inches. Marked: U.S.A.

Smiley Pig with gold trim, flower decals, and original Painter's Palette label. Marked: U.S.A.

Chrysanthemum Smiley Pig with fired-on red neckerchief, gold trim, and a Painter's Palette label on the neckerchief, 11 inches. Marked: U.S.A.

Apple Smiley Pig with hand painted apples and leaves, gold trim on buttons. Marked: U.S.A.

Apple Smiley Pig with hand painted apples and leaves, gold trim. Note difference in leaves from previous Apple Smiley. Marked: U.S.A.

Smiley Pig, also known as Flat Head, with blue china paint neckerchief, gold trim, flower decals. Marked: U.S.A.
From The Collection of Paul and Joy Schneider

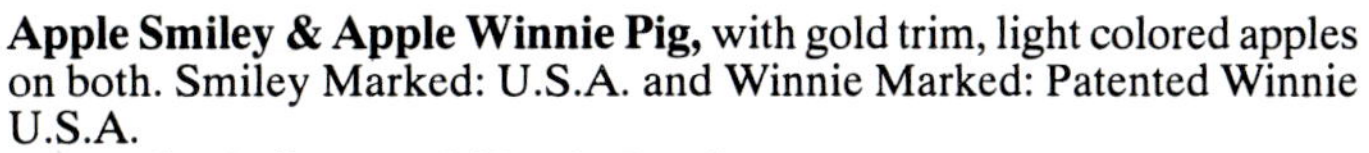

Apple Smiley & Apple Winnie Pig, with gold trim, light colored apples on both. Smiley Marked: U.S.A. and Winnie Marked: Patented Winnie U.S.A.
From The Collection Of Linda Romberg

Plum Smiley Pig, no gold trim, with hand-painted plums and green buttons on overalls. Marked: U.S.A. *From The Collection of Paul and Joy Schneider*

Apple Smiley & Apple Winnie Pig, with gold trim, darker colored apples on both. Note white feet on Winnie. Smiley Marked: U.S.A. and Winnie Marked: Patented Winnie U.S.A.
From The Collection Of Linda Romberg

Apple Smiley Pig, no gold trim, with large hand-painted apples and green buttons on overalls. Marked: U.S.A.

Winnie Pig

Design Patent 140,172 applied for April 20, 1944

Winnie Pig came along about a year and a half after Smiley Pig, when Shawnee was using underglaze decorating techniques. To date, no Winnie's have ever turned up decorated with cold paint. Winnie is white, wears a ruffle-collared coat and a flower-adorned hat, has her left hand in her coat pocket, and carries a purse with her right hand.

The Winnie Pig cookie jars shown in this book all exhibit differences in decoration, though some of these may be subtle. Remember that these jars were hand decorated by various artists, each with their own style.

There are three immediately noticeable features of a **Shamrock Winnie** to distinguish it from a **Clover Blossom Winnie:** 1) green shamrock on left coat pocket; 2) round flower for top coat button instead of a clover blossom and three leaves; 3) several clover flowers with leaves on hat, instead of a single clover blossom. Once you become accustomed to Shawnee colors, you will then notice a distinctive green that is only on the Clover Blossom Winnie's.

Winnie Pig, blue collar on coat, blue flower on hat and on purse. 11-1/4 inches
Left: plain Blue Winnie, Marked: U.S.A.
Right: gold trim Blue Winnie, Marked: Patented Winnie U.S.A.

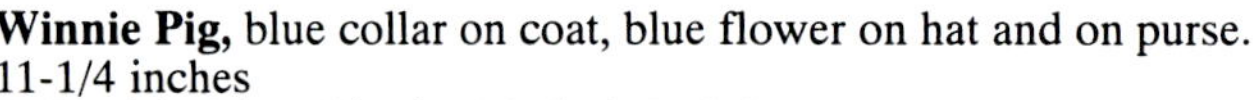

Winnie Pig, peach collar on coat, peach and blue flowers on hat and peach flower on top coat button. Purse has blue flower.
Both jars Marked: Patented Winnie U.S.A.
Left: plain Peach Winnie.
Right: gold trim Peach Winnie with red feet.

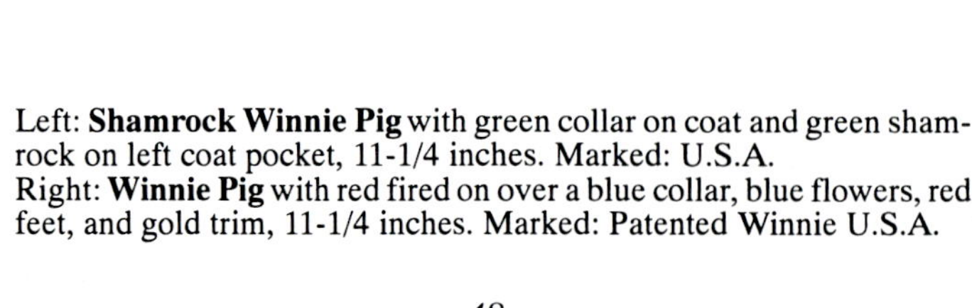

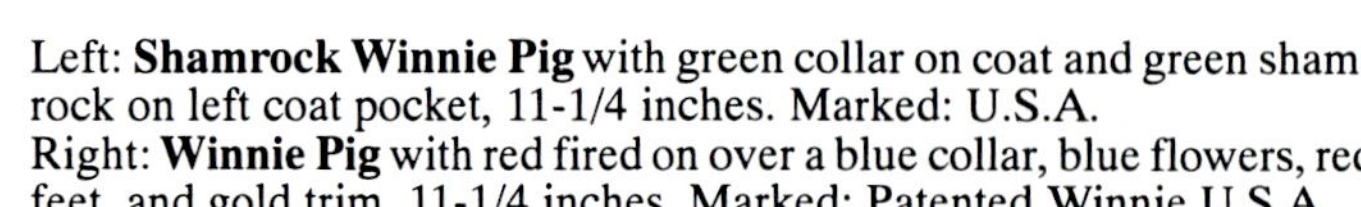

Left: **Shamrock Winnie Pig** with green collar on coat and green shamrock on left coat pocket, 11-1/4 inches. Marked: U.S.A.
Right: **Winnie Pig** with red fired on over a blue collar, blue flowers, red feet, and gold trim, 11-1/4 inches. Marked: Patented Winnie U.S.A.

Left: **Winnie Pig** with blue collar, gold trim, and red flower on coat and purse. Marked: U.S.A.
Right: **Winnie Pig** with peach collar, gold trim, and red flower on coat and purse. Marked: Patented Winnie U.S.A.

Winnie Pig, gold trim blue Winnie, with single red flower hand painted on hat. Marked: Patented Winnie U.S.A.

Left: **Winnie Pig** with red fired on over a blue collar, red flowers on coat and purse, gold trim. Marked: Patented Winnie U.S.A.
Right: **Winnie Pig** with blue collar, gold trim, and blue flower on coat and purse. Marked: Patented Winnie U.S.A.

Winnie Pig, gold trim blue Winnie. Marked: Patented Winnie U.S.A.

Winnie Pig, gold trim peach Winnie, with lime green collar, red flower on coat and on purse. Marked: Patented Winnie U.S.A.
Rare jar!

Winnie Pig, gold trim peach Winnie, with red flower on coat and on purse. Marked: Patented Winnie U.S.A.

Shamrock Winnie Pig, with gold trim, fired-on red collar over green. Marked: U.S.A.

Shamrock Winnie Pig, with gold trim, fired-on rust collar over green. Marked: U.S.A.

Winnie Pig, gold trim, fired-on red collar over blue. Marked: Patented Winnie U.S.A.

Clover Blossom Winnie Pig, plain, with 'Cookies' decal on coat. Marked: Patented Winnie U.S.A.

Apple Winnie Pig, plain, with emerald green leaves, buttons, and coat trim. Marked: Patented Winnie U.S.A.
From The Collection Of Linda Romberg

Clover Blossom Winnie Pig with gold trim, 11 inches. Marked: Patented Winnie U.S.A.
From The Collection of Paul & Joy Schneider

Clover Blossom Winnie Pig with gold trim. Marked: Patented Winnie U.S.A.

Apple Winnie Pig, gold trim, purse outlined in brown. Marked: Patented Winnie U.S.A.

Blueberry Winnie Pig, gold trim. Marked: Patented Winnie U.S.A.

Blueberry Winnie Pig gold trim, fired-on red over blue collar. Marked: Patented Winnie U.S.A.
From The Collection of Paul and Joy Schneider

Blueberry Winnie Pig with gold trim, Painter's Palette label.
Marked: Patented Winnie U.S.A.
From The Collection Of Hughy & Chris Mahloch

Apple Winnie Pig with gold trim, purse outlined in green. Marked: Patented Winnie U.S.A.

Bank Head Cookie Jars

These Shawnee bank head cookie jars had slots in the top of the head for coins, with the base of the head closed off to keep coins in. The bottoms of the jars were intended for cookies. All of the Winnie and Smiley heads appear to be decorated the same way, so are interchangeable with either butterscotch bases or chocolate bases.

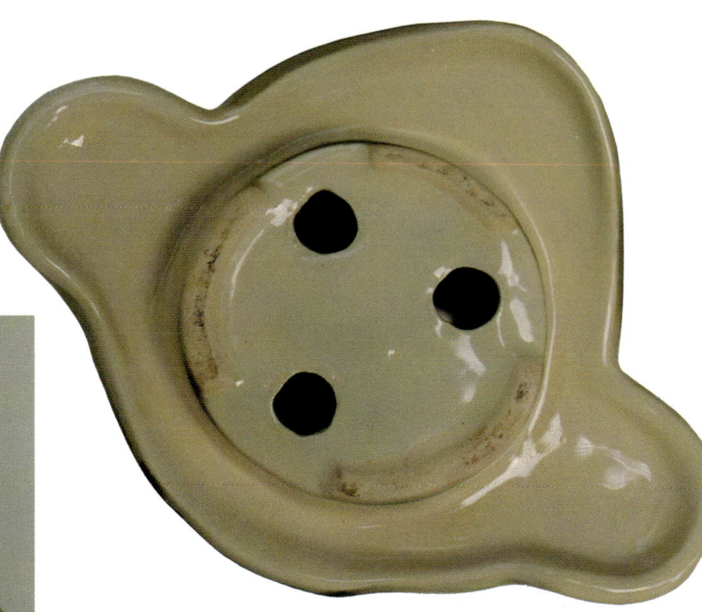

Butterscotch Smiley bank head shown from bottom, with three holes to make it easier to knock out the bottom and remove the money. Collectors prefer that these bottoms be intact. This head has a glazed bottom, and could also be used as a free-standing bank; most are unglazed where the three holes are.

Left: **Butterscotch Winnie** bank head cookie jar, 10-1/2 inches. Marked: Patented Winnie Shawnee 61 U.S.A.
Right: **Butterscotch Smiley** bank head cookie jar, 10-1/2 inches. Marked: Patented Smiley Shawnee 60 U.S.A.

Butterscotch Smiley bank head cookie jar with gold trim. A gold number 3 is written inside the head and the bottom of this jar. A gold trimmed Butterscotch Winnie bank/cookie jar may also be found. Marked: Patented Smiley Shawnee 60 U.S.A.
From The Collection of Paul and Joy Schneider

Left: **Chocolate Winnie** bank head cookie jar, 10-1/2 inches. Marked: Patented Winnie Shawnee 61 U.S.A.
Right: **Chocolate Smiley** bank head cookie jar, 10-1/2 inches. Marked: Patented Smiley Shawnee 60 U.S.A.

Chocolate Smiley bank head cookie jar, gold trim, 11 inches. Marked: U.S.A.

Chocolate Winnie bank head cookie jar, gold trim. Marked: Patented Winnie Shawnee 61 U.S.A.

Green Coat Winnie Pig bank head cookie jar, gold trim, 10-1/2 inches high. Marked: Patented Winnie Shawnee 61 U.S.A.
From The Collection of Paul and Joy Schneider

Green Coat Winnie Pig bank head cookie jar, gold trim. Marked: Patented Winnie Shawnee 61 U.S.A.

Green Coat Winnie Pig bank head cookie jar, gold trim. *Photo Courtesy of Jazz'e Junque Cookie Jar Shop, 3831 N. Lincoln Ave., Chicago, IL 60613*

Butterscotch Smiley cookie jar only with no money slot in head. Marked: Patented Smiley Shawnee 60 U.S.A.

Platinum Winnie Pig bank head cookie jar, chocolate bottom, platinum trim. Marked: Patented Winnie Shawnee 61 U.S.A.
From The Collection of Melvin and Jean Gibson
Too rare to determine value.

Chocolate Smiley and Winnie cookie jars only, no bank in heads. The bottoms are marked identically to the bank head cookie jars.

Top view of the Chocolate Smiley and Winnie with no money slots in head.

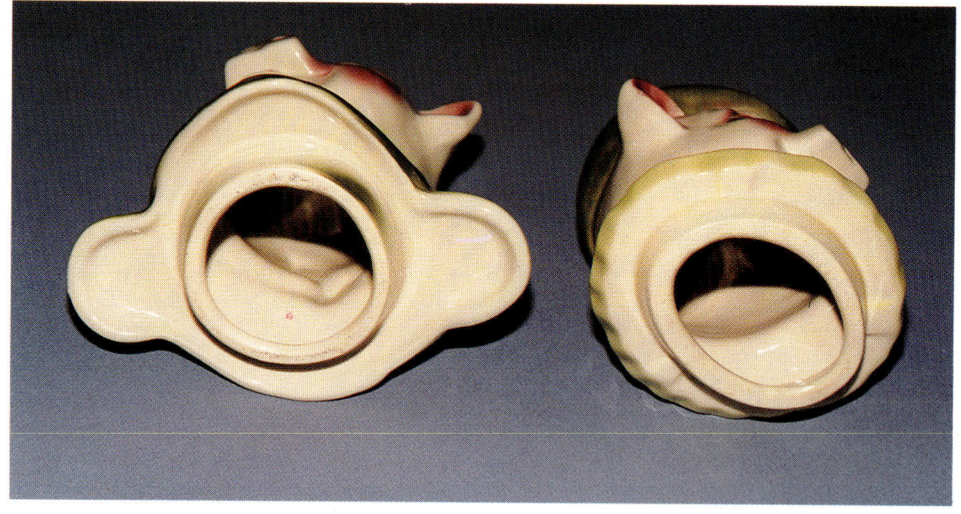

Bottom view of the Chocolate Smiley and Winnie showing normal opening for cookie jar heads.

Puss'n Boots

Design Patent 141,322 applied for February 28, 1945

Puss 'n Boots is approximately 10-1/4 inches high, has a white body, knitted booties on her front paws, a shawl over her shoulders, a bow at her neck, and a yellow bird on her hat. Marks will not be listed for individual jars, as all jars shown are marked with the impressed words: **Patented Puss 'n Boots U.S.A.**

Puss 'n Boots with long tail extending over her right front paw; all other details match the short tail jar.
From The Collection of Robert and Lois Duvall

Puss 'n Boots with short tail.

Puss 'n Boots with gold trim and flower decals, tail and lower body hand painted.

Puss 'n Boots with gold trim and flower decals, and hand painted tail. This is the harder-to-find white bow outlined with gold trim, which is actually the absence of red painted on the original bow.

Puss 'n Boots with gold trim and flower decals, with the tail and lower body airbrushed with color.

Puss 'n Boots with gold trim and flower decals, with tail and lower body hand painted.

Puss 'n Boots with gold trim and flower decals, with tail and lower body hand painted.

Puss 'n Boots with long tail, gold trim and flower decals, tail and lower body airbrushed.

Puss 'n Boots with short tail, white bow, gold trim and flower decals, hand painted tail and lower body.

Puss 'n Boots with long tail, gold trim and flower decals, airbrushed body. Note wedge-shaped space between front feet.

Puss 'n Boots with short tail, white bow, gold trim and flower decals, hand painted tail and lower body.

Puss 'n Boots with solid gold decoration, long tail. Marked: Patented Puss 'n Boots U.S.A. *Too rare to determine value.*

Muggsy

Design Patent 139,094 applied for June 30, 1944.

Muggsy, Shawnee's favorite canine, obviously has a toothache. His head is wrapped with a blue scarf that covers his left jaw, and is tied in a bow on top. Muggsy can be found marked with his name, or simply with a U.S.A.

Muggsy decorated plain, with the standard blue scarf, 11-1/4 inches. Marked: Patented Muggsy U.S.A.

Muggsy with gold trim and flower decals, and hand decorated black on tail and ears, 11-1/4 inches. Marked: U.S.A.
From The Collection of Rich & Linda Guffey

Muggsy with his fur detailed with gold trim decoration, 11-1/4 inches. Marked: Patented Muggsy U.S.A.

Muggsy with his fur detailed with wavy gold trim decoration, 11-1/4 inches. Marked: Patented Muggsy U.S.A.
From The Collection Of Hughy & Chris Mahloch

Muggsy with gold trim and White Rose decals, 11-1/4 inches. *Rare!*

Muggsy with rare green scarf, gold trim and flower decals, 11-1/4 inches. Marked: Patented Muggsy U.S.A.
Rare!

Left: **Muggsy** with gold trim and flower decals, 11-1/4 inches, Marked: Patented Muggsy U.S.A.
Right: **Muggsy** with gold trim and flower decals, and original Painter's

Muggsy with gold trim and hand painted black fur decoration. Marked: Patented Muggsy U.S.A. *Rare!*
From The Collection of Paul & Joy Schneider

Muggsy with gold trim and flower decals. Marked: Patented Muggsy U.S.A. *From The Collection of Robert & Lois Duvall*

Muggsy with gold trim and flower decals. Marked: Patented Muggsy U.S.A.

Lucky Elephant

Design Patent 134,514 applied for October 9, 1942

This caricature of a sitting elephant cookie jar was one of the five original figural cookie jars that Shawnee produced. Elephant is white, has a bent trunk that forms a handle for lifting the lid, with cold painted black eyes and feet, pink ears and mouth, and either a red or blue bow tie.

Lucky Elephant with gold trim, flower decals, and hand painted black bug on his right tusk, 11-3/4 inches. Marked: U.S.A.

Left: **Elephant** decorated plain, with red bow tie. Some cold paint wear, which is typical with these early jars, 11-3/4 inches. Marked: U.S.A. Right: **Lucky Elephant** with gold trim and flower decals, and a gold decal with his name *Lucky* on his chest, 11-3/4 inches. Marked: U.S.A.

Lucky Elephant with gold trim and flower decals, original Painter's Palette label. Hand painted flowers around back and side, 11-3/4 inches. Marked: U.S.A.

Another view of previous Lucky with flowers delicately hand painted around his back and sides.

Lucky Elephant with gold trim, flower decals, hand painted black bug on his right tusk, and hand painted flowers on his left side and foot, 11-3/4 inches. Marked: U.S.A.
From The Collection of Linda Romberg

Lucky Elephant with gold trim, flower decals, and rare red collar, Painter's Palette label, 11-1/2 inches. Marked: U.S.A.
From The Collection of Paul & Joy Schneider

Lucky Elephant with gold trim, and all hand painted flowers. Marked: U.S.A. *Rare!.*
From The Collection Of Hughy & Chris Mahloch

Sailor Boy with black hair, and decorated with gold trim, 11-1/4 inches. Marked: U.S.A.

Sailor Boy

Design Patent 134,512 applied for October 9, 1942

Sailor Boy is a caricature of a little boy dressed up in sailors' garb. He is white, with cold painted black eyes, necktie, and shoes, red lips, and blue stars on his hat and blouse collar. It is believed that production did not extend beyond the war years of the mid-forties. Little Sailor Boy is one of the original five figural Shawnee cookie jars.

The gold trim decorated Sailor Boy cookie jars done by outside decorators sometimes had a gold decal of the letters **GOB** applied to him. Research by Master Chief Richard Guffey, U.S.N., has turned up the following information from the book *Naval Ceremonies, Customs, and Traditions* published by Naval Institute Press, Annapolis, Maryland:

> *Excerpts from Miscellaneous Historical Facts:*
> "The word GOB as meaning a sailor of the United States Navy is most probably an abbreviation of the Chinese transcription of the Spanish word 'Captain', pronounced 'kia-pi-tan' in Pekingese (Mandarin), but which the people in Canton and Hongkong pronounce 'gob-bid-dan'. The term was applied, certainly as long ago as the first decade of this century, if not earlier, to 'captains' of foreign ships, and loosely, to all foreign sailors on their ships in the ports of South China or ashore. The longer word was later shortened to the first syllable 'gob' and thus found a pretty general monosyllabic use."

Sailor Boy with white dots painted over the black on his necktie, 11-1/2 inches. Marked: U.S.A.

Sailor Boy with blond hair, and decorated with gold trim, 11-1/2 inches. Marked: U.S.A.

Left: **Sailor Boy** with reddish blond hair, gold trim, and flower decals. Marked: U.S.A.
Right: **Sailor Boy** with blond hair, gold trim, and flower decals. Marked: U.S.A.
From The Collection of Linda Romberg

Sailor Boy with solid gold decoration. Marked: U.S.A.
Too rare to determine value.

Sailor Boy with some cold paint wear, 11 inches. Marked: U.S.A.

Sailor Boy with blond hair, gold trim, flower decals, and a hand painted bug on the top of his hat that overlaps onto the side. Marked: U.S.A.

Sailor Boy with black hair, gold trim, 11-1/2 inches. Marked: U.S.A.

Jack (Dutch Boy)

Design Patent 134,511 applied for October 9, 1942

Jack was one of the five original figural cookie jars that Shawnee produced. He was first decorated with cold paint, though his pants were often blue or yellow underglaze. Later, Jack was underglaze decorated with blue stripes on his pants, and paired with Jill who displayed a tulip on her apron. It is here that they are most often referred to as *Dutch Boy and Girl*, probably because of the tulip, combined with Jack's dutch bob haircut. All of the gold trim jars of Jack have gold decals declaring his name to be *Happy*.

Jill (Dutch Girl)

Design Patent 134,579 applied for October 9, 1942

Jill was one of the five original figural cookie jars that Shawnee produced. She was first decorated with cold paint, though her skirt and apron were often blue or yellow underglaze. Later, Jill was underglaze decorated with a tulip on her apron, and became known to collectors as *Dutch Girl.* Gold trim varieties of Jill are numerous, and it's here where she displays a gold decal declaring her name to be *Cooky.*

Note: Confused about names? In this book, cold painted original jars are Jack and Jill. The later underglaze decorated jars, with a tulip on the girl and stripes on the boy, will be as they've always been called by collectors .... Dutch Boy and Dutch Girl. Gold trim jars will be Happy and Cooky.

Dutch Boy with crisscross striped pants, underglaze decorated, 11 inches. Marked: U.S.A.
Dutch Girl with tulip on apron, underglaze decorated, 11-1/2 inches. Marked: U.S.A.

Jack and **Jill,** with matching yellow bottoms. Jack's paint has been touched up, and Jill's paint has been washed away.
Jack is 11-1/4 inches, Marked: U.S.A.
Jill is 11-1/2 inches, Marked: U.S.A.

Left: **Happy (Dutch Boy)** with gold trim and flower decals. Marked: U.S.A.
Right: **Cooky (Dutch Girl)** with gold trim and flower decals. Marked: U.S.A.

Left: **Happy** decorated with gold trim and flower decals, and two hand painted flowers on the back of his pants. Marked: U.S.A.
Right: **Happy** decorated with gold trim and hand painted patches on his pants. Marked: U.S.A.

Jack and **Jill** with matching blue bottoms, original cold paint wear on both.
Jack is 11-1/4 inches, Marked: U.S.A.
Jill is 11-1/2 inches, Marked: U.S.A.

Happy with gold trim, rust scarf, patches. Marked: U.S.A.

Happy with gold trim, blue scarf, patches. Marked: U.S.A.

Hand painted flowers on the white pants of previous Happy.

Happy with gold trim and flower decals. Marked: U.S.A.

Happy with gold trim and flower decals.
Marked: U.S.A.
From The Collection of Robert & Lois Duvall

Cooky with gold trim and flower decals. Marked: U.S.A.

Happy (Dutch Boy) with gold trim and flower decals. Marked: U.S.A.

Dutch Boy with double stripes on pants. Marked: U.S.A.

Cooky (Dutch Girl) with gold trim and flower decals. Hand painted flowers on shoulder and arm. Marked: U.S.A.

Hand painted flowers on previous Cooky (Dutch Girl) cookie jar.

Left: **Cooky (Jill)** decorated with gold trim and hand painted flowers in her hands. Marked: U.S.A.
Right: **Cooky (Jill)** decorated with gold trim and flower decals. Marked: U.S.A.

Cooky with gold trim. Marked: U.S.A.

Cooky with gold trim and flower decals. Marked: U.S.A.

Jill decorated with beautiful hand painted flowers, stems, and leaves.
Too rare to determine value.

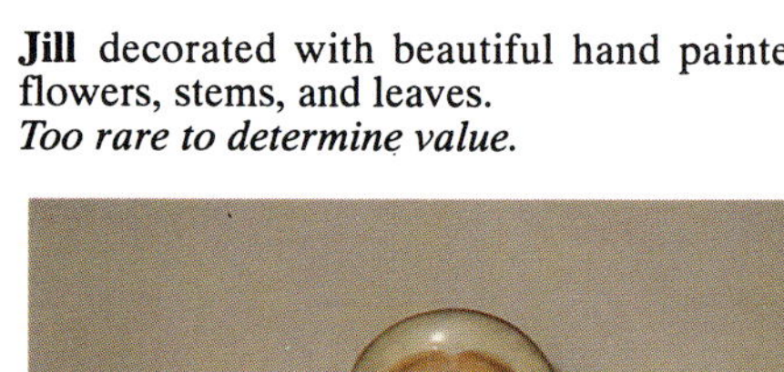

Cooky decorated with gold trim and flower decals, 11-1/2 inches. Marked: U.S.A.

Cooky with gold trim and flower decals, hand painted flowers in her hands. Marked: U.S.A.

Left: **Cooky (Dutch Girl)** with gold trim and flower decals. Marked: U.S.A.
Right: **Cooky (Dutch Girl)** with tulip, gold trim and flower decals. Marked: U.S.A.
From The Collection of Linda Romberg

Left: **Great Northern Dutch Boy** with butterscotch bottom, yellow top. Marked: Great Northern U.S.A. 1025
Right: **Great Northern Dutch Girl** in two shades of green. Marked: Great Northern U.S.A. 1026

Great Northern Dutch Girl, with unusual beige skirt, yellow and green top. Marked: Great Northern U.S.A. 1026
From The Collection of Shirley Legum

Great Northern Dutch Girl, white with blue trim.
Marked: Great Northern U.S.A. 1026

Great Northern Dutch Girl, also known as Mimi, with unusual beige skirt, black and orange top. Marked: Great Northern U.S.A. 1026
From The Collection of Paul and Joy Schneider

Drum Major

Design Patent 151,810 applied for March 14, 1947

Drum Major extends out of a round drum cookie jar, which is adorned with toy soldiers carrying rifles. A catalog for Butler Brothers dated February 1950 offers this jar. An important point here is that this jar was decorated using BOTH spray painted and brush painted techniques. The red, yellow, and blues were sprayed on, while the black features were applied with a brush. This method of spray decorating was implemented years before the 1954 time-frame that has always been reported up to now.

Tip: Drum Major's head often broke off quite cleanly at the neck, so check for a reglued head.

Jo Jo Clown

Jo Jo the Clown is shown tumbling with a seal atop a ball; and the seal is balancing his own ball on the tip of his nose. This jar, which appears in a 1951 Shawnee catalog, also implements the combination of spray and brush decorating techniques.

Tip: the yellow ball on the seal's nose is often found damaged, so check closely for repairs.

Jo Jo Clown and **Seal** plain, 9 inches high.
Marked: Shawnee U.S.A. 12

Drum Major, plain, 10 inches high. Marked: U.S.A. 10

Drum Major, gold trim, 10 inches high. Marked: U.S.A. 10

Jo Jo Clown and **Seal** with gold trim, 9 inches high. Marked: Shawnee U.S.A. 12

Owl

Design Patent 139,098 applied for March 1, 1944

Winking Owl has only been found underglaze decorated, with no cold-painted versions turning up to date.

Winking Owl with gold trim and hand decorated, 11-1/2 inches high. Marked: U.S.A.

Left: **Winking Owl** decorated plain, 11-1/2 inches. Marked: U.S.A.
Right: **Winking Owl** with gold trim and hand decorated features, 11-1/2 inches. Marked: U.S.A.

Winking Owl with gold trim and hand decorated, 11-1/2 inches high. Marked: U.S.A.

Little Chef

Design Patent 157,511 applied for March 18, 1948

Hexagonal jar with embossed chefs, gingerbread boys, and the word COOKIES, all underglaze decorated.

Left: **Little Chef** in green color, 8-1/2 inches. Marked: U.S.A.
Right: **Little Chef** in white, with red and gold trim decorated, 8-1/2 inches. Marked: U.S.A.

Left: **Little Chef,** decorated, with white background, 8-1/2 inches. Marked: U.S.A.
Right: **Little Chef,** decorated, with cream background, 8-1/2 inches. Marked: U.S.A.

Little Chef in caramel (or butterscotch) color, 8-1/2 inches. Marked: U.S.A.

Little Chef in yellow, 8-1/2 inches. Marked: U.S.A.

Carousel

The Carousel is circular, embossed with four animals riding around it. The word COOKIES is embossed on two sides of this jar.

Carousel decorated with red and blue cold paint, which is greatly worn, 9-3/4 inches high. Marked: U.S.A. S4

Carousel that appears to have been repainted, 9-3/4 inches high. Marked: U.S.A. S4

Pennsylvania Dutch, 8-1/4" high. Marked: U.S.A. 75
The complete line of Pennsylvania Dutch can be seen in chapter 15.

Corn King & Corn Queen

The complete lines of Corn King and Corn Queen dinnerware can be seen in chapters 17 and 19.

Left: **Corn King**, 10-1/4 inches. Marked: Shawnee U.S.A. 66
Right: **Corn Queen**, 10-1/4 inches. Marked: Shawnee U.S.A. 66

Jug, blue, with hand painted flowers, 8-1/2 inches. Marked: U.S.A. 75

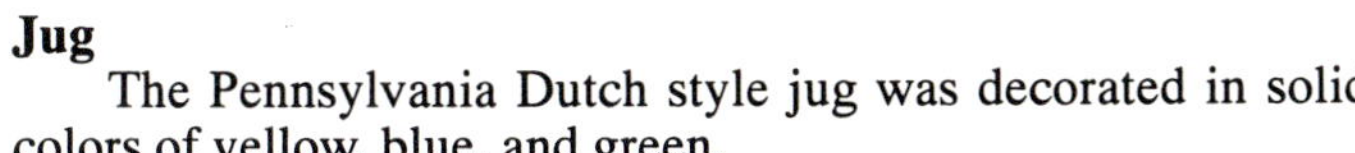

Jug

The Pennsylvania Dutch style jug was decorated in solid colors of yellow, blue, and green.

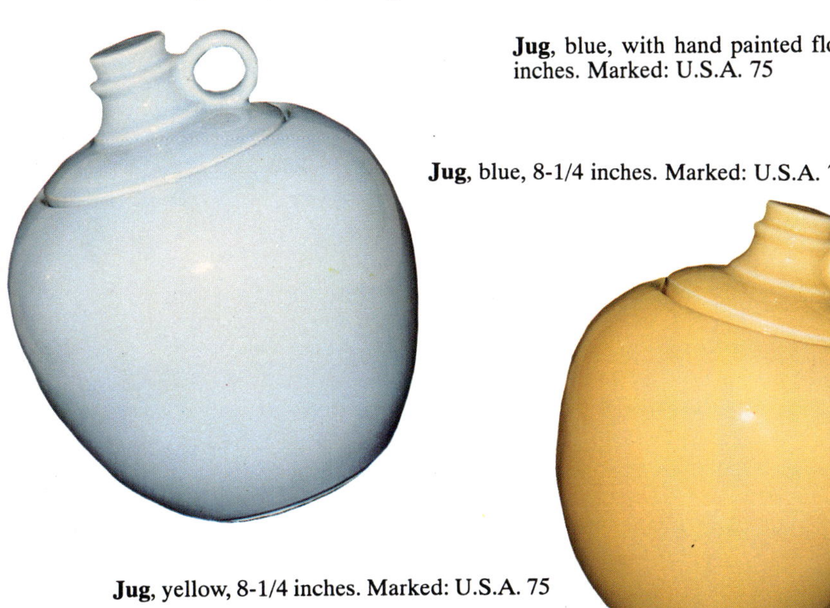

Jug, blue, 8-1/4 inches. Marked: U.S.A. 75

Jug, yellow, 8-1/4 inches. Marked: U.S.A. 75

Jug, blue, hand painted flowers, 8-1/2 inches. Marked: U.S.A. 75

Fruit and Basket, gold trim on fruit, 8-1/4 inches. Marked: Shawnee U.S.A. 84. The complete line of Fruit and Basket can be found in chapter 15.

Fern octagonal cookie jar, 8-3/4 inches. Marked: U.S.A. More items in the Fern Ware line can be found in chapter 15.

Snowflake beanpot-style cookie jar, 7-1/4 inches. Marked: U.S.A. More items in the Snowflake line can be found in chapter 15.

Lobster Snack Jar or Bean Pot, 40 oz. Marked: Kenwood Oven Proof U.S.A. 925
More items in the Lobster line can be found in chapter 18.

Basketweave

This hexagon jar with a basketweave pattern, was made during Shawnee's early years. Some decals were applied to these jars at the factory, and were fired on at low temperatures. However, additional gold trim, decals, and hand painted flowers, were most likely applied by outside decorators.

Left: **Basketweave** jar in powder blue, with no decal decoration, 7-3/4 inches. Marked: U.S.A.
Right: **Basketweave** jar with gold trim and flower decals, 7-3/4 inches. Marked: U.S.A.

Left: **Basketweave** jar with Pennsylvania Dutch style decal, 7-3/4 inches. Marked: U.S.A.
Right: **Basketweave** jar with Basket of Flowers decal, 7-3/4 inches. Marked: U.S.A.

Left: **Basketweave,** green, gold trim, with hand painted flowers, 7-1/2 inches. Marked: U.S.A.
Right: **Basketweave,** blue, gold trim, with hand painted flowers, 7-1/2 inches. Marked: U.S.A.
From The Collection of Terry & Sandra Bauer

Chapter 6: Canisters

The four-sided canisters with rounded corners were made during Shawnee's early years. Decals were applied to these canisters at the factory and fired on at low temperatures. However, additional gold trim, decals, and hand painted flowers were most likely applied by outside decorators.

Left: **Canister**, blue, with gold stenciling and hand painted saddle, horn, and whip, 7 inches, original Painter's Palette label. Marked: U.S.A.
Right: **Canister**, blue, with gold stenciling and hand painted tobacco leaves, 7 inches. Marked: U.S.A.
From The Collection Of Terry & Sandra Bauer

Left: **Canister**, blue, with Dutch Boy and Girl decal, 7 inches. Marked: U.S.A.
Right: **Canister**, yellow, with Rose decal, 7 inches. Marked: U.S.A.

Canisters, blue, with Fruit decal, each is 7 inches high. Marked: U.S.A.

Canister, green, with gold stenciling and hand painted top hat, cane, and lighted cigarette, 7 inches. Marked: U.S.A.
From The Collection Of Tom & Kathy Bulmer

Canister bottom and lid of previous item.

Canister, yellow, with gold stenciling and hand painted top hat, cane, and lighted cigarette, 7 inches. Marked: U.S.A.
From The Collection of Melvin and Jean Gibson

Chapter 7: Pitchers Figural

Apple Smiley Pig with red neckerchief, plain, 7-3/4 inches. Marked: Patented Smiley U.S.A.

Smiley Pig

Design Patent 140,203 applied for November 17, 1944

Left: **Smiley Pig** with burgundy and blue flowers, plain, 7-3/4 inches. Marked: Patented Smiley U.S.A.
Right: **Smiley Pig** burgundy, gold trim, fired-on red feet, 7-3/4 inches. Marked: Patented Smiley U.S.A.

Clover Blossom Smiley Pig with gold trim. Marked: Patented Smiley U.S.A. *Courtesy Of Paul & Linda Spenst*

Left: **Smiley Pig** with peach and blue flowers, plain, 7-3/4 inches. Marked: Patented Smiley U.S.A.
Right: **Smiley Pig** peach, with gold trim, red feet, 7-3/4 inches. Marked: Patented Smiley U.S.A.

Clover Blossom Smiley Pig with gold trim. Marked: Patented Smiley U.S.A.

Smiley Pig with flowers on chest and solid platinum decoration, Essex China label. Marked: Patented Smiley U.S.A. *Rare!*

Clover Blossom Smiley Pig with solid platinum decoration, 7-1/2 inches. Marked: Patented Smiley U.S.A.
Goblets with solid platinum decoration, 3-1/4 inches high.
Rare!
Courtesy of Melvin & Jean Gibson

Clover Blossom Smiley Pig with solid gold decoration, 7-1/2 inches. Marked: Patented Smiley U.S.A.
Goblets with solid gold decoration, 3-1/4 inches high. All four goblets were found with the Smiley pitcher; apparently were sold as a set. Marked with a stamp: Le Mieux China Hand Decorated 24 Karat Gold
Rare!

Chanticleer

Design Patent 147,541 applied for April 20, 1946

All Chanticleer Rooster pitchers shown are marked exactly the same, with the impressed words: **Patented Chanticleer U.S.A.**

Chanticleer with gold trim and flower decals.

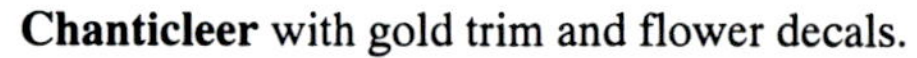

Left: **Chanticleer** decorated plain, 7-1/2 inohes high.
Right: **Chanticleer** with gold trim and flower decals; red on comb and wattles is fired on over the burgundy.

Chanticleer with gold spatter, solid gold handle and neck feathers.
Courtesy Of Robert & Lois Duvall

Chanticleer with gold trim and flower decals, 7-1/2 inches high.
Courtesy of Rich & Linda Guffey

Chanticleer with gold trim and poppy decals.

Chanticleer with gold trim and airbrushed colors.

Chanticleer with gold trim and airbrushed colors.

Chanticleer with gold trim and airbrushed colors.

Chanticleer with hand painted scene of New Orleans, LA.

Chanticleer, back side hand painted with words *Old Slark House* 1779 New Orleans La.

Left: **Chanticleer** with gold trim, flower decals, burgundy wings.
Right: **Chanticleer** with gold trim, flower decals, yellow wings.
Courtesy of Linda Romberg

Left: **Chanticleer** with gold spatter and solid gold handle.
Right: **Chanticleer** with gold feathers, comb, wattles, and beak.
Courtesy of Linda Romberg

Chanticleer pitcher with solid gold decoration.
Goblets with solid gold decoration, 3-1/4 inches high.
Rare!
Courtesy of Melvin & Jean Gibson

Bo Peep

Design Patent 139,093 applied for June 30, 1944

The Little Bo Peep pitchers shown are 8 inches high, have hand decorated details, and are often referred to by collectors as the "large" Bo Peep. Note the variations in the color of her hair from blond to strawberry blond. All Little Bo Peep pitchers shown have the impressed mark: **Patented Bo Peep U.S.A.**

Left: **Bo Peep** with gold trim, flower decals, red over peach.
Right: **Bo Peep** with gold trim, flower decals, blue over peach.

Left: **Bo Peep** with blue bonnet and peach coat trim, plain.
Right: **Bo Peep** with blue bonnet, gold trim, flower decals, red over peach.

Left: **Bo Peep** with lavender bonnet and green coat trim, plain.
Right: **Bo Peep** with gold trim, purple pansy decals, lavender bonnet.

Left: **Bo Peep** with gold trim, flower decals.
Right: **Bo Peep** with gold trim, flower decals.

Left: **Bo Peep** with gold trim and hand decorated; note red ribbon under her right arm.
Right: **Bo Peep** with gold trim, flower decals.

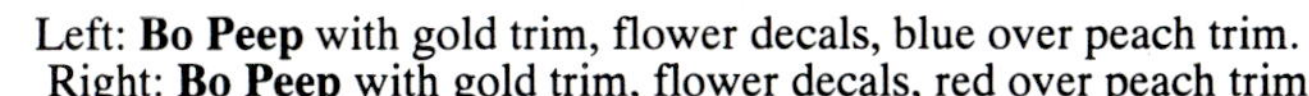

Left: **Bo Peep** with gold trim, flower decals, blue over peach trim.
Right: **Bo Peep** with gold trim, flower decals, red over peach trim.

Left: **Bo Peep** with gold trim, flower decals.
Right: **Bo Peep** with gold trim, flower decals.

Bo Peep with gold trim, flower decals.

Top: **Little Bo Peep** with gold trim. Marked: Shawnee U.S.A. 47
Bottom: **Little Boy Blue** with gold trim. Marked: Shawnee U.S.A. 46
Courtesy of Linda Romberg

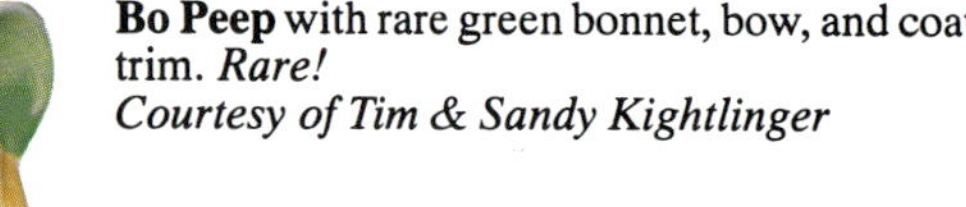

Bo Peep with rare green bonnet, bow, and coat trim. *Rare!*
Courtesy of Tim & Sandy Kightlinger

Bo Peep and Boy Blue

This Little Bo Peep and Little Boy Blue combination appear in a 1951 Shawnee catalog, making this a later version of the original Bo Peep. Collectors often refer to this Bo Peep as the "small" Bo Peep, as she is 7-1/2 inches high, and holds 30 ounces. Little Boy Blue is also 7-1/2 inches high, and holds 20 ounces. The red, yellow, and blue colors here are spray decorated, with facial features done by brush.

Left: **Little Bo Peep** Marked: Shawnee U.S.A. 47
Right: **Little Boy Blue** Marked: Shawnee U.S.A. 46

Bo Peep with rare blue airbrushed dress, gold trim. *Rare!*
Courtesy of Don & De Anderson

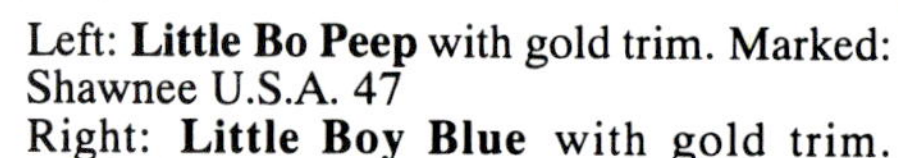

Left: **Little Bo Peep** with gold trim. Marked: Shawnee U.S.A. 47
Right: **Little Boy Blue** with gold trim. Marked: Shawnee U.S.A. 46
Courtesy of Terry & Sandra Bauer

Chapter 8: Pitchers Non-Figural

Additional pitchers may also be found in specific lines such as: **Fern, Fruit, Laurel Wreath, Valencia, Wave, White Corn,** and **Miscellaneous Kitchen Ware.**

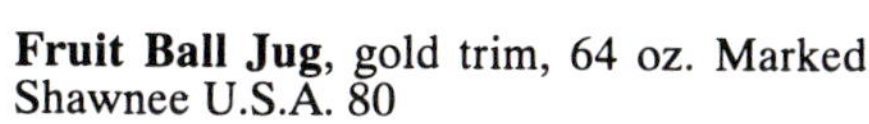

Fruit Ball Jug, gold trim, 64 oz. Marked: Shawnee U.S.A. 80

Ribbed Utility, 5" high. Marked: U.S.A.

Pennsylvania Dutch ball jug, 64 oz. Marked: U.S.A.

Left: **Space Saver Jug**, 20-oz capacity, hand decorated flowers, 6 inches. Marked: U.S.A. 35
Right: **Space Saver Jug**, 20-oz capacity, spray decorated embossed flower, 6 inches. Marked: U.S.A. 40

Sunflower ball jug, 7-1/4 inches. Marked: U.S.A.

Flower & Fern, dark green, 5-1/2 inches high. Marked: U.S.A.

Valencia ball jug. Marked: U.S.A.

Oval Ball Jug, plain, 40 oz. capacity, 5-1/2 inches high, 7-1/4 inches long. (H153 circa 1941) Marked: U.S.A.
Author's Note: Be sure that measurements on this item match those listed here, and make note that the U.S.A. mark is incised. I have handled and measured MANY similar jugs, before this one was found and confirmed.

Left: **White Corn**, 8 inches, hand painted green husks. Marked: U.S.A.
Center: **Corn King**, 8 inches. Marked: Shawnee U.S.A. 71
Right: **Corn Queen**, 8 inches. Marked: Shawnee U.S.A. 71

Fern ball jug. Marked: U.S.A.

Snowflake ball jug, 7-1/4 inches. Marked: U.S.A.

Chapter 9: Creamers

Additional creamers may be seen in the following chapters or sections: **Fern, Flower & Fern, Laurel Wreath, Lobster, Pennsylvania Dutch, Snowflake, Sunflower, Valencia, Wave**.

Smiley Pig, peach flower with gold trim, red feet, 4-1/2 inches. Marked: Patented Smiley U.S.A.

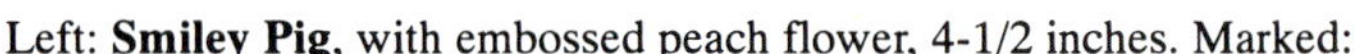

Left: **Smiley Pig**, with embossed peach flower, 4-1/2 inches. Marked: Patented Smiley U.S.A.
Center: **Child's Smiley Pig** with red neckerchief.
See Miscellaneous Rare section
Right: **Clover Blossom Smiley Pig**, 4-1/2 inches. Marked: Patented Smiley U.S.A.

Clover Blossom Smiley Pig, gold trim, 4-1/2 inches. Marked: Patented Smiley U.S.A.

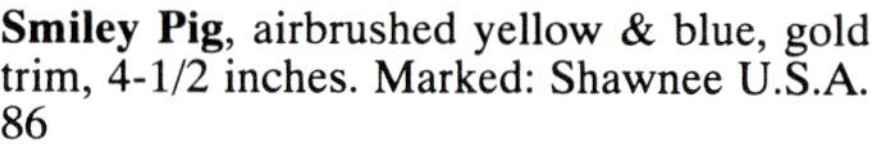

Smiley Pig, airbrushed yellow & blue, gold trim, 4-1/2 inches. Marked: Shawnee U.S.A. 86

Smiley Pig, airbrushed yellow & blue over Clover Blossom Smiley, 4-1/4 inches. Marked: Shawnee U.S.A. 86

Clover Blossom Smiley Pig, solid gold decorated, 4-1/2 inches. Marked: Shawnee U.S.A. 86

Puss 'n Boots, shown in White and Cream colors, 4-1/2 inches high. Marked: Patented Puss 'n Boots U.S.A.

Puss 'n Boots, white with gold trim. Marked: Patented Puss 'n Boots U.S.A.
Left: Eyes Open Puss 'n Boots.
Right: Eyes Closed Puss 'n Boots.

Puss 'n Boots, gold trim and roses decals. Marked: Patented Puss 'n Boots U.S.A.

Puss 'n Boots, airbrushed yellow & green, 4-3/4 inches. Marked: Shawnee U.S.A. 85
Left: Yellow Cat.
Center: Orange Cat.
Right: Yellow Cat with Gold Trim.

Puss 'n Boots, gold trim and flower decals, 4-1/2 inches. Marked: Patented Puss 'n Boots U.S.A.

Puss 'n Boots, all white, 4-1/2 inches. Marked: Patented Puss 'n Boots U.S.A.

Puss 'n Boots, solid gold decorated, 4-3/4 inches. Marked: Patented Puss 'n Boots U.S.A.

Elephant, 4-3/4 inches. Marked: Patented U.S.A.
Design Patent 141,324 Applied For February 28, 1945.
Left: **Elephant**, gold trim and flower decals, no cheek coloring.
Center: **Elephant**, plain.
Right: **Elephant**, gold trim and flower decals.

Elephant, 4-3/4 inches. Marked: Patented U.S.A.
All shown with gold trim and flower decals, fired-on red painted ears.

Elephant, solid gold decorated, 4-3/4 inches.
Marked: Patented U.S.A.

Elephant, 4-3/4 inches. Marked: Patented U.S.A.
Left: Elephant with gold trim and flower decals.
Right: Elephant, all white with gold trim.

Elephant, with gold trim and flower decals.
Marked: Patented U.S.A.

Spiral Pitcher, dark green, 3-1/2 inches high. Marked: U.S.A.

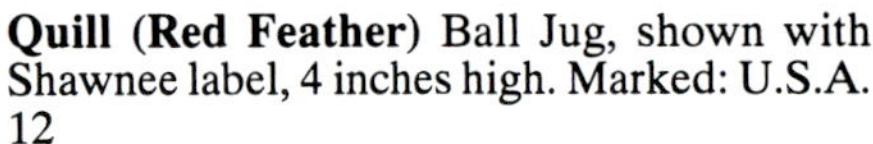

Quill (Red Feather) Ball Jug, shown with Shawnee label, 4 inches high. Marked: U.S.A. 12
Reportedly, this creamer was made for a special fund-raising event or banquet for the United Way. This is unconfirmed, but certainly logical.

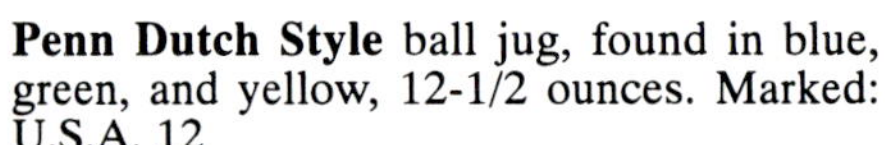

Penn Dutch Style ball jug, found in blue, green, and yellow, 12-1/2 ounces. Marked: U.S.A. 12

Penn Dutch Style tilt creamer with hand painted flowers, 10 ounces. Marked: U.S.A. 10

Penn Dutch Style tilt creamer, found in blue, green, and yellow, 10 ounces. Marked: U.S.A. 10

Left: **White Corn**, 5 inches, with hand painted husks. Marked: U.S.A.
Center: **Corn King**, 5 inches. Marked: Shawnee U.S.A. 70
Right: **Corn Queen**, 5 inches. Marked: Shawnee U.S.A. 70

Chapter 10: Utility / Sugar / Grease Jars

The intended use of jars shown in this chapter could be as varied as the decorations and shapes we find them in. Most catalogs show them as covered sugar bowls, and on occasion they are paired with range size salt & pepper shakers and referred to as Range Sets. Range shakers were handy on the stove for seasoning, and the jars were used to save grease from cooking, which was set aside for later use. Range Sets have also been placed on the kitchen table, with sugar in the covered jar, and salt and pepper in the shakers. The covered jar could also contain jam or jelly, while the range shakers could contain powdered sugar or cinnamon, all to be used for making toast or other breakfast foods.

Some of the utility jars are shown with range shakers that match. The shakers will also appear in the Salt & Pepper Shakers chapter. Not every covered jar made at Shawnee has shakers to match.

For additional jars, either open or covered, or range sets, refer to the following chapters or sections: **Clover Blossom, Corn King & Queen, Cottage, Fern, Flower & Fern, Fruit and Basket, Laurel Wreath, Lobster, Pennsylvania Dutch, Snowflake, Sunflower, Valencia, Wave,** and **White Corn.**

Oval Basket and **Smiley Pig** shakers, gold trim and flower decals.
Basket is 4-3/4 inches high, Marked: U.S.A.
Smiley shakers are 5 inches high, no mark.
From The Collection of Paul & Joy Schneider

Oval Basket with gold trim and flower decals. Marked: U.S.A.

Oval Basket with gold trim and flower decals. Marked: U.S.A.

Oval Basket with gold trim and flower decals. Marked: U.S.A.
From The Collection of Linda Romberg

Oval Basket, white with blue trim, 4-3/4 inches. Marked: U.S.A.

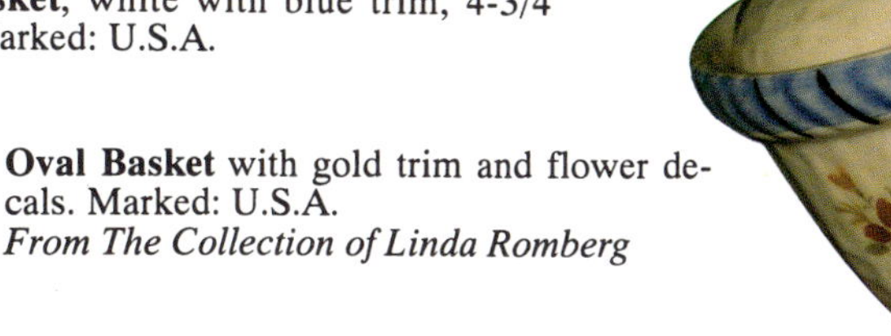

Oval Basket with gold trim and flower decals. Marked: U.S.A.
From The Collection of Linda Romberg

Oval Basket with gold trim and flower decals, 4-3/4 inches. Marked: U.S.A.
From The Collection of Arthur & Rita Bee

Oval Basket with gold trim and flower decals, fired-on red trim over blue, 4-3/4 inches. Marked: U.S.A. (This decal has also been found on a Smiley Pig cookie jar.)
From The Collection of Rich & Linda Guffey

Oval Basket, white with green trim, 4-3/4 inches. Marked: U.S.A.

Oval Basket with gold trim and flower decals. Marked: U.S.A.

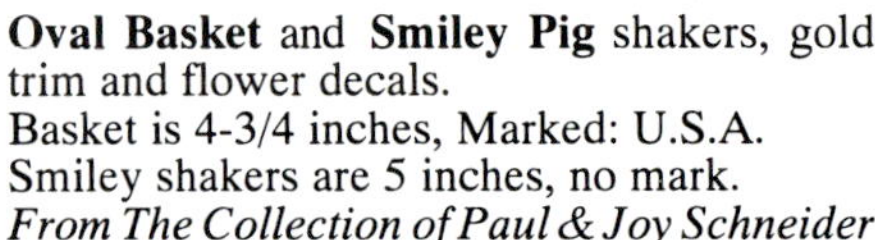

Oval Basket and **Smiley Pig** shakers, gold trim and flower decals.
Basket is 4-3/4 inches, Marked: U.S.A.
Smiley shakers are 5 inches, no mark.
From The Collection of Paul & Joy Schneider

Round Basket, white with green trim, 5-1/4 inches. Marked: U.S.A.

Round Basket with gold trim and flower decals. Marked: U.S.A.

Water Bucket and **Dutch Boy & Girl** shakers, white with blue trim.
Bucket is marked: U.S.A.
Shakers are 5 inches high, no mark.

Great Northern Water Bucket and **Dutch Boy & Girl** shakers. Note the different position of the blue stripes on the bucket, from the previous one. Also note the straight line on the girl's apron, and the difference on the boy's shoes.
Bucket is marked: Great Northern U.S.A. 1042
Shakers are 5 inches, no mark.

Water Bucket and **Dutch Boy & Girl** shakers, gold trim and flower decals.
Bucket is marked: U.S.A.
Shakers are 5 inches high, no mark.
From The Collection of Paul & Joy Schneider

Water Bucket with gold trim and flower decals. Marked: U.S.A.

Water Bucket with gold trim and flower decals. Marked: U.S.A.

Water Bucket with gold trim and flower decals. Marked: U.S.A.

Penn Dutch Style Grease Jar, found in green, blue, and yellow. Marked: U.S.A.

Decorative Set, to date this is the entire line known with this decoration, though the blue rope pattern appears on the rare Tulip pitcher and creamer.
Left: Small Shakers, 3-1/4 inches, no mark.
Center: Covered Grease Jar, 5 inches, Marked: U.S.A.
Right: Large Shakers, 5 inches, Marked: U.S.A.

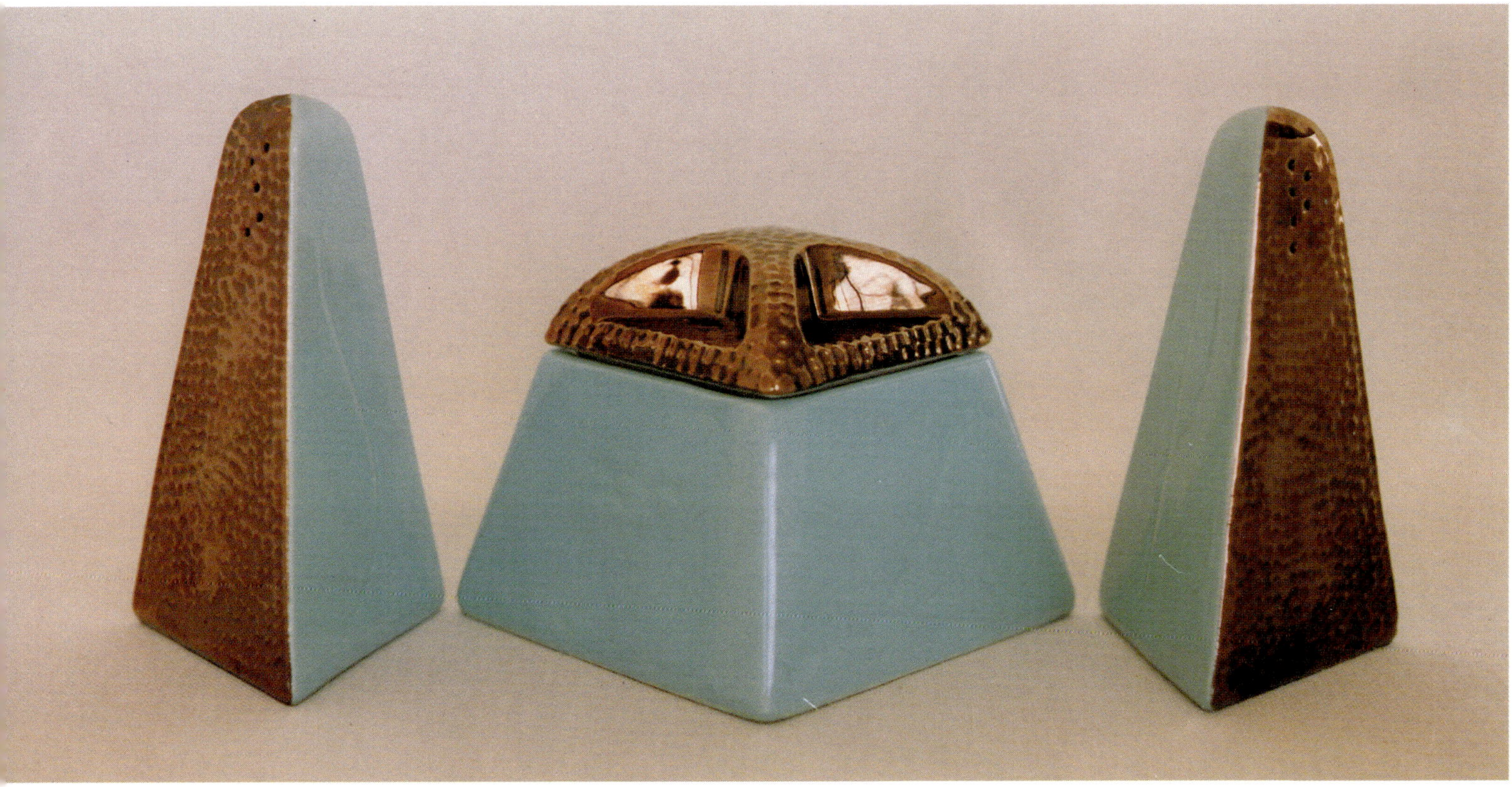

Sahara Range Set, pyramid-shaped shakers and grease jar, embossed palm tree on side, turquoise with hammered copper decorated lid. Grease Jar is 3-3/4 inches high. Marked: Kenwood U.S.A. 977 Shakers have incised **S** and **P** on one side.

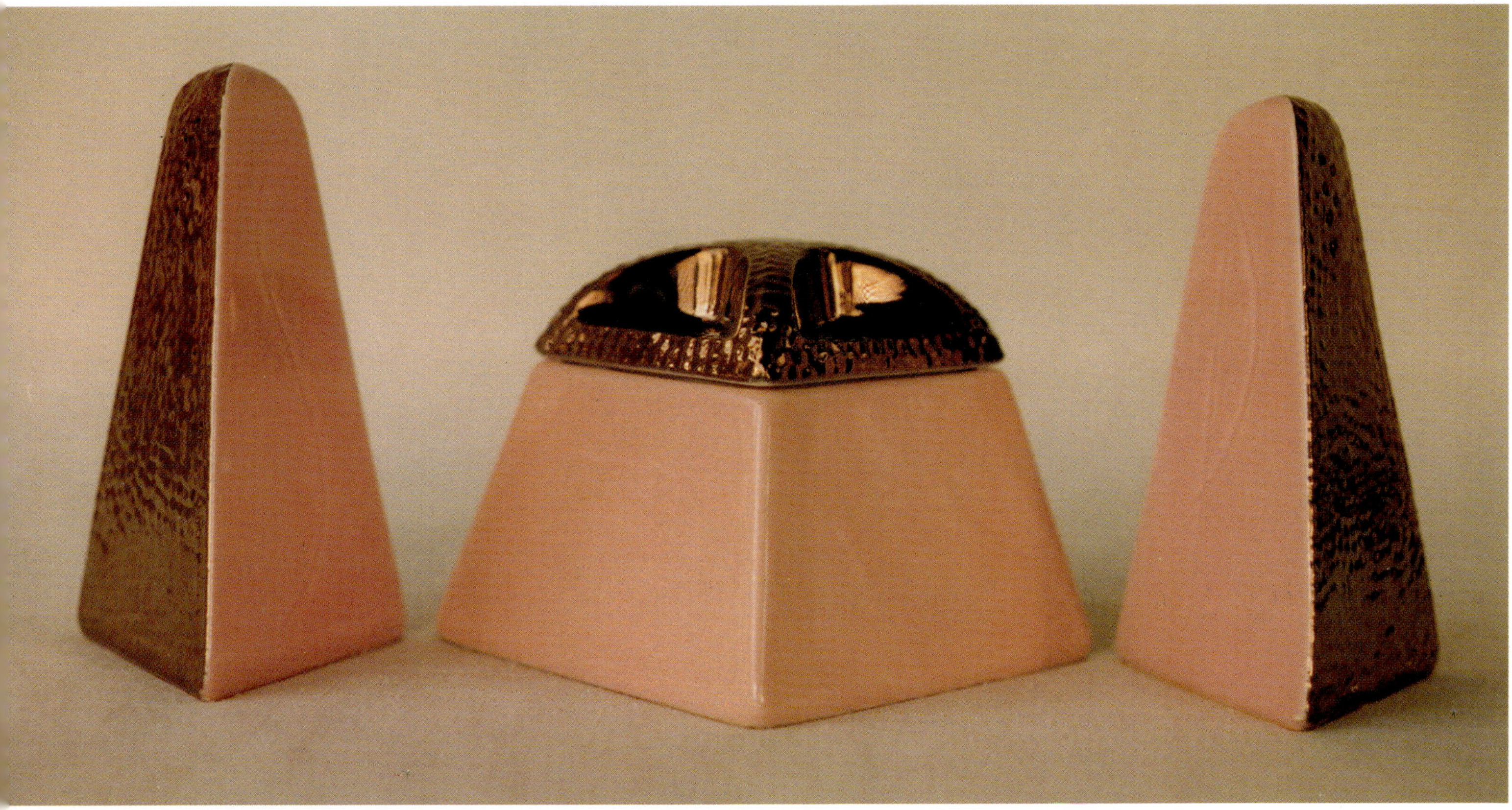

Sahara Range Set, pyramid-shaped shakers and grease jar, embossed palm tree on side, pink with hammered copper decorated lid. Grease Jar is 3-3/4 inches high. Marked: Kenwood U.S.A. 977 Shakers have incised **S** and **P** on one side.

Chapter 11: Teapots Figural

Granny Ann

Design Patent 139,092 applied for June 29, 1944

Granny Ann wears a flowing dress with apron, a shawl (cape) over her shoulders, a flowered hat, carries a basket in her right hand (which forms the spout), a cane in her left hand, and is 8 inches high. Some teapots are marked **Patented Granny Ann U.S.A.**, while others only have a **U.S.A.** mark.

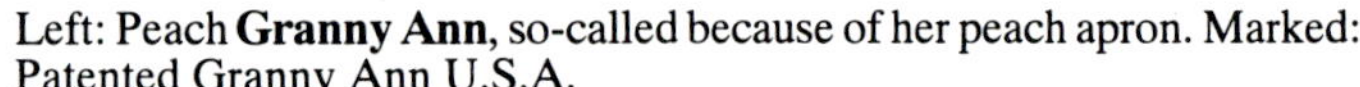

Left: Peach **Granny Ann**, so-called because of her peach apron. Marked: Patented Granny Ann U.S.A.
Right: Peach **Granny Ann** with gold trim, rose decals, and red shawl trim. Marked: Patented Granny Ann U.S.A.

Top: Lavender **Granny Ann**, so-called because of her lavender apron. Essex China label intact. Marked: Patented Granny Ann U.S.A.
Bottom: Lavender **Granny Ann** with gold trim and flower decals, and gold trim on her shawl. Marked: Patented Granny Ann U.S.A.

Left: Green **Granny Ann**, so-called because of her green apron. Marked: Patented Granny Ann U.S.A.
Right: Green **Granny Ann** with gold stenciled trim on shawl. Marked: Patented Granny Ann U.S.A.

Left: Peach **Granny Ann** with gold stencil and flower decals.
Right: Peach **Granny Ann** with gold trim and flower decals.

Left: Peach **Granny Ann** with gold trim and flower decals.
Right: Peach **Granny Ann** with gold trim and flower decals.

Top: Lavender **Granny Ann** with gold trim and flower decals.
Bottom: Lavender **Granny Ann** with gold trim and flower decals.

Left: Lavender **Granny Ann** with matt airbrushed colors, gold trim.
Right: Lavender **Granny Ann** with gold trim and flower decals.
From The Collection of Linda Romberg

Left: Lavender **Granny Ann**, decorated plain.
Right: Lavender **Granny Ann** with gold trim and flower decals.

Peach **Granny Ann** with gold and decals, including one on her apron. Marked: Patented Granny Ann U.S.A.
From The Collection of Melvin & Jean Gibson

Lavender **Granny Ann** with red hair, gold trim, and flower decals. Marked: Patented Granny Ann U.S.A.
Hard to find!
From The Collection Of Terry & Sandra Bauer

Lavender **Granny Ann** with red hair, gold trim, and flower decals. Marked: Patented Granny Ann U.S.A.
Hard to find!

Green **Granny Ann** with gold trim, green matt finish. Marked: Patented Granny Ann U.S.A. (In order to show an outstanding close-up of Granny, we had to sacrifice the teapot handle. Handle is beautiful solid gold trim.) *Rare!*
From The Collection Of Joe & Florence Cristiano

Lavender **Granny Ann** with red hair, gold trim, and flower decals. Marked: U.S.A. *Hard to find!*

Green **Granny Ann**, Marked: U.S.A.

Peach **Granny Ann** with gold trim and flower decals. Marked: U.S.A.

Tom The Piper's Son

Tom, Tom, The Piper's Son, stole a pig and away he run! The pig is in his right hand (which forms the spout), and an ear of corn is in his left. Collectors generally refer to this little guy as Tom Tom for short.

Tom with matt blues and reds, and gold trim decoration. Marked: Tom The Piper's Son Patented U.S.A. 44

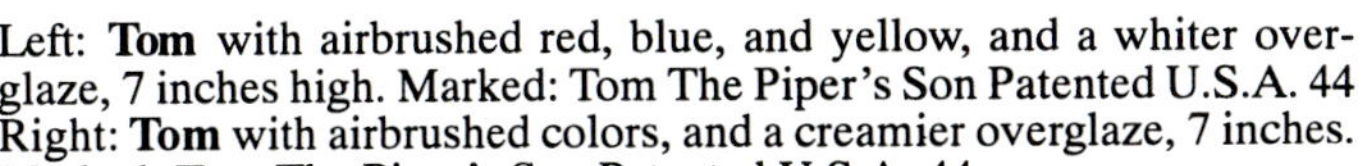

Left: **Tom** with airbrushed red, blue, and yellow, and a whiter overglaze, 7 inches high. Marked: Tom The Piper's Son Patented U.S.A. 44
Right: **Tom** with airbrushed colors, and a creamier overglaze, 7 inches. Marked: Tom The Piper's Son Patented U.S.A. 44

Tom with white body and hand painted details, original Shawnee label. Marked: Tom The Piper's Son Patented U.S.A.
From The Collection Of Robert & Lois Duvall

Tom with gold trim. Marked: Tom The Piper's Son Patented U.S.A. 44.

Tom with airbrushed matt colors. Marked: Tom The Piper's Son Patented U.S.A. 44
From The Collection of Paul & Joy Schneider

Tom with gold trim, and hand decorated red patch. Marked: Tom The Piper's Son Patented U.S.A.

Tom with gold trim, and hand decorated blue patch. Marked: Tom The Piper's Son Patented U.S.A.
From The Collection Of Robert & Lois Duvall

Yellow **Elephant** with gold trim, 6-1/2 inches. Marked: U.S.A.
From The Collection of Paul & Joy Schneider

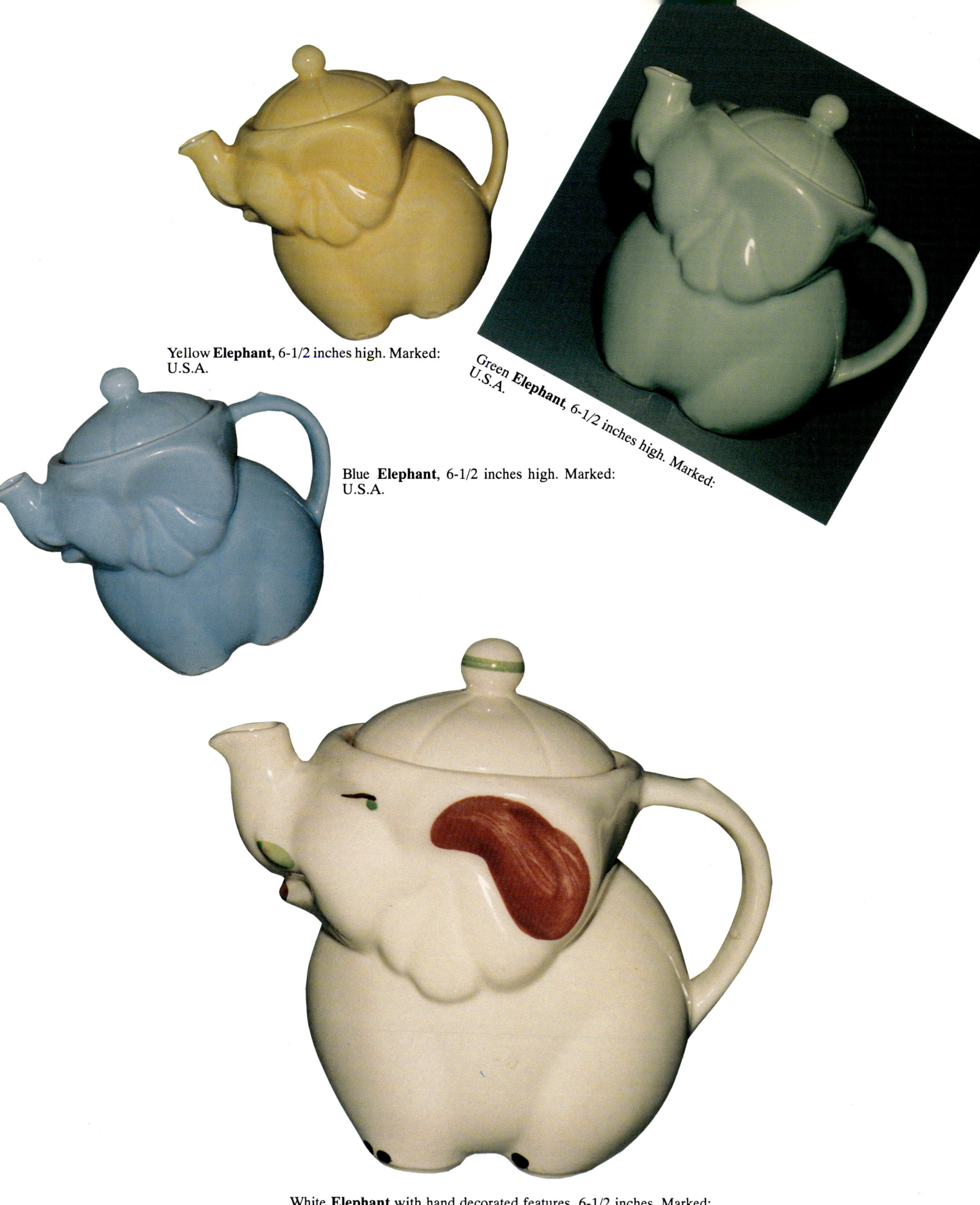

Yellow **Elephant**, 6-1/2 inches high. Marked: U.S.A.

Green **Elephant**, 6-1/2 inches high. Marked: U.S.A.

Blue **Elephant**, 6-1/2 inches high. Marked: U.S.A.

White **Elephant** with hand decorated features, 6-1/2 inches. Marked: U.S.A.
From The Collection of Paul & Joy Schneider

Chapter 12: Teapots Non-Figural

Additional teapots will also be found under specific lines such as **Clover Blossom**, **Corn King & Queen**, **Cottage**, **Fern**, **Flower & Fern**, **Laurel Wreath**, **Snowflake**, **Sunflower**, **Valencia**, **Wave**, and **White Corn**. However, any gold trimmed teapots from the above lines may appear in this section.

Research indicates that all of the teapots in this first section were made in the early years of Shawnee's production. Generally, they are solid colors, with embossed designs. Wherever possible, we have given them the names given in Shawnee catalogs; otherwise we tried to give them a descriptive name based on their decoration or design. Early colors were pretty basic, and it is possible for any of these items to turn up in any of the following colors: Dark Green, Dark Blue, Yellow, Burgundy, Bright White, Matt White, Bright Turquoise, Old English Ivory, Flax Blue, Powder Blue, Dusty Rose, Shell Pink, Peach.

Rosette, cobalt blue, full flower finial, 6-1/4 inches. Marked: U.S.A.

Rosette, dark green, half-flower finial, 6 inches. Marked: U.S.A.

Drape, white, 5-3/4 inches. Marked: U.S.A.

Rosette, yellow, full flower finial, 6-1/4 inches. Marked: U.S.A.

Criss Cross, yellow, 6 inches. Marked: U.S.A. Shown is the teapot with full-length diagonal embossed lines. Another teapot variation shows diagonal embossed lines on the lid and just over the top of the teapot, leaving the lower half plain.

Swirl, 6-1/2 inches. Marked: U.S.A.

Round Conventional with horizontal rings, burgundy, 5-1/2 inches. Marked: U.S.A.

Bell Flower with 8 panels, blue, 6-3/4 inches. Marked: U.S.A.

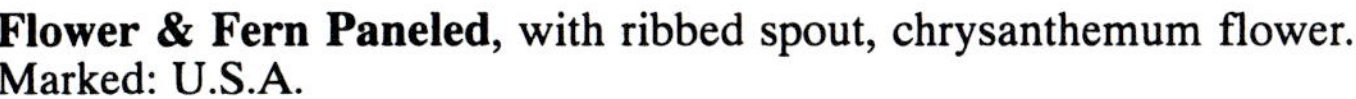

Flower & Fern Paneled, with ribbed spout, chrysanthemum flower. Marked: U.S.A.

Flower & Fern Paneled, with ribbed spout, daisy flower, opposite side of previous teapot.

Decorative Ribbed with layered petals, 5 inches. Marked: U.S.A.

Horizontal Ringed Marked: U.S.A.

Fern Embossed with gold trim and hand painted decoration, 6-3/4 inches. Marked: U.S.A. *This is a large teapot, and is usually found in solid color, without the decoration. So far, two of these teapots have been found with a black metal coffee maker insert.*

The following teapots are all decorated under the glaze, indicating that they are mid-to-post World War II era products.

Elite, 6-3/4 inches high. Marked: U.S.A.

Elite with gold trim and decals, 6-3/4 inches. Marked: U.S.A.

Embossed Rose, coral rose and light green leaves, 6-1/4 inches. Marked: U.S.A.

Embossed Rose, pink rose and dark green leaves, 6-1/4 inches. Marked: U.S.A.

Conventional, round handle with pinky rest, hand painted flowers, 6-1/2 inches. Marked: U.S.A.

Horizontal Ribbed Base, squared handle and ribbed spout, with heart-shaped flower and gold trim, 6 inches. Marked: U.S.A.

Embossed Rose, pink with gold trim, 6-1/4 inches. Marked: U.S.A.

Horizontal Ribbed Base, squared handle and ribbed spout, hand painted flowers, 6 inches. Marked: U.S.A.

Horizontal Ribbed Base, squared handle and ribbed spout, hand painted flower and gold trim, 6 inches. Marked: U.S.A.

Conventional, round handle with pinky rest, hand painted flowers and gold trim, 6-1/2 inches. Marked: U.S.A.

Paneled with ribbed spout, hand painted flowers, 6 inches. Marked: U.S.A.

Tulip with ribbed collar, 6 inches. Marked: U.S.A.

Vertical Ribbed Base and ribbed spout, Penn-Dutch-style hand decorated flower, gold trim, 6 inches. Marked: U.S.A.

Ribbed Collar with embossed spout and finial, hand painted flowers. Marked: U.S.A.
From The Collection of Sue Blodgett

Ribbed Collar with embossed spout and finial, hand painted flowers and gold trim, 6-3/4 inches. Marked: U.S.A.

Clover Blossom with gold trim, 6-1/2 inches. Marked: U.S.A.
From The Collection of Hughy and Chris Mahloch

Sunflower with gold trim showing gold wear on handle, 6-1/4 inches. Marked: U.S.A.
From The Collection of Terry & Sandra Bauer

Clover Blossom with gold trim, shown from back.

Platinum Sunflower Teapot with bottom stamp reading *Le Mieux China Platinum Hand Decorated.* Marked: U.S.A.
From The Collection of Paul & Joy Schneider

White Corn with gold trim, mostly on spout and handle, 6-1/2 inches. Marked: U.S.A.
From The Collection of Marvin L. Mulligan

Left: **Corn King** individual teapot, 10 oz, 4-1/2 inches. Marked: U.S.A. 65
Right: **Corn King** teapot, 30 oz, 6-1/2 inches. Marked: Shawnee U.S.A. 75
This item also found in solid gold and gold trimmed decoration.
See Corn King & Queen dinnerware for additional items in corn.

Pennsylvania Dutch teapots, left to right graduating sizes of 10 oz, 14 oz, 18 oz, 27 oz, all in Boston Shape; 30 oz in round shape & handle.
See Pennsylvania Dutch section for additional items.

Penn Dutch Style, called the Boston Shape, found in yellow, green, and blue.
Left: Individual Teapot, 10 ounce. Marked: U.S.A. 10
Right: Teapot, 14 ounce. Marked: U.S.A. 14

Penn Dutch Style (Boston Shape), gold trim with some wear on handle, 5 inches. Marked: U.S.A.
From The Collection of Terry & Sandra Bauer

Penn Dutch Style (Boston Shape), 27 oz, shown with original Shawnee label. Marked: U.S.A. 27
From The Collection of Marvin L. Mulligan

Chapter 13: Coffee Makers & A.D. Carafes

After Dinner Coffee Pots (Carafes)

Ribbed and Waves Coffee Carafe, dark green, 7-1/4 inches high. Marked: U.S.A.

Ribbed Coffee Carafe, yellow, 7-1/4 inches. Marked: U.S.A.

Ribbed Coffee Carafe, burgundy, 7-1/4 inches. Marked: U.S.A.

Coffee Makers

The following were all French Drip coffee makers, with water boiled in other utensils and then poured through these drip baskets to brew coffee. Some baskets were ceramic, just like the pot, while other baskets were made of aluminum. The ceramic makers had a perforated combination plain shape coffee basket, water holder, and water spreader. Lid fits both pot and water holder. Designed to be used with filter papers.

Fern Coffee Maker, 9 inches, 5 cup capacity. (H316M, circa 1942) Marked: U.S.A.

Snowflake Coffee Maker, 6 cup capacity. (H126M, circa 1941) Marked: U.S.A.

Bell Flower Coffee Maker, 7 cup capacity. (H328M, circa 1942) Shown in Turquoise and Blue. Yellow also available. Marked: U.S.A.
From The Collection of Arthur & Rita Bee

Flower & Fern Paneled Coffee Maker, shown with Ceramic Coffee Makers, yellow and turquoise. Marked: U.S.A. Also shown is paper DIRECTIONS sheet found inside the yellow pot.
From The Collection of Linda M. Nelson

Flower and Fern Coffee Maker, circa early 1940s. Marked: U.S.A.

DIRECTIONS (found in Flower & Fern Paneled Coffee Maker)

1. Place filter paper on inside of perforated bottom of coffee basket.
2. Spread drip ground coffee evenly over entire filter paper.
3. Use one tablespoon of coffee for the first cup, and one-half tablespoon for each additional cup. If stronger coffee is desired, use a larger amount of coffee per cup. If weaker coffee is desired, us a lesser amount of coffee per cup.
4. Place water spreader on ledge above coffee.
5. Heat water in a separate vessel until boiling, and pour into coffee maker.
6. To obtain best results, warm maker before starting to make coffee.
7. **Warning.** Pottery utensils should never be placed over an open flame. To have coffee hot, place coffee maker on a heating pad, preferably asbestos, over a low flame, and allow to heat while coffee is filtering.

Bottom of coffee maker insert for previous Flower & Fern Paneled pot.

Fern Coffee Maker yellow with gold trim and decals. A blue Fern coffee maker with these same decals and gold trim has also been found, with the Painter's Palette label intact. Marked: U.S.A. *From The Collection of Rich & Linda Guffey*

Pennsylvania Dutch Coffee Maker, aluminum maker, 42 ounces, bottom of pot stamped with words: *Do not place over direct heat. Use pad.*
Marked: U.S.A. 52

Penn Dutch Style Coffee Jug, 52 ounces.
Marked: U.S.A. 52

Sunflower Coffee Maker, aluminum maker, 42 ounces. Marked: U.S.A.

Patio Carafe, mirror-black with white stopper and matching white warmer. Triple-plated brass stand, 8 cup capacity. (#945).
Marketed by Kenwood Ceramics. Original List Price $4.95.
From The Collection of Melvin & Jean Gibson

Embossed Flower Coffee Jug, 52 ounces. Shape is same as Sunflower and Pennsylvania Dutch jugs. Marked: U.S.A. 52
Left: Flower Jug decorated plain.
Right: Flower Jug with gold trim.

Chapter 14: Salt & Pepper Shakers

There are a few interesting facts about Shawnee shakers that will help you in making an informed purchase. First, in order to be a matched set of shakers, they should have an uneven number of shaker holes. For example, small shakers *generally* have three holes and four holes to make a matched set; large shakers *generally* have four holes and five holes to make a matched set. This rule does have exceptions! Whenever possible, I placed the number of correct holes for that set of shakers in the description (e.g.: 5/4 or 4/3 or 3/2, etc.).

Clover Blossom Smiley and Winnie.
Large (5/4)
Small (4/3)

Heart Winnie and Smiley, large, gold trim and decal, blue on top of Winnie's hat.

Heart Smiley and Winnie.
Large (5/4)
Small (4/3)

Heart Winnie and Smiley, large, gold trim and flower decal.

Heart Winnie and Smiley, large, gold trim and flower decal.

Smiley, large, gold trim and decals.

Smiley, large, blue neckerchiefs. (5/4)

Matched sets of paired Smiley Pig shakers are more common than the matched sets of Smiley Pig with Winnie Pig shakers. Why? Smiley was designed and produced before Winnie. There are no known sets of two Winnie Pig shakers; once she arrived, Smiley was her mate. Smiley was the Salt with five holes in large shakers, and four holes in small shakers. Winnie was the Pepper with four holes in large shakers, and three holes in small shakers.

Another point to be aware of is that the color of Winnie Pig's top coat button should match Smiley Pig's neckerchief color to be a set. But again, there are known exceptions to this rule.

Going back to the days of Five and Dime Stores, most items were displayed loosely in open bins, and customers paired their own items as sets. Keep this in mind when someone says they've had a pair of shakers, mismatched, since they were brand new. There may have been little regard at the time for the number of shaker holes, or whether two Winnie's looked better together than a Smiley and a Winnie.

Most salt and pepper shakers had too little space on the bottom of them for markings. So, with most shakers being unmarked, I will make note of marks only on those few sets that have them.

Smiley, large, gold trim and decals.

Smiley, large, gold trim and decals.

Smiley, large, red neckerchiefs. (5/4)
Smiley and Winnie, small. (4/3) (Mismatched? Maybe, but they've been a couple for years!)

Smiley, large, gold trim and decals.

Smiley, large, green neckerchiefs. (5/4)
Smiley and Winnie, small. (4/3)
These sets are generally paired with Shamrock Smiley and Winnie cookie jars.

Smiley, large, gold trim and decals.

Large shakers, known as **Range Shakers**, are 5 inches high.
Small shakers, or **Table Shakers**, are 3-1/4 inches high.

Size, as always, is approximate, and will not be noted with each set shown. The only time size will be given, is when it differs from the above.

Additional salt and pepper shakers may be seen in the following chapters: **Corn King & Queen**, **Fern**, **Flower & Fern**, **Fruit & Basket**, **Laurel Wreath**, **Lobster**, **Pennsylvania Dutch**, **Snowflake**, **Sunflower**, **Valencia**, **Wave**, and **White Corn**. Range shakers may also be found in the chapter on **Utility / Sugar/ Grease Jars**.

Smiley, large, gold trim and decals.

Smiley, large, gold trim and decals.

Smiley, large, gold trim and decals.

Smiley, large, gold trim and decals.

Smiley, large, gold trim and decals.

Smiley, large, mismatched, though were bought as a pair.
Left: Red over Peach neckerchief, Gold Trim and Decal (5/4)
Right: Red over Green neckerchief, Gold Trim and Decal (5/4)

Smiley, large, gold trim and decals.

Heart Smiley and Winnie, small, gold trim.

Left: **Smiley**, small, peach neckerchief. (4/3)
Center: **Smiley**, large, peach neckerchief. (5/4)
Right: **Smiley**, small, peach neckerchief, gold trim. (4/3)

Smiley Design Patent 135,785 applied for April 27, 1943. This was the original Smiley Pig shaker set with pointed neckerchief and elbows, decorated with cold paint. Red and Blue neckerchiefs were available. (3/2)
There are look-alike shakers that may confuse the Shawnee collector. See different bottom finishes.

Smiley and Winnie, small, fired-on red over green, gold trim. (4/3)

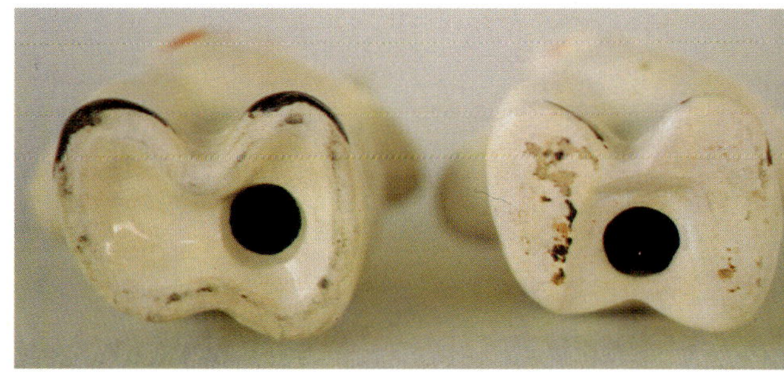

Smiley Shaker Bottom.
Left: Shawnee Smiley shaker with glazed bottom and fill hole to one side.
Right: Look-alike Smiley shaker with unglazed U-shaped bottom and fill hole centered.

Clover Blossom Smiley and Winnie, small, gold trim.

Smiley and Winnie, small, gold trim.

Smiley, small older version, gold trim.

Winnie and Smiley, small, gold trim, yellow dot flowers.

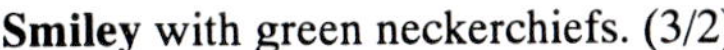

Smiley with green neckerchiefs. (3/2)

Clover Blossom Winnie and Smiley, small, gold trim and decorated with hats and coats. (4/3)

Smiley with yellow neckerchiefs. (3/2)

Clover Blossom back shown, Smiley has written on him: *Little Switzerland, Ohio.*

Smiley, peach and red neckerchiefs, blue stripes on pants, bought as a set, though they have 4/4 shaker holes.

Farmer Pig with shovel, small, shown front and side view. (4/3)
Left: Farmer Pig, plain.
Right: Farmer Pig, gold trim.

Left: **Muggsy**, large. (5/4)
Right: **Muggsy**, small. (4/3)

Muggsy, large, gold trim decorated. (5/4)

Left: **Muggsy**, large, gold trim decorated.
Right: **Muggsy**, small, gold trim decorated.

Muggsy, large, gold trim decorated.

Muggsy, small, unusual Muggsy shakers with left ear cropped close to his body. (4/3)
From The Collection of Toni Crittenden

Muggsy, small, gold trim decorated. (4/3)

Puss 'n Boots decorated plain, with original Shawnee labels on back. This shaker has only been found in the small size. (4/3)

Puss 'n Boots with gold trim decorated.

Puss 'n Boots with gold trim decorated.

Left: **Grey-Eyed Owls** decorated plain. (4/3)
Right: **Green-Eyed Owls**, original Shawnee labels, green toes. (4/3)
This shaker has only been found in the small size.

Puss 'n Boots with gold trim decorated.

Owls, gold trim decorated. (4/3)

Owls, gold trim decorated, left has peach eye feathers, right has yellow eye feathers. (4/3)

Ducks. This shaker has only been found in the small size. (4/3)

Left: **Owls**, gold trim decorated; gold is straight band with vertical feathers.
Right: **Owls**, gold trim decorated; gold is wavy with horizontal feathers.

Chanticleer, large, gold trim decorated.

Left: **Owls**, gold trim decorated.
Right: **Owls**, gold trim decorated.

Chanticleer, large, gold trim decorated.

Left: **Chanticleer**, large, plain. (5/4)
Right: **Chanticleer**, small, note the red speckles on chest. (4/3)

Left: **Chanticleer**, small, plain.
Right: **Chanticleer**, small, gold trim decorated.

Left: Brown **Dutch Boy and Girl**, large. (3/2)
Right: Blue **Dutch Boy and Girl**, large. (3/2)
These shakers have only been found in the large size.
These also appear as figurines on the Wishing Well planter.

Left: Brown **Dutch Boy and Girl**, gold trim.
Right: Blue **Dutch Boy and Girl**, gold trim.

Blue **Dutch Boy and Girl**, gold trim.

Sailor Boy and Bo Peep, small. (4/3)

White **Dutch Boy and Girl**, large, with wavy band on girls' apron. (5/4)

Swiss Boy and Girl, large. (3/2)
These shakers have only been found in the large size.

Great Northern Dutch Boy and Girl, large, with straight band on girls' apron, and decorated shoes on boy. (5/4)

Swiss Boy and Girl, gold trim decorated.

Dutch Boy and Girl, large, gold trim and decals.

Dutch Boy and Girl, large, gold trim and decals.

Dutch Boy and Girl, brown trim decorated instead of blue.

Dutch Boy and Girl, large, gold trim and decals.

Dutch Boy and Girl, rust color fired on pants and skirt.

Dutch Boy and Girl, large, gold trim and decals.

Left: **Chef S & P**, small, plain. (5/4)
Right: **Chef S & P**, small, gold trim. (5/4)

Flower Cluster, gold trim, 2-1/4 inches high. (3/2)

Left: **Flower Pots**, small, plain. (3/2)
Right: **Flower Pots**, small, gold trim. (3/2)

Flower Cluster, plain, shown front and back, 2-1/4 inches high. (3/2)

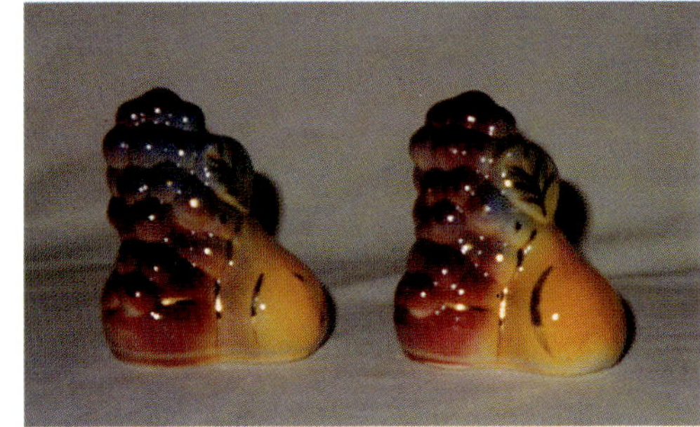

Fruit, large, gold trim, 3-1/2 inches high. Marked: U.S.A. 85 (4/4)

Left: **Fruit**, large, 3-1/2 inches high, with lip to nestle up to utility jar. Marked: U.S.A. 85 (4/4)
Right: **Fruit**, small, 2-1/2 inches high. Marked: U.S.A. 82 (3/3)
These shakers defy the rules, by continually being 4-hole large pairs, and 3-hole small pairs. It was once thought that perhaps a large and small shaker comprised a pair, but Shawnee catalogs disproved that.

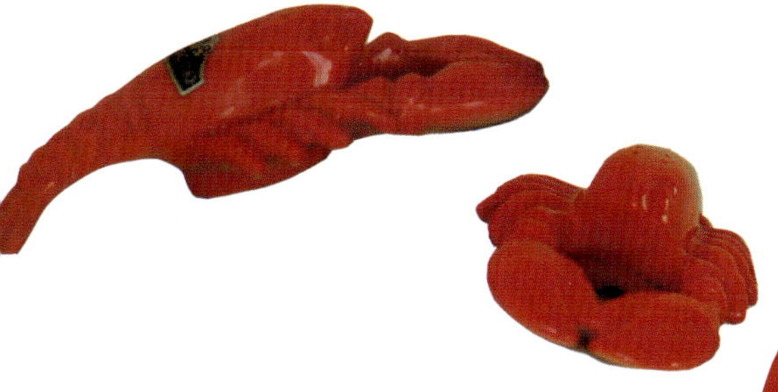

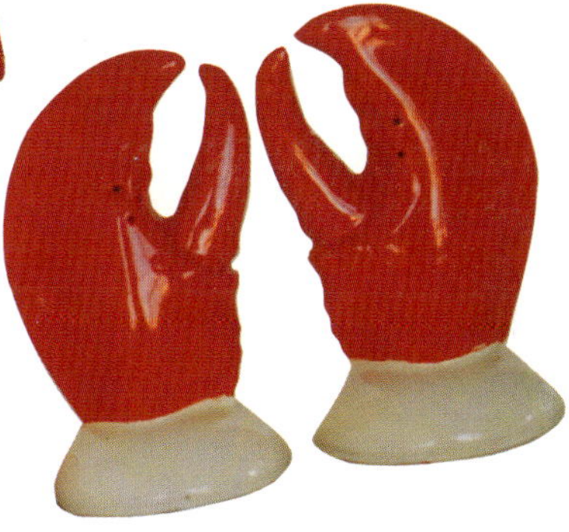

Left: **Lobster,** full body, Kenwood label, 7-1/4 inches long. Marked: U.S.A. (5/4)
Right: **Lobster Claw**, 5 inches high, no mark. (3/2)

Cottage, shown front and back, 3-3/4 inches. Marked: U.S.A. 9 (5/4)

Left: **Watering Cans**, plain, small. (4/3)
Right: **Watering Cans**, gold trim and decals, small. (4/3)

Left: **Milk Cans**, plain, Shawnee label, small. (4/3)
Right: **Milk Cans**, gold trim and decals, small. (4/3)

Decorative, large, with gold trim.
See the chapter on Utility/Sugar/Grease Jars for the rest of this line.

Left: **Wheelbarrows**, plain, small. (4/3)
Right: **Wheelbarrows**, gold trim, small. (4/3)

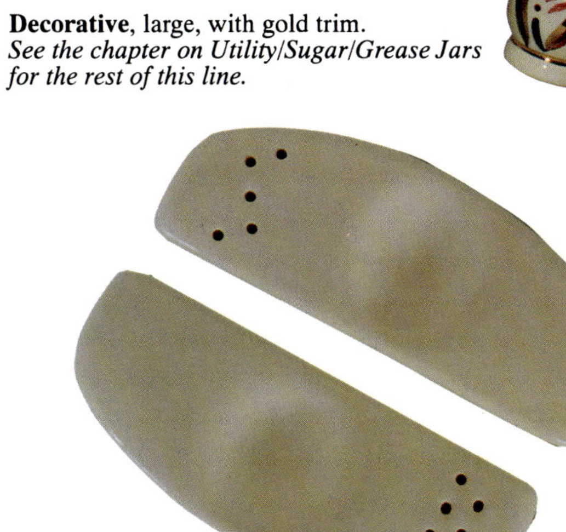

Susan Set Shakers, white, 1-1/4 inches high, 3-3/4 inches long, holes are shaped as **S** and **P**, no mark.
See the chapter on Kitchenware, Casual Living, for use of these shakers.

Sahara, pink and medallion, 5 inches, impressed **S** and **P** on sides, holes are shaped as **S** and **P**.
See the chapter on Utility/Sugar/Grease Jars for the rest of this line.

Penn Dutch Style Jug, large, found in blue, green, and yellow. (5/4)

Left: **White Corn**, single shaker, small. (3/2)
Center: **Corn King**, single shaker, small. (3/2)
Right: **Corn Queen**, single shaker, small. (3/2)
See each of the corn chapters for more items in these lines.

Modern Ribbed Base, chartreuse, 3-1/2 inches, no mark. (5/4)

All of the following are early Shawnee, mainly the pre-World War II years, and have been produced as figurines or flower bowl inserts as well. See the chapter on Figurines.

White Corn, large, gold trim decorated. (5/4)

Stippled Birds, 3 inches high, no mark. (2/1)
Colors found: Powder Blue, Off White.

The two previous sets of birds have been shown in Butler Brothers catalogs with several variations: tail up and down as a set, tails up as a set, tails down as a set. The key here seems to be matching uneven holes to make a set!

Rabbit, ears down, 3 inches high, no mark, (A584). (2/1)
Colors: Bright White, Turquoise, Dusty Rose.

Elephant, 3 inches high, no mark, (A593). (2/1)
Colors: Bright White, Turquoise, Flax Blue, Old English Ivory, Shell Pink.

Stippled Fish, found as a set, Old Ivory, no mark. (2/1)

Stippled Tropical Fish, 2-3/4 inches high, no mark.
Colors: Off White, Turquoise.
Courtesy of Marvin Mulligan

Stippled Blow Fish, 2-1/2 inches high, no mark.
Colors: Off White, Turquoise.

Grecian Pitcher, 2-1/2 inches high, no mark. (3/2)

Ribbed Ewer, 2-1/2 inches high, no mark. (3/2)

Jug with Bug, 2-1/2 inches high, no mark. (3/2)

Ribbed-Neck Pitcher, 2-3/4 inches high, no mark. (3/2)

Pitcher, 2-3/4 inches high, no mark. (3/2)

Section IV: Kitchenware Lines

Chapter 15: Lines

Clover Blossom

This line was advertised in a Butler Brothers catalog for the January 1947 issue, replacing one issued for July 1946. These china pigs were promoted as having *"Great sales potentialities for your store now that the Smiley - Winnie combination has expanded into a COMPLETE FAMILY LINE. Dressed in new garb, these vitrified china pigs are now 'In Clover'."*

Butler Brothers suggested that retailers also promote the cookie jars for pretzels, crackers, and popcorn. The 5-inch range shakers had a suggested use of cinnamon in one, and powdered sugar in the other, to be placed beside the toaster for making cinnamon toast. Another idea was for the large Smiley pitcher to be placed next to a waffle iron, and used as a batter jug, while two small Smiley creamers could be used for melted butter and syrup.

All Items In The Clover Blossom Line May Be Found Trimmed With Gold

Check Specific Categories For Examples

Note: **Apple** decorated Winnie cookie jars and Smiley pitchers are variations of the embossed **Clover Blossom** design, and in some instances could be a judgment call. Thus far, the **Apple** Smiley cookie jar has only been found with hand painted apples.

Smiley Pig Cookie Jar.
This is the only Smiley Pig cookie jar with an embossed design on him. *Original Retail $3.29.*
11-1/2 inches, 3 pint capacity, Marked: Patented Smiley U.S.A.

Winnie Pig Cookie Jar.
Identifying features for Winnie are a single Clover Blossom on her top coat button, on her hat, and on her purse, along with the absence of any flower or shamrock on her left coat pocket. *Original Retail $3.29.*
12 inches, 3 pint capacity, Marked: Patented Winnie U.S.A.

Smiley Pig Pitcher (Jug).
This is the only Smiley pitcher designed with a neckerchief, and having the embossed Clover Blossom on his rump. *Original Retail $2.45.*
7-1/2 inches, 2 quart capacity, Marked: Patented Smiley U.S.A.

Teapot.
Embossed Clover Blossoms adorn both sides of this teapot, as well as the lock-lid finial. No-drip spout; comfortable handle. *Original Retail $1.95.*
6-1/2 inches, 6-cup capacity, Marked: U.S.A.

Smiley Pig Creamer.
This Smiley creamer, designed with a neckerchief and embossed clover blossom, was reissued later in spray-decorated yellow and blue colors. *Original Retail 95¢.*
4-1/2 inches, 10-ounce capacity, Marked: Patented Smiley U.S.A.

Sugar / Jam / Drip Jar.
Embossed Clover Blossom on two sides, and the lid finial of this jar. *Original Retail $1.50.*
4-3/4 inches, Marked: U.S.A.

Winnie & Smiley Range Salt & Pepper Set.
Again, the embossed Clover Blossom sets these shakers apart from other sets, as well as the fact that Smiley's overall buttons are green. Smiley has 5 holes on the top of his head; Winnie has 4 holes in the top of her hat. *Original Retail $1.65 / Pair.*
5 inches high - No Discernible Marks.

Winnie & Smiley Table Salt & Pepper Set.
This Smiley lacks the embossed Clover Blossom on his pants, but the telling signs that he is of the Clover Blossom set are the green buttons on his overalls, and green crossed straps in back, along with the red neckerchief. Winnie has a large red button at the top of her coat, and a single green clover painted on her purse and hat. Smiley has 4 holes; Winnie has 3 holes. *Original Retail 59 Cents / Pair.*
3-1/4 inches high - No Discernible Marks.

Matching Three-Piece Range Set.
Consisting of the **Drip Jar** and **Range Size Smiley & Winnie Shakers**, this was offered as a combination set to retailers.
Original Retail $2.89 / Set.

Cottage

This line, also called Cookie House, is one of the most elusive and challenging lines for Shawnee collectors to acquire. These square-shaped Cottage pieces are most readily identified by taking note of the *rounded* red door. Square blue windows appear on both front and back, and the brown shingled roof lifts off as the lid on all but the shakers.

We have been unable to pinpoint exact year(s) of production on this line, but it can be confined to between 1946 and 1954, with the late 1940s as the most likely. Square-shaped items such as these had problems with the walls collapsing during production, and there is a problem with ill-fitting lids on some pieces. Many pieces have been found with original Essex China labels still intact.

Top Left: **Cottage Cookie Jar**, 7 inches high. Marked: US.A. 6

Top Right: **Cottage Sugar Bowl**, 4-1/2 inches high. Marked: U.S.A. 8

Bottom Left: **Cottage Salt & Pepper Shakers**, 3-3/4 inches high, 5 & 4 shaker holes. Marked: U.S.A. 9

Bottom Right: **Cottage Teapot**, 5-1/2 inches high. Marked: U.S.A. 7

Fern (Wheat)

Documented as early as July 1942, this line had often been referred to by collectors as **Wheat**, until catalogs turned up describing it as **Fern Leaf**.

Fern ware is an octagonal shape with a vertical fern leaf design embossed on the panels, with an embossed ring of beads around the top. Teapots have a fluted spout with a lid to match. Listed colors are Yellow, Flax Blue, and Turquoise, with Dusty Rose and Old Ivory colors added to the mixing bowl sets.

Based on catalog information currently available, all items in the Fern Leaf line are represented here. Whenever possible, the catalog number of each item is noted in parenthesis following the description. Every item has been found marked with a **U.S.A.**, so this will not be noted with each listing.

Mixing Bowl Set, listed from the smallest: 5-inch Yellow; 6-inch Flax Blue; 7-inch Dusty Rose; 8-inch Old Ivory; 9-inch Turquoise.
From The Collection of Sharon Figura

Note: Mixing Bowls were marketed in a number of combinations, with three, four, or five bowls comprising a set. All sizes listed are diameters.

3-Pc Bowl Set of 5" 7" 9" bowls
4-Pc Bowl Set of 5" 6" 7" 8" bowls
4-Pc Bowl Set of 6" 7" 8" 9" bowls
5-Pc Bowl Set of 5" 6" 7" 8" 9" bowls

Ball Jug, 7-1/4 inches high, 2 quart capacity (H434).

Left: **Creamer**, 3-1/4 inches high, 9 ounce capacity (H3512) *Matches Teapot H316.*
Right: **Sugar Bowl**, 3 inches high, 9 ounce capacity (H3612) *Matches Teapot H316.*

Pitcher, 5-1/2 inches high, 1-1/2 pint capacity (H382).

Match Box Holder, 5-1/2 inches high, can hang on wall or set on stove (H456).

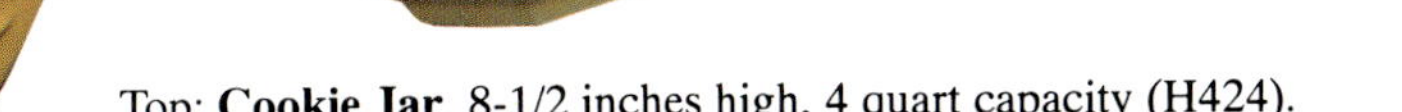

Top: **Cookie Jar**, 8-1/2 inches high, 4 quart capacity (H424).
Bottom: **Canister**, 7-1/4 inches high, 2-1/2 quart capacity (H412).

Salt Box, 5 inches high, 6 inches long, designed to hang on wall or set on stove (H446).

Grease Jar, 4-1/2 inches high, 16 ounce capacity (H401).

Teapot, 6 inches high, 6 cup capacity (H316). Shown in Coffee Maker section with ceramic basket coffee maker.

Salt & Pepper Shakers, 4 inches high, holes form **S** and **P** (H393).

Teapot, 2 cup capacity (H372).

Salt Box, 4-3/4 inches high, can be hung on wall or set on stove.

Flower and Fern

Flower and Fern is a name that collectors have given to this line, for lack of catalog information from Shawnee. However, *Butler Brothers* marketed this line in their 1942 catalog as **Mexican Floral**.

A daisy-like flower and fern frond are embossed on one side, while the other side displays an embossed chrysanthemum-like flower and fern frond. Colors found so far are: Dark Green, Dark Blue, Yellow, Off White, Old Ivory, Turquoise, Flax Blue. All pieces shown are marked with **U.S.A.**, except for the small and large shaker sets, which have no discernible marks.

Left: **Open Sugar Bowl** 3 inches high.
Right: **Creamer** 3 inches high.

Salt Box with gold trim, 4-3/4 inches high.

Ball Jug Pitcher with gold trim and flower decals, 5-1/2 inches high, 40 ounces.
From The Collection Of Arthur & Rita Bee

Salt Box with gold trim, 4-3/4 inches high.
From The Collection Of Linda Romberg

Match Box Holder, 5-1/2 inches high.

Grease Jar 3-1/2 inches high.

Left: **Aladdin Creamer**, turquoise, 3 inches high.
Right: **Aladdin Sugar Bowl**, turquoise, 3 inches high.

Range Salt & Pepper Shakers, white, 4-1/2 inches high.

Ball Jug Pitcher, 5-1/2 inches high, 40 ounces.

Table Salt & Pepper Shakers, turquoise, 3 inches high.

Ball Creamer 4 inches high.

Teapot, 5-cup capacity, 5-1/4 inches high.

Teapot, 6-cup capacity.
Shown in Coffee Maker section with aluminum insert as a coffee maker.

Jardiniere 5 inches high.
Following are listed Flower & Fern embossed jardinieres and flower pots known to date. As always with pottery, sizes may vary slightly. Examples may possibly be found in the chapter on Flower Pots and Jardinieres.
Jardinieres: 4-1/2 inches, 5-1/2 inches, 6-1/2 inches.
Flower Pot with Saucer: 2-3/4 inches, 4-1/2 inches, 5 inches.

Fruit and Basket

Appearing in a 1951 Shawnee catalog, this colorful and popular line was designed by Robert Heckman.

Heckman was responsible for introducing color blending, a decorating technique using the spray gun method. Three basic colors were blended to decorate the fruit in this line, with random touches of a brush to highlight lines of pear stems or bananas, etc. The fruit design is embossed on the ball jug, and spray decorated.

The large shakers were made with a hook extension at the top, so that they could be nestled up to the sugar bowl. The rule of thumb is that in order to be a matched set, shakers have to have an unmatched number of holes. The Fruit shakers defy this rule: the small shakers have three holes each; the large shakers have four holes each. The only exception found so far are the large shakers pictured in this section that are owned by designer Bob Heckman .... they have five holes each.

Top Row:
Fruit & Basket Casserole, 6-1/2 inches. Marked: Shawnee U.S.A. 83.
Fruit Salt & Pepper Shakers, small, 2-1/2 inches high, both 3-hole. Marked: U.S.A. 82
Fruit & Basket Cookie Jar, 8-1/2 inches. Marked: Shawnee U.S.A. 84

Bottom Row:
Fruit Ball Jug, embossed, 6-1/2 inches, 48-ounce capacity. Marked: Shawnee U.S.A. 80
Fruit & Basket Sugar Bowl / Grease Jar, 5-1/2 inches. Marked: Shawnee U.S.A. 81
Fruit Salt & Pepper Shakers, large, 3-1/2 inches high, both 4-hole. Marked: U.S.A. 85

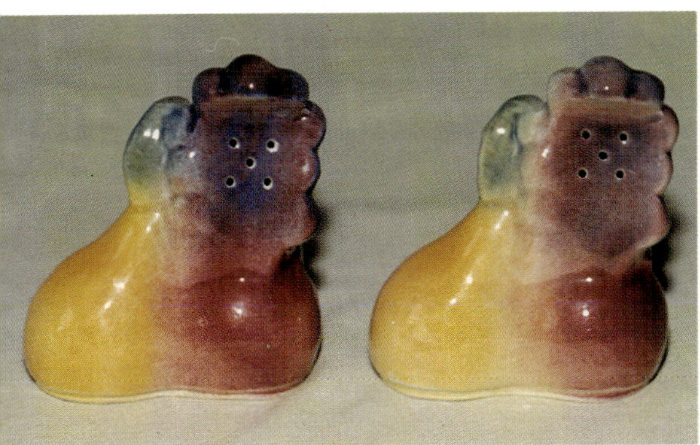

Fruit Salt & Pepper Shakers, large, both have 5 shaker holes. *Courtesy of Robert & Pauline Heckman*

Fruit & Basket line shown decorated with gold trim. Note the difference in gold trim on the two casseroles, as one has a gold band around the basket, while the other does not. Also, on some items such as the casserole on the right with the gold band, the leaves are solid gold trimmed, while other pieces may have gold trim outlining the item. Photo is missing the second small shaker.
From The Collection Of Terry & Sandra Bauer
Cookie Jar, gold trim.
Casserole, gold trim.
Ball Jug, gold trim.
Sugar Bowl, gold trim.
Large Salt & Pepper Shakers, gold trim.
Small Salt & Pepper Shakers, gold trim.

Laurel Wreath

Collectors call this limited kitchenware line Laurel Wreath because of the embossed laurel leaves pattern. On a historical note, in ancient times the laurel wreath was bestowed as a mark of honor to poets, athletes, and heroes.

Colors found to date are yellow, blue, and green. All items shown, including the shakers, are marked with an incised **U.S.A.**

Utility Pitcher 7-1/2 inches.

Creamer 3-1/2 inches.

Open Sugar Bowl 3-1/2 inches.

Range Set.
Salt & Pepper Shakers, 4 inches, 5 & 4 holes.
Grease Jar, 4 inches.

Teapot 6-1/4 inches.

The two teapots at right are different heights, and note the difference in position of the top part of the handle to the body of the teapot.

Teapot 6-3/4 inches.

Pennsylvania Dutch

Patents were filed on January 13, 1948, for this kitchen pottery line designed by Robert Heckman. Very popular with collectors, it is a challenge to acquire the entire set, though to date, no examples of the Beater Jug have been documented.

All ware for this line was cast plain, then laid in the mold in which ink had been placed, and lines were transferred onto pieces. The design was then hand painted on, glazed, and fired.

Examples of this line have appeared elsewhere under a few specific categories such as cookie jars, teapots, or coffee makers.

The shapes of the Pennsylvania Dutch line were also produced in solid colors of blue, green, and yellow. See specific categories for examples.

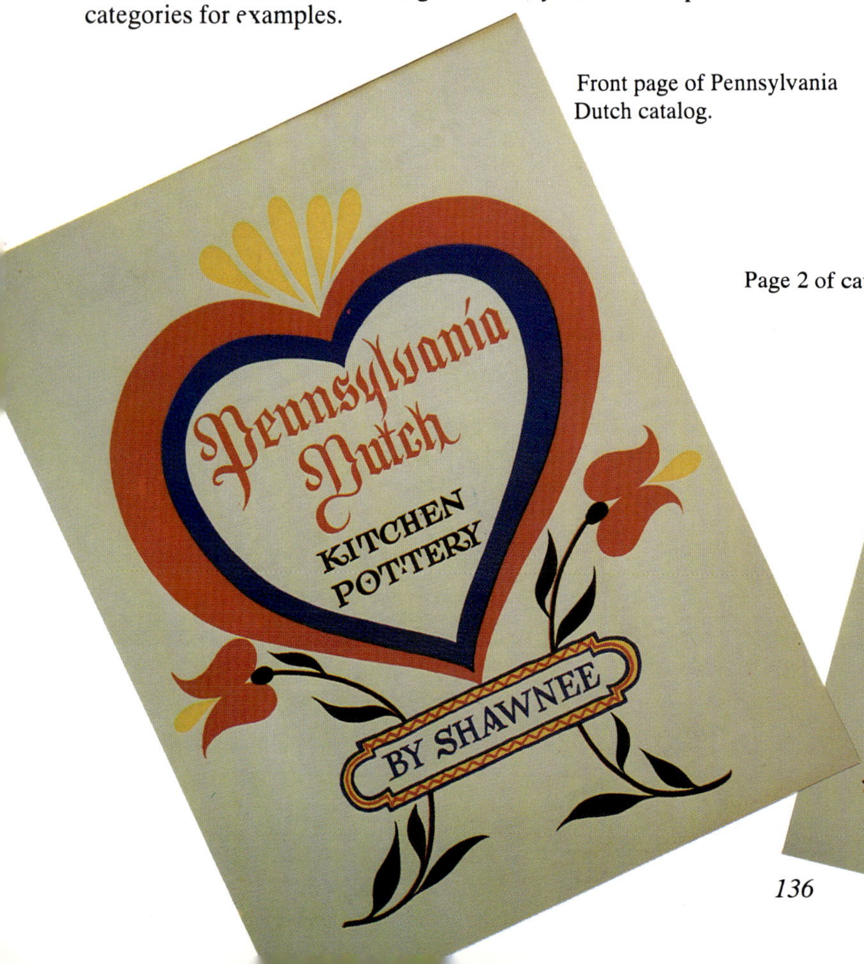

Pennsylvania Dutch
KITCHEN POTTERY
BY SHAWNEE

Front page of Pennsylvania Dutch catalog.

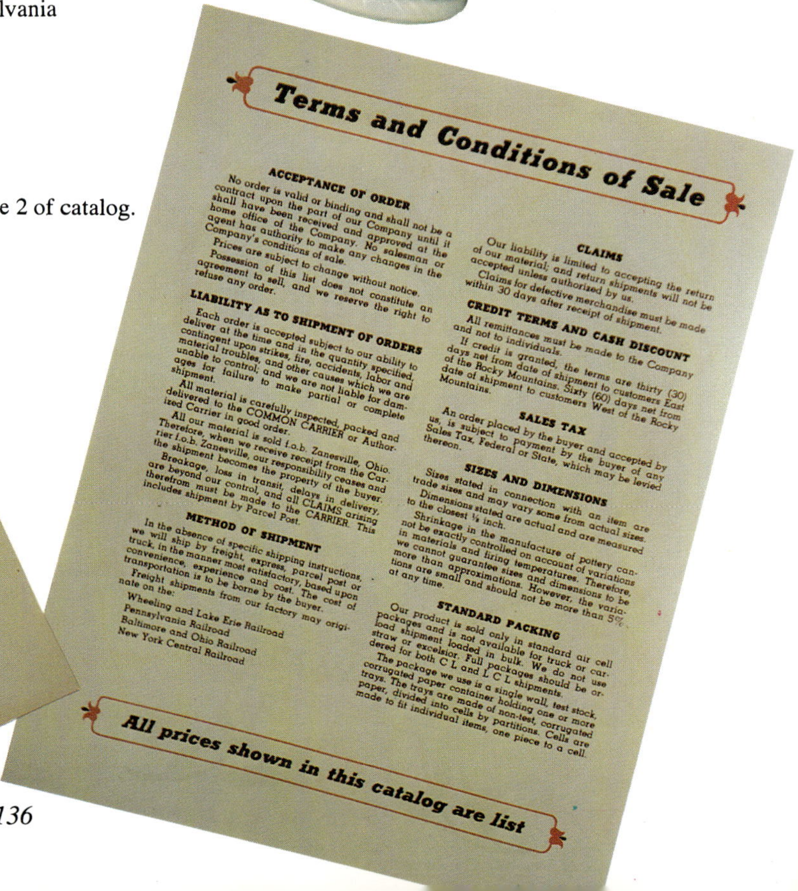

Terms and Conditions of Sale

ACCEPTANCE OF ORDER

No order is valid or binding and shall not be a contract upon the part of our Company until it shall have been received and approved at the home office of the Company. No salesman or agent has authority to make any changes in the Company's conditions of sale.

Prices are subject to change without notice.

Possession of this list does not constitute an agreement to sell, and we reserve the right to refuse any order.

LIABILITY AS TO SHIPMENT OF ORDERS

Each order is accepted subject to our ability to deliver at the time and in the quantity specified, contingent upon strikes, fire, accidents, labor and material troubles, and other causes which we are unable to control; and we are not liable for damages for failure to make partial or complete shipment.

All material is carefully inspected, packed and delivered to the COMMON CARRIER or Authorized Carrier in good order.

All our material is sold f.o.b. Zanesville, Ohio. Therefore, when we receive receipt from the Carrier f.o.b. Zanesville, our responsibility ceases and the shipment becomes the property of the buyer.

Breakage, loss in transit, delays in delivery, are beyond our control, and all CLAIMS arising therefrom must be made to the CARRIER. This includes shipment by Parcel Post.

METHOD OF SHIPMENT

In the absence of specific shipping instructions, we will ship by freight, express, parcel post or truck, in the manner most satisfactory, based upon convenience, experience and cost. The cost of transportation is to be borne by the buyer.

Freight shipments from our factory may originate on the:

Wheeling and Lake Erie Railroad
Pennsylvania Railroad
Baltimore and Ohio Railroad
New York Central Railroad

CLAIMS

Our liability is limited to accepting the return of our material; and return shipments will not be accepted unless authorized by us.

Claims for defective merchandise must be made within 30 days after receipt of shipment.

CREDIT TERMS AND CASH DISCOUNT

All remittances must be made to the Company and not to individuals.

If credit is granted, the terms are thirty (30) days net from date of shipment to customers East of the Rocky Mountains. Sixty (60) days net from date of shipment to customers West of the Rocky Mountains.

SALES TAX

An order placed by the buyer and accepted by us, is subject to payment by the buyer of any Sales Tax, Federal or State, which may be levied thereon.

SIZES AND DIMENSIONS

Sizes stated in connection with an item are trade sizes and may vary some from actual sizes.

Dimensions stated are actual and are measured to the closest ⅛ inch.

Shrinkage in the manufacture of pottery cannot be exactly controlled on account of variations in materials and firing temperatures. Therefore, we cannot guarantee sizes and dimensions to be more than approximations. However, the variations are small and should not be more than 5% at any time.

STANDARD PACKING

Our product is sold only in standard air cell packages and is not available for truck or carload shipment loaded in bulk. We do not use straw or excelsior. Full packages should be ordered for both C L and L C L shipments.

The package we use is a single wall, test stock, corrugated paper container holding one or more trays. The trays are made of non-test, corrugated paper, divided into cells by partitions. Cells are made to fit individual items, one piece to a cell.

All prices shown in this catalog are list

Page 2 of catalog.

Page 3 of catalog.

Re-introducing the folk art of a quaint group of European immigrants who started bringing their influence to America during the 17th Century.

The Land of the Pennsylvania Dutch has contributed more than any other community to the folk lore of early America. Comparatively few original pieces have escaped destruction since this Pre-Revolutionary period; however, Shawnee has restored a favorite motif of heart and tulip decoration to pottery which blends modern kitchen utility with striking Early American Pennsylvania Dutch color decorations of yellow, red, green and blue.

All decorations are hand-painted under transparent glaze on a china, cream-colored body.

Page 4 of catalog - centerfold showing products in line.

Page 5 of catalog - centerfold showing products in line.

DESCRIPTIVE PRICE LIST

★ ITEM: J-6052-M Name: COFFEE MAKER
CAPACITY: 42 ounces under Aluminum Basket.
DESCRIPTION: Each with Aluminum Basket.
PACKING: 1/12 dozen to individual chip board carton; ½ dozen to shipping carton.
WEIGHT PACKED: 21 pounds per carton.
PRICE: $39.04 Per Dozen Pieces

★ ITEM: J-6052-J Name: COVERED JUG
CAPACITY: 52 ounces.
PACKING: 1 dozen to carton.
WEIGHT PACKED: 39 pounds per carton.
PRICE: $28.80 Per Dozen Pieces

★ ITEM: J-6010-T Name: TEAPOT
CAPACITY: 10 ounces.
DESCRIPTION: Boston Shape.
PACKING: 2 dozen to carton.
WEIGHT PACKED: 22 pounds per carton.
PRICE: $14.40 Per Dozen Pieces

★ ITEM: J-6014-T Name: TEAPOT
CAPACITY: 14 ounces.
DESCRIPTION: Boston Shape.
PACKING: 2 dozen to carton.
WEIGHT PACKED: 27 pounds per carton.
PRICE: $16.00 Per Dozen Pieces

★ ITEM: J-6018-T Name: TEAPOT
CAPACITY: 18 ounces.
DESCRIPTION: Boston Shape.
PACKING: 2 dozen to carton.
WEIGHT PACKED: 30 pounds per carton.
PRICE: $17.28 Per Dozen Pieces

★ ITEM: J-6027-T Name: TEAPOT
CAPACITY: 27 ounces.
DESCRIPTION: Boston Shape.
PACKING: 1 dozen to carton.
WEIGHT PACKED: 26 pounds per carton.
PRICE: $23.36 Per Dozen Pieces

★ ITEM: J-6034-J Name: BEATER JUG
CAPACITY: 34 ounces.
PACKING: 2 dozen per carton.
WEIGHT PACKED: 43 pounds per carton.
PRICE: $18.56 Per Dozen Pieces

★ ITEM: J-6075-K Name: COOKY JAR
CAPACITY: 80 ounces.
DIMENSIONS: 8¼" high, 7½" diameter.
DESCRIPTION: Jug Shape.
PACKING: 1 dozen to carton.
WEIGHT PACKED: 46 pounds per carton.
PRICE: $35.20 Per Dozen Pieces

★ ITEM: J-6012-J Name: BALL JUG
CAPACITY: 12½ ounces.
PACKING: 2 dozen to carton.
WEIGHT PACKED: 20 pounds per carton.
PRICE: $10.88 Per Dozen Pieces

★ ITEM: J-6064-J Name: BALL JUG
CAPACITY: 2 quarts.
DESCRIPTION: With Ice Lip.
PACKING: 1 dozen to carton.
WEIGHT PACKED: 37 pounds per carton.
PRICE: $25.60 Per Dozen Pieces

Page 6 of catalog.

DESCRIPTIVE PRICE LIST

★ ITEM: J-6030-T
Name: TEAPOT
CAPACITY: 30 ounces.
PACKING: 1 dozen per carton.
WEIGHT PACKED: 25 pounds per carton.
PRICE: $23.68 Per Dozen Pieces

★ ITEM: J-6008-R
Name: SUGAR BOWL
CAPACITY: 8½ ounces, 2¾" high.
PACKING: 2 dozen per carton.
WEIGHT PACKED: 16½ pounds per carton.
PRICE: $9.28 Per Dozen Pieces

★ ITEM: J-6009-J
Name: CREAMER
CAPACITY: 10 ounces, 4¾" high.
PACKING: 2 dozen per carton.
WEIGHT PACKED: 17½ pounds per carton.
PRICE: $9.92 Per Dozen Pieces

★ ITEM: J-6050-R
Name: UTILITY OR GREASE JAR
CAPACITY: 14 ounces.
DESCRIPTION: Jug Shape.
PACKING: 2 dozen per carton.
WEIGHT PACKED: 28 pounds per carton.
PRICE: $14.40 Per Dozen Pieces

★ ITEM: J-6055-R
Name: RANGE SIZE SALT & PEPPER
SIZE: 4¾" high.
DESCRIPTION: Jug Shape.
PACKING: 1 dozen pair to carton.
WEIGHT PACKED: 12 pounds per carton.
PRICE: $14.40 Per Dozen Pair

ASST. No. J-6001-A
Name: GIFT ASSORTMENT
Composed of:
2 Only—J-6010-T 10 oz. Teapot
3 Only—J-6027-T 27 oz. Teapot
3 Only—J-6012-J 12½ oz. Jug
2 Only—J-6064-J 2 qt. Ball Jug
1 Only—J-6052-M Coffee Maker
1 Only—J-6052-J 52 oz. Covered Jug
3 Only—J-6008-R Sugar Bowl
3 Only—J-6009-J 10 oz. Creamer
2 Only—J-6075-K Cooky Jar
TOTAL—20 PIECES TO ASSORTMENT.
WEIGHT PACKED: 36 pounds.
PRICE: $33.92 Per Assortment
NOTE: Above assortment is priced slightly higher than solid pack of individual sizes to cover additional container costs.

ASST. No. J-6000-A
Name: STARTER ASSORTMENT
DESCRIPTION: Composed of:
2 Only—J-6075-K Cookie Jar
2 Only—J-6064-J 2 qt. Ball Jug
3 Only—J-6012-J 12½ oz. Ball Jug
2 Only—J-6052-J 52 oz. Covered Jug
3 Only—J-6010-T 10 oz. Teapot
2 Only—J-6014-T 14 oz. Teapot
2 Only—J-6018-T 18 oz. Teapot
2 Only—J-6027-T 27 oz. Teapot
TOTAL: 18 PIECES TO ASSORTMENT.
PACKING: 1 Assortment.
WEIGHT PACKED: 34 pounds per carton.
PRICE: $32.96 Per Assortment
NOTE: Above assortment is priced slightly higher than solid pack of individual sizes to cover additional container costs.

ASST. No. J-60487-T
Name: TEAPOT ASSORTMENT
DESCRIPTION: Boston Shape.
Each Assortment composed of:
6 Only—J-6010-T 10 oz.
6 Only—J-6014-T 14 oz.
6 Only—J-6018-T 18 oz.
4 Only—J-6027-T 27 oz.
TOTAL: 24 PIECES.
PACKING: 1 Assortment.
WEIGHT PACKED: 24 pounds per carton.
PRICE: $35.60 Per Assortment
NOTE: Above assortment is priced slightly higher than solid pack of individual sizes to cover additional container costs.

Page 7 of catalog.

DESCRIPTIVE PRICE LIST

ASST. No. J-6005-A
Name: KITCHEN ASSORTMENT
DESCRIPTION:
Composed of:
4 Only—J-6075-K Cooky Jar
4 Only—J-6064-J 2 qt. Ball Jug
4 Only—J-6052-J 52 oz. Covered Jug
TOTAL: 12 PIECES TO ASSORTMENT.
PACKING: 1 Assortment.
WEIGHT PACKED: 38 pounds per assortment.
PRICE: $32.00 Per Assortment
NOTE: Above assortment is priced slightly higher than solid pack of individual sizes to cover additional container costs.

ASST. No. J-6011-R
Name: SUGAR AND CREAMER SET
Each Set composed of:
1 Only—J-6008-R Sugar Bowl
1 Only—J-6009-J Creamer
PACKING: 1 dozen sets per carton.
WEIGHT PACKED: 20 pounds per carton.
PRICE: $19.20 Per Dozen Sets

ASST. No. J-6002-A
Name: TEA SET
Each Set composed of:
1 Only—J-6030-T 30 oz. Teapot
1 Only—J-6008-R Sugar Bowl
1 Only—J-6009-J 10 oz. Creamer
TOTAL: 3 PIECES TO SET.
PACKING: ½ dozen sets to carton.
WEIGHT PACKED: 23 pounds per carton.
PRICE: $45.12 Per Dozen Sets
NOTE: Above assortment is priced slightly higher than solid pack of individual sizes to cover additional container costs.

ASST. No. J-6057-R
Name: RANGE SET
Each Set composed of:
1 Only—J-6050-R Grease Jar
1 Only—Pair J-6055-R Salt and Pepper
PACKING: 1 dozen sets to carton.
WEIGHT PACKED: 22 pounds per carton.
PRICE: $28.80 Per Dozen Sets

Shawnee Pottery Co.
ZANESVILLE OHIO

Back page 8 of catalog.

Pennsylvania Dutch Kitchenware Line.

Coffee Maker, 52 ounces, or 42 ounces with aluminum basket inserted. Marked: U.S.A. 52, and bottom is stamped with words: *Do not place over direct heat. Use pad.*

Covered Jug, 52 ounces, Marked: U.S.A. 52, and bottom is stamped with words: *Do not place over direct heat. Use pad.*

Cooky Jar, 8-1/8 inches high, 80 ounces. Marked: U.S.A. 75

Beater Jug, 34 ounces.
No examples have turned up to date.
Too rare to determine value!

Teapot, 10 ounce Boston Shape. Marked: U.S.A. 10

Teapot, 14 ounce Boston Shape. Marked: U.S.A. 14

Teapot, 18 ounce Boston Shape. Marked: U.S.A. 18

Teapot, 27 ounce Boston Shape. Marked: U.S.A. 27

Teapot, 30 ounce. Marked: U.S.A.

Ball Jug, 2 quarts, with ice lip. Marked: U.S.A. 64

Utility / Grease Jar, 14 ounces. Marked: U.S.A.

Range Size Salt & Pepper Shakers, 4-3/8 inches, no mark.

Ball Jug Creamer, 12-1/2 ounces. Marked: U.S.A. 12

Creamer, tilt, 10 ounces. Marked: U.S.A. 10

Sugar Bowl, 2-3/4 inches, 8-1/2 ounces. Marked: U.S.A.

Snowflake

This kitchenware line was made around 1941 and 1942, but was dropped from production by October 1942. A difficult line to photograph, it consists of horizontal ribbed lines with incised snowflakes interspersed all over. Two variations of the snowflake design have been noted: one has six points, and the other has eight points. Reportedly, the creamer and sugar were give-aways of the Procter & Gamble Company.

In July of 1941, the mixing bowl set consisted of 5" 6" 7" 8" and 9" diameter bowls, made with a ***handy grip top***. This top was a wide, flat band around the outer top circumference of the bowl. By January of 1942, the design of these bowls was changed to a narrower, more rounded, top band. It is possible that production changes were made due to problems with the grip top bowls either chipping, or just not fitting right when stacked in one another. Even though the rest of the line was dropped in late 1942, production of the mixing bowls continued.

Colors listed are: Bright White, Old English Ivory, Powder Blue, Turquoise, Flax Blue, Yellow. The mixing bowl sets had these possible colors listed plus Dark Green, Dark Blue, Burgundy, Dusty Rose.

Based on catalog information currently available, all items in the Snowflake line are represented here, with catalog numbers included with each piece, placed in parenthesis after the description. All items shown are marked with **U.S.A.**, except the large salt and pepper shakers, which have no discernible marks.

Ball Jug, 7-1/4 inches, 2 quart (H254).

Mixing Bowls, Set of Five, later design of rounded band tops. Mixing Bowls: 5" yellow H175, 6" flax blue H176, 7" dusty rose H177, 8" old ivory H178, 9" turquoise H179.
From The Collection of Rich & Linda Guffey

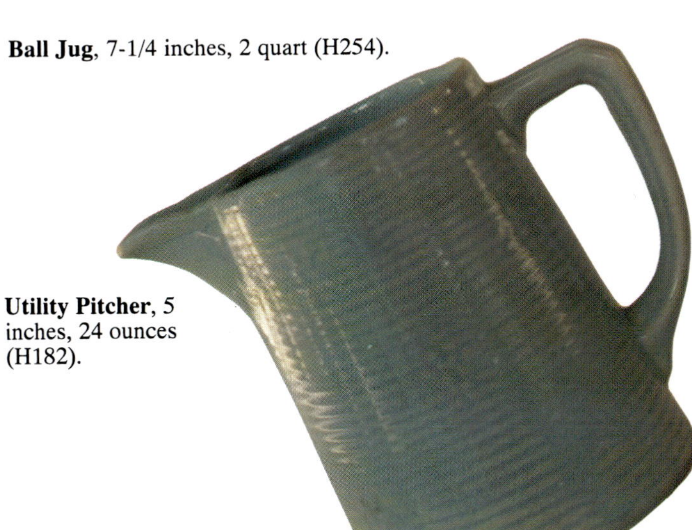

Utility Pitcher, 5 inches, 24 ounces (H182).

Canister (Cookie Jar), 7 inches, 2 quart (H222).

Note: Mixing bowls were marketed in a number of combinations, with three, four, or five bowls comprising a set. All sizes listed are diameters:

3-Pc. Bowl Set of 5" 7" 9" bowls
4-Pc. Bowl Set of 5" 6" 7" 8" bowls
4-Pc. Bowl Set of 6" 7" 8" 9" bowls
5-Pc. Bowl Set of 5" 6" 7" 8" 9" bowls

Grip Top Mixing Bowl, earliest design, 7 inches diameter (H177).
From The Collection of Melvin & Jean Gibson

Mixing Bowls, Set of Five, later design of rounded band tops. Colors: 5" burgundy, 6" old ivory, 7" dark green, 8" dark blue, 9" yellow.
From The Collection of Ron Brown

Teapot 4 inches, 2 cup (H122).

Teapot 7 inches, 8 cup (H126).
When used with aluminum coffee maker, this pot has 6-cup capacity.
See Coffee Maker section for example.

Teapot 5-1/2 inches, 5 cup (H125).

Left: **Creamer** 3 inches, 7 ounces (H107).
Right: **Open Sugar** 3 inches, 7 ounces (H117).

Range Salt & Pepper Shakers 4 inches high (H205).

Grease Jar 3-1/2 inches, 12 ounces (H214).
The Grease Jar and Salt & Pepper Shakers were sold as a Range Set.

Sunflower

Popular with collectors, this line is relatively easy to compile, with the Coffee Jug seeming to be the most difficult piece to acquire. Designed by Robert Heckman in the late 1940s, the teapot Design Patent 149,623 was filed March 7, 1947.

The Coffee Maker/Jug holds 52 ounces if used as a covered jug only. When the aluminum basket is used to make coffee, the liquid volume is reduced to 42 ounces. See Coffee Maker section for example.

The Sunflower pattern is embossed and hand decorated. All items listed are marked **U.S.A.**

Top Row:
Ball Jug, 7-1/4 inches, 2-quart.
Range Salt & Pepper Shakers, 5 inches, 4 & 5 holes.
Covered Jug / Coffee Maker, 7-3/4 inches, 52 ounces.

Bottom Row:
Ball Jug Creamer.
Teapot, 6-1/4 inches, 30-ounce.
Table Salt & Pepper Shakers 3-1/4 inches.
Covered Sugar / Grease Jar 4-3/4 inches.

Wave

The embossed wave pattern on this line inspires the name used by collectors. In addition to the items shown, the teapot may be found with the French Drip coffee maker. Colors found are yellow, blue, and green.

Top Row:
Range Salt & Pepper Shakers, 5 inches, Marked: U.S.A.
Utility Pitcher, 5-1/2 inches, Marked: U.S.A. 32
Grease Jar, 5 inches, Marked: U.S.A.

Bottom Row:
Open Sugar, 3-1/8 inches, Marked: U.S.A.
Creamer, 4 inches, Marked: U.S.A. 13
Teapot, 6 inches, Marked: U.S.A. 30

Wave Pitchers.
Creamer, blue, 4 inches, Marked: U.S.A. 13
Utility, green, 5-1/2 inches, Marked: U.S.A. 32
Utility, green, 6-1/2 inches, Marked: U.S.A. 60

White Corn

White Corn kitchenware was the predecessor to the later popular line of Corn King dinnerware.

First produced in the mid-1940s, White Corn was not a great seller, so the line was never expanded. Bob Heckman worked on improving the White Corn line by changing the colors to pale yellow kernels with lighter green husks. The sugar shaker was the one original piece of the White Corn line that was never carried over to the later Corn King or Corn Queen lines.

The green husks were hand painted, and the finials of the teapot and sugar bowl were painted brown.

Tip: How do you know you have White Corn with gold trim, as opposed to either Corn King or Corn Queen with gold trim? Look inside. All White Corn will still have white interiors, while the other lines have yellow interiors.

Top Row:
Table Salt & Pepper Shakers, 3-1/4 inches, no marks.
Pitcher, 8 inches, 40 ounces, Marked: U.S.A.
Teapot, 6-1/2 inches, 30 ounces, Marked: U.S.A.

Bottom Row:
Creamer, 4-3/4 inches, 12 ounces, Marked: U.S.A.
Sugar Shaker, 5-1/4 inches, Marked: U.S.A.
Sugar Bowl, 5 inches, Marked: U.S.A.
Range Salt & Pepper Shakers, 5 inches, no marks.

White Corn with Gold Trim.
Note two variations of gold trim on the Range Shakers: the front left set has more yellow and brown, while the front right set has more of the white kernels left exposed.

Note two variations on the Covered Sugar Bowls in the right rear; one has more brown than the other.
From The Collection Of Terry & Sandra Bauer

Gold Trim Teapot.
Gold Trim Pitcher.
Gold Trim Sugar Shaker.
Gold Trim Sugar Bowl.
Gold Trim Creamer.
Gold Trim Range Shakers.
Gold Trim Table Shakers.

Section V: Dinnerware Lines

Chapter 16: Valencia

Soon after Shawnee Pottery began production in 1937, a Sears Roebuck Co. representative approached president Addis E. Hull, Jr., asking for a dinnerware line that would compete with Fiesta ware. Shawnee designer Louise Elizabeth Bauer created Valencia, the first dinnerware line produced at the pottery.

Sears promoted this line by giving away a 20-Piece Starter Set with every new refrigerator purchase. This set consisted of Service for Four; each setting was made up of one Cup, Saucer, Bread and Butter Plate 6-1/2", Dinner Plate 9-3/4", and Sauce Dish 5". Customers could then purchase additional pieces, as well as the Starter Set, through the stores and catalogs. Valencia dinnerware displays in the Sears stores were enhanced by a Spanish Dancers display figurine, also the design of Louise Elizabeth Bauer.

Production of Valencia cannot be precisely dated, but was limited to around two or three years. Unfortunately, it did not adequately withstand day to day use.

Because all pieces of Valencia shown in advertisements have not been found, there is some question whether every piece was produced. Some pieces shown in the Sears ad, have actually turned up designed differently. For example, the Ice Pitcher became a Ball Jug shape somewhere in the design process. Some bowls, nappies, and plates found, have never conformed to the listed sizes, leaving doubt about whether all pieces were produced in all sizes. With time, perhaps sharp-eyed collectors will come forward with new discoveries. To this end, all items in the ad have been listed and priced, in the hopes that they do exist.

Very few pieces have been found with the word **Valencia**, or a **U.S.A.** impressed on the bottom; most pieces are unmarked. Colors listed: Tangerine, Blue, Green, Yellow, with Burgundy added later.

Warning: A Valencia look-alike, named *Corinthian,* was marketed in the late 1940s by China & Glass Distributors, Inc. of New York. Documented are a Ball Jug in 1 qt. and 2 qt. sizes, and a Carafe, done in the Valencia swirl pattern. Colors listed were Sunset Red, Yellow, Green, Blue, but were decorated with white interiors. Shawnee Valencia interiors will be the same color as the exterior.

Sears Valencia advertisement.

Colorful Valencia.

Spanish Dancers Display Figurine.
Tangerine, 11-1/4" high, 5-1/2" diameter base, no mark on bottom. Embossed word Valencia on front of pedestal base. *Rare!*
From The Collection of Rich & Linda Guffey

Spanish Dancers Display Figurine shown from back.

10 inch Dinner Plates.

6-3/4 inch Plates.

13 inch Chop Plate.

Not Shown, Same Pattern As Previous:
15" Chop Plate.
9-3/4" Plate.
7-3/4" Plate.

Teacup and Saucer.
Teacup 2-3/4 inches high.
Saucer 6-1/2 inches diameter.

Teacup Saucers 6-1/2 inch.

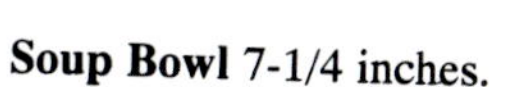

Soup Bowl 7-1/4 inches.

Bowl 9 inches.

Tumblers 5-1/4 inches, Yellow, Green, Blue, Tangerine.
Very hard to find! Additional Tumblers in Miscellaneous Rare chapter.

Carafe with lid.

6-Piece Relish Tray Yellow tray holds four wedge inserts and one round insert, 1-1/4 inches high, 10-1/4 inches diameter, no mark.

Salt & Pepper Shakers Salt has 6 holes in a circle, with a 7th hole in center of circle; pepper has 6 holes in a circle, 3 inches high.

Teapot 7-1/2 inches.

Covered Sugar 4 inches high.
Creamer 3-1/4 inches high.

Batter Jug, no lid, 7-1/2 inches.

Ice Pitcher (Ball Jug).
7 inches high, 64 ounce, ice lip.

Mixing Bowl 9 inches diameter, one of a set of eight nesting bowls, ranging from 5" to 12" diameter.

Ice Pitcher (Ball Jug).
7 inches high, 64 ounce, ice lip.

Bud Vase 7 inches.

Ice Pitcher (Ball Jug).
7 inches high, 64 ounce, ice lip.

Ice Pitcher (Ball Jug).
7 inches high, 64 ounce, ice lip.

Ice Pitcher (Ball Jug).
7 inches high, 64 ounce, ice lip.

Additional Valencia ware listed on advertisement:

Ash Tray.
Bowl, footed, punch/salad.
Bowl, marmite, w/lid, 4-1/2".
Bowl, mixing 5".
Bowl, mixing 6".
Bowl, mixing 7".
Bowl, mixing 8".
Bowl, mixing 9".
Bowl, mixing 10".
Bowl, mixing 11".
Bowl, mixing 12".
Bowl, 9-1/2".
Bowl, lug, w/lid.
Candle Holder, bulb, pair.
Candle Holder, tripod, pair.
Casserole, 7-1/2".
Casserole, 8-1/2".
Casserole, footed, 8".
Casserole, lug.
Coaster.
Coffee Pot.
Coffee Pot, A.D.
Compote, footed, 12".
Compote, pedestal.
Cookie Jar.
Cup, A.D.
Cup, cream soup, lug.
Cup, tall.
Dish, 5".
Dish, 6".
Egg Cup.
Jug, ball, 32 ounce.
Jug, syrup.
Marmalade.
Mustard.
Pie Baker, 9-1/4".
Pie Baker, 10-1/2".
Plate, compartment.
Saucer, A.D.
Saucer, off-center ring.
Stack Set, round, 4-piece.
Tray, for batter set.
Utensil, fork.
Utensil, pie server.
Utensil, spoon.
Utility tray, rectangular.
Vase, footed, 8".
Vase, footed, 10".
Vase, footed, 12".

Chapter 17: Corn King

The most successful and enduring line produced at Shawnee was the Corn King dinnerware. Created in a limited number of pieces in 1946 by Robert Heckman, it eventually became a complete table and kitchen ware line sold in five-and-dime stores by the single piece or in boxed sets. This made it easy for the homemaker to replace a broken piece, or add to the line as needed. Sale of Corn King continued until around 1955 when the colors were changed and the line was renamed Corn Queen.

The earliest pieces of Corn King were hand decorated by brush, but later it was decorated using a mask which covered the kernels, allowing the husks to be sprayed green. Then the entire piece was dipped into a unique translucent yellow glaze mixed at Shawnee, and fired. Early corn ware was cast, but once the Ram Press was installed at Shawnee, all plates and items 4 inches and under were produced on this press.

Jess Parentice was responsible for the idea of marketing boxed sets of corn ware, the first of which was the Pop Corn Set. Bob Heckman worked with the box company in designing special cartons that had die cut lids which could fold open for store displays, or be closed for transporting the ware safely. These special display cartons were expensive, and undoubtedly cost nearly as much as the pottery itself.

Since there are many look-alike corn items on the market, including some obvious reproduction pieces, there is a tip to recognizing the real Corn King items. A close look at the Shawnee corn kernels reveals a realistic staggered pattern to them, whereas most other corn has straight horizontal and vertical lines on the kernels. Salt & pepper shakers are the most commonly misidentified items, so keep in mind that there were only two sizes made by Shawnee ..... the 5-1/4 inch range shakers and the 3-1/4 inch table shakers.

Original catalog sheets of Corn King show all of the items in this line, although the color printed in the catalog is not accurate. Additional examples of this line may be seen in specific categories such as cookie jars.

Corn King Catalog Sheet.

Corn King Dinnerware.

- #5 Mixing Bowl 5".
- #6 Mixing Bowl 6-1/2".
- #8 Mixing Bowl 8".
- #65 Individual Teapot 10 oz.
- #66 Cookie Jar 9-3/4".
- #68 Plate 9-3/4".
- #69 Mug 8 oz.
- #70 Creamer.
- #71 Pitcher / Jug 40 oz.
- #72 Covered Butter Dish.
- #73 Individual Casserole.
- #74 Casserole 11"
- #75 Teapot 30 oz.
- #76 Salt & Pepper 3-1/4".
- #77 Salt & Pepper 5-1/4".
- #78 Sugar Bowl / Utility Jar.
- #79 Corn Holder / Relish Tray.
- #90 Teacup 5 oz.
- #91 Saucer 5-1/2".
- #92 Fruit Dish 6".
- #93 Salad / Dessert Plate 7-1/2".
- #94 Soup / Cereal Bowl 6-3/4"
- #95 Vegetable Dish 8-7/8".
- #96 Platter 11-3/4".

Polly Ann's Pop Corn Set catalog.

Corn King with Gold Trim.
Left: **Sugar Bowl**, gold trim, 5-1/4 inches. Marked: U.S.A. 78
Center: **Teapot**, gold trim, 6-1/2 inches. Marked: Shawnee U.S.A. 75
Right: **Creamer**, gold trim, 5 inches. Marked: Shawnee U.S.A. 70
From The Collection of Paul & Joy Schneider

Polly Ann's T-V Time Pop Corn Set in original display box.
Consists of four 6-1/2 inch bowls, 12 ounce jug for melted butter, 5 inch salt shaker, and 10 ounce can of Betty Zane pop corn.
From The Collection of Melvin & Jean Gibson

Indian Corn King Shakers, 5 inches, underglaze decorated.
Rare!
From The Collection of Paul & Joy Schneider

TOWN AND COUNTRY
8 piece
SNACK SET
4 MUGS 4 PLATES
PICNICS PARTIES
BARBECUES

101 Snack Set — 8 Pc. Town & Country Set
4 Only #69 — 8 oz. mugs
4 Only #68 — 9¾" plates
Each Set in its own display carton
4 Sets to shipping carton. Wt. 36 lbs.

Corn-King OVENPROOF KITCHENWARE

- For patio or picnic, for kitchen or outdoor entertaining, for the "Casual Living Set"—a complete line of ovenproof bake and serve ware in the colorful Corn-King pattern.
- All semi-porcelain, the decoration is under the glaze which means it is not affected by detergents. Available in two assortments plus standard-pack. All cartons are 200# test.

SHAWNEE POTTERIES
ZANESVILLE, OHIO U.S.A.
Catalog 15K

Town and Country Snack Set catalog.

Town and Country Snack Set in original display box. Consists of four plates, #68, and four mugs, #69, each with an original Corn King label. Original Montgomery Ward price sticker intact, listing set for $4.98, on sale for $3.95.
From The Collection of Melvin & Jean Gibson

Left: **Corn King Individual Casserole**, 4 inches high, 9 ounces. Marked: Shawnee Oven Proof U.S.A. 73
Right: **Corn King Casserole**, 5-1/2 inches high. Marked: Shawnee Oven Proof U.S.A. 74
These casseroles have the green lids, with a curled husk forming the finial.

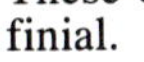

Three corn shakers, two of which are Shawnee Corn King, and one is a look-alike.
Left: **Shawnee Corn King** 5-1/4" range shaker with rounded top, original label, and staggered kernels.
Center: **Corn** shaker by unknown maker. Note the even horizontal and vertical lines of the kernels, a peaked top, and brush strokes on the green husk indicating that it was not spray decorated. Also, Shawnee did not make a medium size shaker like this.
Right: **Shawnee Corn King** 3-1/4" shaker with rounded top, and staggered kernels.
Warning: There is a lot of corn dinnerware being passed off as Shawnee today, mainly because of the high prices that Shawnee commands.

Corn King Casserole with Kernels on Lid, 5-1/2 inches high. Marked: Shawnee U.S.A. 74 *Very Rare!*
It is believed that this is an early design that was changed to eliminate having to hand decorate both pieces of this item.
From The Collection of Melvin & Jean Gibson

Corn King Corn Holder, or Relish Tray, or Spoon Holder, 8-1/2 inches long. Marked: Shawnee Oven Proof U.S.A. 79

The ends of these Corn Holders / Relish Trays are quite different. On the right is the earlier cast version, with a thick and uneven end. On the left is the later version, produced on the Ram Press, where the ends were thinner and more even.

Chapter 18: Lobster

The Lobster dinnerware line was the only one that Shawnee Pottery marketed under their Kenwood Ceramics Division. It was introduced in a 1954 catalog, and featured a full range of coordinated table and kitchen items.

When Arthur K. Grindley was hired as the new Shawnee president in July of 1953, it was hoped that he would infuse some new production ideas into Shawnee. Coming from his family's pottery, Grindley Artware Company of Sebring, Ohio, he carried over ideas for a line of lobster-decorated dinnerware. Just how many items were produced by Grindley Artware, and in what colors, is uncertain, but Shawnee Pottery subsequently altered and/or added to the line. The french-handled casseroles with stands, range set, and small french casseroles were designed by Robert Heckman at Shawnee. Again, die cut display boxes were created for marketing related items of Lobster ware.

Lobster ware was one which had to have three separate firings during production: the first was in the bisque kiln; the second was in the tunnel kiln after being glazed; and the third was to fire the red on the lobster at a lower temperature. Of course, any items without the red lobster had only two firings.

Shawnee catalogs listed two colors available for Lobster ware; a Satin Charcoal glaze, or glossy Van Dyke Brown glaze. When neither of these colors seemed to appeal to the public, a glossy Mirror Black glaze was introduced in 1955. Reportedly, early production samples were done in white, but never went into full production in this color.

Despite concentrated efforts to market Lobster ware, it did not prove to be a popular line with the public back in the mid 1950s. Today, however, it is quite popular with collectors of Shawnee Pottery, with some items commanding very high prices.

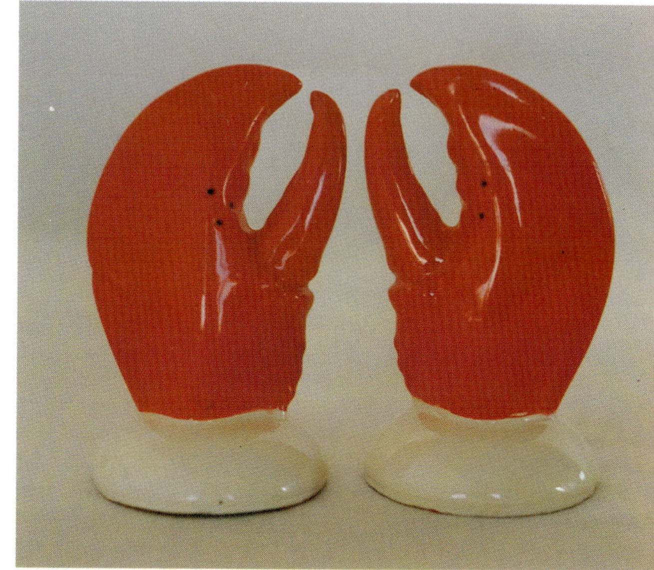

Claw Shakers, 5 inches high, no mark. (3/2)

Snack Jar or Bean Pot, often referred to as the Cookie Jar, Satin Charcoal, 40 oz. Marked: Kenwood U.S.A. 925
From The Collection of Paul & Joy Schneider

Lobster Pin, ceramic, made at Shawnee as a giveaway at the 1954 Pittsburgh China and Glass Show promoting the new Lobster ware line. Approximately 2-1/2 inches long, it is stamped on the back with the words, *Kenwood Ceramics Shawnee Potteries Zanesville, Ohio*, though not all words are legible on all pins.

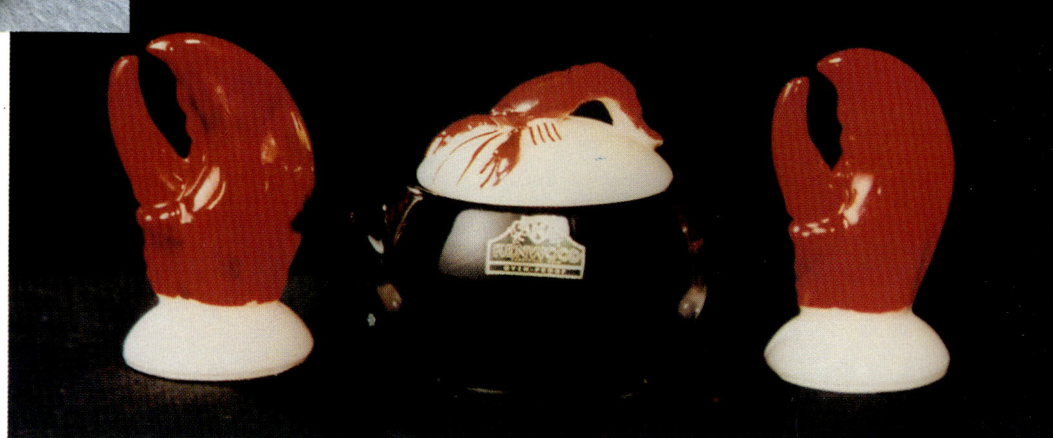

Range Set, Gold Trim, original Kenwood label, Mirror Black utility jar.
From The Collection of Lanny & Shawn Jones

Back of the ceramic Lobster Pin.

Lobster Shakers, full body, 7-1/4 inches long, with label. Marked: U.S.A. (5/4)

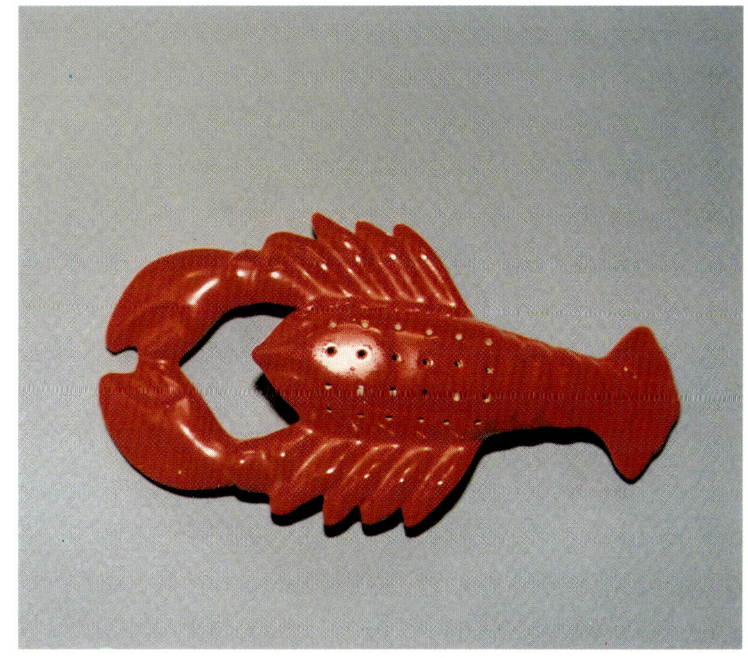

Hors d'oeuvre Holder 7-1/4 inches long. Marked: U.S.A.

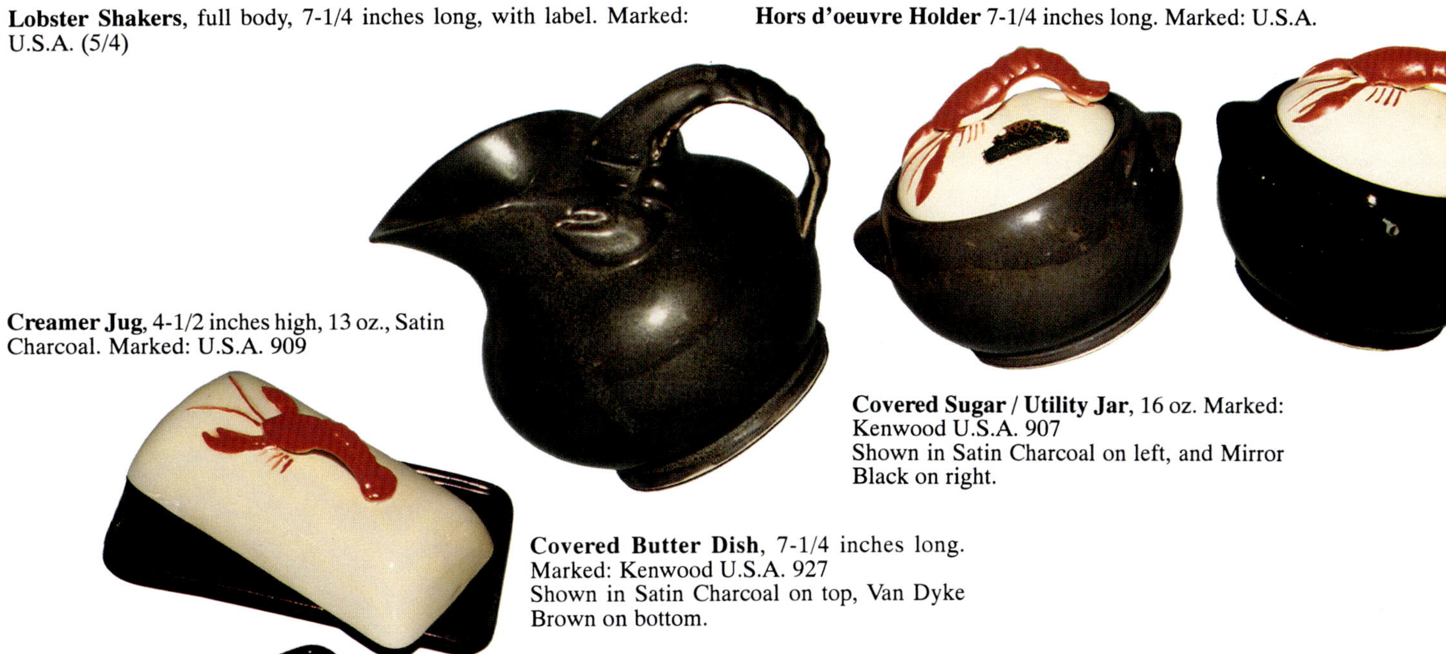

Creamer Jug, 4-1/2 inches high, 13 oz., Satin Charcoal. Marked: U.S.A. 909

Covered Sugar / Utility Jar, 16 oz. Marked: Kenwood U.S.A. 907
Shown in Satin Charcoal on left, and Mirror Black on right.

Covered Butter Dish, 7-1/4 inches long. Marked: Kenwood U.S.A. 927
Shown in Satin Charcoal on top, Van Dyke Brown on bottom.

Mug, 8 oz., 3-1/4 inches high, no mark.

Covered Relish Pot, 5-1/2 oz. Marked: Kenwood U.S.A. 926

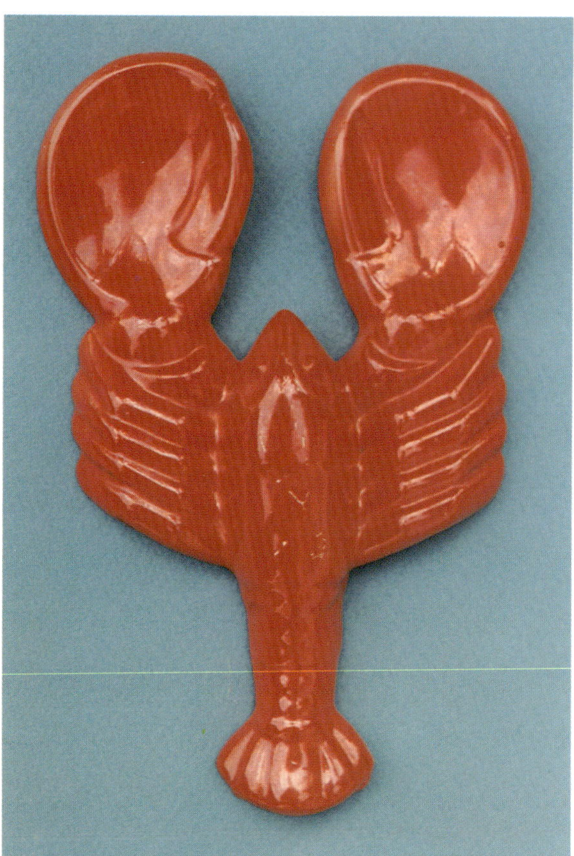

Double Spoon Holder, 8-1/2 inches long.
Marked: U.S.A. 935

Compartment Plate, green & brown, 11-3/4 inches long. Marked: Kenwood U.S.A. 912
Note that the plate is the shape of the large lobster claw. Will also be found in Satin Charcoal and Van Dyke Brown.

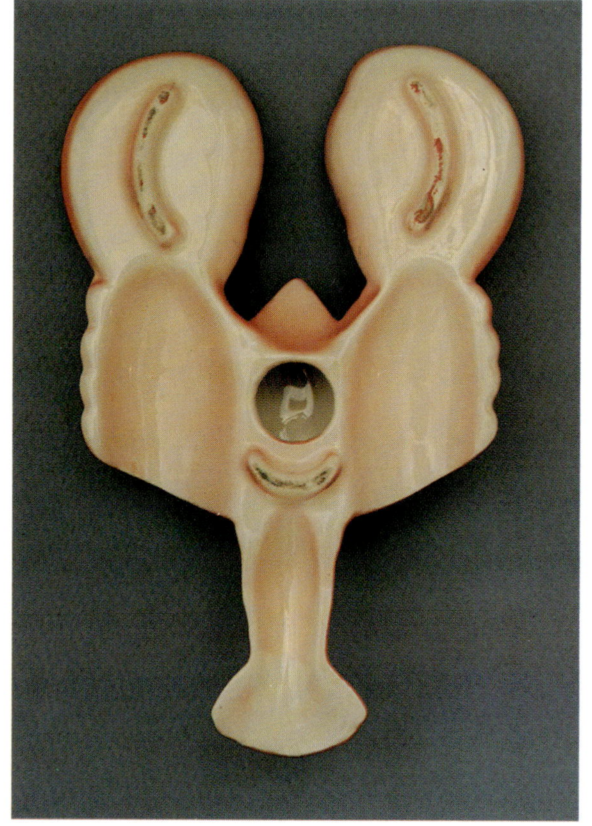

Back of Double Spoon Holder.

Back of Compartment Plate.

French Casseroles, all shown in Mirror Black, ranging in size from 10 ounce, 16 ounce, 1 quart, 2 quart.

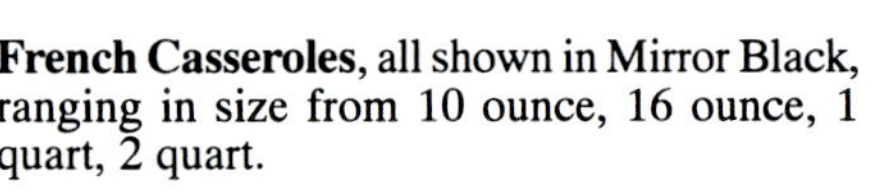

lobster

casseroles by KENWOOD

Real conversation pieces, these french-type lobster casseroles are striking to behold yet delightfully practical and in perfect taste. All pieces are scarlet, eggshell white and mirror-black, *oven-proof*, semi-porcelain. Stands are sturdy triple-plated brass.

No. 996 16-oz. Lobster Casserole, wt. 3 lbs. List $5.95

No. 997 1-qt. Lobster Casserole, wt. 5 lbs., List $6.95

No. 998 2-qt. Lobster Casserole, wt. 6 lbs., List $7.95

All numbers are individually packed in air-cell, 200 lb. test cartons that meet parcel post requirements for reshipment.

KENWOOD CERAMICS

Division of Shawnee Potteries, Zanesville, Ohio, U.S.A.

Lobster Casserole Catalog.

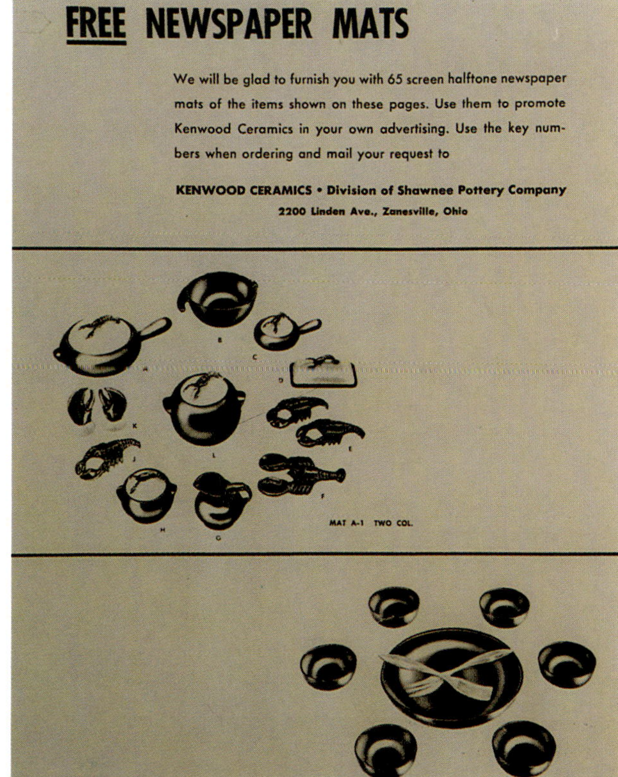
FREE NEWSPAPER MATS

We will be glad to furnish you with 65 screen halftone newspaper mats of the items shown on these pages. Use them to promote Kenwood Ceramics in your own advertising. Use the key numbers when ordering and mail your request to

KENWOOD CERAMICS • Division of Shawnee Pottery Company
2200 Linden Ave., Zanesville, Ohio

MAT A-1 TWO COL.

MAT A-7 TWO COL.

Lobster Catalog Page showing newspaper mats available.

Additional items listed that are not pictured, except in catalog pages:

#915 Mixing Bowl or Open Baker, 5" diameter.

#917 Mixing Bowl or Open Baker, 7" diameter.

#919 Mixing Bowl or Open Baker, 9" diameter.

#921 Salad, Soup, or Chili Bowl, 5-3/4" diameter.

#922 Salad or Spaghetti Bowl, 14" diameter.

#928 Handled Batter Bowl, 8" diameter.

lobster

sets by KENWOOD

Add color to your table or kitchen with a set of lobster claws that resemble the real thing—but contain salt and pepper. Delight your guests with individual casserole dishes that are different—and oven-proof. The perfect gift for gourmets and their ladies.

No. 906 Range Set, Lobster Claw Salt and Pepper Set plus Utility Bowl, in display carton, packed 4 cartons per master carton, wt. 12 lbs. List $4.95 set.

No. 901 10-oz. French Casseroles, set of 4 in display carton, packed 4 cartons per master carton, wt. 23 lbs. List $9.95 set.

Both sets are packed in handsome durable display cartons of special snow-white corrugated board printed in two colors as shown. Sells at point-of-sale; eliminates packing for take-home sales or local delivery.

KENWOOD CERAMICS

Division of Shawnee Potteries, Zanesville, Ohio, U.S.A.

Range Set and Casserole Set Catalog.

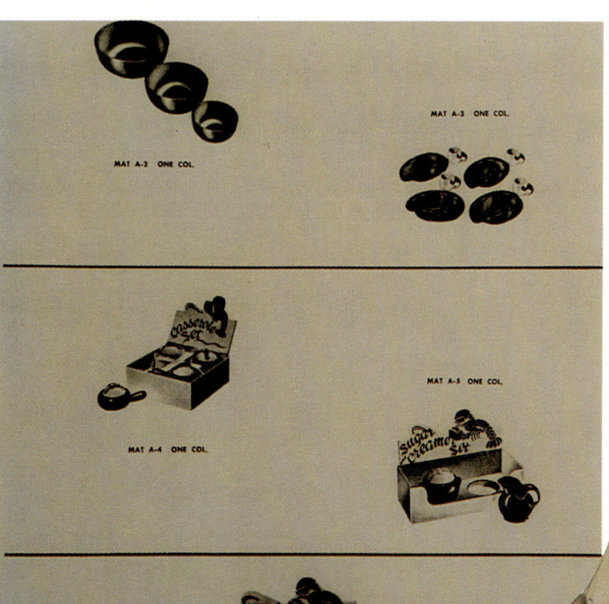
MAT A-2 ONE COL.

MAT A-3 ONE COL.

MAT A-4 ONE COL.

MAT A-5 ONE COL.

MAT A-6 ONE COL.

Lobster Catalog Page showing newspaper mats available.

Boxed Casserole Set, with original die cut display box, four 10-ounce french casseroles.

Chapter 19: Corn Queen

Corn Queen is the later version of Shawnee's corn dinnerware line, with all pieces of the original Corn King line being carried over to Queen.

After John F. Bonistall became president of Shawnee, he determined that changes were needed to lower production costs and increase sales of the Corn King dinnerware. By 1955, changes were being made in the glaze colors, with the husks made a darker green, the kernels made a lighter yellow, and the name changed to Corn Queen.

Boxed sets continued to be marketed, though the boxes no longer were the expensive die cut ones used for Corn King. The boxes were plain and rugged to protect the pottery from damage, but the written literature was printed on a thinner cardboard sleeve which fit over the plain box.

Corn Queen was met with some renewed interest from the buying public, and was marketed right up until the time Shawnee closed, but it never attained the popularity of Corn King.

Original catalog sheets of Corn Queen show all of the items in this line, although the color in the catalog is not accurate. Additional examples of this line may be seen in specific catagories such as cookie jars.

Cover to the Corn Queen catalog.

Corn Queen catalog depicting entire line of dinnerware.

Corn Queen Dinnerware.
#5 Mixing Bowl 5".
#6 Mixing Bowl 6-1/2".
#8 Mixing Bowl 8" .
#65 Individual Teapot 10 oz.
#66 Cookie Jar.
#68 Plate 10".
#69 Mug 8 oz.
#70 Creamer.
#71 Pitcher / Jug 1 qt.
#72 Covered Butter Dish.
#73 Individual Casserole.
#74 Casserole 1-1/2 qt.
#75 Teapot 30 oz.
#76 Salt & Pepper 3-1/4".
#77 Salt & Pepper 5-1/4".
#78 Sugar Bowl / Utility Jar.
#79 Corn Holder / Relish Tray.
#90 Teacup 5 oz.
#91 Saucer 5-1/2".
#92 Fruit Dish 6".
#93 Salad / Dessert Plate 8".
#94 Soup / Cereal Bowl.
#95 Vegetable Dish 9".
#96 Platter 12".

Corn Queen catalog depicting entire line of boxed sets.
#100 Pop Corn Set.
#101 Snack Set.
#102 Table Set.
#103 Mixing Bowl Set.
#106 Place Setting.
#108 Corn Roast Set.

Corn Queen Corn-Roast Set, consisting of large platter, 4 corn holders, covered butter dish, and small salt & pepper shakers, boxed in plain box (has colorful printed sleeve propped up against the open cover).
From The Collection of Melvin & Jean Gibson

Corn-Roast Set box closed, with outer printed sleeve replaced over the box.

SECTION VI: KITCHENWARE - CASUAL LIVING

CHAPTER 20: LINES

BRUNCH BOWLS

By Kenwood Ceramics

The **Brunch Bowl Casserole** served triple duty as a batter bowl, a mixing bowl with easy-hold handle and pouring lip, and elegant casserole with its' own warming stove. Genuine copper glaze in rich hammered design sets off the ceramic cover. Charming incised designs of tea kettles, roosters, cups and saucers, eating utensils, etc., decorate the oven proof bowl.

Brunch Bowl Casserole, 1-1/2 quart, pink and copper, pink stove, copper stand, bowl marked: Kenwood Oven Proof U.S.A. 940.

Kenwood-crafted originals...of oven-proof, semi-porcelain

Sahara **RANGE SET**

ORIGINAL, in every sense, yet eminently practical. Capacious salt and pepper shakers are easy to handle, firmly stable. Unique utility jar with hammered-copper decorated ceramic cover. In pink with copper, or turquoise with copper. Beautifully boxed in sturdy self-displayer.

NO. 976-P—Sahara Range Set in Pink and Copper.

NO. 976-T—Sahara Range Set in Turquoise and Copper.

Packed one 3-piece set to individual display carton. 4 cartons per master carton. Wt. 10 lbs. per master carton. Also available in parcel post re-shipper.

Brunch bowl **CASSEROLE**

TRIPLE DUTY; batter bowl, mixing bowl (featuring easy-hold handle and pouring lip) and elegant casserole with its own stove. Genuine copper glaze in rich hammered design sets off the ceramic cover. Charming incised designs decorate the bowl of pink, oven-proof, semi-porcelain.

NO. 943—Brunch Bowl Casserole. Pink and Copper. Copper stand. Pink stove. 1½ Quart Capacity.

Packed one to a carton (mailable), wt.—5 lbs.

Brunch bowl **SET**

A JOY in the kitchen and at the party table, too. Clever culinary symbols march 'round each bowl in smart intaglio design. Bowls are 8", 7" and 6" in diameter; nest perfectly. Of genuine oven-proof semi-porcelain in pink, turquoise, and canary yellow.

NO. 941—Brunch Bowl Set in Pink, Turquoise and Yellow.

One set to an individual carton (mailable), wt.—6 lbs.

KENWOOD CERAMICS
Division of Shawnee Potteries, Zanesville, Ohio, U.S.A.

Sahara Range Set, see Utility/Sugar/Grease Jars.
Brunch Bowl Set, 6", 7", 8" diameter bowls in set, with kitchen culinary symbols, in pink, turquoise, yellow.

SUNDIAL

By Kenwood Ceramics

These Casseroles and Chafing Dishes, made of oven proof high-fired semi-porcelain, were available in three sizes. Each had a smart triple-plated brass stand and matching warmer for candle, alcohol, or Sterno. Two color combinations of Pink and Black, and Turquoise and Black were produced.

sundial

casseroles and chafing dishes by KENWOOD

Something new and lovely under the sun, these handsome chafing dishes are appealingly novel, fabulously beautiful. Each is of flawless high-fired semi-porcelain, and *oven-proof*. Each has its own smart triple-plated brass stand and matching warmer for candle, alcohol or Sterno. Three sizes —each available in two striking color combinations (pink and black, turquoise and black).

No. 991-P 16-oz., pink and black, ind. carton, wt. 3 lbs.,
No. 991-T Same in turquoise and black

No. 992-P One-quart, pink and black, ind. carton, wt. 5 lbs.,
No. 992-T Same in turquoise and black

No. 993-P Two-quart pink and black, ind. carton, wt. 6 lbs.,
No. 993-T Same in turquoise and black

Each chafing dish, with stand and stove, individually packed in air-cell 200 lb. test cartons that meet parcel post requirements for reshipment.

KENWOOD CERAMICS
Division of Shawnee Potteries, Zanesville, Ohio, U.S.A.

Sundial catalog sheet.

No. 991 - 16 ounce Tab Handle Chafing Dish - *Orig. List $4.95.*
No. 992 - One-Quart Tab Handle Chafing Dish - *Orig. List $5.95.*
No. 993 - Two-Quart Tab Handle Chafing Dish - *Orig. List $6.95.*

a glee-some threesome...in rich ceramics and gleaming copper

Saucy Susan

Proved a best-seller, Saucy Susan is the one complete condiment susan that's right for every season—every seasoning. One unit that revolves for easy serving, provided with salt and pepper, stoppered oil and vinegar cruets, and four individual sauce or preserve cups with covers and servers. Three stunning color combinations with copper or brass frame.

NO. 985-P—Saucy Susan in Pink, White, and Copper.

NO. 985-T—Saucy Susan in Turquoise, White, and Copper.

NO. 985-B—Saucy Susan in Black, White, and Brass.

ipped one to a carton (mailable), —6 lbs.

Salad Susan

Serves two salads in high style at buffet, table or patio. Styled in striking pink, or turquoise, with accents of rich copper and black. Has oil and vinegar cruets, salt and pepper shakers, two 9" salad bowls, all of semi-porcelain ceramics, revolving on a triple-plated copper frame mounted on ball bearings. Serving accessories included. Imposing size and made with genuine craftsmanship; as a gift, for the hostess "who has everything."

NO. 959-P—24" Salad Susan. Pink, White, Black, with Copper.

NO. 959-T—24" Salad Susan. Turquoise, White, Black, with Copper.

Shipped one to a carton (mailable), wt.—10 lbs.

Toastee Susan

The warmth of copper, the elegance of semi-porcelain ceramics (in pink or turquoise) to make breakfast an event. As a napkin holder or toast server. One covered dish holds butter (regular or California size); the other has two compartments for preserves. Carrying handle. Revolves. A gift in the most-wanted price range.

NO. 955-P—Toastee Susan in Pink, White, and Copper.

NO. 955-T—Toastee Susan in Turquoise, White, and Copper.

NO. 955-B—Toastee Susan in Black, White, and Brass.

Shipped one to a carton (mailable), wt.—5 lbs.

KENWOOD CERAMICS

Division of Shawnee Potteries, Zanesville, Ohio, U.S.A.

Susan Sets

By Kenwood Ceramics

The **Salad Susan** serves two salads at buffet, table, or patio. Two 9-inch salad bowls, oil and vinegar cruets with stoppers, salt and pepper shakers, all of semi-porcelain, revolve on a triple-plated copper frame mounted on ball bearings. Serving accessories included. *Original Retail $19.95.*

No. 959-P - Pink, White, and Black, with Copper Frame.
No. 959-T - Turquoise, White, and Black, with Copper Frame.

Salad Susan, 24 inches, pink, white, black, with copper frame.
Courtesy of Rich & Linda Guffey

Salad Susan, 24 inches, pink, white, black, with black frame.
Courtesy of Ron Brown

Sundial Casserole, 11" long. Marked: Kenwood Oven Proof U.S.A. 997 *Top view showing Roman numerals and sundial lid; french handle.*

Kenwood Bowl, 9" diameter. Marked: Kenwood Oven Proof U.S.A. 964
Bottom view showing indented rim for setting bowl into Salad Susan frame.

The **Saucy Susan** is a complete condiment unit that provides salt and pepper shakers, oil and vinegar cruets with stoppers, and four individual sauce or preserve cups with covers and servers. Three color combinations on a revolving brass or copper frame. *Original Retail: $11.95 with Copper Frame and $9.95 with Brass Frame.*

No. 985-P - Pink and White, with Copper Frame.
No. 985-T - Turquoise and White, with Copper Frame.
No. 985-B - Black and White, with Brass Frame.

Saucy Susan, pink and white, copper frame. Original shipping box with label from Kenwood Ceramics, Division of Shawnee Pottery. One cup lid has original Kenwood label intact.
Courtesy of Terry & Sandra Bauer

Saucy Susan, black and white, brass frame.

The **Supper Susan** combines the best features of the chafing dish and lazy susan. Consists of a one-quart chafing dish, six small and large serving dishes, ceramic stove for candle, sterno, or alcohol, all of oven proof semi-porcelain ceramic, and triple-plated brass frame that revolves on ball bearings. *Original Retail: 18-inch $19.95 and 16-inch $14.95.*

Supper Susan, 16-inch, Turquoise and White. Marked: Kenwood U.S.A. 972

No. 965-B - 18" Supper Susan - Black and White decorated.
No. 965-P - 18" Supper Susan - Pink and White decorated.
No. 975-P - 16" Supper Susan - Pink and White.
No. 975-T - 16" Supper Susan - Turquoise and White.

Chafing Dishes

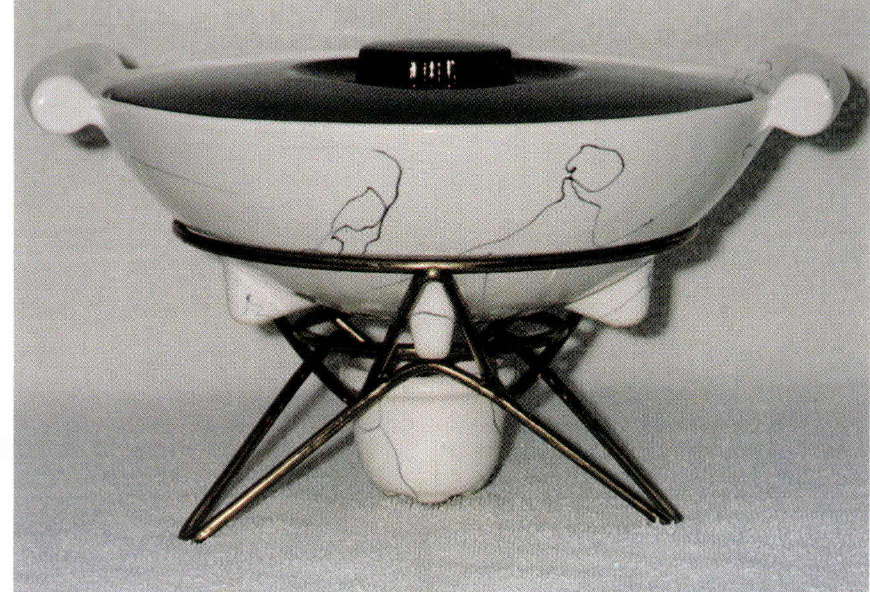

Party Chafing Dish in Classic Ionic, has mirror-black cover and unique vined-white casserole and warmer. Star-Stand of triple-plated brass. Dish rests in stand or on feet when used as casserole. Catalog No. 999 - Black and Vined White, Brass Frame - *Orig. List $7.95.* Marked: Kenwood Oven Proof 962 U.S.A. *Courtesy of Rich & Linda Guffey*

The **Toastee Susan** was designed to hold either napkins or toast, while one covered dish holds butter in its single compartment, and the other covered dish has two compartments for preserves. The brass or copper frame has a carrying handle, and revolves. *Original Retail: $9.95 with Copper Frame and $7.95 with Brass Frame.*

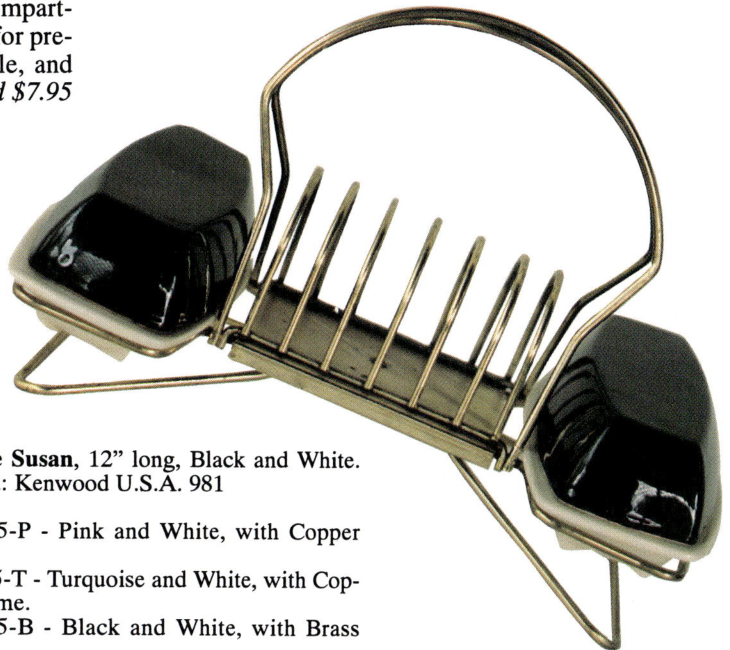

Toastee Susan, 12" long, Black and White. Marked: Kenwood U.S.A. 981

No. 955-P - Pink and White, with Copper Frame.
No. 955-T - Turquoise and White, with Copper Frame.
No. 955-B - Black and White, with Brass Frame.

Section VII: Planters & Vases

Chapter 21: Planters of Animals

Nearly all Shawnee planters were made with glazed bottoms, having an unglazed rim. Any planters that vary from this will be duly noted.

Any planter could turn up in a variety of colors typical of the era in which it was produced. Any planter could be found with gold trim decoration. Some were done within the Shawnee Pottery, while others were done by outside decorators.

Whenever possible, I chose to represent more than one color combination, or showed opposite sides to a piece for easier identification. I also pictured an example of the gold trim pieces when available.

All dates listed are to give a general time frame, though the items could have been produced before and after the listed year.

(*) Denotes Not Catalog Confirmed.
(XXX) Letter and/or number in parenthesis is catalog number when known. On later pieces, the catalog number is the 3 or 4 digit number impressed on the bottom marks.

Two Birds And Nest. Marked: U.S.A. *Courtesy of Marvin Mulligan*

Caricature Bird, 4", cold paint decorated. (P294) Marked: U.S.A.

Bird On Shell, tail up, 4-1/2" high. Marked: U.S.A.
Bird On Shell, tail down, 4" high. Marked: U.S.A.
Dusty Rose, Off-White, Turquoise. *Courtesy of Arthur & Rita Bee*

Top Row:
Caricature Duck, Marked: U.S.A., 3-1/2" high, Bright White, Old English Ivory, decorated orange feet and bill and black eyes (P304).
Caricature Bird, Marked: U.S.A., 4" high, Flax Blue decorated red beak, black eyes (P465).
Bottom Row:
Duckling, Marked: U.S.A., 4" high, Bright White, Old English Ivory, decorated orange feet and bill, black eyes (A654).
Duckling, Marked: U.S.A., 4-1/2" high, Bright White.
Duck, Marked: U.S.A., 7" high, Bright White, Old English Ivory, decorated orange bill and feet, black eyes (P287).

Two Parakeets On Stump, 5-1/2" high (P396) Marked: U.S.A.
Left: variegated colors, shown from back.
Right: turquoise, shown from front.

Duck and Planting Dish Marked: Shawnee U.S.A.

Bird On Planting Dish, 2-1/2" high, dish 6-1/2" square. Marked: Shawnee U.S.A. 767

Birds On Driftwood 7-1/2" high, chickadees on gray high gloss branch. Marked: Shawnee U.S.A. 502

Dove and Planting Dish, Marked: U.S.A. 2025, 8-1/2" long. White Dove with Avocado, Black, or Cherry Dish.

Birds On Driftwood, 7-1/2" high, Marked: Shawnee U.S.A. 502
Left: Chickadees on light brown bisque driftwood.
Right: Chickadees on light brown bisque, with gold trim.

Left: **Flying Mallard** 5-1/2", Marked: U.S.A. 707
Right: **Flying Mallard** 5-1/2", gold trim. Marked: U.S.A. 707

Flying Goose 6" high, Marked: Shawnee U.S.A. 820

Left: **Duckling** 5-1/2", Marked: Shawnee U.S.A. 720
Right: **Duckling** 5-1/2", gold trim. Marked: Shawnee U.S.A. 720

Duckling and Egg 3-1/4" high, no mark, gold trim, flat unglazed bottom (753).

Duckling and Egg 3-1/4" high, no mark, flat unglazed bottom (753).

Duck and Cart 5" high, Marked: Shawnee U.S.A. 752
Feather in kerchief is missing.

Chick and Egg 4-3/4" high. Marked: Shawnee U.S.A. 730

Duck and Cart 5" high, Marked: Shawnee U.S.A. 752
Feather in kerchief is missing.

Bird Planter, 2-1/2" high, 5-1/2" long, Marked: U.S.A. 508
Ebony, Vined Avocado, Vined White.

All Circa Early 1940s; 3-4 inches high.

Top Row:
Pig and Basket, Marked: U.S.A., cold paint decorated (P514).
Duckling, Marked: U.S.A.
Penguin, Marked: U.S.A. *

Center Row:
Rabbit and Cabbage, Marked: U.S.A. (P524).
Goose, Marked: U.S.A.
Kitten and Yarn, Marked: U.S.A.

Bottom Row:
Rabbit and Basket, Marked: U.S.A.
Sitting Pig, Marked: U.S.A. (P404).
Squirrel at Stump, Marked: U.S.A. *

All Old Ivory (Antique Brown) Decorated, Circa 1955.

Top Row:
Parakeet (also called Cockatiel) 4" high. Marked: Shawnee U.S.A. 523
Rooster 6" high. Marked: Shawnee U.S.A. 503
Butterfly 3-3/4" high. Marked: Shawnee U.S.A. 524

Bottom Row:
Ram 6-1/2" high. Marked: Shawnee U.S.A. 515
Giraffe 7" high. Marked: Shawnee U.S.A. 521

Striped Kitten 4-1/4" high. Marked: U.S.A. 723

Rooster 6-1/2" high. Marked: Kenwood U.S.A. 1503
Courtesy of Melvin & Jean Gibson

Cat and Sax 4-1/2" high. Marked: Shawnee U.S.A. 729

Kitty with Bow 8" long (P268) Marked: U.S.A.

Top Row:

Pig 3" high. Marked: U.S.A. 760
Hound and Jug 4" high. Marked: Shawnee U.S.A. 610

Bottom Row:
Squirrel 3-1/2" high. Marked: Shawnee U.S.A. 664
Bird Planter 2-3/4" high. Marked: U.S.A. 502

Kitten and Basket, 6" high, 7-1/2" long, Marked: Kenwood U.S.A. 2026

Open back planter and bottom view of flat bottomed Blackie the Cat.

Blackie the Cat, no marks, 4" high, flat unglazed bottom (642).
Left: Blackie, blue bow, gold trim.
Center: Blackie, blue bow, plain.
Right: Blackie, red bow, gold trim.

Fawn and Stump, 5-3/4" high. Marked: U.S.A. 535

Cat and Sax 4-1/2" high. Marked: Shawnee U.S.A. 729

Left to right:
Fawn, no mark, 8-7/8" high (P209).
Fawn, no mark, 7" high (P207).
Fawn, no mark, 6-1/4" high (P205).
Colors: Matt White, Shell Pink, Old English Ivory, Powder Blue, Turquoise, with painted eyes and tongue.

Deer In Shadowbox, 9" high. Marked: Shawnee U.S.A. 850

Left: **Fawn and Fern**, 6" high, Tropical Green base with black fawn. Marked: Shawnee U.S.A. 737
Right: **Fawn and Fern**, 6" high, Chartreuse base with brown fawn. Marked: Shawnee U.S.A. 737
Courtesy of Robert & Lois Duvall

Top Row: **Fawn and Stump** 7" high. Marked: Shawnee U.S.A. 624 *Two color variations.*
Bottom Row: **Deer and Fawn Planting Dish** 6" high. Marked: Shawnee U.S.A. 669 *Two color variations.*

Lying Deer Marked: U.S.A. *

Left:**Fawn and Log** 6-1/2" high, gold trim. Marked: Shawnee U.S.A. 766
Right: **Fawn and Log** 6-1/2" high, plain. Marked: Shawnee U.S.A. 766
Courtesy of Robert & Lois Duvall

Two Fawns, 5-1/2" high. Marked: Shawnee U.S.A. 721

Hound Dog, no mark, 3 " high, 7" long (P434). Cold paint is missing on this piece, but this dog can sometimes be found with brown spots.

Dachshund, no mark, 5" long, Dusty Rose and Flax Blue (A793).

Ibex, 4-1/4" high. Marked: U.S.A. 613

Gazelle on Base, 10" high, Marked: Shawnee U.S.A. 522 Satin Pink and White gazelles on Ebony bases, circa 1955. *Courtesy of Melvin & Jean Gibson*

Puppy with Bee, no mark, 3-1/4" high, shown front and back. Cold paint decorated, this puppy was a very popular seller, and is easily found today.

Puppy Dog, no mark, 5" high, flat unglazed bottom (662).

Crouching Spaniel, 4-1/2" high (P228) Marked: U.S.A.

Queenie the Beagle, no mark, 3-3/4" high, flat unglazed bottom (643).
Left: Queenie with gold trim.
Right: Queenie plain.

Open back planter and bottom view of flat bottomed Queenie.

Poodle and Carriage, 4-1/2" high. Marked: U.S.A. 704
Left: Poodle & Carriage plain.
Right: Poodle & Carriage gold trim.

Hound and Pekingese, 4-1/2" high, Marked: U.S.A. 611
Left: Hound & Peke plain.
Right: Hound & Peke gold trim.

Sitting Terrier, 7-1/4" high. Marked: U.S.A. *(Also made as a Figurine, having no opening in back for plants.)*

Puppy Dog, no mark, 5" high, flat unglazed bottom (662), gold trim.

Dog in Boat 5" high. Marked: Shawnee U.S.A. 736

Chihuahua and Dog House, 4-1/4" high, 8" long (738). Marked: Shawnee U.S.A.
Left: Moss Brown base, no gold trim.
Right: White base, gold trim.

Spaniel and Dog House, 4-1/4" high, 8" long (739). Marked: Shawnee U.S.A.
Left: Hunter Green base, no gold trim.
Right: White base, gold trim (Marked: Shafer 23K gold guaranteed).

Terrier and Dog House, 4-1/4" high, 8" long (740). Marked: Shawnee U.S.A.
Left: Moss Brown base, no gold trim.
Right: Hunter Green base, gold trim.

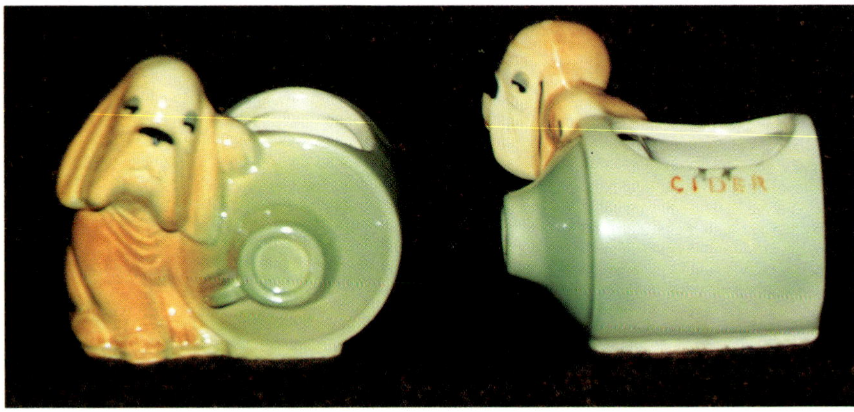

Left: **Hound and Jug**, 4" high, plain. Marked: Shawnee U.S.A. 610
Right: **Hound and Jug**, 4" high, Marked: Shawnee U.S.A. 610 on bottom, gold trim, and word ***Cider*** with **X**'s in red paint under glaze on side of jug.
Courtesy Of Paul & Linda Spenst

Left: **3-Button Shoe and Dog**, 4-1/2" high, 8" long, Marked: U.S.A. Will also be found with 2 buttons on shoe, same pup.
Right: **Frog and Guitar**, 7-3/4" high, Marked: U.S.A.

Poodle on Bicycle, 5-1/2" high.
Marked: U.S.A. 712

Panda and Cradle, 4-3/4" high. Marked: Shawnee U.S.A. 2031. Shown with pink cradle, blue bow & blocks; and blue cradle, pink bow & blocks.

Cub Bear and Wagon, 7-1/4" long. Marked: Shawnee U.S.A. 731
Left: Brown wagon, shown from back.
Right: Avocado wagon, shown from front.

Cub Bear and Wagon, gold trim, brown wagon. Marked: Shawnee U.S.A. 731 *Courtesy of Jerry Schueller*

Cub Bear and Wagon with Chihuahua riding in the wagon! Marked: Shawnee U.S.A. 731 *Courtesy of Jody Kay Adam.*

Elephant with Howdah, 4" high. Marked: U.S.A.

Elephant, no mark, 5" high, Old Ivory, Flax Blue, Powder Blue, decorated black eyes and feet, red mouth, circa early 1940s (P426).

Elephant and Leaf Base, 6" high. Marked: Shawnee U.S.A. Matt Ebony elephant with Satin Pink leaf base.

Bull and Leaf Base, 4-1/4" high. Marked: Shawnee U.S.A. Glossy Black bull with light pink base.

Frog, 3" high. Marked: U.S.A.

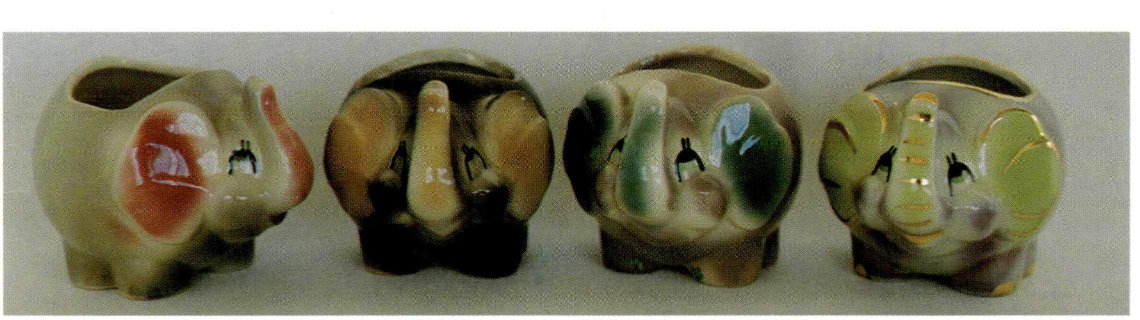

Elephant, 3" high, Marked: U.S.A. 759 Left to Right: #1, #2, #3 plain, #4 with gold trim.

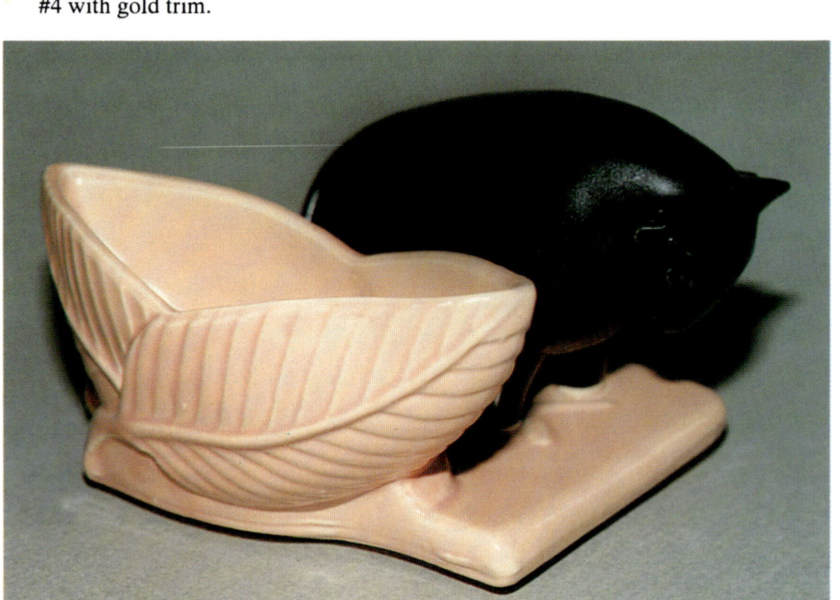

Bull and Leaf Vase, 4-1/4" high, Marked: Shawnee U.S.A. Matt Ebony bull with Satin Pink leaf base.

Frog on Lily Pad, 4" high, 6" long. Marked: Shawnee U.S.A. 726 Circa 1954.

Bull, 3-1/2" high. Marked: 663

Dolphin, 3-1/2" high, variegated colors. Marked: U.S.A. (A674). *Listed as suitable for Planter, Ashtray, or Flower Bowl Insert.*

Dolphin, 5" high, two color variations. Marked: U.S.A. 845 Dolphin on left has "Souvenir of Detroit, Mich." label.

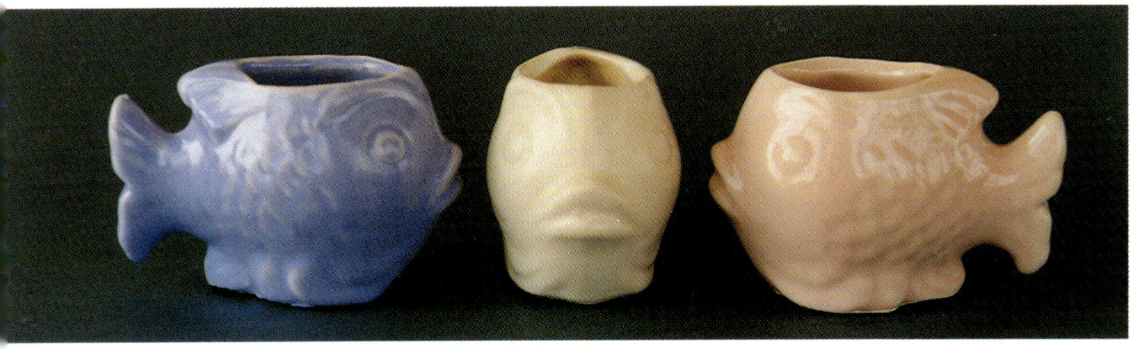

Blow Fish, 3" high. Marked: U.S.A. (P184). Shown in Powder Blue, Matt White, Shell Pink.

Left: **Tropical Fish**, Grey variegated, 7-1/4" high, 10-1/2" long. Marked: U.S.A. 717
Right: **Tropical Fish**, Van Dyke Brown with gold trim, 7-1/4" high. Marked: U.S.A. 717
Circa 1954, listed as Planter or Vase.

Turtle, no mark, 3" high, circa 1951, (661). Hunter Green, Yellow, Burgundy.

Angel Fish, 8-1/2" high to top of fin. Marked: U.S.A. Shown in Yellow and Flax Blue; has also been found in Old Ivory and Shell Pink.

Tropical Fish, Surf Green with gold trim, 7-1/4" high. Marked: U.S.A. 717

Lamb with Flower, no mark, 5-1/4" high, cold paint missing. Circa early 1940s.

Tropical Fish, Grey variegated with gold trim, 7-1/4" high. Marked: U.S.A. 717

Lamb with Flower, no mark, 5-3/4" high, Off White with cold painted decoration. Circa early 1940s.

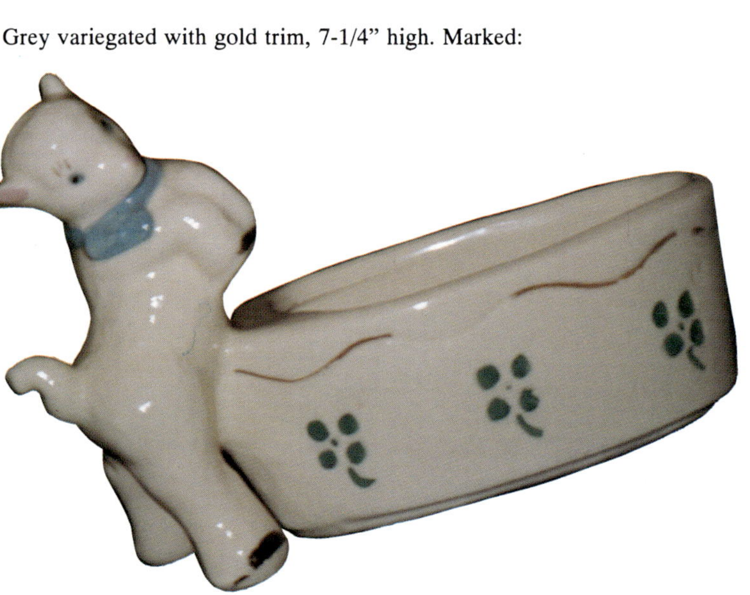

Dancing Lamb with Bowl, 5-1/2" high. Marked: U.S.A. (P506). Bright White with cold painted pink ears and nose, blue eyes and necktie, brown feet; bowl with brown band and four leaf clover and blossoms. *Courtesy of Marvin Mulligan*

Left: **Poodle,** 4-1/4" long, black glaze with gold trim, catalog no. 725, but this planter found with no marks. Right: **Lamb**, 4-1/2" high, black glaze with gold trim. Marked: U.S.A. 724

Flowered Pig, found in turquoise and peach. Marked: U.S.A.

Mouse and Cheese, 4-1/4" high. Marked: U.S.A. 705
Left: Mouse & Cheese plain.
Right: Mouse & Cheese gold trim.

Circus Horse with Pedestal, 6" high. Marked: U.S.A. (P386). *Courtesy of Marvin Mulligan*

Pig and Wheelbarrow, 5-1/2" high. Marked: U.S.A. (P486). Original cold paint intact.

Melancholy Donkey, no mark, 6" high.

Moon-Eyed Calf, no mark, 6-1/4" high, cold paint decorated.

Kentucky Colt, no mark, turquoise, 6-1/2" high shown; also found identical colt 9" high in turquoise.

Frisky Colt, no mark, 5-1/2" high.

Donkey and Basket, 5-1/4" high. Marked: U.S.A. 671

Colt and Stump, 5" high, circa 1953. Marked:
Kenwood U.S.A. 2028
Surf Green Colt, Yellow Stump.
Black Colt, Chartreuse Stump.
Yellow Colt, Surf Stump.

Colt and Stump shown with carved Wooden Horses used as design idea by Robert Heckman.

Top Row:
Pony, 7-1/2" high, Holly Red with Old Ivory mane. Marked: Shawnee U.S.A. 506
Pony, 7-1/2" high, White with Old Ivory mane. Marked: Shawnee U.S.A. 506

Bottom Row:
Pony, 7-1/2" high, Yellow with Green mane. Marked: Kenwood U.S.A. 1509
Pony, 7-1/2" high, Medallion. Marked: Shawnee U.S.A. 506
Also found in Mint Green, marked: Kenwood U.S.A. 1509

Donkey and Mexican Cart, 3-1/4" high. Marked: U.S.A. 538 *This little guy came with the ribbon tied around his neck, and though it's frayed and worn, I have let him keep it on.*

Donkey and Basket, 5-1/4" high, gold trim. Marked: U.S.A. 671
Courtesy of Paul & Linda Spenst

Left: **Sad-Faced Donkey in Hat** with cart, 5-1/2" high. Marked: U.S.A. 709
Right: **Sitting Donkey and Basket**, 5-3/4" high. Marked: Shawnee U.S.A. 722
Courtesy of Robert & Lois Duvall

Left: **Donkey Pulling Cart**, 4" high. Marked: U.S.A. (P248).
Right: **Three Pigs** Looking Over Fence, 4-1/4" high. Marked: U.S.A. (P445).

Fox and Bag, 4-1/2" high. Marked: Shawnee U.S.A. (J-2029). Red Fox with Chartreuse bag. *Courtesy of Rich & Linda Guffey*

Fox and Bag, 4-1/2" high. Marked: U.S.A. (J-2029). Brown Fox with Chartreuse bag.

Left: **Squirrel and Nut**, grey with gold trim. Marked: U.S.A. 713
Right: **Squirrel and Nut**, grey. Marked: U.S.A. 713
Courtesy of Don & De Anderson

Squirrel and Nut, brown, 7-1/2" long. Marked: U.S.A. 713
Courtesy of Rich & Linda Guffey

Squirrel and Nut, brown with gold trim. Marked: U.S.A. 713
Courtesy of Paul & Joy Schneider

Rabbit and Turnip, 4-1/2" high, gold trim. Marked: U.S.A. 703

Rabbit and Turnip, 4-1/2" high, plain. Marked: U.S.A. 703

Rabbit and Stump, 3" high. Marked: U.S.A. 606

Rabbit and Wheelbarrow, no mark, 5 1/4" high (728).

Baby Skunk, 5-1/4" high. Marked: Shawnee U.S.A. 512 Tropical Green base.

Baby Skunk, 5-1/4" high. Marked: Shawnee U.S.A. 512 Satin Pink base.

Chapter 22: Planters of People

Dutch Girl Sprinkling Flowers, 4-1/2" high. Marked: U.S.A. (P375). Some original cold paint remaining.

Left: **Southern Belle**, 8-1/2" high, holding square basket, turquoise. Marked: U.S.A.
Center: **Southern Girl**, 7-1/4" high, holding round basket, Old English Ivory. Marked: U.S.A.
Right: **Southern Girl**, 7-1/4" high, Matt White, same as center girl, but shown from side. Marked: U.S.A.

Children on Shoe, 5" high. Marked: U.S.A. 525

Girl at Wishing Well, 4-1/2" high. Marked: U.S.A. (P365). Shown front and back, in burgundy and turquoise.

Knomes and Log, 3-1/2" high, 8" long. Marked: U.S.A. (P218).

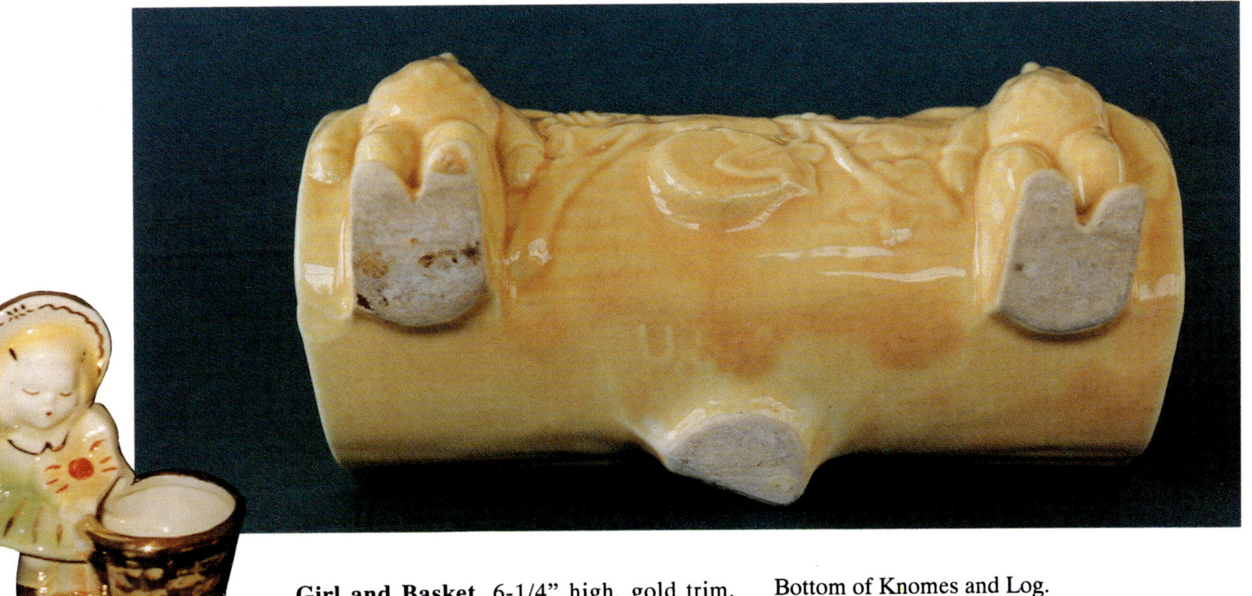

Girl and Basket, 6-1/4" high, gold trim. Marked: U.S.A. 534. *Courtesy of Marvin Mulligan*

Bottom of Knomes and Log.

Girl with Umbrella, 6-1/4" high, three color variations. Marked: U.S.A. 560 *Courtesy of Paul & Linda Spenst*

Boy and Stump, 6-1/4" high. Marked: U.S.A. 533
Left: Low brown stump.
Center: High red stump.
Right: High brown stump.

Colonial Lady, 5-1/2" high, two color variations shown. Marked: U.S.A. 616

Top Row:
Boy and Wheelbarrow, 5-1/2" high, dark face. Marked: U.S.A. 750
Girl with Umbrella, 6-1/4" high. Marked: U.S.A. 560

Bottom Row:
Fishing Boy, 6-1/4" high, high stump. Marked: U.S.A. 532
Girl and Basket, 6-1/4" high. Marked: U.S.A. 534

Boy and Wheelbarrow, 5-1/2" high, light face, gold trim. Marked: U.S.A. 750 *Courtesy of Jerry Schueller*

Left: **Polynesian**, 5-3/4" high. Marked: Shawnee U.S.A. 896
Right: **Polynesian**, 5-3/4", gold trim. Marked: Shawnee U.S.A. 896

Little Kerchief Girl, 5-1/2" high. Marked: U.S.A. 718
Shown front and back, in two color variations. Note the bouquet of flowers behind her back.

Little Kerchief Girl, 5-1/2" high, gold trim. Marked: U.S.A. 718 *Courtesy of Arthur & Rita Bee*

Kneeling Girl with Basket, solid green color. Marked: Shawnee U.S.A. *Courtesy of Randy & Stephanie Adrian*

Mexican Boy, 6" high. Marked: U.S.A. (on back of urn).
Mexican Girl, 6" high. Marked: U.S.A. (on back of urn).
Color variations found: Mexican Boy with orange shirt, black pants; and Mexican Girl with purple shawl, orange skirt.

Bicycle Built For Two, 6" high, plain. Marked: Shawnee U.S.A. 735

Top Row: **Girl and Gate**, no mark, 4" high. **Boy and Gate**, no mark, 4" high.
Bottom Row: **Boy and Dog**, no mark, 4" high. **Pixie**, 3 1/2" high. Marked: U.S.A. 562.

Bicycle Built For Two, 6" high, gold trim. Marked: Shawnee U.S.A. 735 *Courtesy of Rich & Linda Guffey*

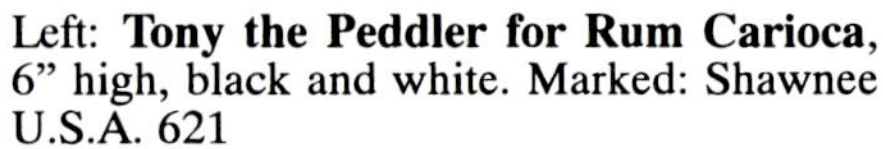

Left: **Tony the Peddler for Rum Carioca**, 6" high, black and white. Marked: Shawnee U.S.A. 621
Center: **Tony the Peddler**, 5-3/4" high. Marked: U.S.A. 621
Right: **Tony the Peddler**, 5-3/4" high, gold trim. Marked: U.S.A. 621

Elf and Shoe, 5-1/2" high, gold trim. Marked: Shawnee U.S.A. 765. This item also found without gold trim.

Buddha, Marked: U.S.A. 524

Swan and Elf, 5-1/2"x 9-1/2"x 6-1/2", Marked: Kenwood U.S.A. Decorated Elf on Textured Chartreuse or White or Textured Black Swan. Circa 1953.

Elf and Wheelbarrow, no mark, 3-1/2" high (762). Shown front and back, in two of several color variations found.

Elf and Flower, no mark, 4" high, flat unglazed bottom.
Left & Center: shown front & back, plain.
Right: gold trim.

Wishing Well with Dutch Boy and Girl, 5-1/2" high, all shown plain. Marked: Shawnee U.S.A. 710 A yellow wishing well has also been found.

Top Row:
Girl and Mandolin, 6-1/2" high. Marked: U.S.A. 576
Chinese Girl and Urn, 6" high. Marked: U.S.A. 701

Bottom Row:
Chinese Boy and Vase, 6" high. Marked: U.S.A. 702
Coolies with Basket, 4" high. Marked: U.S.A. 537

Top Row:
Clown with Blocks, 4-1/4" high. Marked: Shawnee U.S.A.
Clown Planter, 5" high. Marked: U.S.A. 619
Ceramic flower pot 2-1/2" high, came with silk flowers and sold with clown.

Bottom Row:
Jo Jo Clown, 3-1/4" high, plain. Marked: U.S.A. 607
Jo Jo Clown, 3-1/4" high, gold trim. Marked: U.S.A. 607

Chinese Boy and Urn, 6", Marked: U.S.A. 701

Top Row:
Chinese Girl with Book, 3-1/4" high. Marked: U.S.A. 574
Ancient Chinese with Parasol, 5-1/4" high. Marked: U.S.A. 617
Chinese Boy and Girl with Mandolin, 3-1/4" high. Marked: U.S.A. 573

Bottom Row:
Coolie and Cart, 3" high, plain. Marked: U.S.A. 539
Coolie and Cart, 3" high, gold trim iridescent. Marked: U.S.A. 539 A
Coolie and Cart, 3" high, gold trim. Marked: U.S.A. 539

Left: **Boy and Chicken**, green, 5-3/4". Marked: Shawnee U.S.A. 645
Right: **Boy and Chicken**, yellow shirt & green pants, 5-3/4". Marked: Shawnee U.S.A. 645

Coolie & Rickshaw, 4-1/2", Marked: U.S.A.

Left: **Boy and Chicken**, 5-3/4" high, black shirt & green pants. Marked: Shawnee U.S.A. 645
Right: **Boy and Chicken**, 5-3/4", yellow shirt & green pants, gold trim. Marked: Shawnee U.S.A. 645
All of the Boy and Chicken planters are missing the feather from his hat.

Military Boot, 7" high, embossed with top decoration and boot strap, listed as either a planter or vase. Marked: U.S.A. Turquoise, Off White, Burgundy.

Italian Boot, 4-1/2" high. Marked: U.S.A. (P415). Bright White, should have cold paint decoration of red on sides and toe, and black sole.

Button Baby Shoes on Base, 2-1/2" high. Marked: U.S.A.

Button Baby Shoes, 2-1/4" high, matched pair right & left. Marked: U.S.A.

Laced Baby Shoe, 2-1/2" high, Marked: U.S.A. (P174).

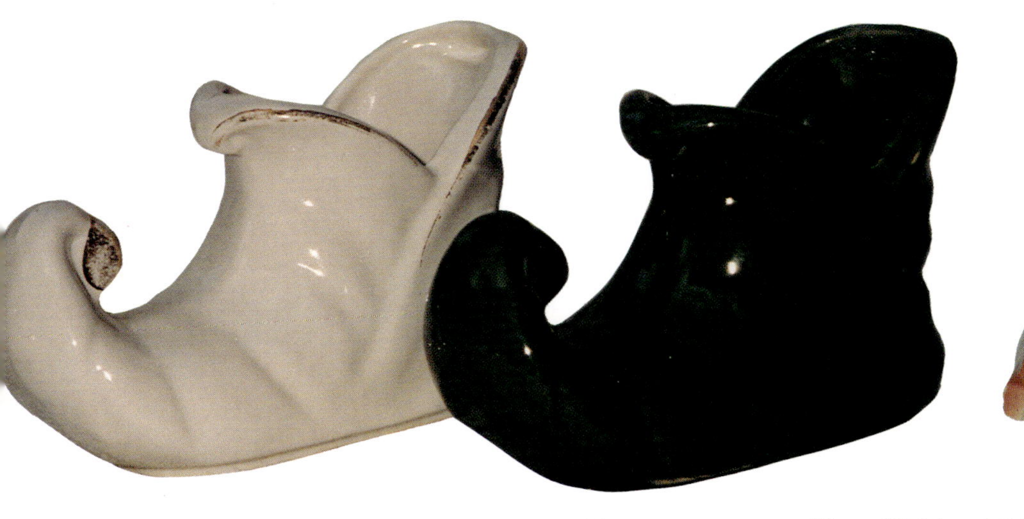

Elf Shoe, 6-1/8" long. Marked: Shawnee U.S.A. 785
Left: Shasta White shoe, gold trim.
Right: Avocado Green shoe, plain.

Piano, 5" high, gold trim. Marked: U.S.A. 528
Courtesy of Robert & Lois Duvall

Shoe and Flower, no mark, 3" high, 4-1/4" long (761).
Left: Grey with red flower, plain.
Center: Charcoal with blue flower, gold trim.
Right: Brown with green flower, gold trim.

World Globe, 7" high.
Marked: Shawnee
U.S.A. 635

Top Row:
Double Flower, 3" high. Marked: U.S.A. 591
Hunter Green, Yellow, Grey.
Lady's Slipper (High Heel), 3-3/4" high.
Marked: U.S.A.
Antique Ivory, Turquoise, White, Dusty Rose.
Slipper often sold for making pin cushions.

Bottom Row:
Piano, 5" high. Marked: U.S.A. 528
Top Hat, 3-1/4" high, with Stars and Stripes pattern. Marked: U.S.A.

Alarm Clock Marked: U.S.A. 1262

Hobby Horse, 3-1/2" high. Marked: Shawnee U.S.A. 660

Double Bowknot, 3" high, white with red polka dot bow. Marked: Shawnee U.S.A. 518

Rocking Horse, 5-3/4" high. Marked: U.S.A. 526 Shown in Powder Blue and Peach.

Sea Shell, 3-1/4" high, 5" long. Marked: U.S.A. 665

Leaf, 3" high, 5-3/4" long. Marked: U.S.A. 509 Ebony, Vined Avocado, Vined White.

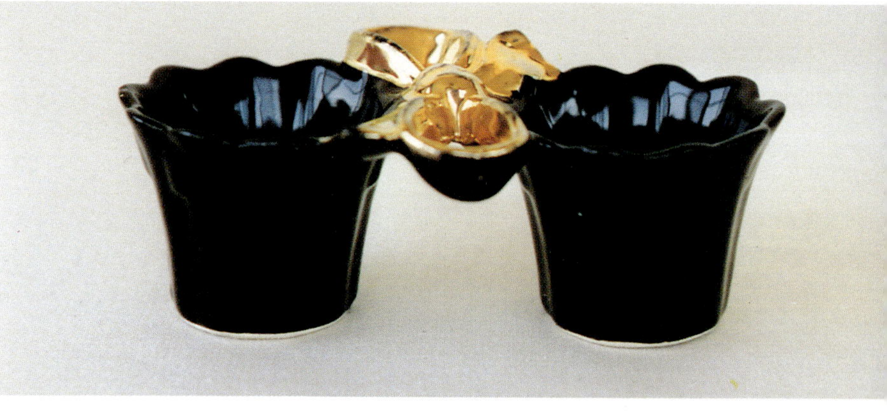

Double Bowknot, 3" high, black with gold bow. Marked: Shawnee U.S.A. 518

Three Pots and Trellis, 7" high. Marked: Shawnee U.S.A. 517 Ebony or Avocado Green Pots with Tropical Green Trellis.

Shadowbox with Yellow Rose, 9" high. Marked: Shawnee U.S.A. 850 *Courtesy of Sue Blodgett*

Canopy Bed, 7-3/4" high, 8" long, pink canopy. Marked: Shawnee U.S.A. 734
Left: Canopy Bed, plain.
Right: Canopy Bed, gold trimmed.

Canopy Bed, 7-3/4" high, 8" long, yellow canopy. Marked: Shawnee U.S.A. 734 *Courtesy of Paul & Linda Spenst*

Canopy Bed, 7-3/4" high, 8" long, yellow canopy, gold trim. Marked: Shawnee U.S.A. 734 *Courtesy of Robert & Lois Duvall*

Basket Cradle with embossed flowers, 4-1/2" high, 8" long. Marked: U.S.A. (P258).

High Chair with Kitten, 6-1/4" high, pink with cold paint decoration. Marked: U.S.A. 727

Basket, 5-1/2" high, shown in White Decorated and Brown & Green. Marked: Shawnee U.S.A. 640

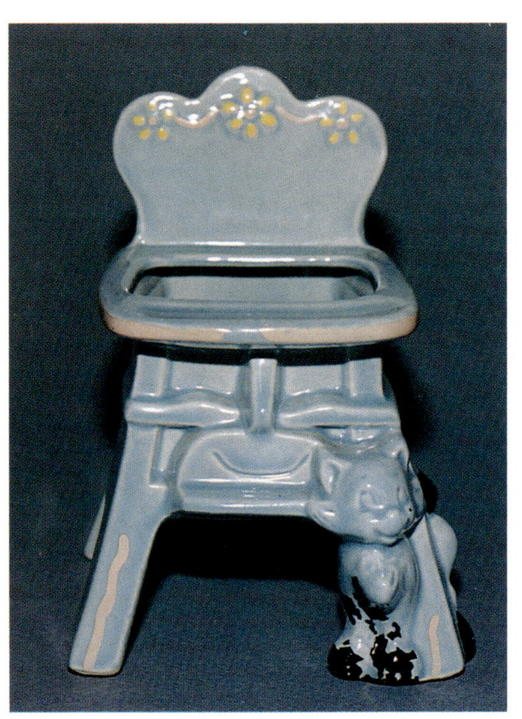

High Chair with Kitten, 6-1/4", blue with cold paint decoration. Marked: U.S.A. 727

Sprinkling Can, embossed basketweave with iris, 5-1/4" high and 6" high. Marked: U.S.A.

Coal Bucket with embossed flower. Marked: U.S.A. *Courtesy of Don & De Anderson*

Wheelbarrows Marked: U.S.A.
Left: Cold Paint worn; Center: Cold Paint intact;
Right: Underglaze Decorated.
Courtesy of Marvin Mulligan

J P Planter Series, so-called because each piece is marked on the bottom with a three-digit number preceded by a **J** and ending with a **P**.

Left: **Picnic Basket** Marked: U.S.A. J540P
Center: **Coal Bucket** Marked: U.S.A. J541P
Right: **Cradle** Marked: U.S.A. J542P

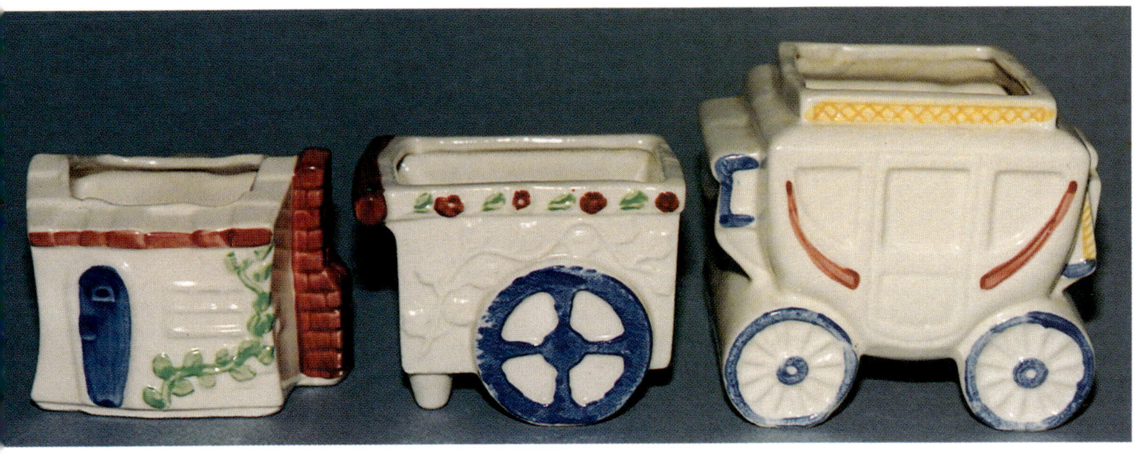

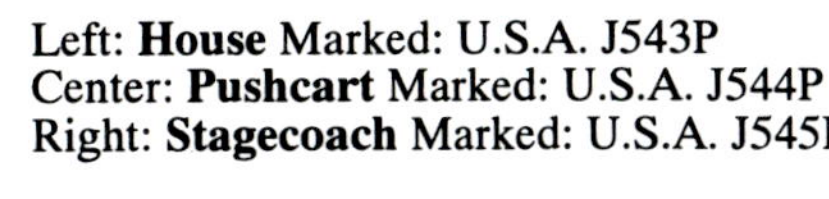

Left: **House** Marked: U.S.A. J543P
Center: **Pushcart** Marked: U.S.A. J544P
Right: **Stagecoach** Marked: U.S.A. J545P

Watering Can, 4" high. Marked: U.S.A.

Pump and Trough, 5-1/4" high, 9-1/2" long. Marked: Shawnee U.S.A. 716 Listed: Surf Green, Moss Brown, Hunter Green.

Dutch Windmill, 6" high, 6-1/2" long. Marked: Shawnee U.S.A. 715
Listed: Surf Green, Moss Brown, Hunter Green.
Left: Dutch Mill, Hunter Green, plain.
Right: Dutch Mill, White, gold trim.

Old Mill and Pond, 6" high, 7" long. Marked: Shawnee U.S.A. 769
Listed: Moss Brown, Hunter Green.
Left: Old Mill, Moss Brown, plain.
Right: Old Mill, White, gold trim.

Bridge, 5" high, 9-1/4" long. Marked: Shawnee U.S.A. 756 Listed: Hunter Green, Chartreuse.
Left: Bridge, Hunter Green, plain.
Right: Bridge, Chartreuse, gold trim.

Chapter 24: Planters of Transportation

4-Piece Train, each piece 4-1/4" long, with **S R R** impressed on sides of each car. This is the most commonly found train set.
Engine Marked: U.S.A. 550
Coal Car Marked: U.S.A. 551
Box Car Marked: U.S.A. 552
Caboose Marked: U.S.A. 553

5-Piece Train set same as previous, with extra White Caboose. *Courtesy of Robert & Lois Duvall*

4-Piece Train set, gold trim, with **S R R** written as **B R R**.
Courtesy of Melvin & Jean Gibson

4-Piece Train, each piece 4-1/4" long, **White Decorated**, harder to find.
Engine Marked: U.S.A. 550
Coal Car Marked: U.S.A. 551
Box Car Marked: U.S.A. 552
Caboose Marked: U.S.A. 553
Courtesy of Melvin & Jean Gibson

19th Century Engine, 6-1/4" high, 10" long. Marked: Shawnee U.S.A. 732

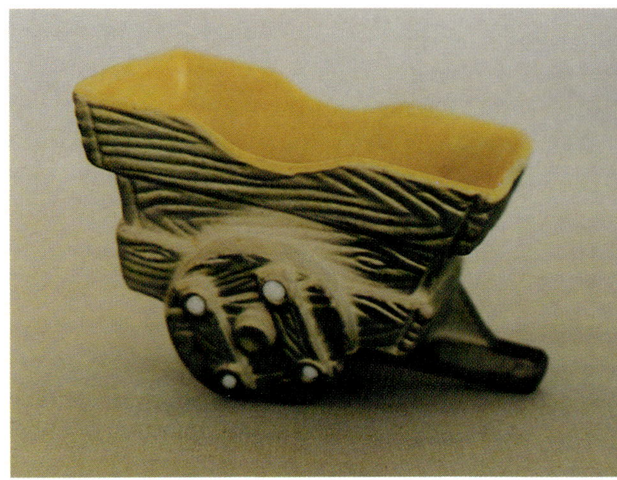

Wood Grain Cart, 4-1/2" high, bisque wood grain exterior, high gloss interior, and enamel wheel studs. Marked: U.S.A. 775 Also produced in light brown bisque wood grain exterior.

Prairie Schooner (Covered Wagon), 7" high. Marked: Shawnee U.S.A. 733 Listed: Old Ivory (shown) and Moss Brown.

Truck and Trailer, two-piece planter.
Truck, 3" high, Burgundy. Marked: Shawnee U.S.A. 680
Trailer, 3-1/4" high, Yellow. Marked: Shawnee U.S.A. 681

Prairie Schooner (Covered Wagon), 7" high. Marked: Shawnee U.S.A. 733 Old Ivory with gold trim and stamped on bottom reading *Shafer 23K gold guaranteed. Courtesy of Arthur & Rita Bee*

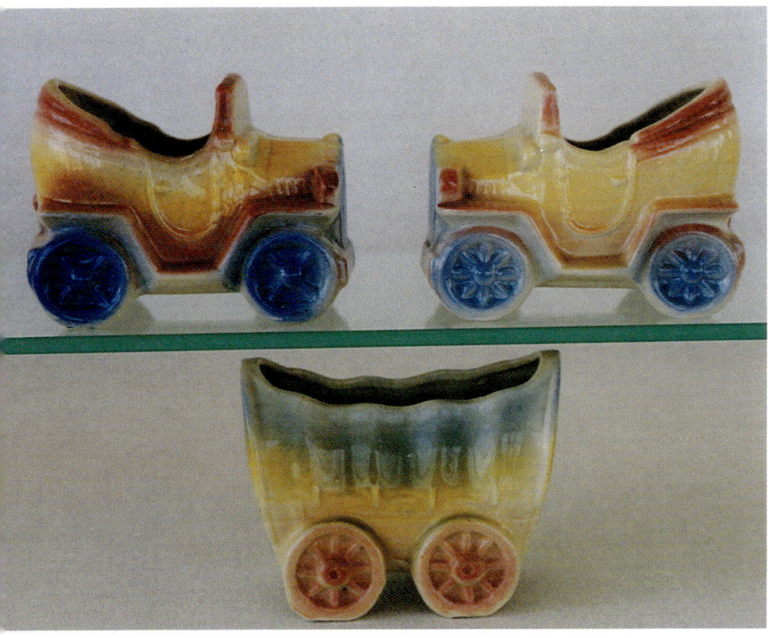

Top Row:
Auto (Four Spoke), 3-1/2" high. Marked: U.S.A. 506 *(Shown in 1951 catalog, indicating later design.)*
Auto (Eight Spoke), 3-1/2" high. Marked: U.S.A. 506 *(Shown in February 1950 catalog, indicating earlier design.)*

Bottom Row:
Covered Wagon, 3-1/2" high, 8-Spoke Wheels. Marked: U.S.A. 514

Circus Wagon, 6" high. Marked: U.S.A.

Gondola, 11-3/4" long. Marked: U.S.A. *Courtesy of Don & De Anderson*

Gondola, 11-3/4" long. Marked: U.S.A.

Chapter 25: Planting Dishes

Early Shawnee catalogs refer to these items as console bowls, flower bowls, flower boxes, bulb bowls, and low flower bowls. Later catalogs referred to these pieces as flower bowls, bulb bowls, planters, planting dishes, and window boxes. Catalog-listed colors are often shown in the description.

Those early Flower Bowls which had Candle Holders to match, have been placed in the **Console Sets** chapter, and several may be found in the chapter on **Flower Frogs**. The remainder fall into this chapter, and there is no set rule for what they are called. Small, rectangular planters were often called window boxes, for display on window sills or other narrow spots. Some oval or round bowls could be utilized for other purposes such as holding fresh fruit, but were often listed simply as Flower Bowls. Most, I'm sure, were used for their intended purpose for plants and flowers.

Embossed Flowers & Leaves, Flax Blue, rectangular. Marked: U.S.A.

Oval Planter, 2-1/2" high, 8-1/4" long. Marked: U.S.A. Shown in Green and Yellow.

Embossed Bulb Bowl, 2-1/2" high, 4-1/2" diameter. Marked: U.S.A. Turquoise, Matt White, Powder Blue, Old English Ivory, footed (FB195). *Courtesy of Toni Crittenden & Art Voorhees*

Oval Planter, underglaze decorated, 2-1/2" high, 8-1/4" long. Marked: U.S.A. *Courtesy of Marvin Mulligan*

Criss Cross Window Box, rectangular, approx. 4". Marked: U.S.A. 170

Oval Planter, embossed shamrocks, 2-1/2" high. Marked: U.S.A. *This same oval planter can be found with an embossed Fleur-de-lis instead of shamrocks.*

Paneled Window Box, rectangular, 3" high, 7" long. Marked: U.S.A.

Wheat Flower Bowl, 3-1/4" high, 9-1/2" long, oval. Marked: U.S.A. Dusty Rose, Matt White, Old Ivory, Turquoise (FB3610).

Ivy Bulb Bowl, 2-1/2" high. Marked: Shawnee U.S.A. 3025 Hunter Green, Tropical Green, Yellow.

Embossed Flower Window Box, rectangular, 2" high, 5-1/2" long. Marked: U.S.A.

Planting Dish, 1-1/4" high, 8-1/2" long. Marked: U.S.A. 3002 Yellow, Grey, Hunter Green. *Courtesy of Ryan Guffey*

Woven Check, 2-1/2" high, 7-1/4" long. Marked: U.S.A. 150 Yellow, Burgundy, Hunter Green.

Shell Bulb Bowl, 2-1/2" high, 6" long. Marked: Shawnee U.S.A. 154 Pastel Blue, Burgundy.

Wood Grain Bisque, yellow glaze interior, 3" high, 5-1/2" long. Marked: Shawnee U.S.A. 400

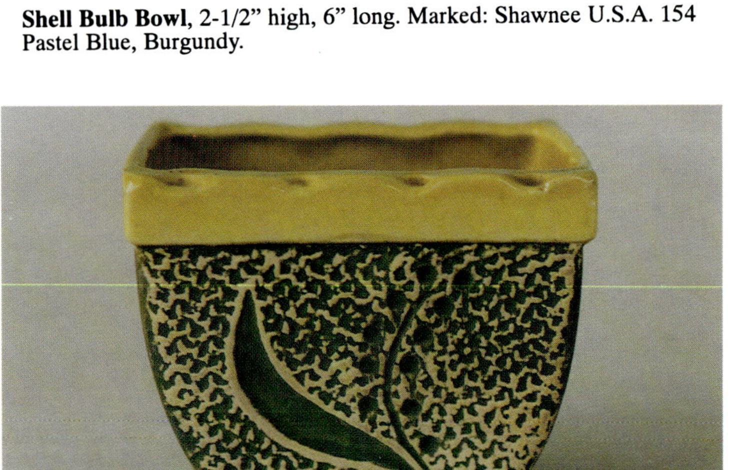

Lily Of The Valley, 3-1/2" high. Marked: U.S.A. 790 Chartreuse glaze interior, Burlap-Textured Green Bisque exterior.

Ribbed Square Bowl, 4" high. Marked: U.S.A. 3005 Butterscotch, Royal Blue, Yellow. *This same pattern also appears on a rectangular planter, 3-1/2" high.*

Square Pointed Planter, 3-3/4", partial label. Marked: U.S.A.

Basket Weave, 5-1/2" long. Marked: U.S.A. 444 Satin Pink glaze interior, Grey Bisque exterior.

Square Planter, 3-3/4" square, two variations shown. Marked: U.S.A. *Examples have turned up with a Shawnee label and original price sticker of 39 cents on this planter.*

Textured high gloss glazes for the following three planters are as listed: Avocado, Canary, Cherry, Chartreuse, Black, Van Dyke Brown, Hunter Green, Surf Green.

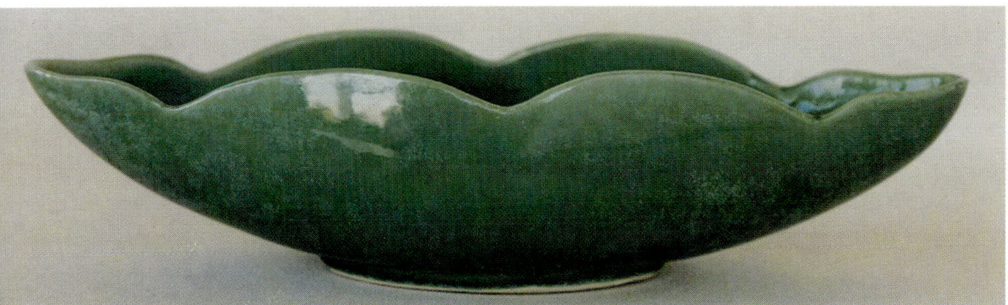

Oval Scalloped Planter, 14-1/4" long. Marked: Kenwood U.S.A. 2002

Square Spatter Planter, 8" square. Marked: Kenwood U.S.A. 2004

Shell Planter, 4-1/4" high. Marked: Kenwood U.S.A. 2005

Leaf Planter with Stem Handles, 3-1/2" high, 14" long. Marked: Shawnee U.S.A. 442 Tropical Green or Ebony. *Note: This can be a wonderful fruit bowl for your table!*

Basket Weave, 5-1/2" long. Marked: U.S.A. 444 Antique Ivory/Brown high gloss glaze.

Red Leaf Planter, 11-1/2" long. Marked: Shawnee U.S.A. 440 Holly Red with White interior.
Same Leaf appears as a 14-1/2" long planter, marked with #441.

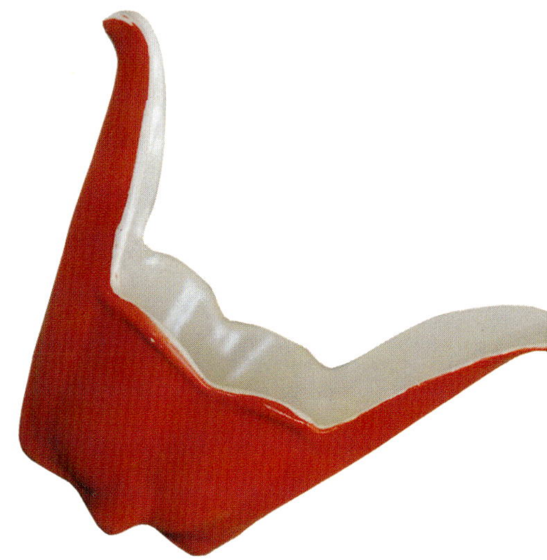

Flared Leaf, 4-3/4" high. Marked: U.S.A. Holly Red with White interior.

Leaf Planting Dish, 4" high, 8-1/2" long. Marked: Shawnee U.S.A. 439 Tropical Green and Satin Pink.

Embossed Feather Bowl, 3-1/2" high, 9-1/2" long, lug handles. Marked: U.S.A. (FB419) Old Ivory, Bright White, Turquoise.

Flower Chain Bowl, round, 6" diameter. Marked: U.S.A.

Flower Bowl with Brass Plated Stand, square, 6-3/4" wide. (2450) Circa 1954. Avocado with Vining, Avocado, Black, Chartreuse. *Courtesy of Melvin & Jean Gibson*

Oval Leaf, 2-1/2" high, 10-1/2" long. No mark. Matt White, Old English Ivory, Turquoise, Powder Blue.

Embossed Daisy, 9-1/2" long. Marked: U.S.A. 152

Planting Dish with Brass Plated Stand, rectangle, 9-1/4" long. (2163) Circa 1954. Avocado, Black, Chartreuse. *Courtesy of Melvin & Jean Gibson*

Embossed Flower Boxes
Top Row:
Calla Lily, plain, 2-1/2" high, 7-1/4" long. Marked: U.S.A. 181
Calla Lily, gold trim. Marked: U.S.A. 181

Bottom Row:
Wild Rose, plain, 2-1/2" high, 8-1/4" long. Marked: U.S.A. 182
Wild Rose, gold trim. Marked: U.S.A. 182

Blue Flower Console, underglaze decorated. Marked: U.S.A.

Blue Flower Cornucopia, 6-1/2" vase, underglaze decorated. Marked: U.S.A.
Blue Flower Planter, underglaze decorated. Marked: U.S.A.

Blue Flower Console with gold trim. Marked: U.S.A. *Courtesy of Donna Buster*

Chapter 26: Flower Pots and Jardinieres

Tulip Jardiniere, yellow, 3-1/2" high. Marked: U.S.A.

Flower Pots and Saucers

#1) **Embossed**, 2-3/4" high. Marked: U.S.A.

#2) & #3) **Ribbon & Bow**, Dusty Rose & Turquoise, 3-1/2" high. Marked: U.S.A.
F594 - 3-1/2" high.
F595 - 4-1/2" high.
F596 - 5-1/2" high.
Colors: Yellow, Bright White, Dark Green, Old Ivory.

#4) **Half Daisy**, Burgundy, 3-1/2" high. Marked: U.S.A.

Embossed Feather Flower Pot, Dusty Rose, 4-1/2" high. Marked: U.S.A.

Half Daisy Jardiniere, Dark Green & Burgundy, 3" high. Marked: U.S.A.

Half Daisy with Rib Corner jardinieres, yellow and turquoise, 3-1/4" high. Marked: U.S.A.

Pot & Saucer, 2-7/8" high, no mark.

Embossed Diamond and Flower
Left: **African Violet Pot and Saucer**, 3" high. Marked: Shawnee U.S.A. 453
Center: **Flower Pot and Saucer**, 4" high. Marked: Shawnee U.S.A. 454
Right: **Flower Pot and Saucer**, 5" high. Marked: Shawnee U.S.A. 455
Not Shown: **Flower Pot and Saucer**, 6" high. Marked: Shawnee U.S.A. 456 Colors listed: Hunter Green, Burgundy, Yellow, Royal Blue.

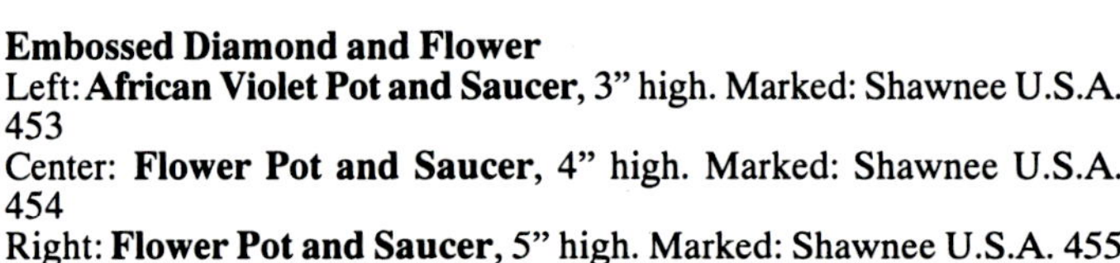

Petal jardiniere, 2-3/4" high. Marked: U.S.A.

Flower Pots and Saucers
#1) **African Violet Pot and Saucer**, 3" high. Marked: Shawnee U.S.A. 463 Colors listed: Avocado, Satin Pink, Tropical Green.

#2) **Diamond Shape Pot and Saucer**, 4" high, 6-1/2" long. (#416). Yellow, Hunter Green. Listed: 3-1/2" high, 5-3/4" long (#415). Listed: 4-1/2" high, 7-3/4" long (#417).

#3) **Duotone Pot and Saucer**, 4" high. Marked: Shawnee U.S.A. 494
Listed: 5" high, #495 and 6" high, #496.

#4) **Two Tone Square Pot and Saucer**, 4" high. Marked: Shawnee U.S.A. 410

Left: **Swirled Leaf**, embossed, footed, 2-3/4" high. Marked: U.S.A.
Center: **Ribbed Vegetable**, embossed, 2-1/2" high. Marked: U.S.A.
Right: **Leaf** with scalloped top, 3-1/2" high. Marked: U.S.A.

Square Jardiniere, 2-1/2" square, fluted sides. Marked: U.S.A. 402 Yellow, Powder Blue, Burgundy.

Left: **Burlap**, 4" high. Marked: Shawnee U.S.A.
Center: **Flared Petal**, 5" high. Marked: Shawnee U.S.A. 466
Right: **Woven Checks**, 4-1/2" high. Marked: Kenwood U.S.A. 1501

Bamboo Style Jardiniere, 6" high. Marked: U.S.A. 4066

Classic Jardiniere, 5-1/2" high. Marked: Shawnee U.S.A. 456

Left: **African Violet Pot & Saucer**, 3" high. Marked: Shawnee U.S.A. 533
Right: **Contiempo** jardiniere, 3-7/8" high. Marked: U.S.A. 438

Flower & Fern jardiniere, 7" high. Marked: U.S.A.

1951 Catalog Page of Pots & Saucers and Jardinieres.

1953 Catalog Page of Pots & Saucers.

Catalog Sheet of Flared and Hydroponic Pot & Saucers, and Classic Jardinieres.

Catalog Sheet of African Violet and Duotone Pot & Saucers, and Classic Jardinieres (with criss-cross).

Chapter 27: Vases

Vases were done in such a variety of colors and shapes, that it is impossible to cover them all in this book. Despite the variety of colors shown here, other colors could always turn up on that same piece. When one color is pictured, known catalog-listed colors are also given in the description. Dimensions given are the heights, and as always, are approximate. Gold trim may be found on any or all of these vases.

Additional vases can be found in the chapter on **1950s Floral Ware**.

Flower Vases, 5", gold trim. Marked: U.S.A. 1135
Courtesy of Marvin Mulligan

5-inch Vases.
Tulip Marked: U.S.A. 1115
Swan Marked: U.S.A. 725
Lily Marked: U.S.A. 705
Flower Marked: U.S.A. 1135
Cornucopia Marked: 735

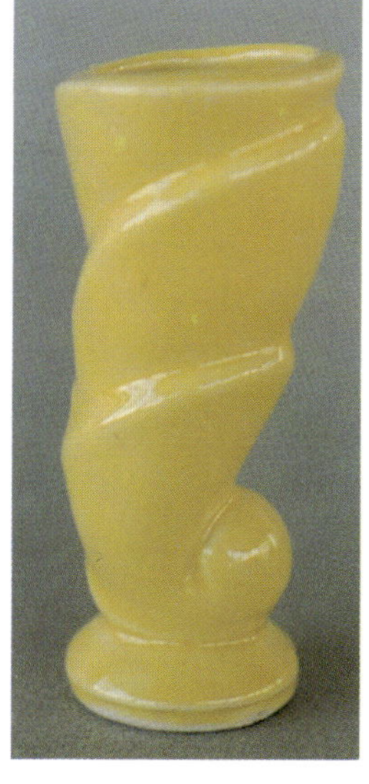

Round Cornucopia, 5". Marked: U.S.A.
Courtesy of Tim & Sandy Kightlinger

Top Row:
Clover Bloom, Burgundy, 5-1/2". Marked: U.S.A.
Fluted Urn, Old Ivory, 5". Marked: U.S.A.
Chain of Flowers, Butterscotch, 5". Marked: U.S.A.
Asters, White, 5". Marked: U.S.A.
Leaf, Yellow, 5-1/4". Marked: U.S.A.
Bottom Row:
Daisy Pitcher, Old Ivory, 6-1/2". Marked: U.S.A.
Embossed Flower & Stems, Cobalt, 5-1/4". Marked: U.S.A.
Double Handled Vase, Old Ivory, 5". Marked: U.S.A.
Ribbed & Embossed Flowers, Burgundy, 5". Marked: U.S.A. (shown, front).
Ribbed & Embossed Flowers, Turquoise, 5". Marked: U.S.A. (shown, back).

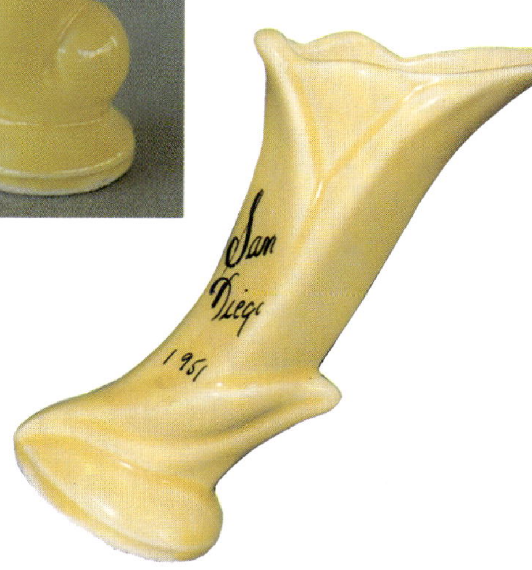

Tilted Flower, 5", decal fired on with *San Diego 1951* written in gold. Marked: U.S.A. 1125
Courtesy of Sue Blodgett

Top Row:
Paneled Two-Handle, oval, Flax Blue, 7". Marked: U.S.A.
Embossed Feather, Matt White, 7", lug handles. Marked: U.S.A.
Swan, Moss & Burgundy, 6". Marked: U.S.A. 806
Bottom Row:
Square Fluted, 8", Green/White/Gold Spatter. Marked: Shawnee U.S.A.
Dolphin, beige, 7-3/4". Marked: Shawnee U.S.A. 828
Hexagon Swirl, Chartreuse, 7-3/4". Marked: U.S.A. J3038
Pedestal Double Handle, round, Turquoise, 8". Marked: U.S.A.

Top Row:
Ribbed V, Yellow, 9". Marked: U.S.A. 809
Flared Swirl, Burgundy, 8-1/2". Marked: U.S.A.
Scalloped, beige, 8-3/4". Marked: Shawnee U.S.A.
Flared Rib with Lug Handles, Burgundy, 9". Marked: U.S.A.
Bottom Row:
Paneled Pitcher, Green, 9". Marked: U.S.A.
Paneled Pitcher, Yellow, 8". Marked: U.S.A.
Embossed Flower with Loop Handle, Burgundy, 7-1/2". Marked: U.S.A.
Bow Knot, Hunter Green, 8-3/4". Marked: U.S.A. 819

Top Row:
Diagonal Swirl, oval, Old English Ivory, 10". Marked: U.S.A.
Diagonal Swirl, oval, Matt White, 10". Marked: U.S.A.
Pedestal Base with Embossed Leaves, Burgundy, 10". Marked: U.S.A.
Bottom Row:
Bulbous with Stardust Texture, Cherry, 10". Marked: U.S.A. 2014
Dove, 9", Yellow & Hunter Green. Marked: U.S.A. 829
Cat-O-Nine-Tails Embossed, Old Ivory, 10". Marked: U.S.A.

Cornucopia Vases
Top Row:
6" Powder Blue, oval base, Marked: U.S.A.
6-1/2" Yellow, oval base, Marked: U.S.A.
6-1/2" Flax Blue, oval base, Marked: U.S.A.
Bottom Row:
6-3/4" Burgundy, rectangle base, Marked: U.S.A.
6-3/4" Dark Green, rectangle base, Marked: U.S.A.

Left: **Embossed Iris Vase**, double handle, 5-1/2". Marked: U.S.A.
Right: **Iris Fan Vase**, 6-1/4". Marked: U.S.A.

Hand Vases, embroidered cuff, 7". Marked: U.S.A.

Left: **Hand Vase,** embroidered cuff, Yellow, 10". Marked: U.S.A.
Right: **Hand Vase,** bow at cuff, *, Turquoise, 7". Marked: U.S.A.

Left: **Rope Vase**, 9". Marked: Shawnee U.S.A. 879
Center: **Burlap Vase**, 8". Marked: Shawnee U.S.A. 868
Right: **Leather Vase**, 5". Marked: U.S.A. 885

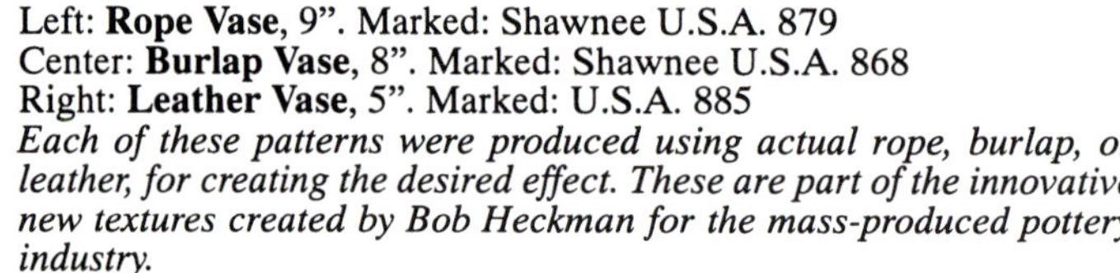

Each of these patterns were produced using actual rope, burlap, or leather, for creating the desired effect. These are part of the innovative new textures created by Bob Heckman for the mass-produced pottery industry.

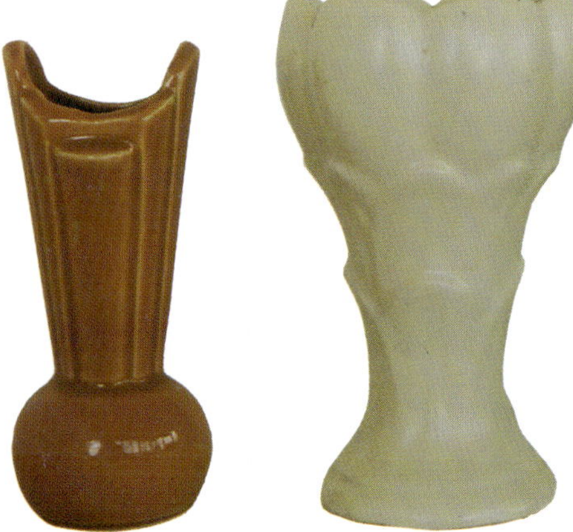

Left: **Geometric**, 5". Marked: U.S.A.
Center: **Tulip**, 5-1/2". Marked: U.S.A.
Right: **Cornucopia**, 5". Marked: U.S.A. 835

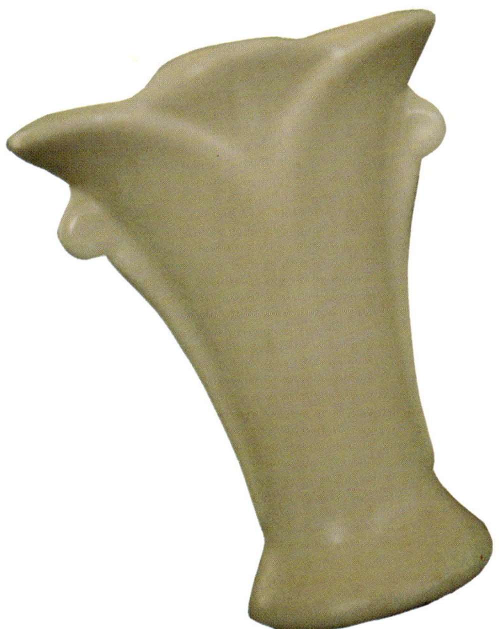

Scalloped Lug Bud Vase, 5". Marked: U.S.A.

Scalloped Top Panel, 4-1/4" high, Matt White. Marked: U.S.A.

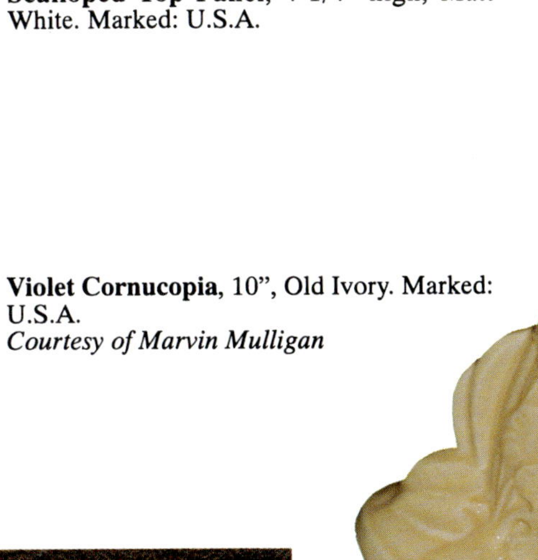

Violet Cornucopia, 10", Old Ivory. Marked: U.S.A.
Courtesy of Marvin Mulligan

Pitcher Bud Vase, 8", plain. Marked: U.S.A. 1168
Double Handle Bud Vase, 8", plain & gold trim. Marked: U.S.A. 1178
Colors known for above items: Grey, Green, Yellow, Burgundy, Blue, Chartreuse.

Philodendron Vase, 6-1/2". Marked: Shawnee U.S.A. 805
Yellow, gold trim; **Green**; **Yellow**, green leaves, gold trim; **Yellow**.
Courtesy of Paul & Linda Spenst

Diamond Pitcher, 8". Marked: U.S.A. 808
Courtesy of Paul & Linda Spenst

Flared Horn with Flowers, 6-1/4". Marked: U.S.A.

Diagonal Ribs with Flowers, 6". Marked: U.S.A.

Flowers & Ribs, 7", scalloped handles. Marked: U.S.A.

Wicker with Chain of Flowers, 8" long, 6" high. Marked: U.S.A.
Listed: Matt White, Old English Ivory, Turquoise, Powder Blue, Yellow. *Courtesy of Rich & Linda Guffey*

Embossed Flower and Leaf, 7" high. Marked: U.S.A. Shown in Turquoise and Shell Pink.

Flowers & Bows, 9-3/4", flared scalloped top. Marked: U.S.A.
Courtesy of Melvin & Jean Gibson

Diamond with Flower, 7", gold trim. Marked: Shawnee U.S.A. 827
Courtesy of Marvin Mulligan

The following are what have become known to collectors as the 1200 Vase Series. All vases have embossed designs, with underglaze decoration.

Top Row:
Tulip, 8-3/4". Marked: U.S.A. 1269
Flower Bud Vase, 3-1/4". Marked: U.S.A. 1201
Fan Vase with Flower, 4". Marked: U.S.A. 1264
Cornucopia, 5-3/4". Marked: U.S.A. 1256
Bottom Row:
3-Flower Lug Handle, 5". Marked: U.S.A. 1205
Chain of Flowers, lug handles, 4-3/4". Marked: U.S.A. 1235
Short Wheat, scalloped top, 4-3/4". Marked: U.S.A. 1215
Embossed Flower, 7", lug handles. Marked: U.S.A. 1257

Diamond with Flower, 7". Marked: Shawnee U.S.A. 827
Listed: Yellow, Hunter Green, Grey.

Tall Wheat, scalloped top. Marked: U.S.A. 1259

Bamboo, Turquoise, 5". Marked: U.S.A.
Bamboo, Antique Ivory, 7". Marked: U.S.A.
Bamboo, Dusty Rose, 5". Marked: U.S.A.
Courtesy of Robert & Linda Giles

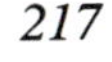

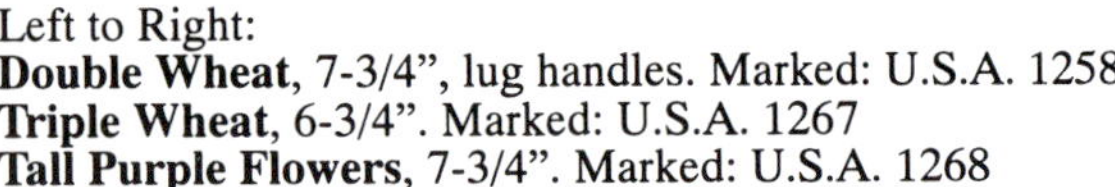

Left to Right:
Double Wheat, 7-3/4", lug handles. Marked: U.S.A. 1258
Triple Wheat, 6-3/4". Marked: U.S.A. 1267
Tall Purple Flowers, 7-3/4". Marked: U.S.A. 1268

Girl at Cornucopia, 5". Marked: U.S.A. 1275
Boy at Cornucopia, 5". Marked: U.S.A. 1276

Left to Right:
Blue Flower Bud Vase, 3-1/4". Marked: U.S.A. 1202
Yellow Flower Bud Vase, 3-1/4". Marked: U.S.A. 1203
Short Purple Flowers, 4-3/4". Marked: U.S.A. 1225
Double Pedestal Vase, 6". Marked: U.S.A. 1266

(End of 1200 Vase series.)

Flower Vase, 5", Chinese Red & Black fired on over glaze. Marked: Shawnee U.S.A. 865

Left to Right:
Leaf, 6-1/2". Marked: U.S.A. 822
Leaf, 7-3/4". Marked: U.S.A. 821
Leaf, 9-1/4". Marked: Shawnee U.S.A. 823
Courtesy of Melvin & Jean Gibson

Left to Right:
Leaf, 6-1/2", gold trim. Marked: U.S.A. 822
Leaf, 7-3/4", gold trim. Marked: U.S.A. 821
Leaf, 9-1/4", gold trim. Marked: Shawnee U.S.A. 823
Courtesy of Melvin & Jean Gibson

Gazelle and Baby, 10" high. Marked: Shawnee U.S.A. 840
Listed: Ebony and Briar-tone, Circa 1955.
Courtesy of Melvin & Jean Gibson

Giraffe and Baby, 10-1/2" high. Marked: Shawnee U.S.A. 841
Shown in Mirror Black, Briar-tone, Matt Ebony, Circa 1955. *Courtesy of Melvin & Jean Gibson*

1953 Shawnee Catalog Page showing several vases not shown previous.
Top Row #1: **Bud Vase Pitcher**, 8" high, #888, Shasta White or Avocado Green.
Top Row #4: **8" Vase** #838, Chartreuse or Grey.
Bottom Row #1: **Flared Vase**, 9" high, #869, Yellow or Avocado Green.
Bottom Row #2: **Cloth Vase**, 9-3/4" high, #880, Yellow or Ivory interior.

Note: The four textured vases of **Leather**, **Burlap**, **Rope**, and **Cloth**, had exterior finishes of either Traditional Glaze (glossy), or Contiempo (bisque).

Section VIII: Miscellaneous

Chapter 28: Banks

In addition to the figural banks shown in this chapter, Shawnee made Bank Head Cookie Jars of Winnie Pig and Smiley Pig. Refer to the **Cookie Jars** chapter.

Howdy Doody Riding A Pig, 6-3/4" high. Marked: Bob Smith U.S.A. Reportedly, this bank was made for only one year around 1950-1951, before production was ceased due to copyright infringement. The money slot is in the back of his neckerchief.

Bulldog, 4-1/2" high, no marks. Money slot is in his head.

Tumbling Bear, 4-3/4" high, original label, no marks. Money slot is in his head.

Chapter 29: Bathroom Accessories

Rondo Bathroom Accessories Catalog.
Circles of Ceramic Beauty listed in colors of: Blue, Pink, White, Gray, Yellow, Black, Melba, Cinnamon, Green, Tan, Lemon Yellow.

Bathroom accessories will not be something the Shawnee collector will rush out to find. Though Shawnee obviously created and marketed ceramic bath accessories, it was not a long-term venture, nor profitable.

Former Shawnee President John F. Bonistall writes: "In 1958 we did make bathroom accessories (toothbrush holders, soap dishes, paper holders, etc.) for Universal Tile Potteries of Cambridge, Ohio (now out of business) for a short time, but it did not work out. Again, there was little profit in it."

Rondo Bathroom Accessories

Shawnee patented a line of bathroom accessories in the 1950s, under the name *Rondo*. Eleven different colors were available, and could be bought in sets or open stock, and were surface-set.

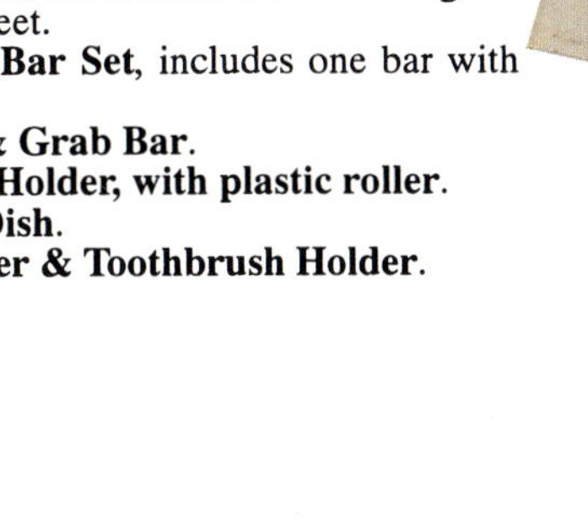

Rondo Bathroom Accessories ordering information sheet.
#500 Towel Bar Set, includes one bar with two holders.
#501 Soap & Grab Bar.
#502 Paper Holder, with plastic roller.
#504 Soap Dish.
#505 Tumbler & Toothbrush Holder.

Left: **Experimental Towel Bar Holder**, Dark Green with gold vining.
Right: Bottom of **Experimental Towel Bar Holder.**
Unglazed area has words *Rondo Pat.Pending 500*.
Glazed area has formula written:
1. Lt. spray gold 6854
2. Ethlyn Acetate Spatter

Simplex Bathroom Accessories

Shawnee produced this line in eleven different colors, which could be bought in sets or open stock. This line was promoted as simple to install, by surface-setting (gluing) them to the wall.

Simplex Towel Bar Holders.
Simplex Toilet Paper Holder with plastic roller.

Chapter 30: Bookends

The **Setter** bookends are smaller than an *identical* design that was produced in Japan. Be sure you are able to match dimensions on these, and to inspect the bottoms to see the mark. I have found some of these have been filled with sand or other material to add weight and stability, and then had the bottoms taped over and perhaps glued with felt.

Setter Head Bookends, 4-3/4" high, with the measurements of the base as just under 3" x 3-3/4". Marked: U.S.A.

RumRill Dealer Sign, 8" high, blue. The swirl vase by the potter was designed for Rumrill by Louise E. Bauer while she was at Shawnee. This sign is pictured for informative purposes only, and we make no claim that RumRill dealer signs were produced at Shawnee Pottery. Some probably were, and others were probably produced by successive potteries who worked with George Rumrill.

Potter's Wheel Bookends, 7-1/4" high. Dark Green.
Left: Shown from front, with embossed *Zanesville, Ohio*.
Right: Shown from back, with impressed mark *Crafted By Shawnee Potteries Zanesville, Ohio 1960*.

Potter's Wheel Bookends, 7" high. Dark Brown.
Left: Shown from front, with no embossed mark.
Right: Shown from back, with impressed mark *Crafted By Shawnee Potteries Zanesville, Ohio 1960*.

The **Potter's Wheel** bookends were originally designed as dealer signs for George Rumrill, and were embossed *Rum Rill* on the front. According to former Shawnee Pottery President John F. Bonistall, the design was resurrected in 1960 and made as bookends. These bookends were never offered for sale, but were presented to V.I.P.'s who visited the pottery, including large-volume customers of Shawnee. These are difficult to acquire.

Flying Geese Bookends, 6" high, 5-1/2" wide. Marked: Shawnee U.S.A. 4000

Flying Geese Bookends, 6", gold trim. Marked: Shawnee U.S.A. 4000.

Chapter 31: Clocks

Clocks were produced in the mid-1950s at Shawnee Pottery, all marketed under the Kenwood Ceramics division. The first, the Trellis Clock, was introduced by designer Robert Heckman. The Pyramid Clock was designed by Mack Holland.

Clocks with non-working or replaced movements will command a lower price than listed.

it's "glamour time" at Kenwood...
and CERAMICLOCKS set off each minute in rich, glowing copper

THE PYRAMID *Ceramiclock*

The timeless sincerity of the pyramids in a lovely living room time-piece. Genuine hammered-copper glaze on semi-porcelain ceramic. Dial is at precisely the right angle for easy viewing, especially when situated in modern, low position. Smart copper, or turquoise face. Guaranteed, synchronous electric movement. In perfect harmony in traditional or modern setting. A unique conversation piece, a beautiful decoration and an excellent clock.

NO. 951-C PYRAMID CERAMICLOCK—Copper face and copper decorated ceramic case.

NO. 951-T PYRAMID CERAMICLOCK—Turquoise face and copper decorated ceramic case. Shipped one to a carton (mailable), wt.—3 lbs.

"COPPER-CLAD" *Ceramiclock*

Styled for the prettiest kitchens, adds a charming note of elegance that never dulls (all-semi-porcelain case cleans like china). Gleaming pink or white with bold design in genuine hammered-copper glaze. Packed in handsome display carton. Guaranteed, synchronous electric movement. Complete with electric cord and brackets for easy hanging. No more beautiful kitchen clock can be imagined; fits into any decor.

NO. 952-P COPPER-CLAD CERAMICLOCK—Pink and Copper.

NO. 952-W COPPER-CLAD CERAMICLOCK—White and Copper.

Packed in individual display cartons. Four cartons per master carton. Wt.—14 lbs. per master carton. Also available packed in parcel post re-shipper at no extra charge.

KENWOOD CERAMICS
Division of Shawnee Potteries, Zanesville, Ohio, U.S.A.

Catalog Sheet.
Pyramid Clock, electric, No. 951-C has copper face and copper finish case.
Pyramid Clock, electric, No. 951-T has turquoise face and copper finish case.

Copper-Clad Clock, electric, No. 952-P has pink and copper exterior.
Copper-Clad Clock, electric, No. 952-W has white and copper exterior.
Packed in die cut display carton, and comes with electric cord and brackets for easy hanging.

Pyramid Clock, 7-1/2" high. Marked: 951 U.S.A. Kenwood. Turquoise face with words *Ceramiclock by Kenwood. Courtesy of Rich & Linda Guffey*

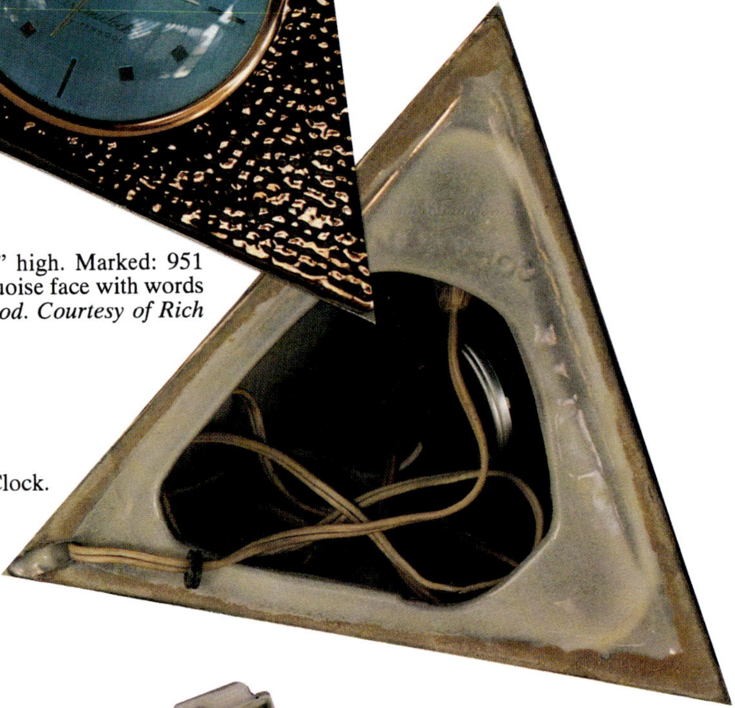

Bottom of Pyramid Clock.

Trellis Clock, 8-1/2" square, no mark, green and white. Not the original clock face and works.

Trellis Clock, 8-1/4" square, no mark, brown and white. Clock face has words *Ceramiclock by Kenwood.*

Grandaughter Clock Catalog Sheet.
Suburbia, Pink/White 825-P.
Heritage, Brown/Beige 825-B.
Electric clock is 10 inches square, semi-porcelain, offered in two-tone ceramic treatments with hand-etched decoration. Triple-plated copper "weight rods" hold matching ceramic planters containing artificial plants. Packaged in a corrugated display carton.

Grandaughter Clock.
Suburbia, pink and white, 10" square. Clock face has words *Ceramiclock by Kenwood.*

Chapter 32: Console Sets & Candle Holders

Early Shawnee catalogs listed a variety of Flower Bowls that could be paired with matching Candle Holders to become Console Sets. The majority were designed and sold as Flower Bowls, and will appear in the **Planting Dishes** chapter.

Whenever possible, catalog numbers are shown in parenthesis. An asterisk (*) means not catalog confirmed. Colors are those listed in catalogs, though any color used during that particular era may turn up.

Additional Console Sets and Candle Holders may be seen in various lines of the **1950s Floral Ware**.

Four Cornucopias Console.
Flower Bowl (FB2811): 4" high, 10-1/4" long. Marked: U.S.A.
Candle Holders (FB404): 3-3/4" high, no mark.
Colors: Matt White, Old English Ivory, Flax Blue, Turquoise, Powder Blue, Dusty Rose.

Four Cornucopias Console with gold trim and decals. Other cornucopia sets decorated identical to this one have turned up in Old Ivory, and Powder Blue. *From The Collection of Francis & Judy VanHooser*

Magnolia Blossom Candle Holders. Bright White underglaze decorated with burgundy and green. Bowl (not shown) is decorated to match. Note that the Magnolia petals on the candle holders are pointed, whereas they are rounded on the bowls.

Magnolia Blossom Console.
Flower Bowl (FB249): 2-1/2" high, 9" diameter. Marked: U.S.A.
Candle Holders (FB253): 3" high, no marks.
Colors: Bright White decorated, Powder Blue, Shell Pink, Old English Ivory, Flax Blue, Dusty Rose.

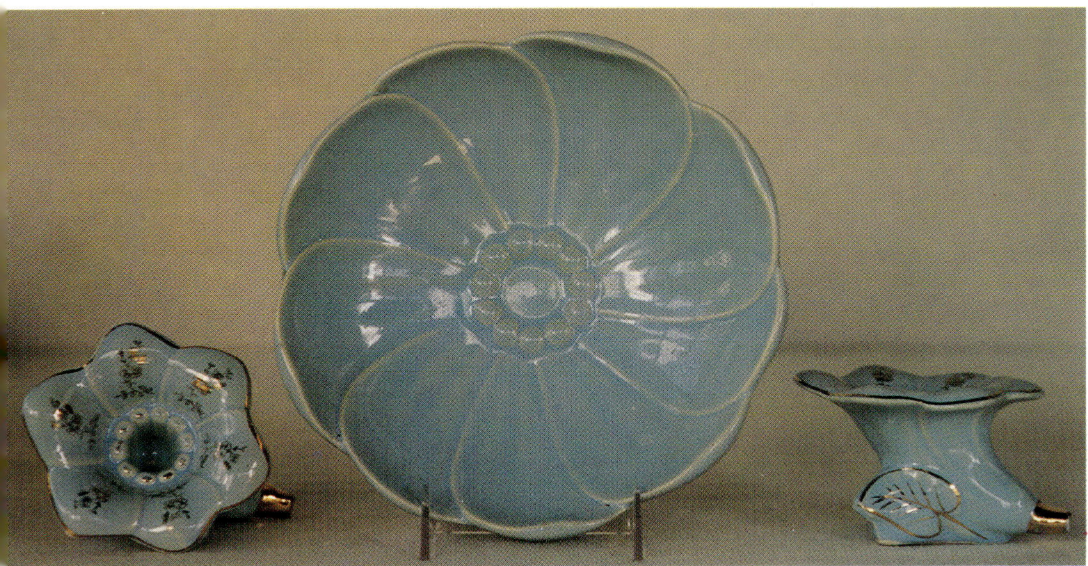

Magnolia Blossom Console. Bowl shown plain; Candle Holders shown with gold trim.

Scallop Top Conventional Console (Blossom).
Flower Bowl (FB188): 3" high, 8" diameter. Marked U.S.A.
Candle Holders (FB233): 3-1/4" high, no marks.
Colors: Matt White, Powder Blue, Old English Ivory, Turquoise, Flax Blue. Collectors have been calling this set **Blossom** for lack of a catalog name.

Scallop Top Conventional Console (Blossom).
Same as previous, but in different color and different view of the bowl design.

Scallop Top Embossed Petals, 3" high, 8" diameter. Marked: U.S.A. **Flower Bowl** (FB178) only, shown in turquoise. Can be paired with Candle Holders (FB233) shown with Blossom Console. Colors: Matt White, Old English Ivory, Powder Blue, Turquoise.

Ribbed Cornucopias with Laurel Wreath.
Flower Bowl, 4" high, 10" long. Marked: U.S.A. **Candle Holders**, 3-1/4" high, no marks. Colors: Matt White, Old Ivory, Flax Blue, Dusty Rose, Turquoise.

Embossed Rectangular Console.
Flower Bowl *, 3' high. Marked: U.S.A. **Candle Holders** (FB233), 3-1/4" high, no marks. *From The Collection of Sandy Kightlinger*

Candle Holder with Handle, 2-1/8" high, 8" long. Marked: Shawnee U.S.A. 3026

Gold Spatter Flared Console.
Flared Bowl, two attached layers, 4" high, 10" diameter. Marked: Shawnee U.S.A. 3504 **Flared Candle Holders**, 2" high. Marked: Shawnee U.S.A. 3522 Shown in black with gorgeous all-over gold spatter. *From The Collection of Melvin & Jean Gibson*

Candle Holder with Handle, green, platinum decorated, 2-1/8" high, 8" long. Marked: Shawnee U.S.A. 3026

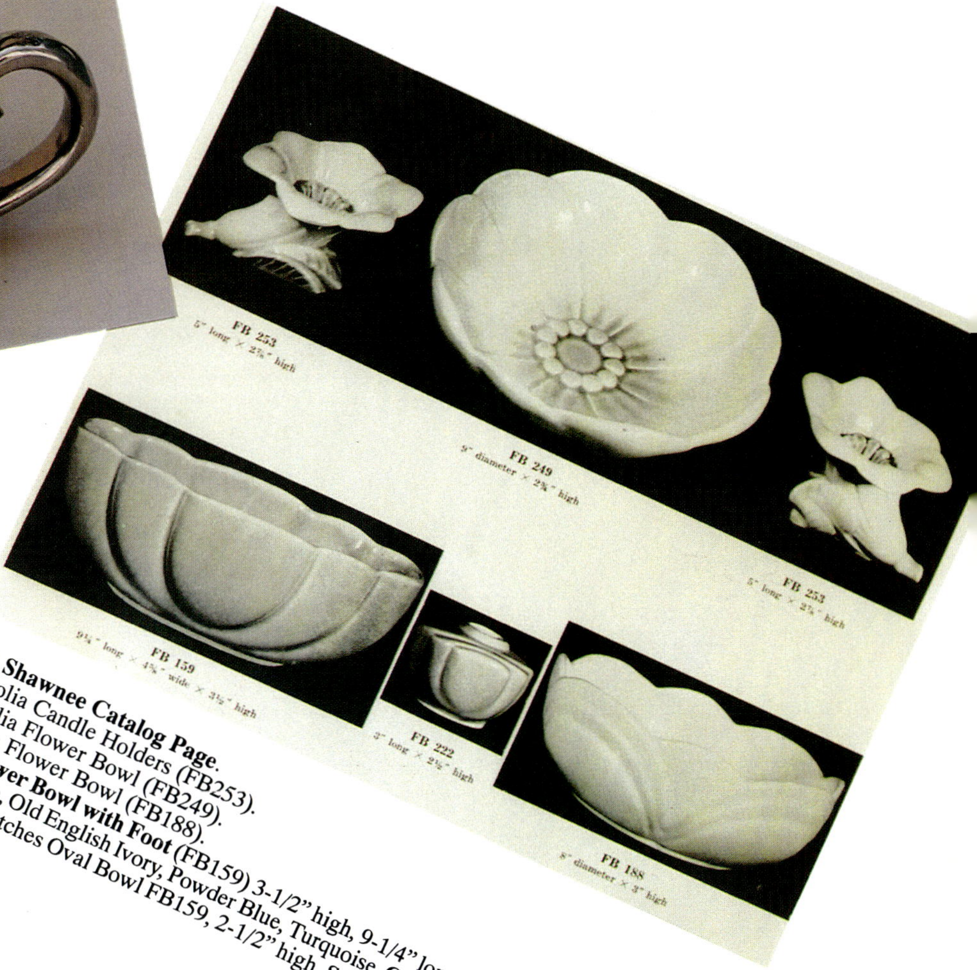

1941 Shawnee Catalog Page. Magnolia Candle Holders (FB253). Magnolia Flower Bowl (FB249). Blossom Flower Bowl (FB188). **Oval Flower Bowl with Foot** (FB159) 3-1/2" high, 9-1/4" long. Listed: Matt White, Old English Ivory, Powder Blue, Turquoise. **Candle Holder** (FB222) matches Oval Bowl FB159, 2-1/2" high. Same colors as bowl.

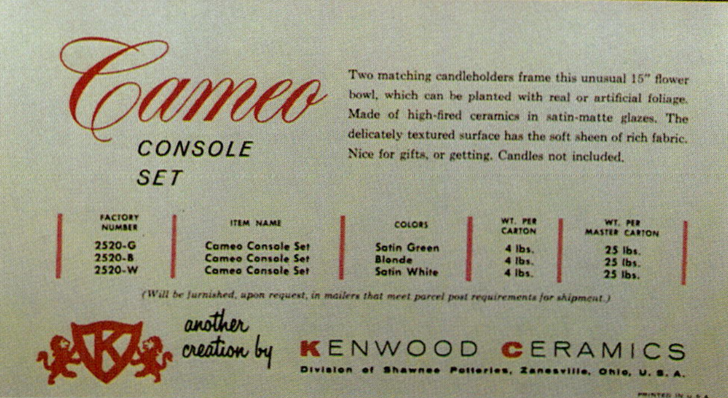

Cameo

CONSOLE SET

Two matching candleholders frame this unusual 15" flower bowl, which can be planted with real or artificial foliage. Made of high-fired ceramics in satin-matte glazes. The delicately textured surface has the soft sheen of rich fabric. Nice for gifts, or getting. Candles not included.

FACTORY NUMBER	ITEM NAME	COLORS	WT. PER CARTON	WT. PER MASTER CARTON
2520-G	Cameo Console Set	Satin Green	4 lbs.	25 lbs.
2520-B	Cameo Console Set	Blonde	4 lbs.	25 lbs.
2520-W	Cameo Console Set	Satin White	4 lbs.	25 lbs.

(Will be furnished, upon request, in mailers that meet parcel post requirements for shipment.)

another creation by KENWOOD CERAMICS

Division of Shawnee Potteries, Zanesville, Ohio, U. S. A.

PRINTED IN U.S.A.

Cameo Console Set Catalog Sheet. Console bowl is 15" long.

Chapter 33: Figurines

The items featured in this chapter were largely ornamental, with catalogs often indicating that items could be used for Flower Bowl Inserts. We will make note of the suggested inserts with the appropriate figural piece. Some of these figurines have also been found with holes drilled in them, intended for use as salt and pepper shakers. See Salt & Pepper Shakers for examples. Figurines have either an open base, or a casting hole in the base, with some glaze of varying degrees on the inside of the piece.

An asterisk (*) denotes not catalog confirmed as Shawnee, though it matches color, size, decoration, and feel of other similar confirmed pieces. All dates listed are to give a general time frame, as each item could have been produced before and after that year. Dimensions are always to be considered approximate. Many early pieces were decorated with cold paint, and collectors are always happy to find examples with the paint intact.

These are the smallest of the miniature animal figurines, and collectors have begun calling them the Mini-Miniatures to distinguish them from the approximately 3-inch high miniatures.

Mini-Miniatures

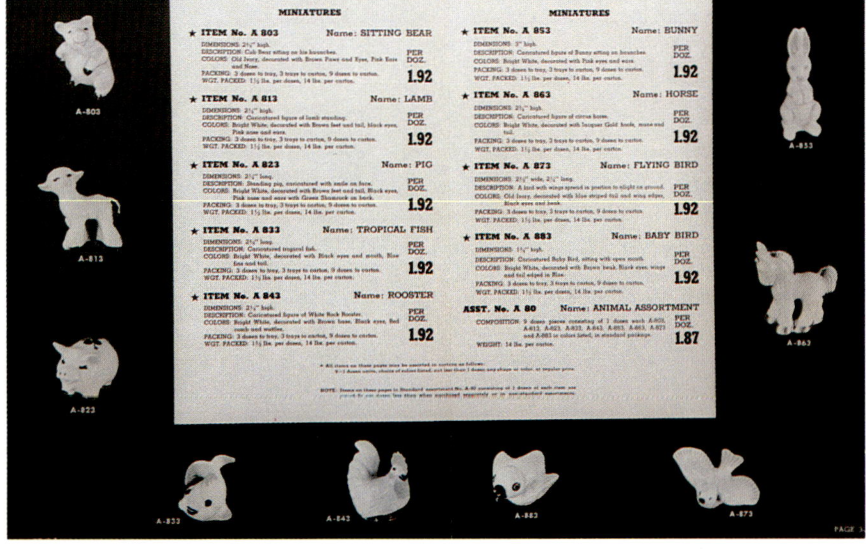

MINIATURES

★ ITEM No. A 803 — Name: SITTING BEAR
DIMENSIONS: 2½" high.
DESCRIPTION: Cub Bear sitting on his haunches.
COLORS: Old Ivory, decorated with Brown Paws and Eyes, Pink Ears and Nose.
PACKING: 3 dozen to tray, 3 trays to carton, 9 dozen to carton.
WGT. PACKED: 1½ lbs. per dozen, 14 lbs. per carton.
PER DOZ. 1.92

★ ITEM No. A 813 — Name: LAMB
DIMENSIONS: 2¼" high.
DESCRIPTION: Caricatured figure of lamb standing.
COLORS: Bright White, decorated with Brown feet and tail, black eyes, Pink nose and ears.
PACKING: 3 dozen to tray, 3 trays to carton, 9 dozen to carton.
WGT. PACKED: 1½ lbs. per dozen, 14 lbs. per carton.
PER DOZ. 1.92

★ ITEM No. A 823 — Name: PIG
DIMENSIONS: 2¼" long.
DESCRIPTION: Standing pig, caricatured with smile on face.
COLORS: Bright White, decorated with Brown feet and tail, Black eyes, Pink nose and ears with Green Shamrock on back.
PACKING: 3 dozen to tray, 3 trays to carton, 9 dozen to carton.
WGT. PACKED: 1½ lbs. per dozen, 14 lbs. per carton.
PER DOZ. 1.92

★ ITEM No. A 833 — Name: TROPICAL FISH
DIMENSIONS: 2½" long.
DESCRIPTION: Caricatured tropical fish.
COLORS: Bright White, decorated with Black eyes and mouth, Blue fins and tail.
PACKING: 3 dozen to tray, 3 trays to carton, 9 dozen to carton.
WGT. PACKED: 1½ lbs. per dozen, 14 lbs. per carton.
PER DOZ. 1.92

★ ITEM No. A 843 — Name: ROOSTER
DIMENSIONS: 2¼" high.
DESCRIPTION: Caricatured figure of White Rock Rooster.
COLORS: Bright White, decorated with Brown base, Black eyes, Red comb and wattles.
PACKING: 3 dozen to tray, 3 trays to carton, 9 dozen to carton.
WGT. PACKED: 1½ lbs. per dozen, 14 lbs. per carton.
PER DOZ. 1.92

★ ITEM No. A 853 — Name: BUNNY
DIMENSIONS: 3" high.
DESCRIPTION: Caricatured figure of Bunny sitting on haunches.
COLORS: Bright White, decorated with Pink eyes and ears.
PACKING: 3 dozen to tray, 3 trays to carton, 9 dozen to carton.
WGT. PACKED: 1½ lbs. per dozen, 14 lbs. per carton.
PER DOZ. 1.92

★ ITEM No. A 863 — Name: HORSE
DIMENSIONS: 2¾" high.
DESCRIPTION: Caricatured figure of circus horse.
COLORS: Bright White, decorated with lacquer Gold hoofs, mane and tail.
PACKING: 3 dozen to tray, 3 trays to carton, 9 dozen to carton.
WGT. PACKED: 1½ lbs. per dozen, 14 lbs. per carton.
PER DOZ. 1.92

★ ITEM No. A 873 — Name: FLYING BIRD
DIMENSIONS: 2½" wide, 2½" long.
DESCRIPTION: A bird with wings spread in position to alight on ground.
COLORS: Old Ivory, decorated with blue striped tail and wing edges, Black eyes and beak.
PACKING: 3 dozen to tray, 3 trays to carton, 9 dozen to carton.
WGT. PACKED: 1½ lbs. per dozen, 14 lbs. per carton.
PER DOZ. 1.92

★ ITEM No. A 883 — Name: BABY BIRD
DIMENSIONS: 1¾" high.
DESCRIPTION: Caricatured Baby Bird, sitting with open mouth.
COLORS: Bright White, decorated with Brown beak, Black eyes, wings and tail edged in Blue.
PACKING: 3 dozen to tray, 3 trays to carton, 9 dozen to carton.
WGT. PACKED: 1½ lbs. per dozen, 14 lbs. per carton.
PER DOZ. 1.92

ASST. No. A 80 — Name: ANIMAL ASSORTMENT
COMPOSITION: 9 dozen pieces consisting of 1 dozen each A-803, A-813, A-823, A-833, A-843, A-853, A-863, A-873 and A-883 in colors listed, in standard package.
WEIGHT: 14 lbs. per carton.
PER DOZ. 1.87

A-803 A-813 A-823 A-853 A-863 A-833 A-843 A-883 A-873

Shawnee Catalog Pages from July 1, 1942.
Bunny on Haunches is the tallest of these mini's at 3" high, ears up,
Bright White with pink eyes and ears.
All other mini's in this catalog have examples pictured.

Bunny with Ears Down *, 2-1/2" high. Old Ivory with cold paint decoration. **Chicken ***, 1-3/4" high. Dusty Rose. *Courtesy of Melvin & Jean Gibson*

Miniature Animals, Circa 1942, no marks, shown left to right:

Standing Pig with Smile, 2-1/4" high. Bright White (A823).
Cub Bear Sitting On Haunches, 2-3/8" high. Old Ivory (A803).
Circus Horse, 2-3/4" high. Bright White (A863).
Terrier *, 2-1/2" high. Old Ivory.
Standing Lamb, 2-1/4" high. Bright White (A813).
White Rock Rooster, 2-1/8" high. Bright White (A843).

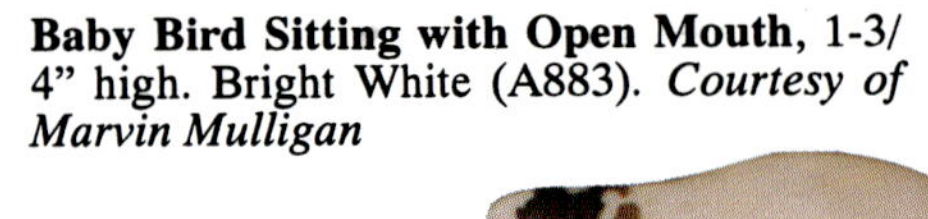

Baby Bird Sitting with Open Mouth, 1-3/4" high. Bright White (A883). *Courtesy of Marvin Mulligan*

Tropical Fish, 2-3/8" long. Bright White (A833). *Courtesy of Linda Guffey*

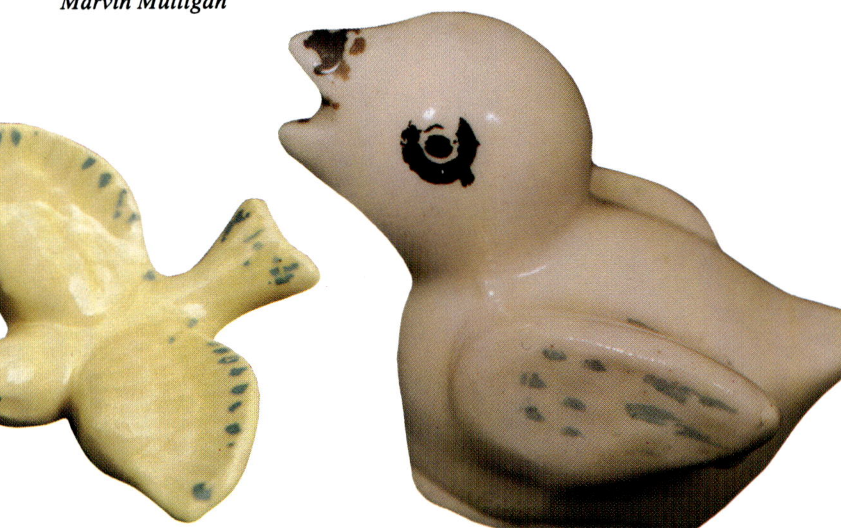

Flying Bird, 2-1/2" wide. Old Ivory (A873). *Courtesy of Paul & Joy Schneider*

Miniatures-Ornamental or flower Bowl Inserts

Catalog Pages from July 1, 1941 showing decorative treatment of dish gardens using some of the following miniatures as flower bowl inserts.

Stippled Bird, no mark. Matt White, Old Ivory, Turquoise. *Courtesy of Marvin Mulligan*

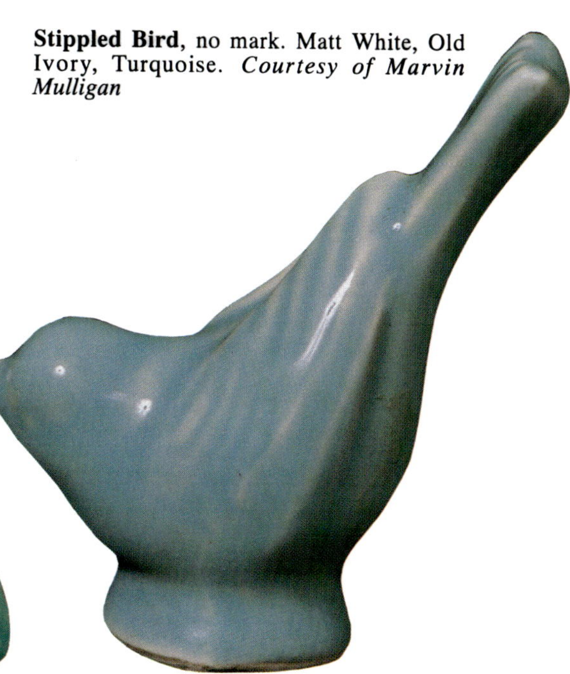

Frog, 2" high, no mark. (A733).

Turtle, 3-1/2" long, no mark. (A743).

Bird, head down, no mark. *Courtesy of Marvin Mulligan*

Birds In Flight, 2-1/2" high, no mark. (A663).

Sitting Canary, head up, 2-3/4" high, no mark.

Feeding Duck, 2" high, no mark. (A713).

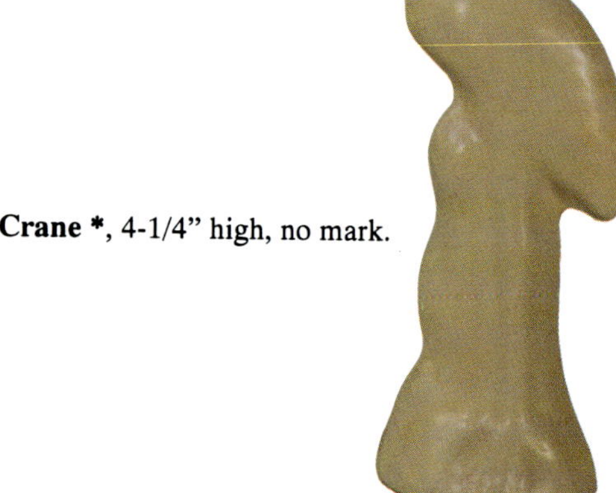

Crane *, 4-1/4" high, no mark.

Left: **Duck**, 4" high, no mark. (A603).
Right: **Duck,** 3" high, no mark.

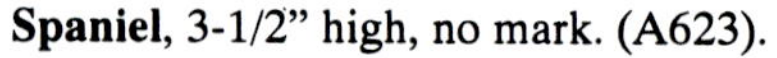

Spaniel, 3-1/2" high, no mark. (A623).

Swimming Swan, 2-1/2" high, no mark. (A723).

Crane, 5-1/4" high, no mark. (A754).

Rabbit with Ears Up, 3-3/4" high, no mark. (A584). *Another version shows rabbit ears down. See Salt & Pepper shakers.*

Pekingese *, 3-1/2" high, no mark.

Parrot on stump, 3-1/2" high, no mark.

Swan Preening Feathers, 3-3/4" high, no mark. (A913).

Standing Bear, 3" high, no mark. (A783).

Dolphin, 1-3/4" high, no mark.

Elephant, 2-3/4" high, no mark. (A593). White Elephant shown with souvenir label.

Fish, 2-1/4" high, no mark.

Tropical Fish, 2-1/2" high, no mark.

Stippled Fish, 2-1/2" high, no mark.

Tropical Fish, no mark.

Owl Sitting On Book, 4" high, no mark. (A613).

Fawn, 4" high, no mark. (A574).

Figurines

Left: **Deer Facing Front**, 6-1/2" high, no mark, cold paint decorated.
Right: **Deer Facing Left**, 6-1/2" high, no mark, cold paint decorated.
This deer appeared later on the Fawn and Stump planters and lamps.

Mumpy Kitty, 5" high, no mark. Cold paint decorated, circa 1942.

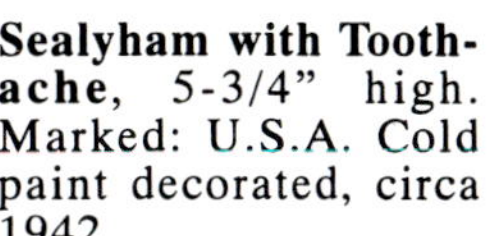

Sealyham with Toothache, 5-3/4" high. Marked: U.S.A. Cold paint decorated, circa 1942.

Baby Donkey, 6-1/2" high, no mark. Left cold painted with brown; right cold painted with black.

Terrier, 7-1/2" high, no mark. Shown back and front, cold paint decorated. *Courtesy of Paul & Linda Spenst*

Terrier with Sore Paw, 5" high, no mark. Cold paint decorated, circa 1942.

Southern Girl, 4" high, no mark.

Sailor Boy, 4" high, open base, no mark. *Rare!*

Dutch Girl, green dress, 4-1/2" high. *This item is also found as a pepper shaker, and as a figurine on the Wishing Well planter.*

Left: **Chinese Girl with Parasol**, 5" high. Marked: U.S.A. 601
Right: **Chinese Boy**, 5" high. Marked: U.S.A. 602
Courtesy of Robert & Lois Duvall

Chinese Girl with Parasol, 5", gold trim. Marked: U.S.A. 601
Chinese Boy, 5", gold trim. Marked: U.S.A. 602
Courtesy of Paul Schneider

Chinese Girl with Parasol, 5", solid gold trim. Marked: U.S.A. 601
Chinese Boy, 5", solid gold trim. Marked: U.S.A. 602
Courtesy of Paul Schneider

Pekingese, 2-1/2" high, no mark, gold trim and flower decals. *Courtesy of Terry & Sandra Bauer*

Squirrel, 2-1/2" high, no mark.
Left: Plain, with Shawnee label.
Center: Gold Trim and flower decals.
Right: Gold Trim.
Courtesy of Paul & Joy Schneider

Deer, no mark, gold trim and flower & wheat decals. *Rare!*
Courtesy of Randy & Stephanie Adrian

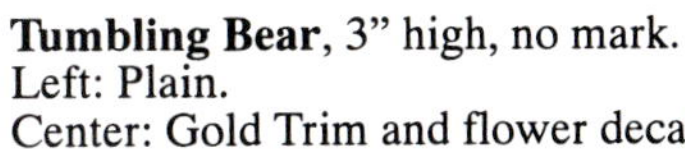

Tumbling Bear, 3" high, no mark.
Left: Plain.
Center: Gold Trim and flower decals.
Right: Gold Trim.
Courtesy of Paul & Joy Schneider

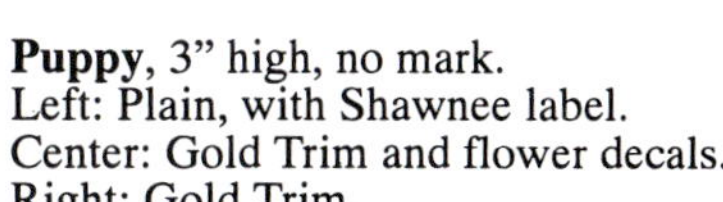

Puppy, 3" high, no mark.
Left: Plain, with Shawnee label.
Center: Gold Trim and flower decals.
Right: Gold Trim.
Courtesy of Paul & Joy Schneider

Rabbit, no mark.
Left: Plain, with Shawnee label.
Right: Gold Trim with Shawnee label.
Courtesy of Paul & Joy Schneider

Teddy Bear, 3" high, no mark.
Left: Plain, with Shawnee label.
Right: Gold Trim and flower decals.
Courtesy of Paul & Joy Schneider

Teddy Bear, gold trim and flower & wheat decals.
Squirrel, gold trim and flower & wheat decals.
Courtesy of Paul & Joy Schneider

Pekingese, 2-1/2" high, no mark.
Left: Plain, with Shawnee label.
Right: Gold Trim and flower decals.
Courtesy of Paul & Joy Schneider

Deer, no mark.
Hard to find!

Lamb, 6-1/4" high, no mark. Circa 1950.
Left: Plain.
Right: Gold Trim.

Terrier, 6-1/4" high, no mark. Circa 1950.
Left: Plain.
Right: Gold Trim.

Gazelle, with gold trim, 7" high, 10-1/2" long.
Marked: U.S.A. 614

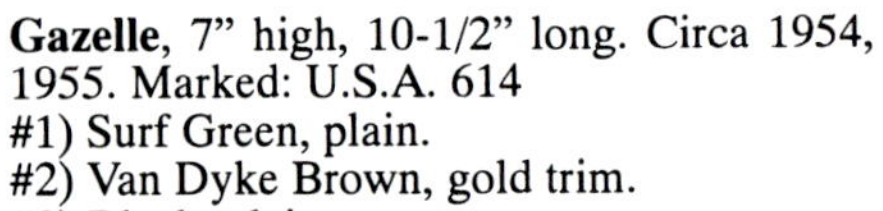

Gazelle, 7" high, 10-1/2" long. Circa 1954, 1955. Marked: U.S.A. 614
#1) Surf Green, plain.
#2) Van Dyke Brown, gold trim.
#3) Black, plain.
#4) Van Dyke Brown with white mottling, gold trim.
Courtesy of Melvin & Jean Gibson

Chapter 34: Flower Frogs

Flower Frogs were made during Shawnee's early years, and were often referred to as Flower Bowl Inserts. Additional flower bowl inserts may be found in the **Figurines** chapter.

Swan, 3-3/4" high, no marks. Turquoise, Old English Ivory, Flax Blue.

Sea Horse, 3-3/4" high, no marks. Turquoise, Old English Ivory, Flax Blue.

Dolphin, 3-3/4" high, no marks. Turquoise, Old English Ivory, Flax Blue.

Snail, 4" high, Gold Trim and flower decals. Marked: U.S.A.
Old English Ivory.

Snail, 4" high, 5" long, Old Ivory. Marked: U.S.A.

Snail, 4" high, 5" long, Matt White. Marked: U.S.A.

Turtle, 4" high, 5" long. Marked: U.S.A. Turquoise.

White **Swan,** White **Dolphin,** Turquoise **Dolphin**, high base, 4-1/2" high, no marks.

Flower Bouquet, 4-1/2" high, no marks.

Flower Bouquet, 4-1/2" high, no marks. Found with a Shawnee label intact.

Dolphin Flower Frog and Round Bowl, bowl 8-1/4" diameter. Marked: U.S.A.

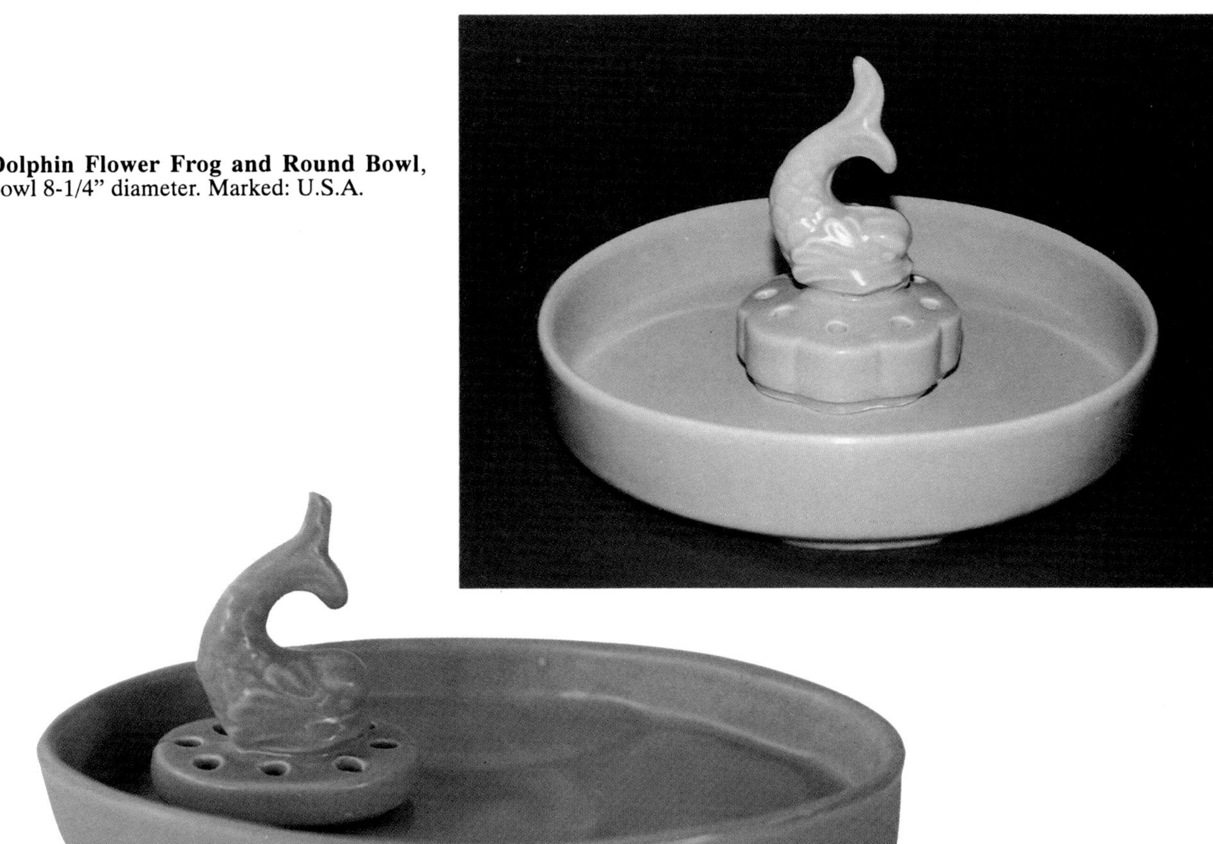

Dolphin Flower Frog and Low Flower Bowl, bowl is 10" long, 1-1/4" high. Marked: U.S.A.

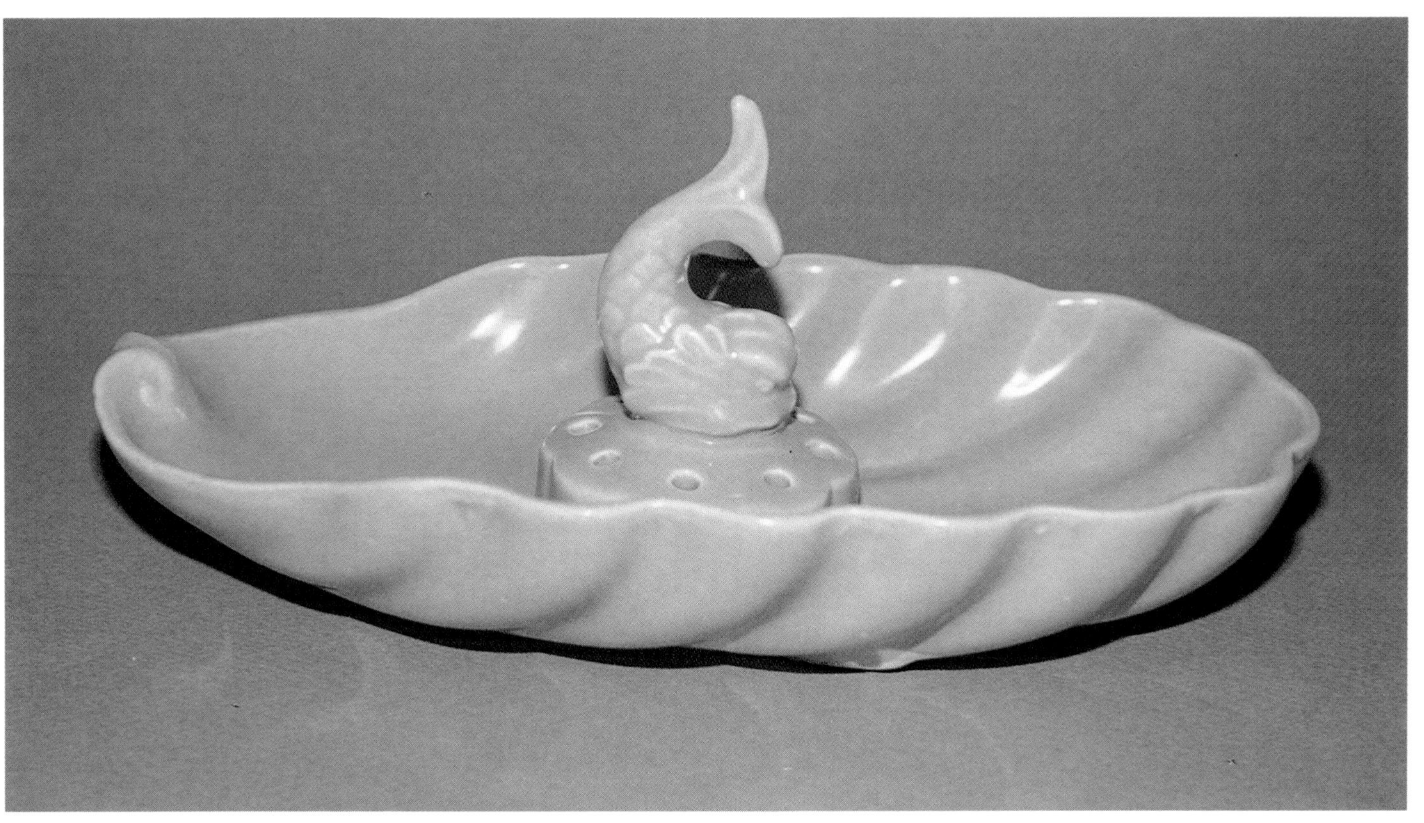

Dolphin Flower Frog and Flower Bowl, 10" long, 8-1/4" wide, no marks. (FB209).

Chapter 35: Lamps

Research has shown that Shawnee produced lamp bases throughout their history, so I have no doubt that we have barely begun to identify all of the lamps that Shawnee made.

More than perhaps any other category of Shawnee, lamps have puzzled the Shawnee collector the most often. Many times I have seen what appear to be identical lamps, but upon close examination, their bases have been finished differently. Through extensive research, including consultation with long-time Shawnee employees, we *know* that many of the lamp molds were provided by outside companies for Shawnee to produce the lamps. We can only *assume* the following: 1) Absolute rigid specifications were given in decorating techniques, glazes, and colors, as well as any gold trim to be applied; 2) The exact same molds and specifications were provided to other potteries as well, explaining the identical products being found, but with different bottoms; 3) or, we can assume that various potteries such as Shawnee only produced the lamp itself, and that these lamps were then all sent to one decorating company.

However, assumption #3 doesn't hold water when you consider the Black Moor Head lamps, which have turned up with several types of bases. The pair pictured in this book were bought by this author a number of years ago, directly from a woman who worked at Shawnee and had decorated the pair. She went to great lengths to tell me about the difficult job it was to apply the gold trim on these pieces. Plus, they meet all the criteria for identifying Shawnee-made lamps that we have established to date.

Experience has given us some guidelines to follow in recognizing some Shawnee lamps: 1) glazed inside; 2) an unglazed bottom rim with a "glazed shelf" or "glazed inner strength ring" that extends inward from the bottom rim. On some lamps it is narrow, while others have a wide inner strength ring, and it's not always even. 3) lamps found so far have a small hole drilled in the back, anywhere from 1/2" to 1-1/2" up from the bottom, from which the cord would extend; 4) I look for the distinctive "step" or baseline ridge that is common to many Shawnee items. This, however, is not mandatory, as there have been many confirmed Shawnee lamps that have lacked this one feature; it's just a plus if it's there.

Lamp shades are another questionable subject. How often have you heard that the shade found on a lamp is the "original shade", so it must be the one that "goes with" that lamp. Lamps are often sold where you can choose a shade to match your own tastes and decor. Keeping this in mind, older lamps can certainly be found with a variety of shades that have been with that lamp for years, and it would be wrong to say that any one shade is the correct one for a particular lamp. Also, shades could have been replaced at any time by the owner of a lamp, and today that shade would look quite old. So ..... Old shade? Probably. Original shade? Possibly. The only "matching" shade? Unlikely!

All dimensions are for the ceramic lamp only, not the electrical hardware.

Elephant with Ball 7-1/2" high, cold paint decoration, no marks.

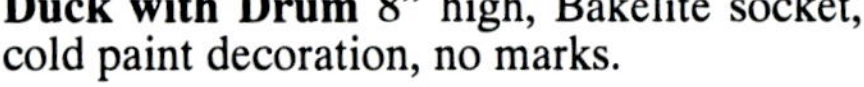

Duck with Drum 8" high, Bakelite socket, cold paint decoration, no marks.

Clown on Drum 7-3/4" high, cold paint decoration, no marks.

Mother Goose * 6-1/2" high, no marks, multi-color goose, blue base.

Puppy 4-3/4" high, no marks, brown puppy, chartreuse base. *Courtesy of Rich & Linda Guffey*

Puppy 4-3/4" high, yellow puppy, brown base.

Rabbit Eating Corn * 6-1/2" high, no marks, blue rabbit, peach base. Also found chartreuse rabbit on butterscotch base. *Note: This rabbit figurine has turned up fired onto a Corn King butter dish bottom. See Miscellaneous Rare section.*

Deer 7-1/4" high, no marks, chartreuse deer, butterscotch base.

Deer 7-1/4" high, no marks, blue deer, peach base.

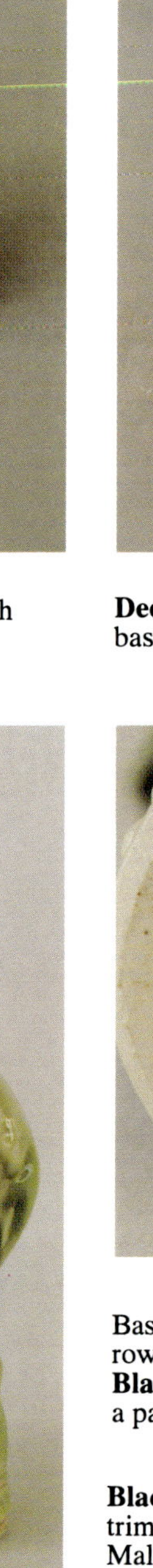

Deer 7-1/4", no marks, yellow deer, brown base.

Deer 7-1/4", no marks, butterscotch deer, chartreuse base.

Base to Black Moor Head lamp, showing narrow and uneven inner strength ring. These **Black Moor Heads** have also been found as a pair of vases, having a glazed bottom.

Black Moor Heads 8" high, no marks, gold trim.
Male on left, with loop on forehead and sword at neck.
Female on right, with star on forehead and flower at neck.

Native Man & Woman gold trim, no marks.
Left: **Male Playing Drum** 8-1/2" high.
Right: **Bare-Breasted Female** 9" high.

Harvest King 9-1/2" high, greens and yellow.

Ballerina on pedestal base, no marks, total height of 11-1/2", or ballerina alone is 10" high. *Courtesy of Melvin & Jean Gibson*

Black Native Man & Woman gold trim, no marks. Very difficult to find. *Courtesy of Melvin & Jean Gibson*

Back view of Black Native Man and Woman.

Harvest King and Queen.
Left: **Harvest King** 9-1/2" high.
Right: **Harvest Queen** 9-1/2" high.
Courtesy of Melvin & Jean Gibson

Spanish Dancers 9" high, no marks, two color variations shown.

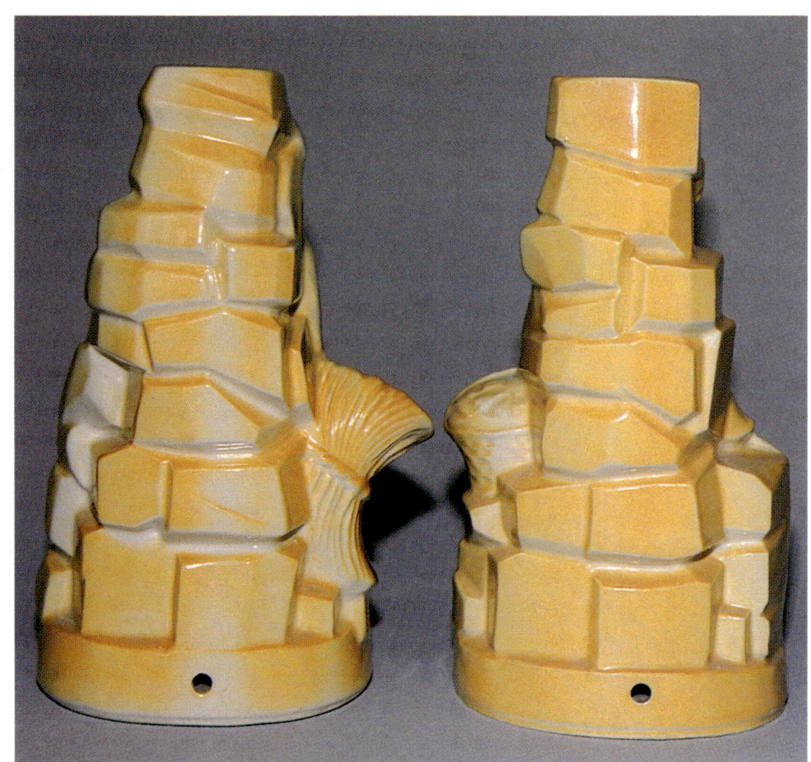

Back view of Harvest King and Queen.

Embossed Flower Wall Lamp 6" wide, 4-1/4" diameter back, shown green base and yellow base, also found with blue base. Marked: U.S.A. *Shawnee Design Patent 149,624 Applied For March 7, 1947*.

Back of Embossed Flower wall lamp.

Ribbon & Bow 7-1/4" high, white with blue bows. Marked: U.S.A. *Designed by Robert Heckman.*

Ribbon & Bow 7-1/2" high, white with pink bows. Marked: U.S.A.

Embossed Flowers 7-3/4" high, no marks.

Bluebird 7-3/4" high, no marks.

Victorian Man & Woman, Doubles 8-1/2" high, no marks. Note that the woman wears a layered ruffle gown, and they are holding hands.

Victorian Man 7-3/4" high, no marks, he holds a hat in his right hand.
Victorian Woman 7-3/4" high, no marks, she wears a hoop gown and holds a basket in her left hand.

Embossed Oriental Woman on cylinder base, 8" high, no marks. Two color variations shown.

Oriental Man with Mandolin on pedestal base, 11-1/2" high on base, lamp alone is 9-1/2", no marks.
Oriental Woman with Mandolin on pedestal base, 11-1/2" high on base, lamp alone is

Oriental Boy 8-1/4" high, no marks.
Oriental Girl 8-1/4" high, no marks.

Oriental Girl & Boy, Doubles 9" high each, pink & yellow and green & yellow shown, no marks.

Oriental Man & Woman with Mandolin, same as previous in different colors on pedestal bases.

Oriental Man & Woman, Doubles, with flowing robes, 8-1/2" high each, no marks, two color variations shown.

Stagecoach with red and black cold paint decoration.
Courtesy of Sandy Kightlinger

Oriental Man with Mandolin 8" high, no marks.
Oriental Woman with Mandolin 8" high, no marks.

Different view of Anchor, Rope, & Stars lamp.

Anchor, Rope, and Stars shown in burgundy.
Marked: U.S.A. *Courtesy of Sandy Kightlinger*

Chapter 36: Miniatures

Among the first items that Shawnee produced were ornamental miniatures shown in this chapter. Some of these were designed specifically for the RumRill line, and were carried on in the Shawnee line through the early 1940s. Most are non-figural, with two known exceptions ..... the swan and the snail.

Miniatures have turned up with a variety of decorations added to them: cold painted flowers, decals, and souvenir labels. Most are found in plain solid pre-World War II colors.

Additional miniatures drilled with holes for use as **Salt & Pepper Shakers** will be found in that chapter.

Most miniatures are around **3 inches** in height, though a few do vary depending upon their design. I will make note only of those that differ considerably from this. All should be found with a glazed bottom and an impressed **U.S.A.** mark, though not all marks are legible on all pieces.

This shows a variety of **colors**, though some shapes are repeated:

Poinsettia Jug Flax Blue.
Embossed Basket Bright White.
Beaded Pedestal Vase Dark Green.
Poinsettia Jug Powder Blue.
Grecian Pitcher Burgundy.
Star Pitcher Yellow.
Poinsettia Jug Matt White.
Grecian Pitcher Shell Pink.
Urn Old English Ivory.
Jug with Bug Dusty Rose.
Flared Cornucopia Turquoise.

View of glazed bottoms and **U.S.A.** mark on miniatures.

Snail 2" high, and very narrow. Marked: U.S.A. Very hard to find! *Courtesy of Linda Guffey*

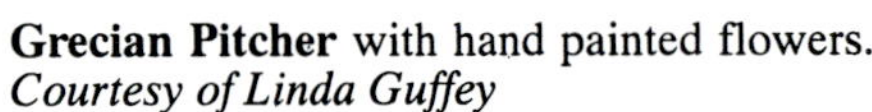

Grecian Pitcher with hand painted flowers. *Courtesy of Linda Guffey*

Star Pitcher with hand painted flowers. *Courtesy of Arthur & Rita Bee*

Display of shapes, left to right, top row to bottom row:

Woven Basket, rectangular.
Fluted Urn.
Embossed Basket, flared top.
Embossed Watering Can.
Double-Grip Urn.
Ribbed Top Bulb Bowl.
Embossed Pitcher on Log.
Shell.
Embossed Flower Pitcher.
Ribbed Top Double Handle Vase.
Embossed Flower & Leaves.
Cornucopia on Double Pedestal.
Pedestal Pitcher.
Swan.

Embossed Flower Pitcher with hand painted flowers. *Courtesy of Marvin Mulligan*

Embossed Watering Can with hand painted flowers. *Courtesy of Marvin Mulligan*

Jug with Bug with hand painted flowers. *Courtesy of Marvin Mulligan*

Embossed Basket, flared top, with hand painted flowers.
Tall Layered Leaf with *Souvenir of Powell, Wyo* label.
Urn with *Souvenir of Lexington, Va* label.

Urn with hand painted flowers.
Vase with hand painted flowers.
Courtesy of Terry & Sandra Bauer

Moon with Stars vase. *Courtesy of Arthur & Rita Bee*

Star Pitcher.

Embossed Loop Handle vase.

Spinning Wheel vase.

Embossed Flower & Leaves.

Feathered Handle vase.

Scalloped Top vase.

Embossed Bud Pitcher.

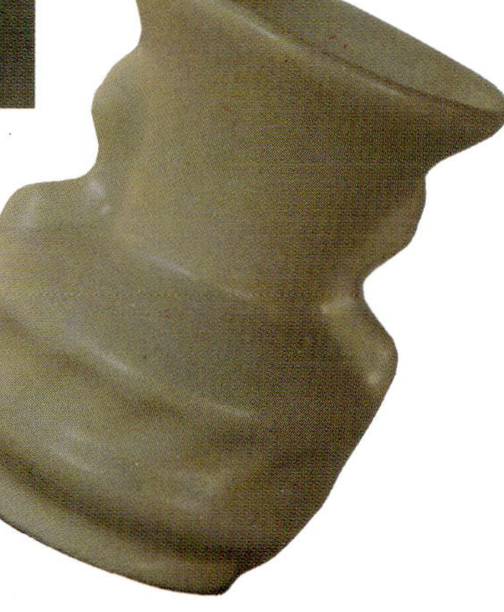

Swirl Bottom vase.

Flat Top Double Handle vase.

Fluted Cornucopia.

Ribbed Ewer.

Cornucopia on Rectangular Pedestal, 3-1/4" high.
Courtesy of Linda Guffey

Short Layered Leaf 2" high.

Tall Layered Leaf 3" high.

Flower Pot & Saucer 2-1/8" high.
Courtesy of Paul & Joy Schneider

Darn-Aide, 5" high, Design Patent 149,625 applied for June 5, 1947. These darning ladies are hollow bodied, open at the base, and come in a pink skirt or blue skirt. Marked: U.S.A.

Kiln Tester Goblets, 3-1/4" high, no discernible marks. Shown in burgundy, white, gray, yellow, and dark green. Various items were glazed and run through the kilns every day to make sure that the glaze colors were mixed properly for that days' production. Then these items were discarded, or placed in the Seconds Room for sale. At a height of 3-1/4", these are the same size and shape goblets that have turned up gilt entirely in gold or platinum, and sold with Smiley Pig or Chanticleer pitchers as beverage sets.
Courtesy of Robert & Betty Winning

Incense Burner, 5" high Oriental man with small hole at hands and round 1" diameter hole in back. Marked: U.S.A.
Left: Pink Incense Burner, plain.
Right: Pink Incense Burner, gold trim.

Incense Burner, 5" high Oriental man same as previous. Marked: U.S.A.
Top: Blue Incense Burner, plain.
Bottom: Blue Incense Burner, gold trim.

Shaving Mug, 3-1/4" high, embossed bust of George Washington on opposite end from handle, embossed stars around base. Marked: U.S.A.

Bottom view of George Washington shaving mug.

Pie Birds (Pie-Chic) 5" high, no discernible marks.
Left: Pie Bird wearing a paper apron which reads: "Directions For Use - Place Pie-chic in center of your pie and fit the upper crust snugly around the base above the slots. While the pie is baking steam will escape thru Pie-chic, the juices will be kept in and filling will not boil over."
Center: **Pink Pie Bird**.
Right: **Blue Pie Bird**.

Toby Mugs, 5-1/4", all marked U.S.A.
Old English Ivory (with some cold paint intact), Dusty Rose, Burgundy, Turquoise. *Other pre-World War II colors have turned up on these items.*

Embossed Ribbed Tumblers, 4-3/4", all marked U.S.A. White, Blue, Peach, Turquoise. *Courtesy of Paul & Linda Spenst*

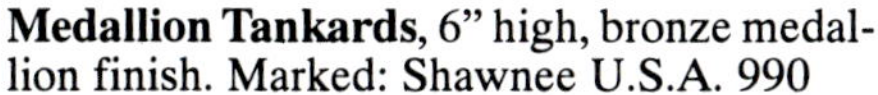

Medallion Tankards, 6" high, bronze medallion finish. Marked: Shawnee U.S.A. 990

Stars & Stripes Pitcher and Goblets.
Pitcher 6-1/4" high, yellow. Marked: U.S.A.
Goblets 3-1/2" high. Marked: U.S.A.

Stars & Stripes Pitcher and Goblets.
Pitcher 6-1/4" high, turquoise. Marked: U.S.A.
Goblets 3-1/2" high. Marked: U.S.A.

Jumbo Ice Server catalog sheet.
Pink Elephant ice server marketed under the Kenwood Ceramics line, 11" high, with a curling trunk handle, and a plastic-gasket seal in the lid for keeping in the cold. Holds two trays of ice cubes. Often, the pink color of the lids and bottoms do not match, making this appear to be mismatched. *Ice servers with the plastic-gasket seal missing will command a slightly lower price.*

Left: **Jumbo** with black collar, 11", Kenwood label. Marked: Kenwood U.S.A. 60
Right: **Jumbo** with white collar, 11". Marked: Shawnee U.S.A. 60

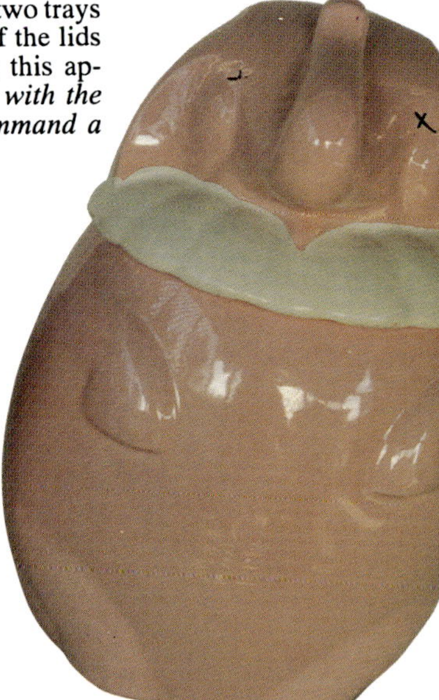

Plastic gasket seal on lid of Jumbo Ice Server.

Bird Candy Dish, 3-3/4" square. Marked: U.S.A.

Bird Candy Dish, Old English Ivory, 3-3/4" square. Marked: U.S.A.

Bon Bon Basket, Turquoise, 2-1/2" high. Marked U.S.A.

Bon Bon Shell, Antique Ivory, 2-1/2" high. Marked U.S.A.

Bon Bon Cornucopia, Turquoise, 2-1/2" high. Marked: U.S.A.

Bon Bon Dishes with fluted edges.
Left: **Oblong Bon Bon**, 5" long. Marked: U.S.A. 352
Right: **Oval Bon Bon**, 4-7/8" long. Marked: U.S.A. 351

Flying Geese Candy Dish, 9" long, also listed as an ashtray. Marked: Shawnee U.S.A. 403

Ribbed Mixing Bowls, set shown in yellow, blue, peach, ivory, and turquoise, with diameters of 5", 6", 7", 8", and 9". All Marked: U.S.A. *Courtesy of Ron Brown*

Back of Spoon Rest.

Spoon Rest, 5-3/4" long, also available in red. Marked: U.S.A.

Kenwood Brunch Bowl, 6" yellow, with criss cross pattern featuring culinary symbols such as teapots and eating utensils. Set of three bowls come in 6", 7", 8" diameters, in yellow, turquoise, and pink. Marked: Kenwood Oven Proof U.S.A. 942

Chapter 39: Miscellaneous - Rare

This chapter was not created to deflect in any way from the wonderful pieces of rare or hard-to-find Shawnee that appear in other chapters throughout this book. What it does contain, however, are items that the average collector will probably never be able to acquire, but can certainly appreciate knowing that they exist. Be sure to make note of all of the wonderful rare cookie jars, corn items, range sets, etc. that are pictured in other chapters of this book. Then perhaps you'll be prepared for the day when *you* will happen upon that rare Shawnee treasure!

Smiley Pig Child's Feeding Dish and Pitcher.
This fabulous pig feeding dish and milk pitcher are the only ones to turn up so far that could possibly be from the Child's Feeding Set, Design Patent 148,012 filed in 1946. It has not been determined if any of the patented feeding sets ever went into production. The dish is obviously a design change from what was drawn, but the pitcher matches the patent exactly. Note the wide-spaced prominent front feet, and the sloped opening on the head of the pitcher. Neither piece has any marking. *Too rare to determine value!*
From The Collection Of Paul & Joy Schneider

Different view of **Smiley Pig Feeding Dish**.

Back view of Smiley Pig Feeding Dish.

Smiley Pig Pitcher with embossed flowers draped over his left shoulder, rather than on his chest. This design matches the patent filed in 1944. Has a Shawnee sample label on the bottom, and is marked: Patented Smiley U.S.A. *Too rare to determine value!*
From The Collection of Sharon F. Figura

Bottom view of Smiley Pig Pitcher with sample label.

Left, Smiley Pig Pitcher with flowers on his chest.
Right, Smiley Pig Pitcher with rare flowers over left shoulder.

Indian Arrowhead Ashtray, 4-1/2" height, 3-1/4" width. Signed on the back with **R. Ganz**, this piece won the *Most Rare And Unusual Shawnee Pottery* award at the January 1993 Shawnee Pottery Collectors Convention in Daytona Beach, Florida.

What sets this particular ashtray apart from most, is that it was signed by designer Rudy V. Ganz. Most of these have been found marked only with the word **Shawnee**. *Too rare to determine value*!
From The Collection Of Francis K. Van Hooser

Back of Arrowhead Ashtray, with **R. Ganz** signature at lower right side of point.

Platter, **one-of-a-kind**, made at Shawnee. Shown is a black platter with etched stems and leaves; approximately 15-1/2 inches in diameter. No marks.
Approximately two dozen sales people and foremen each received a one-of-a-kind platter in a variety of designs and colors. These were originally designed by Bob Heckman for fun, and were never mass-produced. *Too rare to determine value!*
Courtesy of Robert & Pauline Heckman

Back of black etched Platter, no marks.

Muggsy Salt & Pepper Shakers in Original Shipping Carton.
Six brand new sets of Muggsy shakers are on the lower level of this air-cell shipping carton. Each shaker has an Essex China label intact. Sets are matched equally with five and four shaker holes. *Too rare to determine value!*
From The Collection Of Tony & Evadne Serra

Label on Box.
Masback Hardware Company of New York, New York, as distributors, made shipment of the Muggsy shakers to Adams Hardware of Dorchester, Massachusetts.

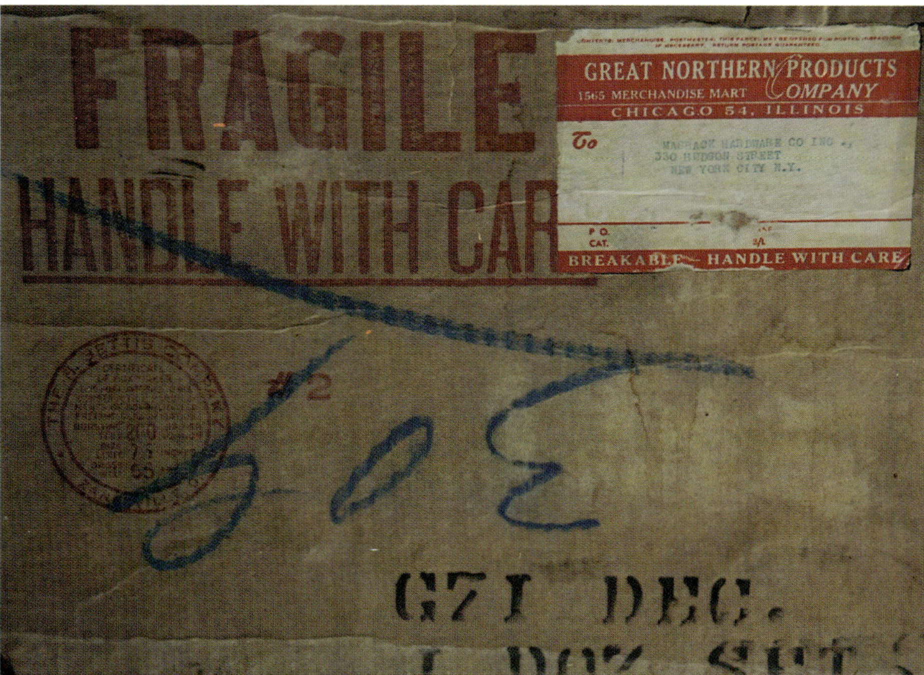

Cardboard Box and Labels.
Box company was A. Bettis Company in Zanesville, Ohio. Stamp indicates that one dozen sets of shakers were originally shipped, with half of those still resting in the box today, a half century later.
Great Northern Products Company of Chicago, Illinois, shows shipment of Muggsy shakers to Masback Hardware Co., Inc., of New York, New York.

Fruit and Basket Range Set - First Sample For Color.
Experimental range set showing the yellow sugar basket with sprayed red trim. The basket was changed to solid yellow to eliminate decorating both pieces. *Too rare to determine value!*
Courtesy of Robert & Pauline Heckman

Valencia Tumblers in pastel colors, 5-1/4" high, no marks. *Rare!*
From The Collection Of Rich & Linda Guffey

Shipping box information.

"Royal Kenwood" Ashtray 12-1/2" square. Marked: Kenwood U.S.A. 3001 4. *Too rare to determine value!*
Courtesy of John F. Bonistall

Mr. John F. Bonistall, former president of Shawnee Pottery writes: "The enclosed ashtray is representative of the **Royal Kenwood** line that was intended to be presented at the Spring 1961 Gift Shows. The colors were **Brown / White / Gold** plus **Green / White / Platinum**, and consisted of **Vases, Flower Bowls, Compotes, Candle Holders, Ashtrays and Planters.**"

This one-of-a-kind test piece was part of a new line to be presented in the Spring of 1961. This offering was never marketed because Shawnee Pottery closed its doors in January 1961. This ashtray was obviously done with the **Riviera** ashtray molds, as the sizes and markings are identical. Marks would have been changed when **Royal Kenwood** went into production. Regarding the size of this piece, Riviera Ashtray catalogs list it as 17", which is a diagonal measurement.

Back of Royal Kenwood test ashtray.

Royal Kenwood ashtray shown in shipping box.

Tulip Creamer and Tulip Ball Jug, underglaze decorated, blue embossed rope design around neck.
Left: **Creamer**, 4-1/4" high, Marked: U.S.A.
Right: **Ball Jug**, 64 oz. Marked: U.S.A.
Very Difficult To Find!
From The Collection Of Paul & Joy Schneider

Pauline's Cannibal planter, designed by Bob Heckman, but never went into production because the bowl was not large enough for a planter. No marks. *Too rare to determine value!*
Courtesy of Robert & Pauline Heckman

Back view of Pauline's Cannibal.

Little Kerchief Girl, standing on Corn King butter dish bottom. Marked: Oven Proof Shawnee U.S.A. 72
Rare!

Rabbit Eating Corn, on Corn King butter dish bottom. Marked: Oven Proof Shawnee U.S.A. 72
Rare!

Chapter 40: Tiles/ Ceramic Plaques

John F. Bonistall had set up a separate Architectural Ceramics Division in the 1950s, to market ceramic plaques for decorative surface treatments. One line was named *Artique*, and it was manufactured in twelve colors, in two styles/designs.

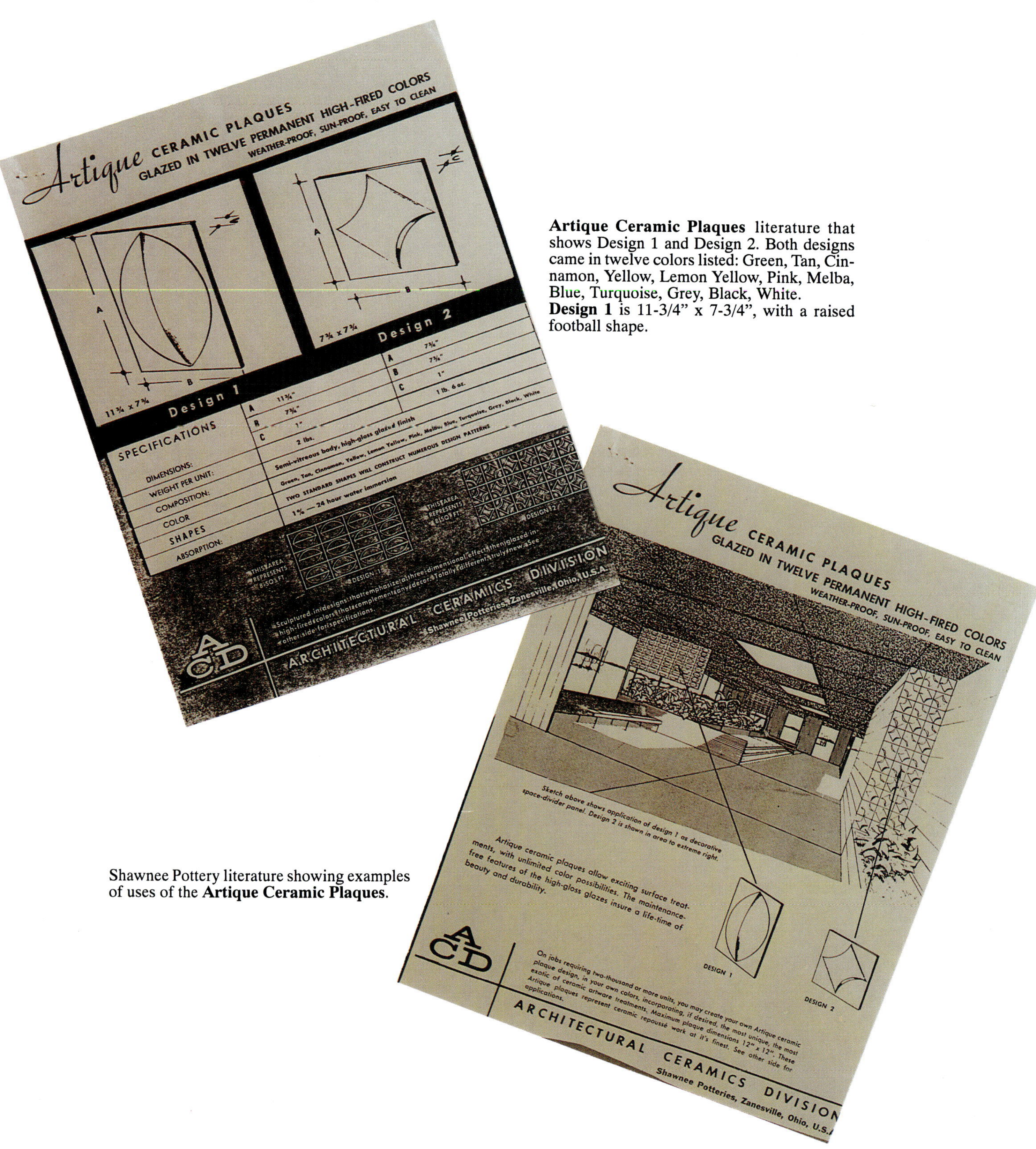

Artique Ceramic Plaques literature that shows Design 1 and Design 2. Both designs came in twelve colors listed: Green, Tan, Cinnamon, Yellow, Lemon Yellow, Pink, Melba, Blue, Turquoise, Grey, Black, White. **Design 1** is 11-3/4" x 7-3/4", with a raised football shape.

Shawnee Pottery literature showing examples of uses of the **Artique Ceramic Plaques**.

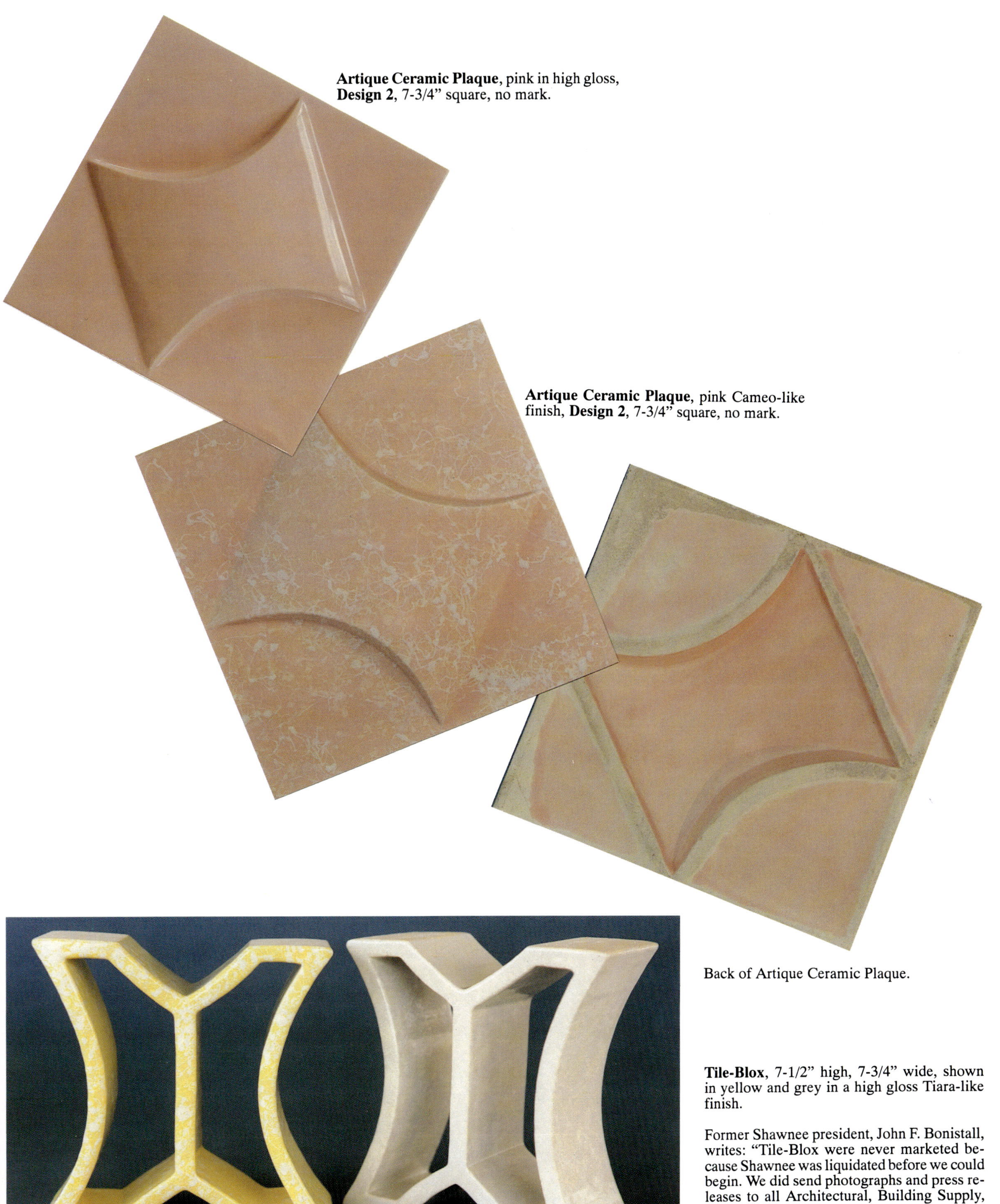

Artique Ceramic Plaque, pink in high gloss, **Design 2**, 7-3/4" square, no mark.

Artique Ceramic Plaque, pink Cameo-like finish, **Design 2**, 7-3/4" square, no mark.

Back of Artique Ceramic Plaque.

Tile-Blox, 7-1/2" high, 7-3/4" wide, shown in yellow and grey in a high gloss Tiara-like finish.

Former Shawnee president, John F. Bonistall, writes: "Tile-Blox were never marketed because Shawnee was liquidated before we could begin. We did send photographs and press releases to all Architectural, Building Supply, and Decorator magazines, and the response was very favorable. These items were never costed-out, nor a retail price determined."

CHAPTER 41: TOBACCIANA

A large number of the ashtrays pictured in this chapter were produced during the 1950s, when every coffee table and end table in America had these displayed. How times have changed!

For additional tobacciana, see the **Miscellaneous Rare** chapter and the **1950s Floral Ware**, most notably the **Confetti** line for an example of the Monte Carlo Ashtray.

Indian Arrowhead Ashtray, 4-1/2" high, 3-1/4" wide. Marked: Shawnee

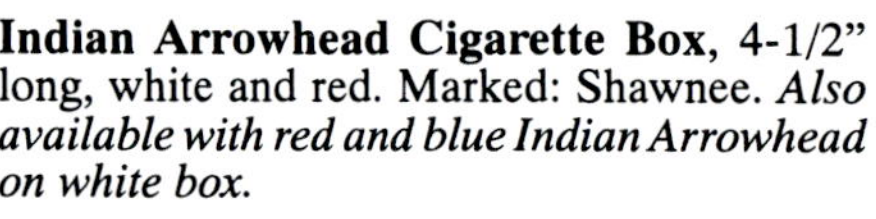

Indian Arrowhead Cigarette Box, 4-1/2" long, white and red. Marked: Shawnee. *Also available with red and blue Indian Arrowhead on white box.*

Cigarette Box, 5-1/2" long, two compartments, Surf Green. Marked: U.S.A. 682

Indian Arrowhead Cigarette Box, 4-1/2" long, 3-1/4" wide, brown. Marked: Shawnee

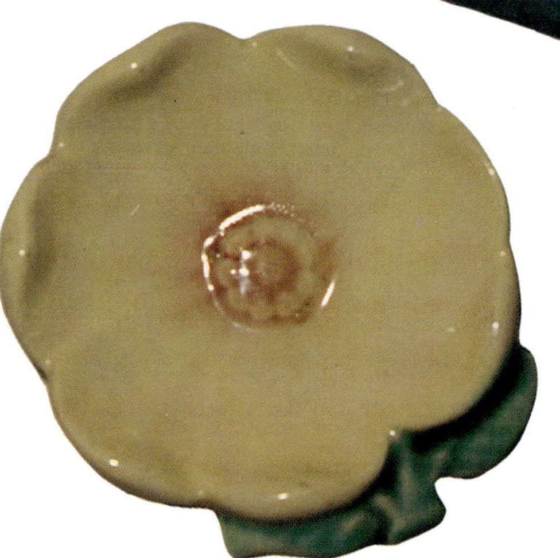

Magnolia Blossom Ashtray, 4-3/4" long. Marked: U.S.A. (A644).

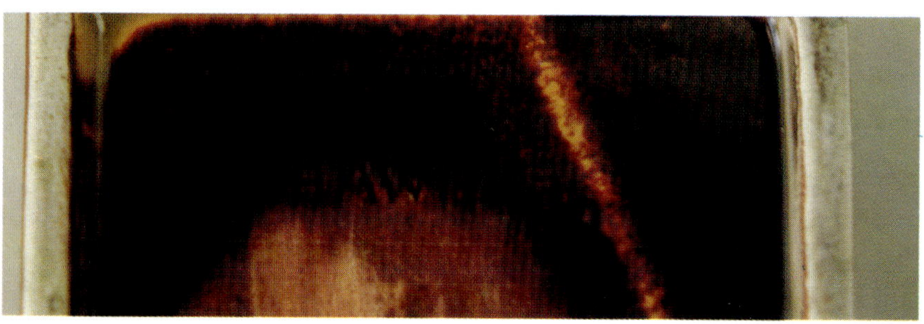

Shawnee mark on Arrowhead cigarette box.

Cigarette Box and Matching Ashtrays, pink with Kashäni bisque exterior.
Cigarette Box, Marked: Kenwood U.S.A. 3016
Ashtrays, Marked: Kenwood U.S.A. 3018

Confetti Cigarette Box and Matching Ashtrays, pink on charcoal.
Cigarette Box, 5-1/2" long. Marked: Kenwood U.S.A. 2120
Ashtrays, 4-1/2" long. Marked: Kenwood U.S.A. 2122

Lid of Confetti cigarette box showing rubber gasket.

Squirrel Ashtray, 3" high, no marks. (A633). Shown in Turquoise, Powder Blue, Dusty Rose. Also Listed: Old English Ivory, Burgundy, Flax Blue.

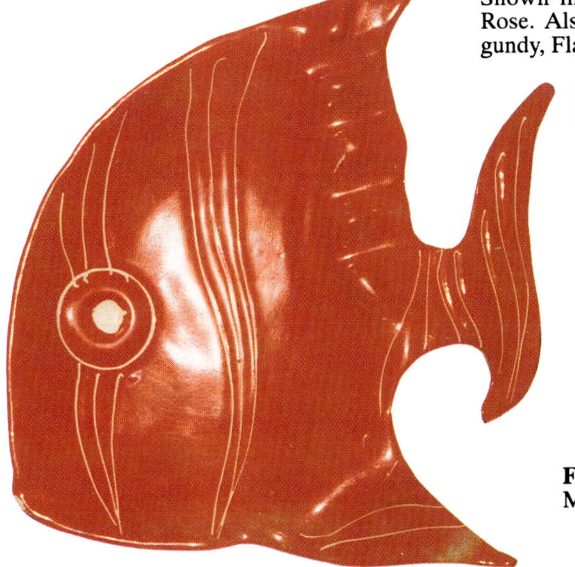

Fish Ashtray, 6" high, 7" long, red & white. Marked: Shawnee U.S.A. 402

Fish Ashtray, 6" high, 7" long, black & white. Marked: Shawnee U.S.A. 402

Maple Leaf Ashtray, 5" wide. Marked: U.S.A. 350

Flying Geese Ashtray, 9" long. Marked: Shawnee U.S.A. 403
Heavily decorated. *Also listed as* ***Candy Dish***.

Panther and Paws Ashtray Set, black and beige, panther ashtray is 12-1/4" long. Marked: Kenwood U.S.A. 2201

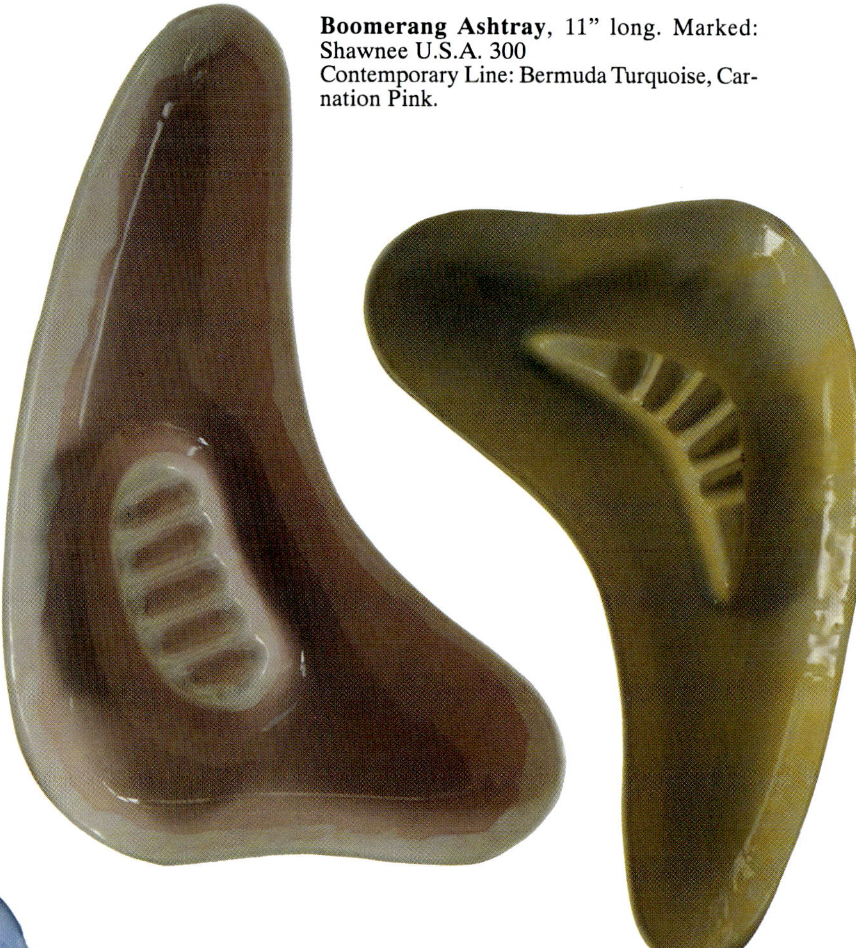

Boomerang Ashtray, 11" long. Marked: Shawnee U.S.A. 300
Contemporary Line: Bermuda Turquoise, Carnation Pink.

Modern Ashtray, 11" long. Marked: Shawnee U.S.A. 301
Hostess Line: Aqua, Pink, Yellow.

Sombrero Ashtray, 10" diameter, no mark.
Pictured with small jardiniere for design comparison.

Flair Ashtray, 9-1/4" long. Marked: Shawnee U.S.A. 408
Contemporary Line: Stardust Pink, Stardust Turquoise.

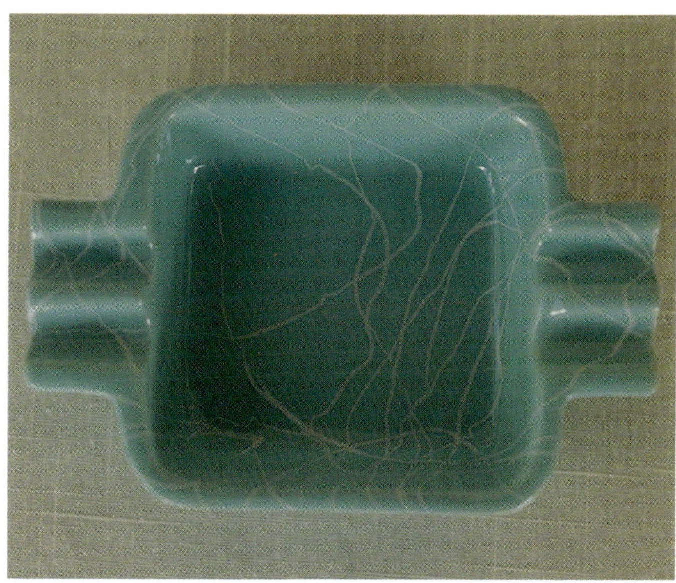

Square Ashtray, 5-1/4" square. Marked: Shawnee U.S.A. 409
Contemporary Line: Vined Turquoise, Vined Pink.

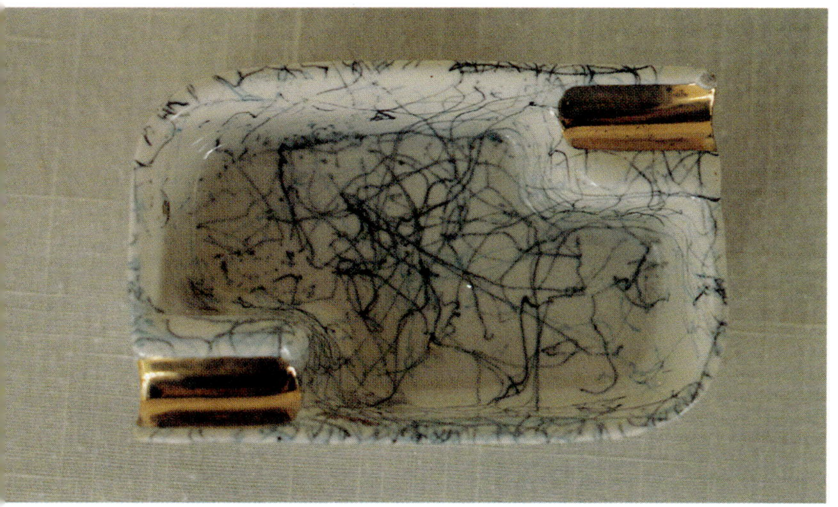

Rectangle Ashtray with Gold, 4-1/2" long,
Vined White. Marked: U.S.A. 401

Square Ashtray, 5" long. Marked: Shawnee U.S.A. 410
Turquoise, Pink, in Stardust Treatment.

Oval Ashtray, 5" diameter. Marked: Shawnee U.S.A. 210
Hostess Line: Onyx, Greenfire, Bronze.

Modern Ashtray, 10" long. Marked: Shawnee
U.S.A. 407
Vined Pink, Vined Turquoise.

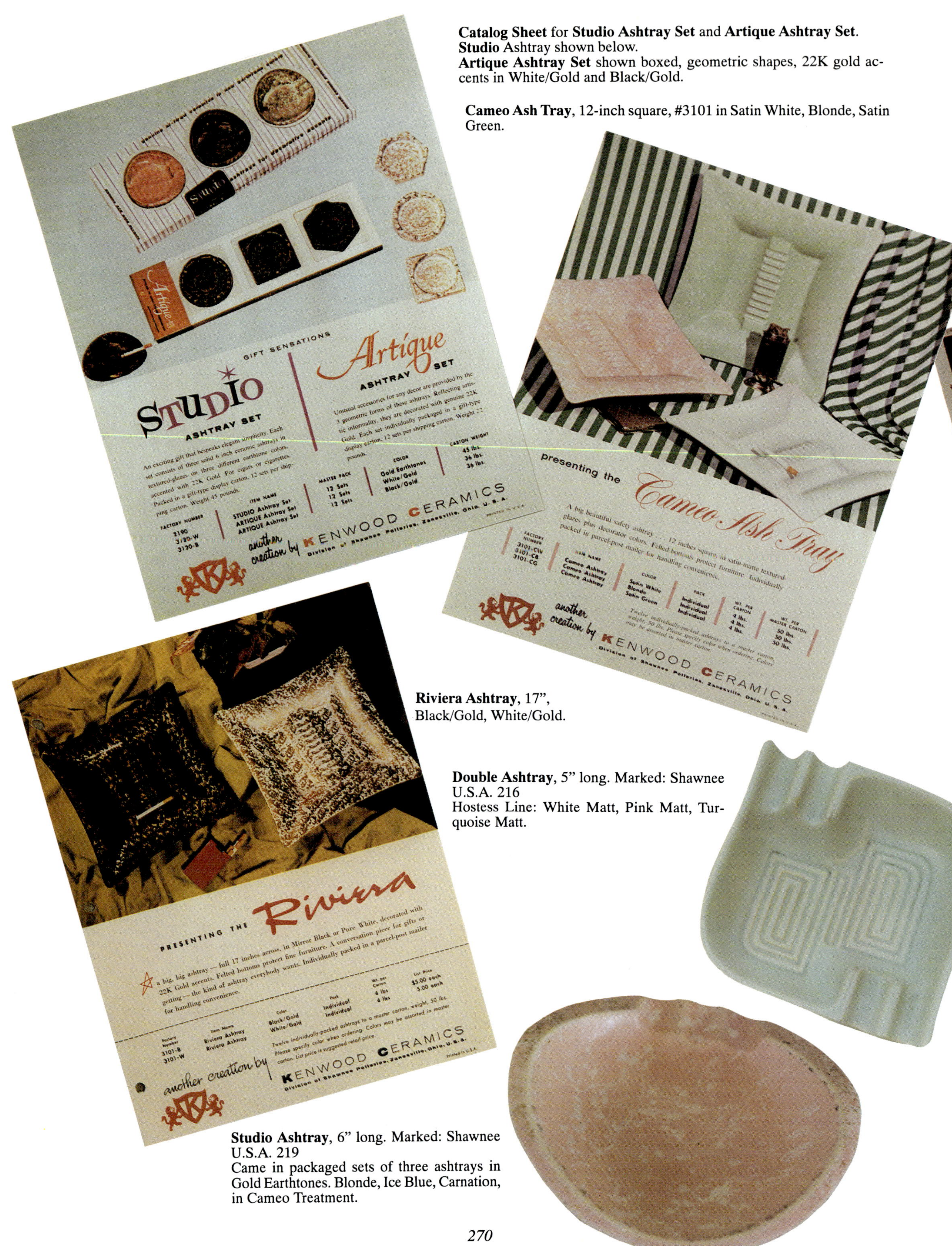

Catalog Sheet for **Studio Ashtray Set** and **Artique Ashtray Set**.
Studio Ashtray shown below.
Artique Ashtray Set shown boxed, geometric shapes, 22K gold accents in White/Gold and Black/Gold.

Cameo Ash Tray, 12-inch square, #3101 in Satin White, Blonde, Satin Green.

Riviera Ashtray, 17", Black/Gold, White/Gold.

Double Ashtray, 5" long. Marked: Shawnee U.S.A. 216
Hostess Line: White Matt, Pink Matt, Turquoise Matt.

Studio Ashtray, 6" long. Marked: Shawnee U.S.A. 219
Came in packaged sets of three ashtrays in Gold Earthtones. Blonde, Ice Blue, Carnation, in Cameo Treatment.

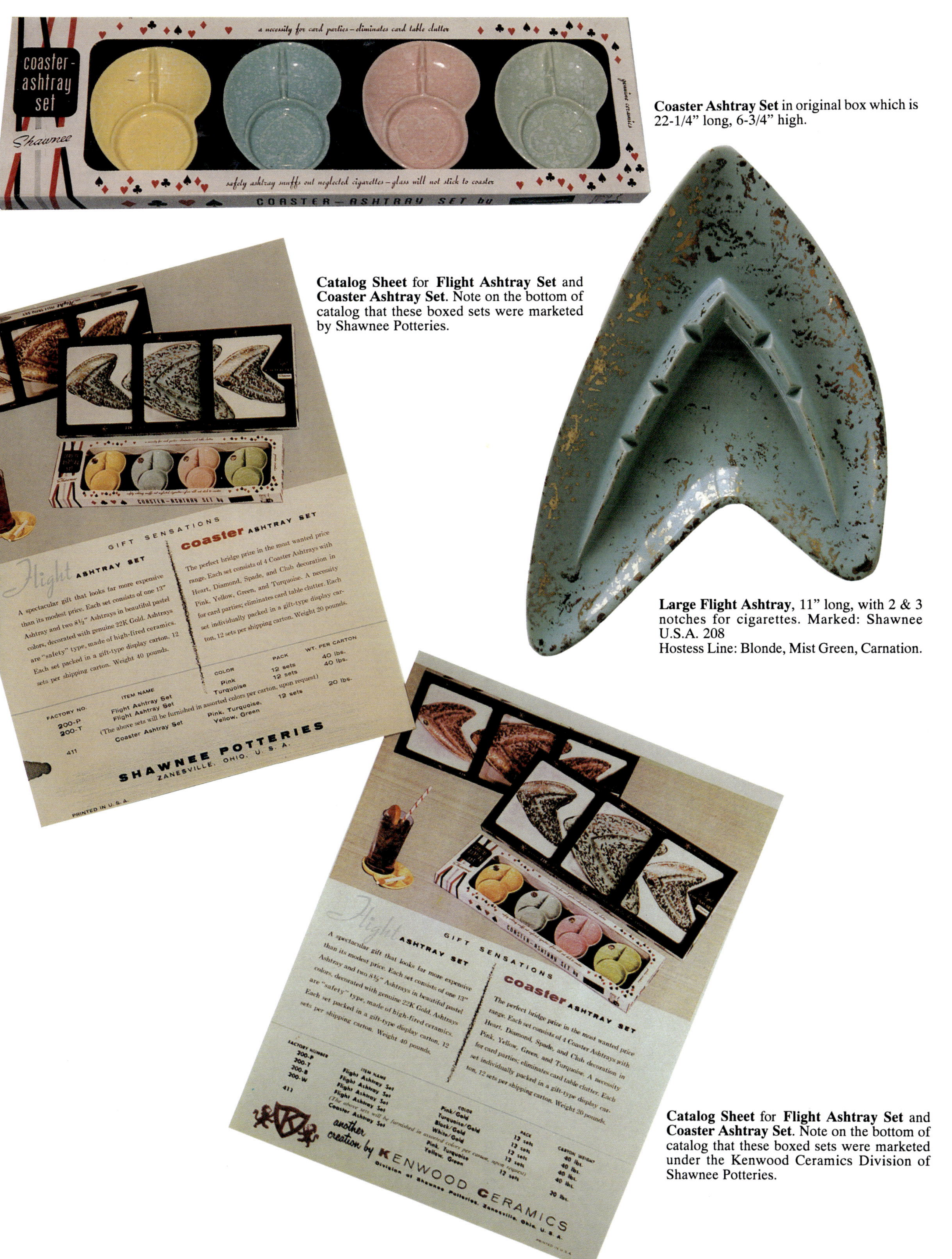

Coaster Ashtray Set in original box which is 22-1/4" long, 6-3/4" high.

GIFT SENSATIONS

Flight ASHTRAY SET

A spectacular gift that looks far more expensive than its modest price. Each set consists of one 13" Ashtray and two 8½" Ashtrays in beautiful pastel colors, decorated with genuine 22K Gold. Ashtrays are "safety" type, made of high-fired ceramics. Each set packed in a gift-type display carton, 12 sets per shipping carton. Weight 40 pounds.

coaster ASHTRAY SET

The perfect bridge prize in the most wanted price range. Each set consists of 4 Coaster Ashtrays with Heart, Diamond, Spade, and Club decoration in Pink, Yellow, Green, and Turquoise. A necessity for card parties; eliminates card table clutter. Each set individually packed in a gift-type display carton, 12 sets per shipping carton. Weight 20 pounds.

FACTORY NO.	ITEM NAME	COLOR	PACK	WT. PER CARTON
200-P	Flight Ashtray Set	Pink	12 sets	40 lbs.
200-T	Flight Ashtray Set	Turquoise	12 sets	40 lbs.
	(The above sets will be furnished in assorted colors per carton, upon request)			
411	Coaster Ashtray Set	Pink, Turquoise, Yellow, Green	12 sets	20 lbs.

SHAWNEE POTTERIES
ZANESVILLE, OHIO, U.S.A.

PRINTED IN U.S.A.

Catalog Sheet for **Flight Ashtray Set** and **Coaster Ashtray Set**. Note on the bottom of catalog that these boxed sets were marketed by Shawnee Potteries.

Large Flight Ashtray, 11" long, with 2 & 3 notches for cigarettes. Marked: Shawnee U.S.A. 208
Hostess Line: Blonde, Mist Green, Carnation.

Flight ASHTRAY SET

GIFT SENSATIONS

A spectacular gift that looks far more expensive than its modest price. Each set consists of one 13" Ashtray and two 8½" Ashtrays in beautiful pastel colors, decorated with genuine 22K Gold. Ashtrays are "safety" type, made of high-fired ceramics. Each set packed in a gift-type display carton, 12 sets per shipping carton. Weight 40 pounds.

coaster ASHTRAY SET

The perfect bridge prize in the most wanted price range. Each set consists of 4 Coaster Ashtrays with Heart, Diamond, Spade, and Club decoration in Pink, Yellow, Green, and Turquoise. A necessity for card parties; eliminates card table clutter. Each set individually packed in a gift-type display carton, 12 sets per shipping carton. Weight 20 pounds.

FACTORY NUMBER	ITEM NAME	COLOR	PACK	CARTON WEIGHT
200-P	Flight Ashtray Set	Pink/Gold	12 sets	40 lbs.
200-T	Flight Ashtray Set	Turquoise/Gold	12 sets	40 lbs.
200-B	Flight Ashtray Set	Black/Gold	12 sets	40 lbs.
200-W	Flight Ashtray Set	White/Gold	12 sets	40 lbs.
	(The above sets will be furnished in assorted colors per carton, upon request)			
411	Coaster Ashtray Set	Pink, Turquoise, Yellow, Green	12 sets	20 lbs.

another creation by KENWOOD CERAMICS
Division of Shawnee Potteries, Zanesville, Ohio, U.S.A.

Catalog Sheet for **Flight Ashtray Set** and **Coaster Ashtray Set**. Note on the bottom of catalog that these boxed sets were marketed under the Kenwood Ceramics Division of Shawnee Potteries.

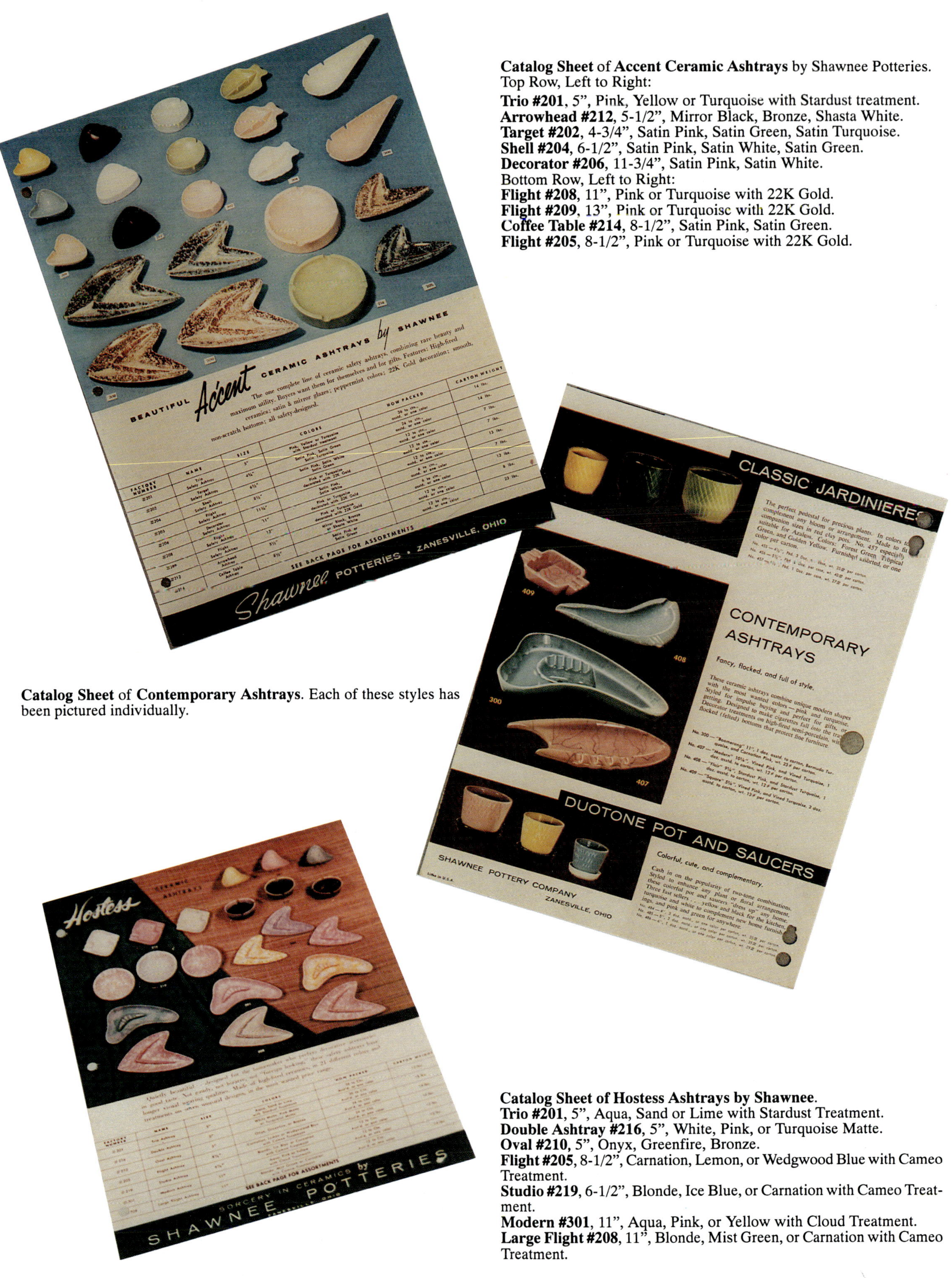

Catalog Sheet of **Accent Ceramic Ashtrays** by Shawnee Potteries.
Top Row, Left to Right:
Trio #201, 5", Pink, Yellow or Turquoise with Stardust treatment.
Arrowhead #212, 5-1/2", Mirror Black, Bronze, Shasta White.
Target #202, 4-3/4", Satin Pink, Satin Green, Satin Turquoise.
Shell #204, 6-1/2", Satin Pink, Satin White, Satin Green.
Decorator #206, 11-3/4", Satin Pink, Satin White.
Bottom Row, Left to Right:
Flight #208, 11", Pink or Turquoise with 22K Gold.
Flight #209, 13", Pink or Turquoise with 22K Gold.
Coffee Table #214, 8-1/2", Satin Pink, Satin Green.
Flight #205, 8-1/2", Pink or Turquoise with 22K Gold.

Catalog Sheet of **Contemporary Ashtrays**. Each of these styles has been pictured individually.

Catalog Sheet of Hostess Ashtrays by Shawnee.
Trio #201, 5", Aqua, Sand or Lime with Stardust Treatment.
Double Ashtray #216, 5", White, Pink, or Turquoise Matte.
Oval #210, 5", Onyx, Greenfire, Bronze.
Flight #205, 8-1/2", Carnation, Lemon, or Wedgwood Blue with Cameo Treatment.
Studio #219, 6-1/2", Blonde, Ice Blue, or Carnation with Cameo Treatment.
Modern #301, 11", Aqua, Pink, or Yellow with Cloud Treatment.
Large Flight #208, 11", Blonde, Mist Green, or Carnation with Cameo Treatment.

CHAPTER 42: WALL POCKETS

Wall pockets were once popular for hanging on the wall with either small plants in them, to root plants with, or make silk flower arrangements in them. Today, an arrangement of wall pockets on a wall can make a very attractive display. Many of Shawnee's later wall pockets were made with flat bases so that they could also be used as vases or planters on a shelf.

Scottie Dog shown from side.

Scottie Dog, 9-1/2" high x 5-1/2" wide, no marks, green.

Cornucopia and Butterfly *, 6" long, no marks. Shown in Bright White with red and black cold painted butterfly.

Scottie Dog, 9-1/2" high x 5-1/2" wide, no marks, Burgundy.
An impressive piece of pottery, and many people are amazed at its large size. Designed by Louise Elizabeth Bauer, it was produced during Shawnee's very early years. Confirmed colors are Old Ivory, Burgundy, Yellow, and Green, and may also be found in any of the solid colors of the early years.
Courtesy of Rich & Linda Guffey

Cornucopia and Bird, 6" long, cold painted eyes and beak, no marks. Shown in Powder Blue, Old Ivory, Dusty Rose (V476).

Star, embossed with Moon, Stars, Clouds, 6" high, no marks. Colors listed: Antique Ivory, Off White, Turquoise.

Daffodil, embossed, 6-3/4" long. Marked: U.S.A. Shown: Dark Green (front), Matt White (back), Turquoise (front).

Bird House, 6" high. Marked: U.S.A. (V466). Bright White with underglaze decoration.

Tropical Fruit, 6-1/2" long, 5-1/2" wide at top. Marked: U.S.A. Colors listed: Turquoise, Antique Ivory, Off White.
Note: Butler Brothers calls this Tropical Fruit, though I think it looks more like a flower.

Sunflower, 6-3/4" diameter. Marked: U.S.A. Colors listed: Antique Ivory, Off White, Turquoise.

Sunflower shown from back.

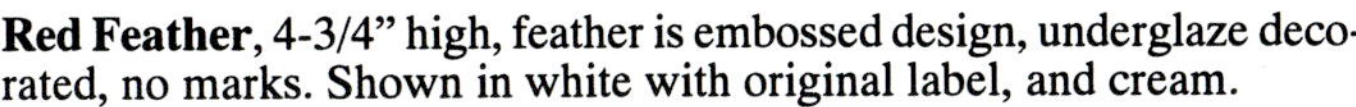

Red Feather, 4-3/4" high, feather is embossed design, underglaze decorated, no marks. Shown in white with original label, and cream.

Fluted Wall Pockets, no marks, shown front, and back with Shawnee Sample Label, chartreuse. *Courtesy of Melvin & Jean Gibson*

Red Feather, 4-3/4" high, no marks. Purple trim outlines entire wall pocket.

Wheat, 4-3/4" high, wheat is embossed design, underglaze decorated, no marks.

Post WW-II Wallpockets, which may be hung on wall or set on shelf. All have sprayed underglaze decoration, and each may also be found with gold trim.

Top Row:
Bow, 4" high. Marked: U.S.A. 434
Lovebirds at House, 5-3/4" high. Marked: U.S.A. 830
Lovebirds at House, 5-3/4" high. Marked: U.S.A. 830

Center Row:
Grandfather Clock, 7" high. Marked: U.S.A. 1261
Mantel Clock, 6" high. Marked: U.S.A. 530
Telephone, 6" high. Marked: U.S.A. 529

Bottom Row:
Mary and Lamb, 5" high. Marked: U.S.A. 586
Little Jack Horner, 5" high. Marked: U.S.A. 585
Girl with Rag Doll, 6-1/4" high. Marked: U.S.A. 810

Girl with Rag Doll. Three color variations. Note the doll's hair matches the little girl's. *Courtesy of Paul & Linda Spenst*

Girl with Rag Doll, 6-1/4" high, gold trim and hand painted flower on hat. Marked: U.S.A. 810
Courtesy of Robert & Lois Duvall

Left: **Girl with Rag Doll**, 6-1/4" high, gold trim. Marked: U.S.A. 810
Right: **Girl with Rag Doll**, 6-1/4" high, gold trim and rose decal on hat. Marked: U.S.A. 810
Courtesy of Paul & Joy Schneider

Lovebirds at House, 5-3/4" high, gold trim. Marked: U.S.A. 830

Mantel Clock, 6" high, gold trim. Marked: U.S.A. 530

Section IX: 1950s Floral Ware

Chapter 43: Lines

Cameo (#2500)

Sorcery In Ceramics By Shawnee
Numbered 2500 Series

Introduced in Catalog No. 26, dated 1960, Cameo was one of the last lines produced at Shawnee. This high-fired, semi-porcelain ceramic artware was shaped and modeled after Fenton Glass.

Cameo Floral Ware.
#2501 Flower Bowl 5".
#2502 Flower Bowl 6".
#2503 Centerpiece Planter 10".
#2504 Fan Planter 6-1/2".
#2505 Windowbox 10".
#2506 Windowbox 14".
#2507 Urn Planter 8-1/2".
#2508 Jardiniere 4".
#2509 Jardiniere 5".
#2510 Jardiniere 6".
#2511 Jardiniere 7".
#2512 Flower Vase 9".
#2513 Bouquet Vase 9".
#2514 Flared Vase 10".
#2515 Bouquet Vase 11".
#2516 Flower Vase 12".

Cameo Catalog Cover.

Cameo Grouping.

Chantilly (#1800)

Sorcery In Ceramics By Shawnee
Numbered 1800 Series

Introduced in Catalog No. 21, dated 1958, Chantilly was described as a cascade of ceramic lace in exquisite colors over capacious designs. Rich, brass-colored bases, with smooth bottoms protect fine furniture. Spray wax from the Sinclair Oil Co. was used to create this texture.

Chantilly.

#1801 Scalloped Planter 3-1/2".
#1802 Pulpit Planter 4-1/2".
#1803 Oblong Planter 7-1/2".
#1804 Square Planter 5".
#1805 Square Planter 6".
#1806 Square Planter 7".
#1807 Flared Jardiniere 4-1/2".
#1808 Flared Jardiniere 6-1/2".
#1809 Flared Jardiniere 8".
#1810 Window Box, rectangular 9".
#1811 Window Box, rectangular 12".
#1812 W[illegible]ndow Box, rectangular 15".
#18[illegible] [illegible]enterpiece Planter 10".
#1814 Pagoda Planter 12".
#1815 Console Planter 17-1/2".
#1816 Bud Vase 10".
#1817 Floral Vase 8".
#1818 Bouquet Vase 9".
#1819 Floral Vase 10".
#1820 Bouquet Vase 11".

Chantilly Catalog Cover.

Chantilly **Pulpit Planter #1802** and Chantilly **Floral Vase #1819**.

Cherie (#1900)

In Autumn Colors By Shawnee
Numbered 1900 Series

Cherie was introduced in Catalog No. 28 as being new for late Fall and Christmas merchandising (this presumably being the 1960 season). Shawnee had taken six of their shapes from the Petit-Point line and created vibrant fall colors for the decorated bisque surface, combined with a white glazed interior, and gold decorated base. The same shape numbers on the bottoms appear in both lines.

Cherie Artware Catalog Sheet.
#1902 Square Planter 5".
#1904 Square Planter 7".
#1905 Windowbox 8".
#1906 Windowbox 11".
#1908 Jardiniere 5".
#1909 Jardiniere 6".

Cherie **Jardiniere #1908** and Cherie **Square Planter #1902**.

Confetti (#2100)

Kenwood Ceramics By Shawnee
Numbered 2100 Series

Kenwood Ceramics, a division of Shawnee Pottery, introduced Confetti as unique beauty in a 3-D glaze. This nubbly-textured line had felted bases to prevent damage to furniture. The three listed colors are White on Black, Pink on Charcoal, and Chartreuse on Brown.

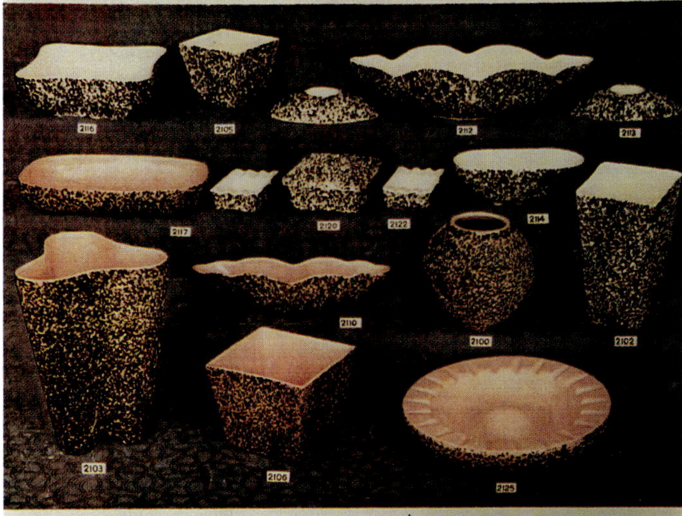

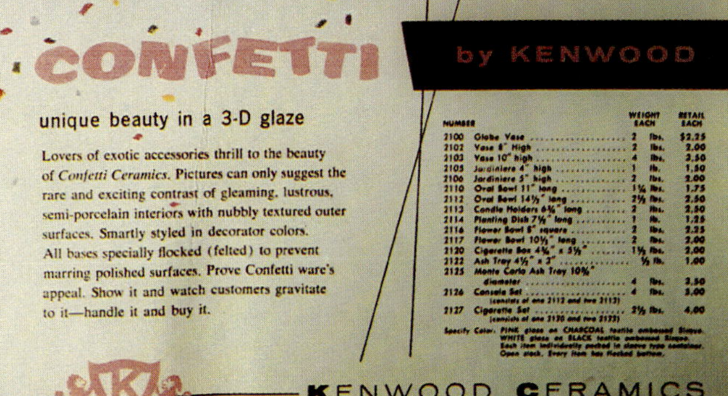

Confetti Catalog Sheet.
#2100 Globe Vase.
#2102 Vase 8".
#2103 Vase 10".
#2105 Jardiniere 4".
#2106 Jardiniere 5".
#2110 Oval Bowl 11".
#2112 Oval Bowl 14-1/2".
#2113 Candle Holders 6-3/4".
#2114 Planting Dish 7-1/2".
#2116 Flower Bowl 8".
#2117 Flower Bowl 10-1/2".
#2120 Cigarette Box.
#2122 Ash Tray.
#2125 Monte Carlo Ash Tray 10-3/4" diameter.

Confetti Oval Bowl #2112 and Candle Holders #2113 (Console Set #2126).

Diora (#1600)

Kenwood Ceramics By Shawnee
Numbered 1600 Series

This textured gold bisque finish is enhanced by white high-fired glazes. We cannot precisely date this line, but the Kenwood Division was created around 1953.

Diora TV Planter #1604 with Kenwood label. *Courtesy of Sue Blodgett*

Diora Catalog Cover.

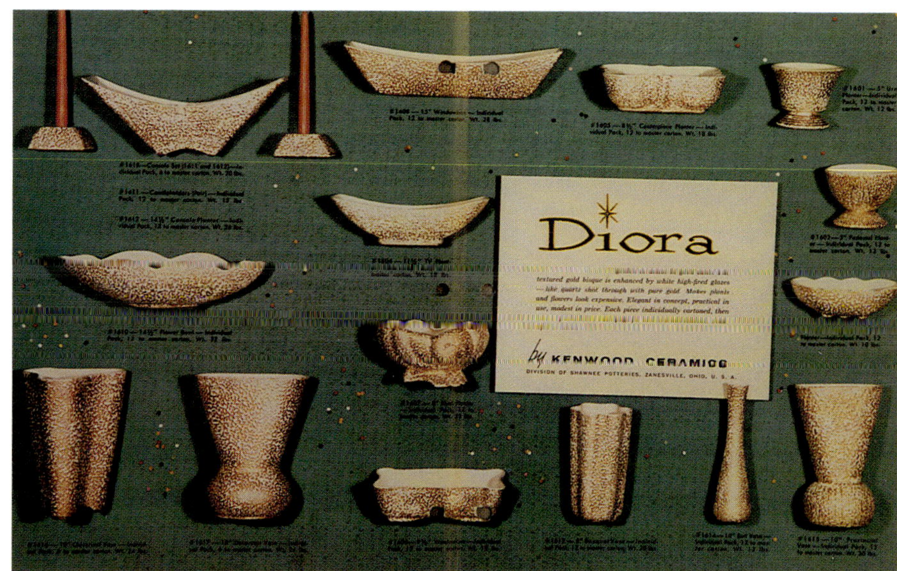

Diora Catalog.
#1601 Urn 5".
#1602 Pedestal Planter 5".
#1603 Scalloped Planter 7-1/2".
#1604 TV Planter 11-1/2".
#1605 Centerpiece Planter 8-1/2".
#1606 Windowbox 9-1/2".
#1607 Shell Planter 8".
#1608 Windowbox 15".
#1610 Flower Bowl 14-1/2".
#1611 Candleholders.
#1612 Console Planter 14-1/2".
#1613 Bouquet Vase 8".
#1614 Bud Vase 10".
#1615 Provincial Vase 10".
#1616 Cloverleaf Vase 10".
#1617 Decorator Vase 10".

Elegance (#1400)

Sorcery In Ceramics By Shawnee
Numbered 1400 Series

Elegance was introduced in Catalog No. 23, dated 1959, as having the gleam of rich silks and satins over classic and contemporary designs. Some of these colors have an almost iridescent look to them, and are listed as: Golden Beige, Satin Pink, Coral, Sterling White, Sable, Crystal Green, Turquoise, Bittersweet, Tropical Green, Canary.

Elegance Cone Planter #1411. *Courtesy of Melvin & Jean Gibson*

Elegance Catalog Cover.

Elegance Catalog.
#1401 Urn Planter 5".
#1402 Bud Vase 11".
#1403 Jardiniere 5".
#1404 Square Windowbox 4".
#1405 Pedestal Planter 5".
#1406 Freeform Planter 7".
#1407 Flared Planter 8-1/2".
#1408 Modern Vase 9".
#1409 Classic Flower Bowl 6".
#1410 Windowbox 9".
#1411 Cone Planter 7".
#1412 Jardiniere 6".
#1413 Flared Planter 12".
#1414 Cone Vase 12".
#1415 Windowbox 15".
#1416 Jardiniere 7".
#1417 Console Planter 18".
#1418 Shell Flower Bowl 8".

Elegance Grouping, Window Box #1404, Candle Holders #1419, Freeform Planter #1406, Bud Vase #1402.

Fairy Wood (#1200)

Sorcery In Ceramics By Shawnee
Numbered 1200 Series

Fairy Wood was introduced in Catalog No. 20, August 1, 1957, as having a decorated bisque exterior, high-fired glazes, and smooth bottoms that protect fine furniture. All planters "nest" to conserve counter space for the retailer. The unique texture of this line was created by using sandblasted plywood, which was then enhanced with beautiful blossom colors. Colors listed are: White, Blonde, Orchid, Blossom Pink, Turquoise, Jonquil Yellow, Meadow Green, Apricot, Apple Green, Driftwood Gray.

Fairy Wood Catalog.
#1201 Square Planter 4-1/2".
#1202 Square Planter 5".
#1203 Square Planter 6".
#1204 Square Planter 7".
#1205 Windowbox 9", rectangular.
#1206 Windowbox 12", rectangular.
#1207 Windowbox 15", rectangular.
#1208 Vase 8".
#1209 Vase 9".
#1210 Modern Vase 10".
#1211 Modern Vase 11".
#1212 Modern Vase 8-1/2".

Fairy Wood Grouping, Vase #1208, Windowbox #1205, Square Planter #1201.

Fairy Wood Catalog Cover.

Fernware (#1700)

By Shawnee
Numbered 1700 Series

Fernware was introduced in Catalog No. 24, which dates it to approximately 1959 or 1960. High-fired glazes were listed in the following colors: Green, White, Yellow, Pink, Turquoise, and Beige.

Fernware Catalog.
#1701 Planter 5".
#1702 Flower Bowl 7-1/2".
#1703 Square Planter 7".
#1704 Windowbox 8".
#1705 Windowbox 11-1/2".
#1706 Windowbox 14".
#1707 Jardiniere 4".
#1708 Jardiniere 5".
#1709 Jardiniere 6".
(Apologies for the glare, but this photo was taken years ago, and could not be duplicated.)

Back side of **Fernware** catalog.

Fernware Windowbox #1705.

Fernware Jardiniere #1708.

Kashäni (#3000)

Studio Ceramics By Kenwood
Numbered 3000 Series

Kashäni is a semi-porcelain ceramic, with high-fired glazes, and a decorated bisque finish. The richly exotic colors listed were: Persian Red with Gold, Black with Gold, and White with Gold; with complementary interior colors. The bottoms were satin-smooth to protect furniture, and the stands were triple-plated brass. Kashäni was named after the exquisite pottery created by ancient Persian potters in Kashän.

Kashäni Lydian Vase #3008.

Kashäni Catalog Cover.

Kashäni Crescent Planter #3009.

Kashäni.

#3001 Chaldean Vase 14".
#3002 Chaldean Vase 11".
#3003 Vestal Vase 9".
#3004 Persian Planter 7".
#3005 Corinth Vase 11".
#3006 Magnum Vase 10".
#3007 Chalice Vase 9".
#3008 Lydian Vase 8".
#3009 Crescent Planter 14".
#3010 Elysian Planter 14".
#3011 Cathay Planter 9".
#3012 Parthian Planter 8".
#3013 Lydian Jardiniere 5".
#3014 Lydian Jardiniere 4".
#3015 3-Pc. Crescent Console Set.
#3016 4-Pc. Cigarette Set.
#3017 Crescent Candleholders.
#3018 Kashäni Ashtrays.

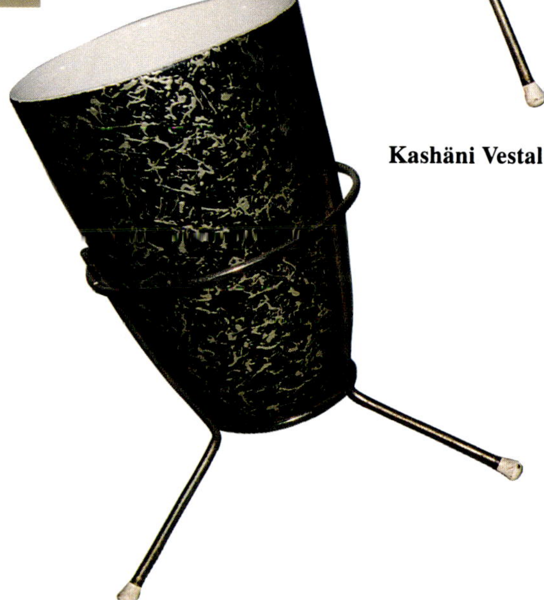

Kashäni Vestal Vase #3003.

Liäna (#1000)

Sorcery In Ceramics By Shawnee
Numbered 1000 Series

Liäna was introduced in Catalog No. 18, dated 1957, as a line of planters and vases. High gloss interiors are contrasted with bisque finish exteriors that have a metallic vining decoration. This vining effect was created by using a rubber cement spray, and was produced in three colors of Gold, Silver, and Copper.

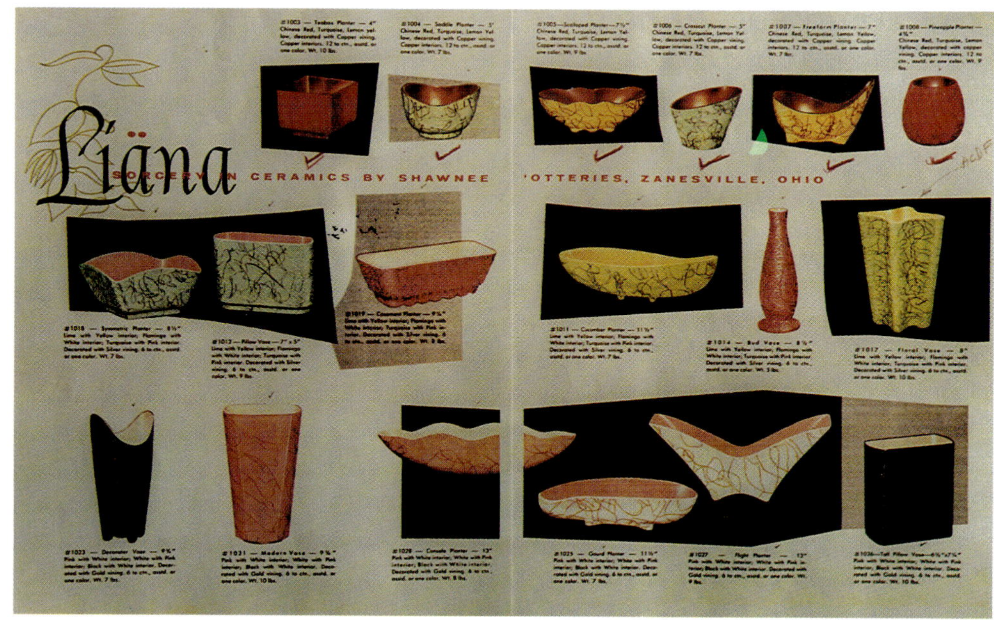

Liäna.

#1003 Teabox Planter 4".
#1004 Saddle Planter 5".
#1005 Scalloped Planter 7-1/2".
#1006 Crosscut Planter 5".
#1007 Freeform Planter 7".
#1008 Pineapple Planter 4-1/4".
#1011 Cucumber Planter 11-1/2".
#1012 Pillow Vase 7" x 5".
#1014 Bud Vase 8-1/2".
#1017 Floral Vase 8".
#1018 Symmetric Planter 8-1/2".
#1019 Casement Planter 9-1/4".
#1021 Modern Vase 9-1/4".
#1023 Decorator Vase 9-1/4".
#1025 Gourd Planter 11-1/2".
#1026 Tall Pillow Vase 6-1/4" x 7-1/4".
#1027 Flight Planter 13".
#1028 Console Planter 13".

Liäna Catalog Cover.

Decorator Vase #1023 with original label, gold vining.

Pillow Vase #1012 with silver vining. **Pineapple Planter #1008** with copper vining.

Medallion (#1500)

Kenwood Ceramics By Shawnee
Numbered 1500 Series

Introduced in 1957, this magnificent line is a rich, glowing statuary bronze over high-fired, semi-porcelain bodies.

magnificent
Medallion
by KENWOOD

UNIQUELY beautiful ceramics, unlike anything you've ever seen . . . Rich, glowing statuary bronze over high-fired, semi-porcelain bodies . . . The sculptored detail creates lustrous highlights, yet never competes with planting or flower arrangements . . . Sure to be 1957's ceramic sensation. Each piece appears to be cast bronze.

#1501—5" Urn Planter—24 to a case, wt. 20 lbs.

#1502—5" Leaf Planter—24 to a case, wt. 22 lbs.

#1503—6" Rooster Planter—12 to a case, wt. 20 lbs.

#1504—11½" Egyptian Planter—12 to a case, wt. 18 lbs.

#1505—8½" Butterfly Planter—12 to a case, wt. 16 lbs.

#1506 — 9½" Basketweave Planter — 12 to a case, wt. 16 lbs.

#1507 — 8" Shell Planter — 12 to a case, wt. 21 lbs.

#1508—15" Windowbox Planter—12 to a case, wt. 35 lbs.

#1509—8½" Pony Planter—12 to a case, wt. 23 lbs.

#1510—14½" Flower Bowl—12 to a case, wt. 25 lbs.

#1511—10½" Prairie Schooner Planter—12 to a case, wt. 41 lbs.

Left—#1512—14½" Flair Planter—12 to a case, wt. 26 lbs.

see back page for Medallion vases

KENWOOD CERAMICS
Division of Shawnee Potteries

Medallion Catalog.
#1501 Urn Planter 5".
#1502 Leaf Planter 5".
#1503 Rooster Planter 6".
#1504 Egyptian Planter 11-1/2".
#1505 Butterfly Planter 8-1/2".
#1506 Basketweave Planter 9-1/2".
#1507 Shell Planter 8".
#1508 Windowbox Planter 15".
#1509 Pony Planter 8-1/2".
#1510 Flower Bowl 14-1/2".
#1511 Prairie Schooner Planter 10-1/2".
#1512 Flair Planter 14-1/2".

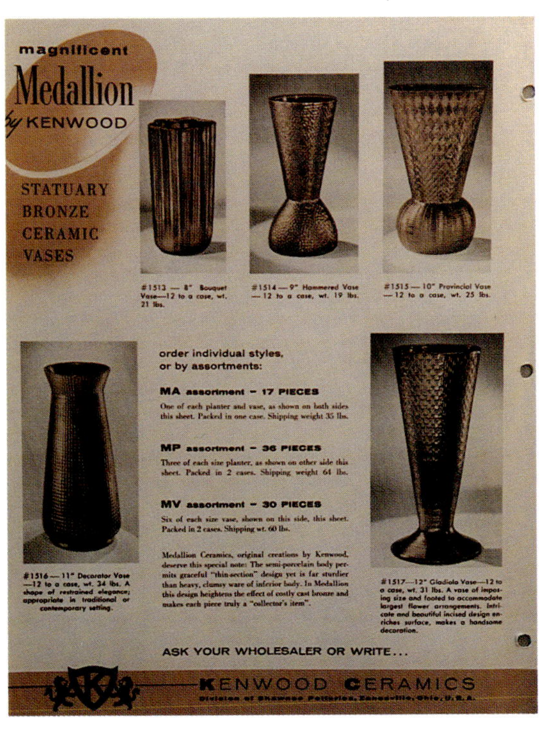

magnificent
Medallion
by KENWOOD

STATUARY BRONZE CERAMIC VASES

#1513 — 8" Bouquet Vase—12 to a case, wt. 21 lbs.

#1514 — 9" Hammered Vase —12 to a case, wt. 19 lbs.

#1515 — 10" Provincial Vase —12 to a case, wt. 25 lbs.

order individual styles, or by assortments:

MA assortment – 17 PIECES

One of each planter and vase, as shown on both sides this sheet. Packed in one case. Shipping weight 35 lbs.

MP assortment – 36 PIECES

Three of each size planter, as shown on other side this sheet. Packed in 2 cases. Shipping weight 64 lbs.

MV assortment – 30 PIECES

Six of each size vase, shown on this side, this sheet. Packed in 2 cases. Shipping wt. 60 lbs.

Medallion Ceramics, original creations by Kenwood, deserve this special note: The semi-porcelain body permits graceful "thin-section" design yet is far sturdier than heavy, clumsy ware of inferior body. In Medallion this design heightens the effect of costly cast bronze and makes each piece truly a "collector's item".

#1516 — 11" Decorator Vase —12 to a case, wt. 34 lbs. A shape of restrained elegance; appropriate in traditional or contemporary setting.

#1517—12" Gladiola Vase—12 to a case, wt. 31 lbs. A vase of imposing size and footed to accommodate largest flower arrangements. Intricate and beautiful incised design enriches surface, makes a handsome decoration.

ASK YOUR WHOLESALER OR WRITE...

KENWOOD CERAMICS
Division of Shawnee Potteries, Zanesville, Ohio, U.S.A.

Prairie Schooner Planter #1511.

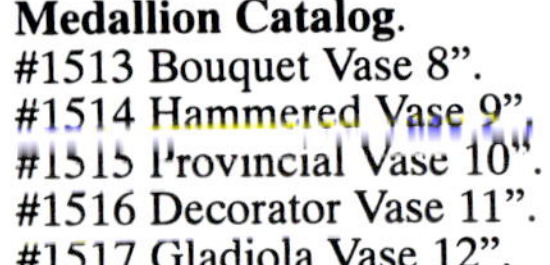

Medallion Catalog.
#1513 Bouquet Vase 8".
#1514 Hammered Vase 9".
#1515 Provincial Vase 10".
#1516 Decorator Vase 11".
#1517 Gladiola Vase 12".

Pastel Medallion Catalog.
#1513P Bouquet Vase 8".
#1514P Hammered Vase 9".
#1515P Provincial Vase 10".
#1516P Decorator Vase 11".
#1517P Gladiola Vase 12".

Pastel Medallion (#1500)

Kenwood Ceramics By Shawnee
Numbered 1500 Series

Medallion ceramics finished in softly-lustrous satin pastels of Peppermint Pink, Green, and White. This line was created especially for florists.

Pastel Medallion Planters Vases
by KENWOOD

in softly-lustrous satin-pastels—Pink, Green and White.

PASTEL MEDALLION ARTWARE
Introductory Assortments

MB assortment – 14 PIECES
Consists of one each, of every number:
1501P 5" Urn Planter
1502P 5" Leaf Planter
1504P 11½" Egyptian Planter
1505P 8½" Butterfly Planter
1506P 9½" Basketweave Planter
1507P 8" Shell Planter
1508P 15" Windowbox Planter
1510P 14½" Flower Bowl
1512P 14½" Flair Planter
1513P 8" Bouquet Vase
1514P 9" Hammered Vase
1515P 10" Provincial Vase
1516P 11" Decorator Vase
1517P 12" Gladiola Vase
Furnished in either Satin-Green, Satin-White, or Satin-Pink. Please specify color when ordering. Packed in one case, weight 27 pounds.

MD assortment – 27 PLANTERS
Consists of three each, of the following items, in assorted pastel colors:
1501P 5" Urn Planter
1502P 5" Leaf Planter
1504P 11½" Egyptian Planter
1505P 8½" Butterfly Planter
1506P 9½" Basketweave Planter
1507P 8" Shell Planter
1508P 15" Windowbox Planter
1510P 14½" Flower Bowl
1512P 14½" Flair Planter
One piece of each number furnished in Satin-Green, Satin-White, and Satin-Pink. Packed in two cases, weight 43 pounds.

MC assortment – 30 VASES
Consists of six each, of the following items, in assorted pastel colors:
1513P 8" Bouquet Vase
1514P 9" Hammered Vase
1515P 10" Provincial Vase
1516P 11" Decorator Vase
1517P 12" Gladiola Vase
Two pieces of each number furnished in Satin-Green, Satin-White, and Satin-Pink. Packed in two cases, weight 60 pounds.

#1514P—9" Hammered Vase —12 to a carton, wt. 19 lbs.

#1513P—8" Bouquet Vase—12 to a carton, wt. 21 lbs.

#1516P—11" Decorator Vase —12 to a carton, wt. 34 lbs.

#1515P—10" Provincial Vase —12 to a carton, wt. 25 lbs.

#1517P — 12" Gladiola Vase — 12 to a carton, wt. 31 lbs.

ASK YOUR WHOLESALER OR WRITE...

PRINTED IN U.S.A.

KENWOOD CERAMICS
Division of Shawnee Potteries, Zanesville, Ohio, U.S.A.

Especially for Florists

#1502P—5" Leaf Planter—24 to a carton, wt. 22 lbs.

#1507P—8" Shell Planter—12 to a carton, wt. 21 lbs.

#1501P—5" Urn Planter—24 to a carton, wt. 20 lbs.

#1504P—11½" Egyptian Planter—12 to a carton, wt. 18 lbs.

#1505P—8½" Butterfly Planter—12 to a carton, wt. 16 lbs.

#1506P—9½" Basketweave Planter—12 to a carton, wt. 16 lbs.

Now, Medallion ceramics in beautiful satin pastels—peppermint Pink, Green, and White in soft tones that make any planting look expensive. All high-fired, semi-porcelain body with richly sculptured detail. The finest for florists—at modest prices.

Pastel Medallion Planters .... by KENWOOD

#1510P—14½" Flower Bowl—12 to a carton, wt. 25 lbs.

#1508P—15" Windowbox Planter—12 to a carton, wt. 35 lbs.

#1512P—14½" Flair Planter—12 to a carton, wt. 26 lbs.

See back page for Medallion vases and assortments

KENWOOD CERAMICS Division of Shawnee Potteries

Pastel Medallion Catalog.
#1501P Urn Planter 5".
#1502P Leaf Planter 5".
#1504P Egyptian Planter 11-1/2".
#1505P Butterfly Planter 8-1/2".
#1506P Basketweave Planter 9-1/2".
#1507P Shell Planter 8".
#1508P Windowbox Planter 15".
#1510P Flower Bowl 14-1/2".
#1512P Flair Planter 14-1/2".

Petit- Point (#1900)

Sorcery In Ceramics By Shawnee
Numbered 1900 Series

Introduced in Catalog No. 22, dated September 1958, Petit-Point has the expensive look of solid brass. Geometric designs complement the embossed pattern; the simple elegance of white-glazed interiors is enhanced by brass-decorated exteriors. A fabric was placed on the mold to create this design.

Petit-Point #1911.

Petit-Point Catalog Cover.

Petit-Point Catalog.

#1901 Square Planter 4".
#1902 Square Planter 5".
#1903 Square Planter 6".
#1904 Square Planter 7".
#1905 Windowbox 8".
#1906 Windowbox 11".
#1907 Windowbox 14".
#1908 Jardiniere 5".
#1909 Jardiniere 6".
#1910 Jardiniere 7".
#1911 Octagon Flower Bowl 10".
#1912 Triangle Flower Bowl 11".

Stardust (#2000)

Kenwood Ceramics By Shawnee
Numbered 2000 Series

Stardust has a high gloss glaze with a spattered look, and comes in four listed colors: Pink, Chartreuse, Avocado, Surf. The bases were flocked to protect furniture. The eight shapes in this line have appeared in other lines.

Stardust Oval Bowl #2001.

Stardust Catalog.
#2001 Oval Bowl 11".
#2002 Oval Bowl 14-1/2".
#2004 Planting Dish 7-7/8".
#2005 Shell Planting Dish 8".
#2007 Planting Dish 7-1/2".
#2012 Vase 8".
#2013 Vase 10".
#2014 Vase 10".

Tiara Arbor Vase #3512 with original label. *Courtesy of Marvin Mulligan*

Tiara (#3500)

Fashions In Ceramics By Shawnee
Numbered 3500 Series

Introduced in Catalog No. 29, Tiara was the last line offered by Shawnee. Inspired by the Danish, this line was in semi-porcelain with high-fired glazes in tones of: Bamboo Green, Lilac, Blonde, Jonquil Yellow, Pumpkin, Forest Green, Cornflower Blue, Violet, Bermuda Green, Sandalwood, Lime, Velvet Pink, Turquoise, and Pearl White.

Tiara.
#3501 Arbor Planter 6".
#3502 Crown Planter 6".
#3503 African Violet Planter 6-1/2".
#3504 African Violet Planter 7-1/2".
#3505 Crown Jardiniere 7".
#3506 Crown Jardiniere 8".
#3507 Flared Windowbox 11-1/2".
#3508 Flared Windowbox 14-1/2".
#3509 Arbor Flower Bowl 10-1/2".
#3510 Bud Vase 11".
#3511 Crown Vase 8".
#3512 Arbor Vase 9".
#3513 Modern Vase 10".
#3514 Arbor Vase 11".
#3515 Crown Vase 12".

Tiara Catalog Cover.

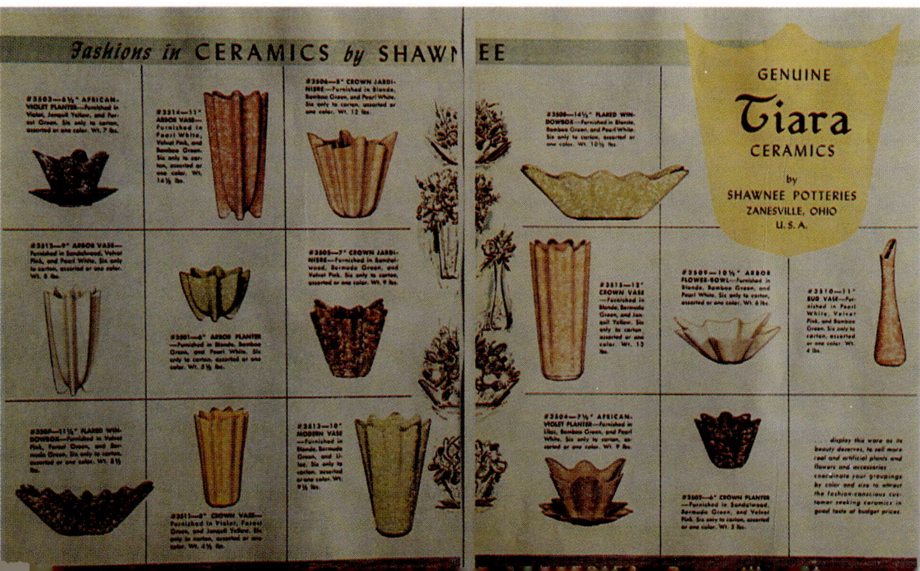

Tiara Flared Windowbox #3508.

Touché (#1000)

Sorcery In Ceramics By Shawnee
Numbered 1000 Series

Introduced in Catalog No. 17, dated 1956, this line has high-fired glazes with a decorated bisque exterior. This was the first florist ware line introduced by President John Bonistall. Many of the shapes numbered in this 1000 series were carried over to the Liäna 1000 series brought out in 1957, catalog no. 18.

Touché. Top Shelf, left to right: Double Planter #1002, Bud Vase #1014, Decorator Vase #1023, Bouquet Vase #1013.
Bottom Shelf, left to right: Flair Planter #1022, Cucumber Planter #1011.

Touché Catalog Cover.

Touché Catalog.
#1001 Pillow Planter 4".
#1002 Double Planter 6-3/4".
#1003 Teabox Planter 4".
#1004 Saddle Planter 5".
#1005 Scalloped Planter 7-1/2".
#1006 Crosscut Planter 4-3/4".
#1011 Cucumber Planter 11-1/2".
#1012 Pillow Vase 7".
#1013 Bouquet Vase 8-1/4".
#1014 Bud Vase 8-1/2".
#1015 Wing Planter 11".
#1016 Conventional Planter 9-1/2".
#1021 Modern Vase 9-1/4".
#1022 Flair Planter 9".
#1023 Decorator Vase 9-1/4".
#1024 Gondola Windowbox 12".
#1025 Gourd Planter 11-1/2".
#1026 Tall Pillow Vase 7-1/4".

Chapter 44: Reproductions & New Products

Shawnee Pottery collectors do not have a serious problem in the reproduction category, yet. The purpose of this chapter is to familiarize you with what has been found on the market today.

Some reproductions are done well, and have the proper markings that leave no doubt that they are new. Other reproductions have been found to be crude and only faintly resembling the original piece. The third category is the most dangerous; the well-done reproductions that closely resemble the original, and are also marked like the original.

There is a new company, whose products we have not pictured, that is making new cookie jars and banks under the name of Shawnee Pottery. The **New** Shawnee Pottery Company of Zanesville, Ohio, is making a limited edition **Farmer Pig®** cookie jar that is the same design as Shawnee's old Farmer Pig salt & pepper shakers. Reports are that the bottom has the word *Shawnee* written exactly the same as the original Shawnee Pottery Company marked their pieces. A second cookie jar has also been produced, a girl pig named **Sowly®**, to go with Farmer Pig®. Sowly® does not look like any other old Shawnee Pottery Company design. These two new cookie jars by the New Shawnee Pottery Company have a 1994 issue price of $175 each. Original Shawnee Pottery figurine designs have also been reproduced as banks. These are the pekingese, squirrel, puppy, rabbit, deer, and teddy bear (they call it a raccoon), being sold as a set of six banks for a 1994 issue price of $200 the set. Literature and/or advertising for these products may lead you to believe that the old and original Shawnee Pottery Company of Zanesville, Ohio, has reopened and is back in business. This is not so ..... this is a new company producing new products.

Another new company whose products we have not pictured is the McCoy Pottery Company of Tennessee. McCoy is currently doing antique reproductions of many old pottery designs, among them Shawnee's Smiley Pig cookie jar. These cookie jars are decorated with gold trim and/or decals, and might be found marked with the word "McCoy". The original retail price on Smiley jars is as low as $20 per jar. Reportedly, there are also Muggsy shakers and a Muggsy cookie jar, though I have not seen these. Just remember that if any known Shawnee designs of cookie jars, shakers, or anything else, turn up with a McCoy mark on them, then they are brand new. McCoy also uses a crackle glaze to make some of their products appear to be old.

In late 1994, I saw a reproduction Chanticleer rooster pitcher that was somewhat smaller than the original Shawnee pitcher. It was made by the Alpine Pottery Co. of Roseville, Ohio, and was selling for $18 retail. This pitcher was really heavy, had a nice cream color, and blue airbrushed head and wing tips and handle. It was stamped on the flat, unglazed bottom with the name and location of the company making it, so there was no problem mistaking it for old Shawnee Pottery.

Buying new products is an individual choice that each of you must make, but there is rarely a happy ending when the collector is misled about the age and origins of a piece. Knowing and trusting the dealer you buy from could possibly save later heartache, and it wouldn't hurt to ask for a return guarantee before investing a significant amount of money. There is absolutely nothing wrong with purchasing new items to add to your collections, provided you are *aware* that the item is new.

New items related to Shawnee collecting are shown here also, as eventually they may end up in the resale market. Documenting when these were made is important to the future of Shawnee collecting.

Indian and Arrowhead Pin
This Shawnee Pottery logo ceramic pin was produced by former Shawnee designer Robert Heckman. It was presented to each member and guest attending the first Shawnee Pottery Collector's Club Convention held in Daytona Beach, Florida, in October 1991. 2-3/4" long - Marked: Shawnee 1991 h

Ear of Corn Pin
Corn King designer Robert Heckman designed and produced a ceramic Ear of Corn pin in the exact colors of the original Corn King. It was presented to each member and guest attending the second Shawnee Pottery Collector's Club Convention held in Daytona Beach, Florida, in January 1993. 2-7/8" long - Marked: Shawnee Convention h 93

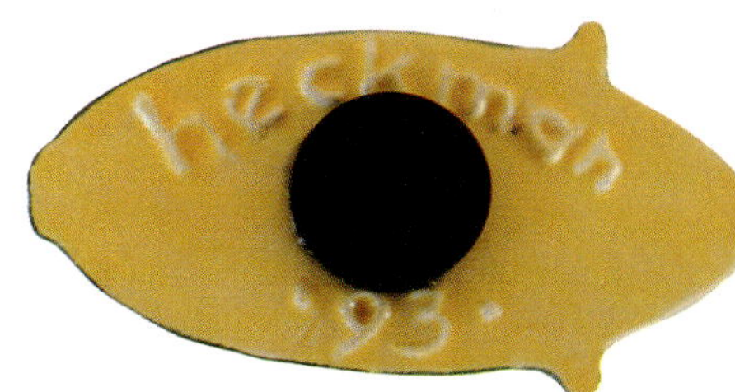

Ear of Corn Magnet
Corn King designer Robert Heckman offered the ceramic Ear of Corn magnet to Shawnee Pottery collectors who were unable to attend the second convention. Produced in a limited quantity, it was offered for sale through the *Exclusively Shawnee* newsletter. 2-7/8" long - Marked: heckman '93'
1993 Issue Price $12 ppd

Lapel or Hat Pins. Four metal lapel or hat pins were offered by Shawnee club member Ron Brown, beginning in 1991 with Smiley Pig. Following Smiley were Winnie Pig, Puss 'n Boots, and Muggsy, 1-1/4" high, no marks.
1991 Issue Price for Smiley $5 ppd
1991 Issue Price for Winnie, Puss'n Boots, & Muggsy set $30 ppd

Muggsy with Red Scarf, 10-1/4" high, gold decal on front reads *Mugnificent Muggsy*. Marked on bottom: Mark Supnick's Commemorative Edition 1992 Muggsy U.S.A. Mark Supnick SA Corl (not part of limited edition). **1992 Issue Price $225.**

Mark Supnick's Commemorative Edition Cookie Jars. First offered to collectors in *Exclusively Shawnee*, this series of limited edition cookie jars was produced beginning in 1992. They are marked and dated on each jar, in addition to having a limited edition number on each. Shirley Corl of Corl's Kiln is the decorator. Each jar is incised on the bottom, for example, with the words *Mark Supnick's Commemorative 1992 Smiley U.S.A.*, and has decal signatures of *Mark Supnick* and *SA Corl*, as well as the edition number. Of course, *1992 Smiley* in the mark would change to *1992 Sailor Boy* etc., on the appropriate jar. All dimensions are approximate.

1992 Edition
Happy 50th Birthday Smiley, 10-3/4" high, gold decal on front reads *Happy 50th Birthday Smiley.* Marked on bottom: Mark Supnick's Commemorative Edition 1992 Smiley U.S.A. Mark Supnick SA Corl.
1992 Issue Price $150; 150 jars in limited edition.

Sailor Boy, Blond Hair, 10-1/2" high, gold decal on front reads *Celebrating 50 Years of Service.* Marked on bottom: Mark Supnick's Commemorative Edition 1992 Sailor Boy U.S.A. Mark Supnick SA Corl.
1992 Issue Price $150; 100 jars in limited edition.

Sailor Boy, Black Hair, 10-1/2" high, gold decal on front reads *Celebrating 50 Years of Service.* Marked on bottom: Mark Supnick's Commemorative Edition 1992 Sailor Boy U.S.A. Mark Supnick SA Corl.
1992 Issue Price $150; 100 jars in limited edition.

Mugnificent Muggsy, 10-1/4" high, gold decal on front reads *Mugnificent Muggsy*. Marked on bottom: Mark Supnick's Commemorative Edition 1992 Muggsy U.S.A. Mark Supnick SA Corl.
1992 Issue Price $150; 150 jars in limited edition.

1993 Edition
Wonderful Winnie, 11" high, gold decal on front reads *Wonderful Winnie*. Marked on bottom: Mark Supnick's Commemorative Edition 1993 Winnie U.S.A. Mark Supnick SA Corl.
1993 Issue Price $175; 150 jars in limited edition.

Purr-fect Puss 'n Boots, 9-3/4" high, gold decal on front reads *Purr-fect Puss 'n Boots*. Marked on bottom: Mark Supnick's Commemorative Edition 1993 Puss 'n Boots U.S.A. Mark Supnick SA Corl.
1993 Issue Price $175; 150 jars in limited edition.

Extremely Lucky, 11" high, gold decal on front reads *Extremely Lucky*. Marked on bottom: Mark Supnick's Commemorative Edition 1993 Lucky U.S.A. Mark Supnick SA Corl.
1993 Issue Price $175; 150 jars in limited edition.

1994 Edition
Smiley Bank Head Cookie Jar, 11" high, gold decal on front reads *Smiley's Stash*. Marked on bottom: Mark Supnick's Commemorative Edition 1994 Smiley U.S.A. Mark Supnick SA Corl.
1994 Issue Price $175; 150 jars in limited edition.

Winnie Bank Head Cookie Jar, 11" high, gold decal on front reads *Windfall Winnie*. Marked on bottom: Mark Supnick's Commemorative Edition 1994 Winnie U.S.A. Mark Supnick SA Corl.
1994 Issue Price $175; 150 jars in limited edition.

Muggsy Bank Head Cookie Jar, 11-1/4" high, gold decal on front reads *Bank On Muggsy*. Marked on bottom: Mark Supnick's Commemorative Edition 1994 Muggsy U.S.A. Mark Supnick SA Corl.
1994 Issue Price $175; 150 jars in limited edition.

Smiley with Black Hair, yellow neckerchief, 10-3/4" high, gold decal on front reads *Happy 50th Birthday Smiley*. Marked on bottom: Mark Supnick's Commemorative Edition 1992 Smiley U.S.A. Mark Supnick SA Corl (not part of limited edition). **1992 Issue Price $225.**

1995 Edition
Berry Smiley, 10-1/2", hand painted strawberries, decal on front reads *Smiley*. Marked on bottom: Mark Supnick's Commemorative Edition 1995 Smiley U.S.A. Mark Supnick SA Corl.
1995 Issue Price $185; 100 jars in limited edition.

Berry Winnie, 10-1/2", hand painted strawberries, decal on front reads *Winnie*. Marked on bottom: Mark Supnick's Commemorative Edition 1995 Winnie U.S.A. Mark Supnick SA Corl.
1995 Issue Price $185; 100 jars in limited edition.

Bottom marks of 1992 Commemorative Smiley shown, representative of all editions.

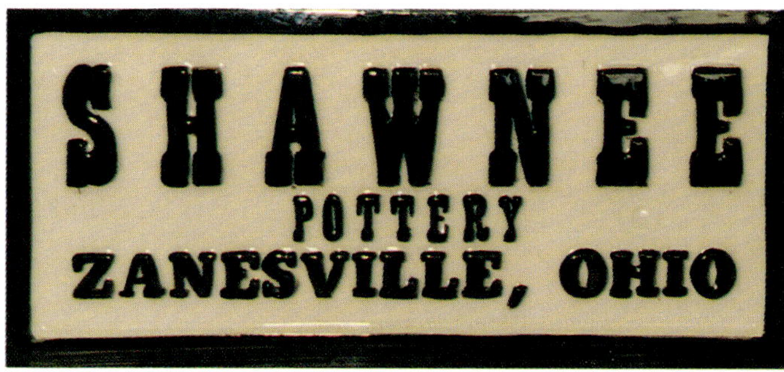

Shawnee Pottery dealer's plaque, produced by the Mangus's, these ceramic plaques were made in 1992, listed in colors of blue, green, or burgundy. Front as shown; back is marked with U.S.A. and date. **1992 Issue Price $25.**

Smiley & Muggsy Magnets, 2" x 3-1/2", produced in 1993 by Terry and Sandra Bauer. Colorful vinyl magnet for refrigerator or desk. **$2.25 ppd per magnet.**

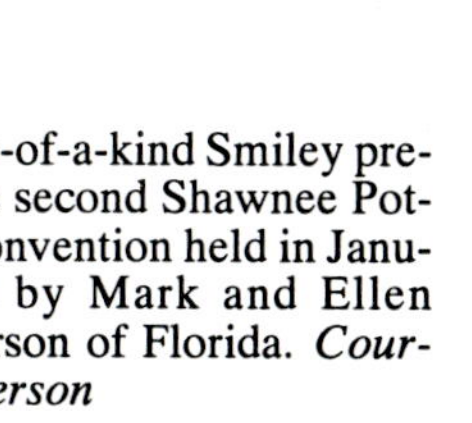

Smiley with Hair, one-of-a-kind Smiley presented as a prize at the second Shawnee Pottery Collectors Club convention held in January 1993. Presented by Mark and Ellen Supnick to Don Anderson of Florida. *Courtesy of Don & De Anderson*

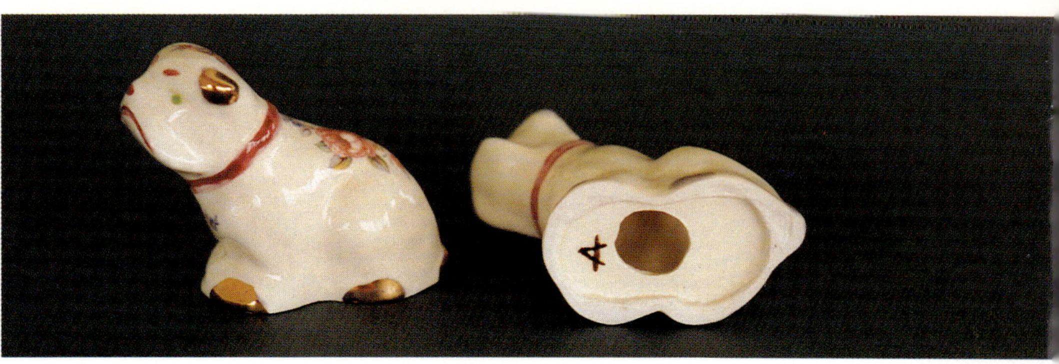

Bulldog figurines, 2-1/2" high, gold trim & decals on left, plain on right. Created in 1992 by Randy and Stephanie Adrian, these ceramic figurines were designed to look like the Bulldog Bank that Shawnee produced. Marked: **A** (later pieces were supposed to have 1992 date added). **1992 Issue Price $15 ppd.**

New Smiley Pig look-alike cookie jar, 10-1/2" high, cold paint decoration, has paper label reading "Made in China". Photo courtesy of Mercedes DiRenzo of Jazz'e Junque Cookie Jar Shop in Chicago, Illinois.

Back of New Smiley Pig cookie jar made in China.

Smiley Pig creamers shown from side. White creamer on left is a reproduction Smiley. Yellow creamer on right is a real Shawnee Smiley.

Bottom marks of **Smiley creamers**, reproduction on left, real Smiley on right. Note that yellow Shawnee Smiley also has the employee #16 bonus stamp.

Granny Ann teapots. Peach apron Granny Ann on left is Shawnee. Purple Granny Ann on right is reproduction.

Again, the reproduction is rather crude, and is considerably smaller than the original. A confusing issue here for the new collector may be that the real Shawnee Granny Ann is only marked **U.S.A.** on the bottom, while the fake Granny Ann actually reads **Patented Granny Ann**. Just keep in mind that Shawnee marked the real Granny Ann's in both ways; with U.S.A., and with the words Patented Granny Ann.

Smiley creamers shown from front, reproduction on bottom, Smiley on right. This is a crudely done reproduction Smiley, with a very rough surface to him. In the photo of the bottom marks, you can see that the embossed Clover Blossom shown on the rump of the real Smiley (yellow one) has been ground off the fake Smiley. The fake Smiley is also considerably smaller than the real one, and this is common with reproductions. the markings are not crisp and clear. The floral decoaration on his chest was meant to resemble the large Smiley pitcher, when the simplest thing they should have done was paint his neckerchief. The most obvious error of all, was that they forgot to cut out his mouth so you could pour from this creamer.

Indian Arrowhead Stained Glass sun-catcher, made by Linda Guffey. Never offered for sale.

Muggsy Stained Glass sun-catcher, made by Linda Guffey. Never offered for sale.

Smiley Pig Stained Glass sun-catcher, made by Linda Guffey. Never offered for sale.

Shawnee T-Shirt offered by Pam Curran to Shawnee Pottery Collector's Club members in 1990, through *Exclusively Shawnee*. **$16.95 ppd.**

Chapter 45: Terrace Ceramics, Inc.

In January of 1961 after Shawnee Pottery closed, John F. Bonistall initiated his own national marketing organization, Terrace Ceramics, and began negotiations with salesmen and suppliers.

On August 28, 1961, American Pottery Company Inc. of Marietta, Ohio, was sold by Joseph Burgess Lenhart to Robert J. Braden. Braden later attended a liquidation auction at Shawnee Pottery and purchased molds, dies, and equipment, which he felt could be used at American Pottery.

By October 12, 1961, Bonistall incorporated Terrace Ceramics, Inc., Zanesville, Ohio, listing four employees. Terrace Ceramics was strictly a marketing company, never a manufacturer.

Robert J. Braden was basically unfamiliar with the making or selling of pottery, so he hired John F. Bonistall in May 1962 as President and General Manager of American Pottery Company. Bonistall remained in this position until 1964.

Terrace Ceramics, Inc. became the sole marketing agent for American Pottery products from May 1962 until their closing. Terrace also marketed their own lines that were produced by many different manufacturers, some of which were Haeger Potteries of Dundee, Illinois, American Pottery of Marietta, Ohio, and McNicol China Company of Clarksburg, West Virginia.

Shawnee molds, owned by Braden at American Pottery, resulted in the production of familiar cookie jars such as Smiley Pig, Winnie Pig, Muggsy (Dismal Doggie), and Corn, all sold by Terrace Ceramics. The corn dinnerware was also marketed by Terrace, though the colors were changed from familiar Shawnee colors. One line called *Corn-Ware* was done in a pale yellow and green glaze; while another line, with some design changes on several items, was done in a brown drip glaze and called *Maize-Ware*. Occasionally, a piece of Terrace corn still has the name Shawnee on the bottom too, the result of neglecting to remove the Shawnee name from the original die.

John Bonistall has reported that Terrace Ceramics ceased selling in 1975, but remained a programmed marketing company.

Playtime Cookie Jars marketed by Terrace Ceramics.

Corn-Ware Butter Dish marketed by Terrace Ceramics.

Bottom marks of Corn-Ware butter dish.

Maize-Ware Catalog Cover.

Maize-Ware Corn Dinnerware marketed by Terrace Ceramics.

Chapter 46: Patent Reports

Design Patents issued to the Shawnee Pottery Company of Zanesville, Ohio, during the 1940s and 1950s.

All patents will show a date filed, and a date when the Design Patent number was issued. During World War II, patent numbers were issued rather quickly, often in a matter of months. Note that after the war, some designs took as much as two years to have a patent number issued.

Patent dates should be used only as a guideline for production times. Many items were most likely produced long before and/or long after patents were filed and issued.

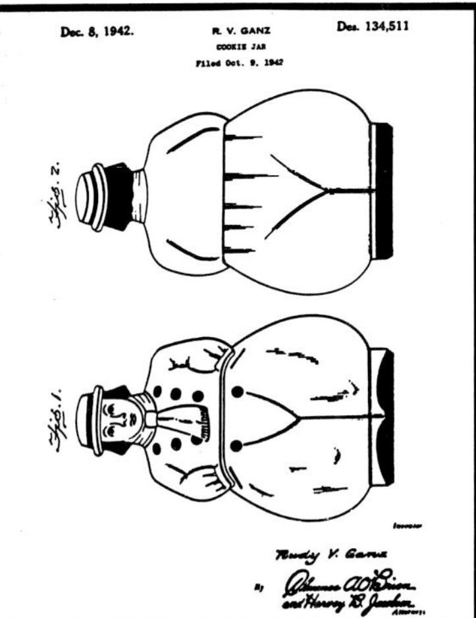

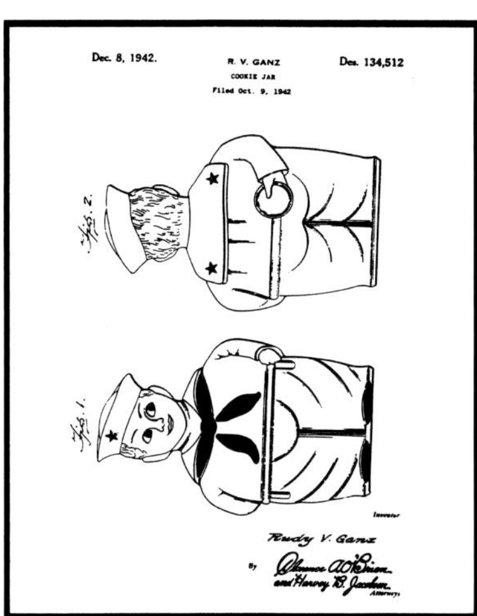

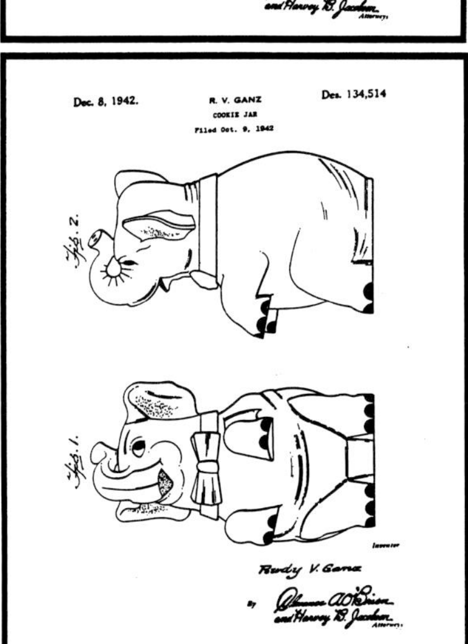

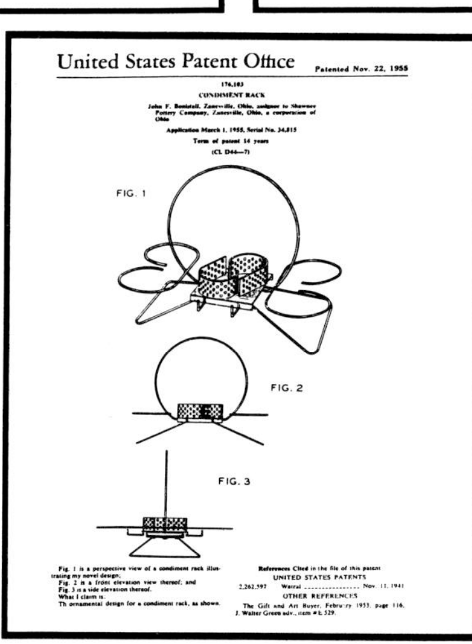

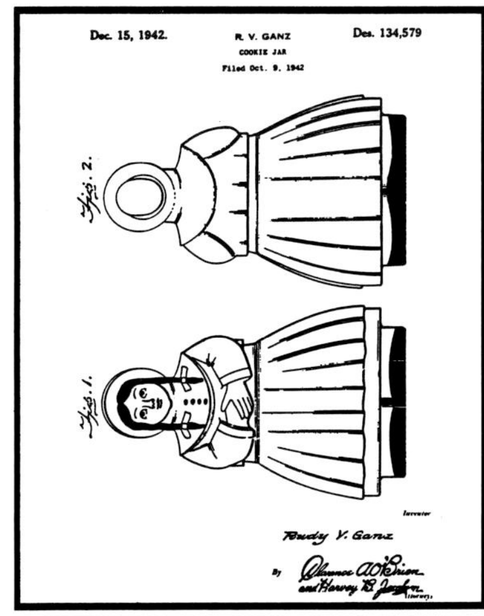

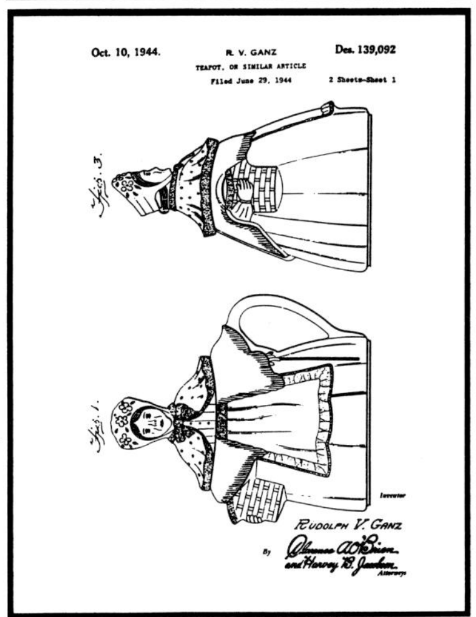

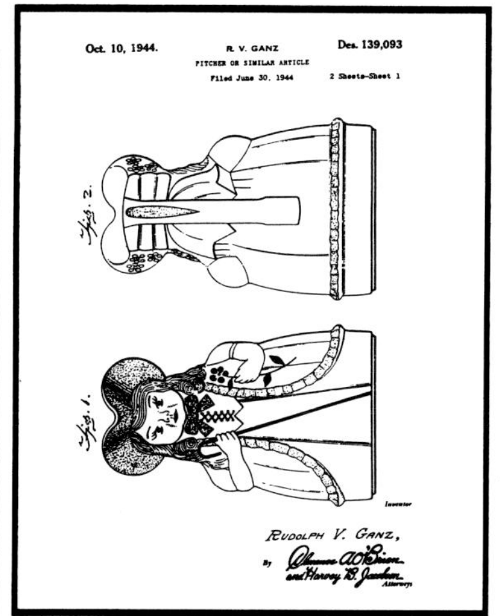

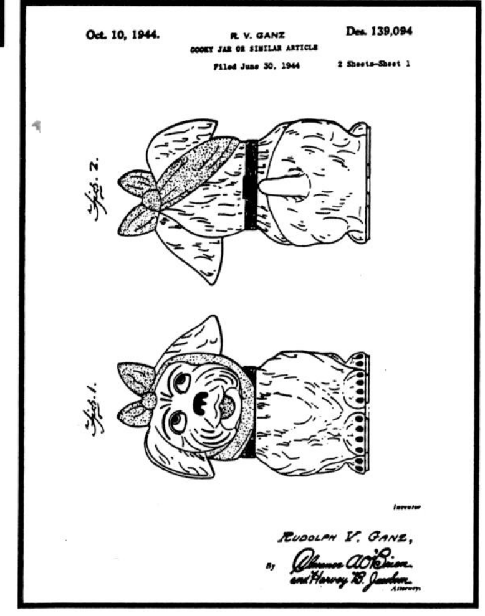

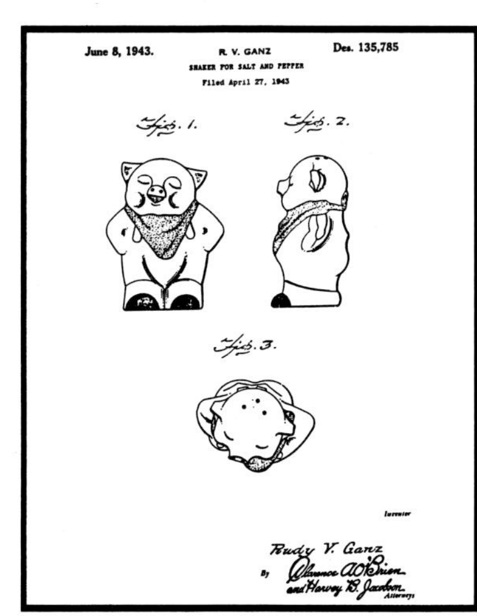

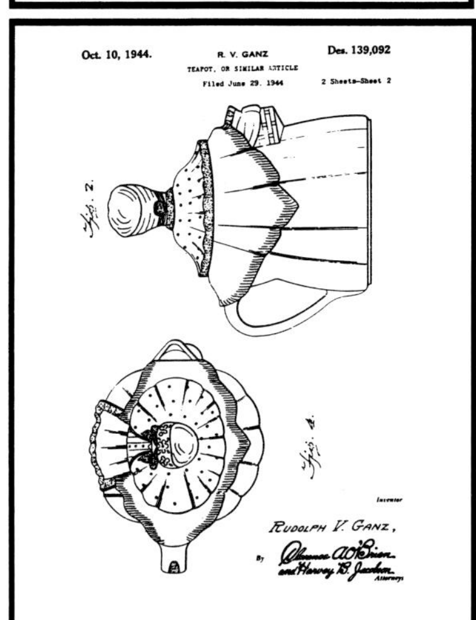

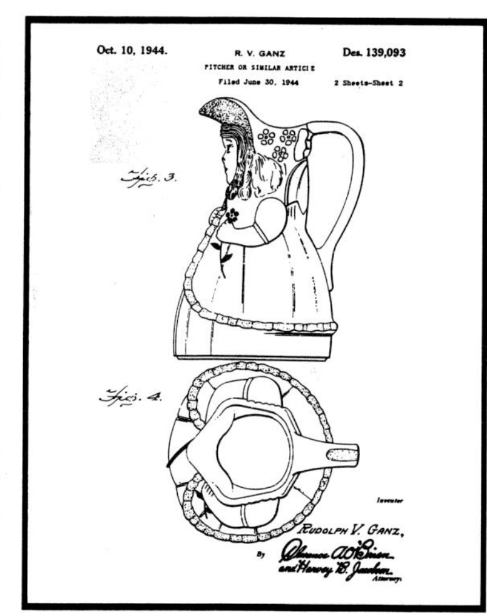

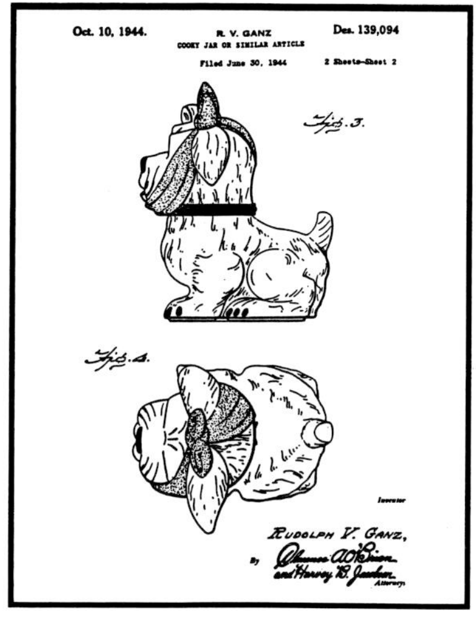

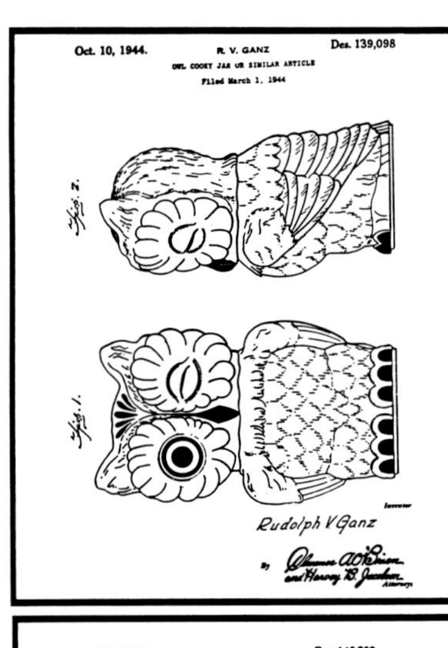
Oct. 10, 1944.
R. V. GANZ
Des. 139,098
OWL COOKY JAR OR SIMILAR ARTICLE
Filed March 1, 1944
Rudolph V Ganz

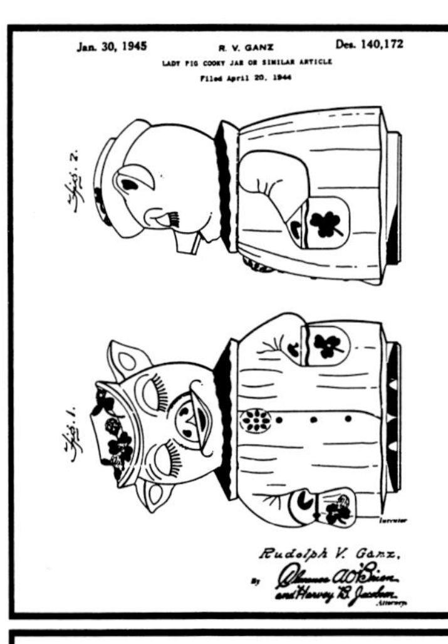
Jan. 30, 1945
R. V. GANZ
Des. 140,172
LADY PIG COOKY JAR OR SIMILAR ARTICLE
Filed April 20, 1944
Rudolph V. Ganz.

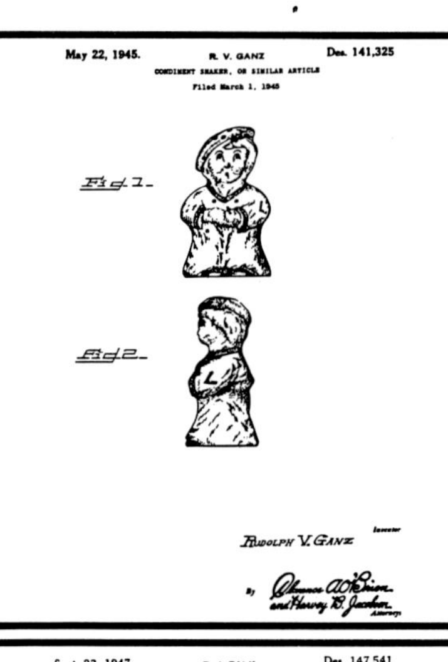
May 22, 1945.
R. V. GANZ
Des. 141,325
CONDIMENT SHAKER, OR SIMILAR ARTICLE
Filed March 1, 1945
RUDOLPH V. GANZ

May 22, 1945.
R. V. GANZ
Des. 141,339
CONDIMENT SHAKER, OR SIMILAR ARTICLE
Filed March 2, 1945
RUDOLPH V. GANZ

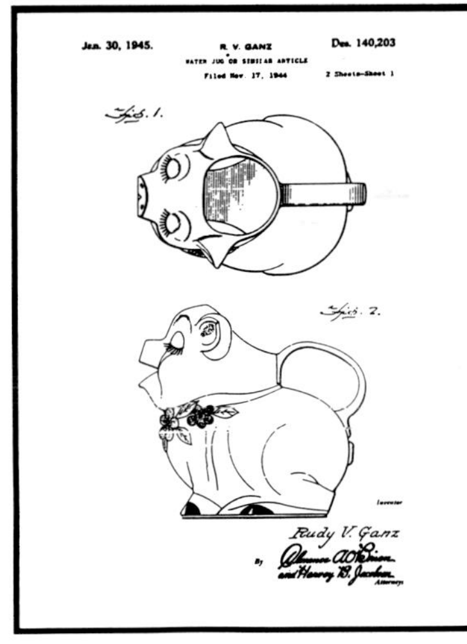
Jan. 30, 1945.
R. V. GANZ
Des. 140,203
WATER JUG OR SIMILAR ARTICLE
Filed Nov. 17, 1944
2 Sheets-Sheet 1
Rudy V. Ganz

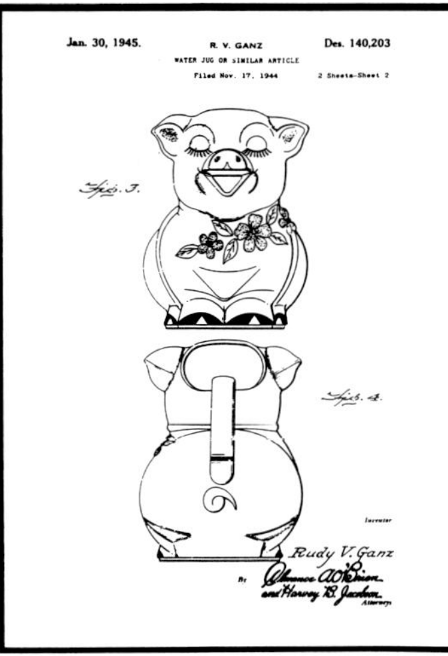
Jan. 30, 1945.
R. V. GANZ
Des. 140,203
WATER JUG OR SIMILAR ARTICLE
Filed Nov. 17, 1944
2 Sheets-Sheet 2
Rudy V. Ganz

Sept. 23, 1947.
R. J. FALK
Des. 147,541
PITCHER
Filed April 20, 1946
FIG. 1
FIG. 2
R. J. FALK

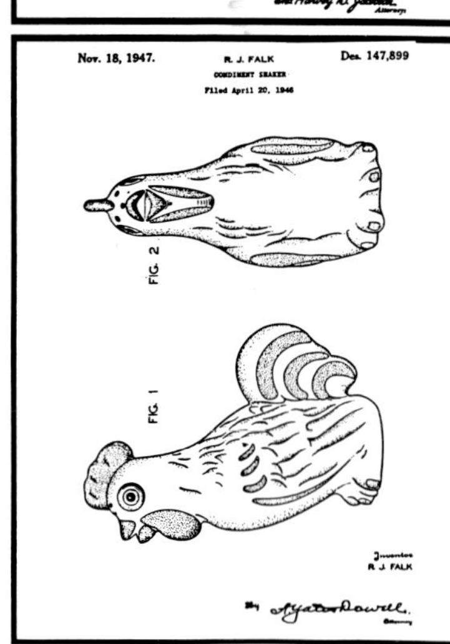
Nov. 18, 1947.
R. J. FALK
Des. 147,899
CONDIMENT SHAKER
Filed April 20, 1946
FIG. 2
FIG. 1
R. J. FALK

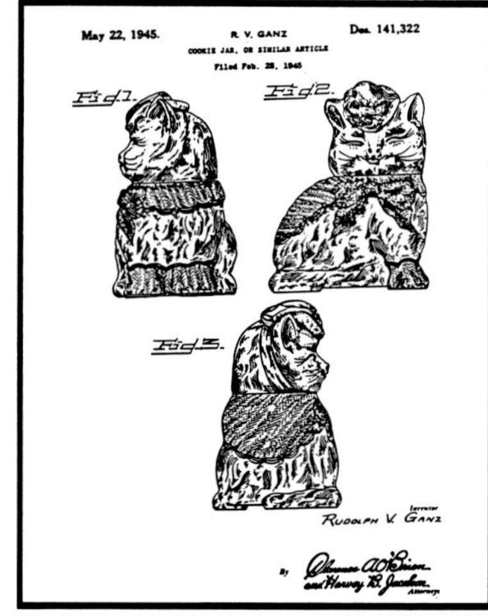
May 22, 1945.
R. V. GANZ
Des. 141,322
COOKIE JAR, OR SIMILAR ARTICLE
Filed Feb. 28, 1945
RUDOLPH V. GANZ

May 22, 1945.
R. V. GANZ
Des. 141,323
CONDIMENT SHAKER, OR SIMILAR ARTICLE
Filed Feb. 28, 1945
RUDOLPH V. GANZ

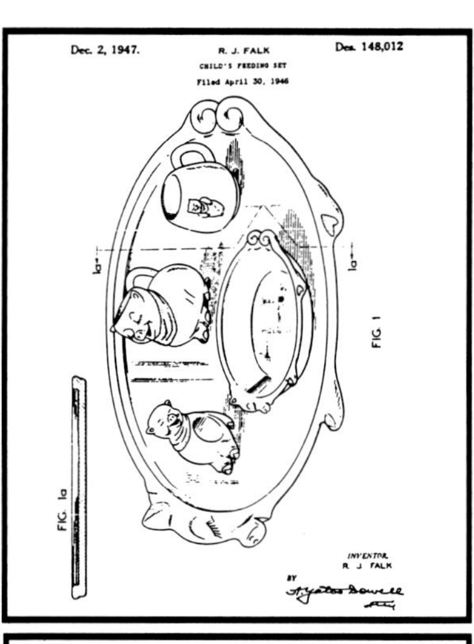
Dec. 2, 1947.
R. J. FALK
Des. 148,012
CHILD'S FEEDING SET
Filed April 30, 1946
FIG. 1
FIG. 1a
INVENTOR
R. J. FALK

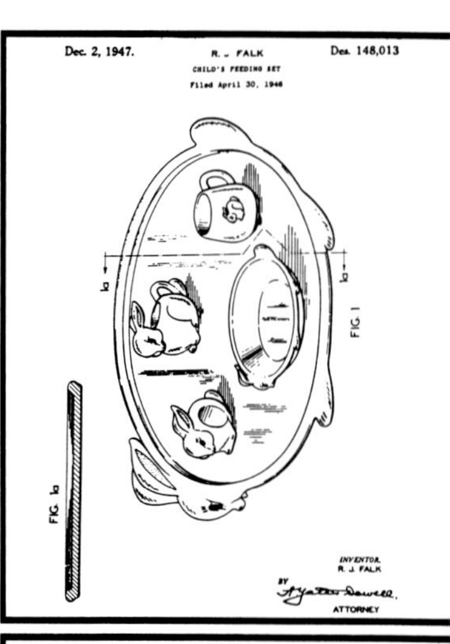
Dec. 2, 1947.
Des. 148,013
CHILD'S FEEDING SET
Filed April 30, 1946
FIG. 1
FIG. 1a
INVENTOR
R. J. FALK
ATTORNEY

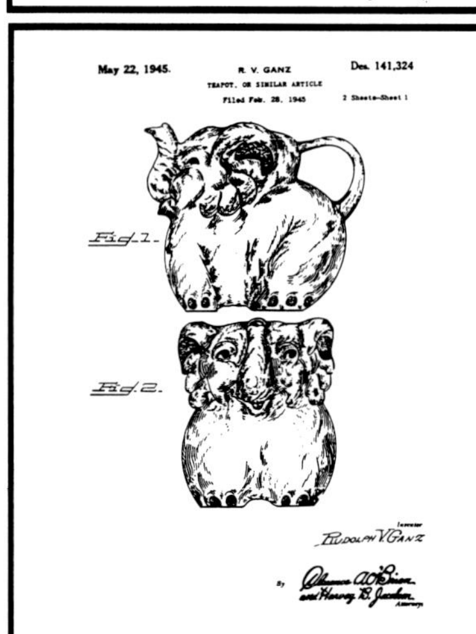
May 22, 1945.
R. V. GANZ
Des. 141,324
TEAPOT, OR SIMILAR ARTICLE
Filed Feb. 28, 1945
2 Sheets-Sheet 1
RUDOLPH V. GANZ

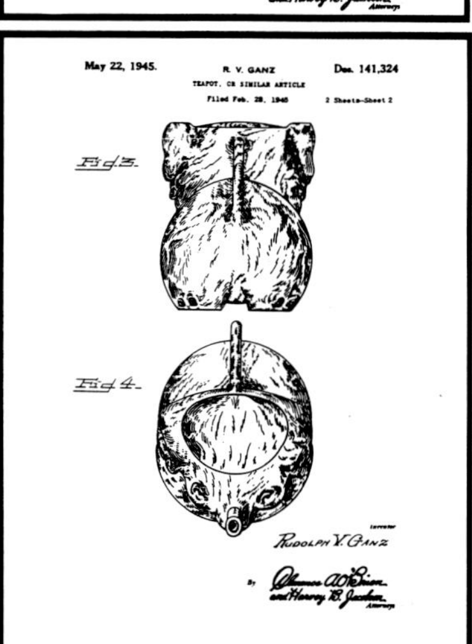
May 22, 1945.
R. V. GANZ
Des. 141,324
TEAPOT, OR SIMILAR ARTICLE
Filed Feb. 28, 1945
2 Sheets-Sheet 2
RUDOLPH V. GANZ

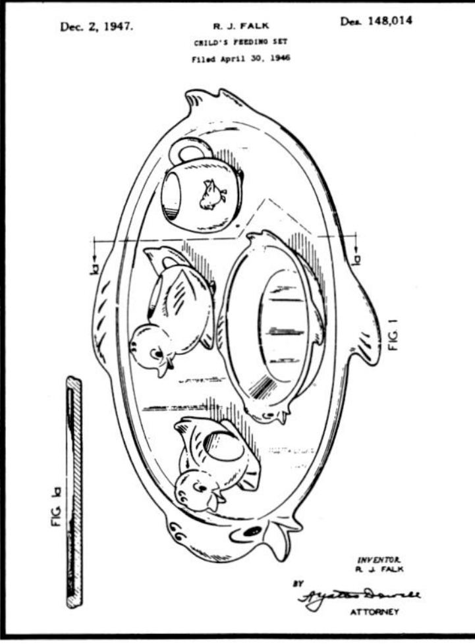
Dec. 2, 1947.
R. J. FALK
Des. 148,014
CHILD'S FEEDING SET
Filed April 30, 1946
FIG. 1
FIG. 1a
INVENTOR
R. J. FALK
ATTORNEY

Dec. 9, 1947.
R. J. FALK
Des. 148,056
Filed April 20, 1946
2 Sheets-Sheet 1
FIG. 1
R. J. FALK

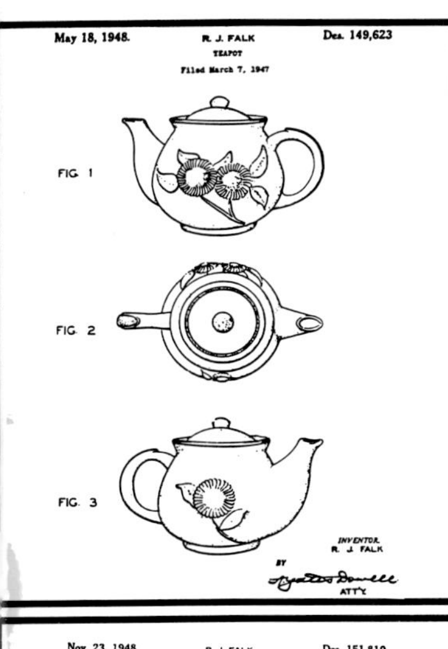
May 18, 1948.
R. J. FALK
Des. 149,623
TEAPOT
Filed March 7, 1947
FIG. 1
FIG. 2
FIG. 3
INVENTOR.
R. J. FALK
BY
ATT'Y

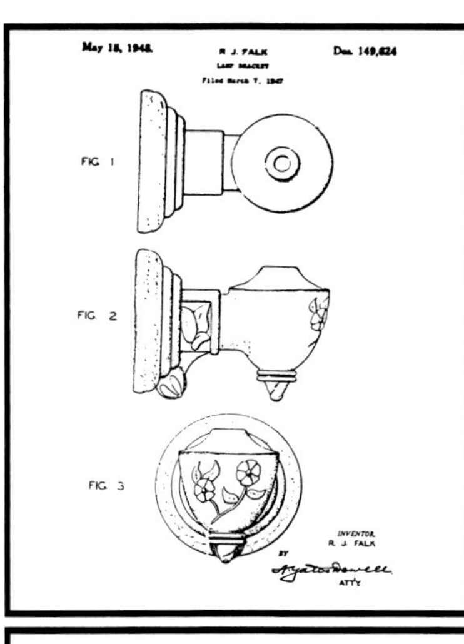
May 18, 1948.
R. J. FALK
Des. 149,624
LAMP BRACKET
Filed March 7, 1947
FIG. 1
FIG. 2
FIG. 3
INVENTOR.
R. J. FALK
ATT'Y

Feb. 21, 1950
J. L. PARENTICE
Des. 157,411
BEATER JUG
Filed Jan. 13, 1948
FIG. 1
FIG. 2
INVENTOR.
J. L. PARENTICE
BY
ATTORNEY

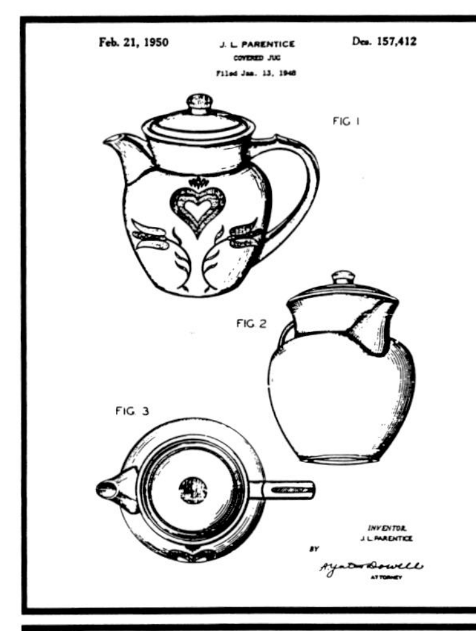
Feb. 21, 1950
J. L. PARENTICE
Des. 157,412
COVERED JUG
Filed Jan. 13, 1948
FIG. 1
FIG. 2
FIG. 3
INVENTOR.
J. L. PARENTICE
BY
ATTORNEY

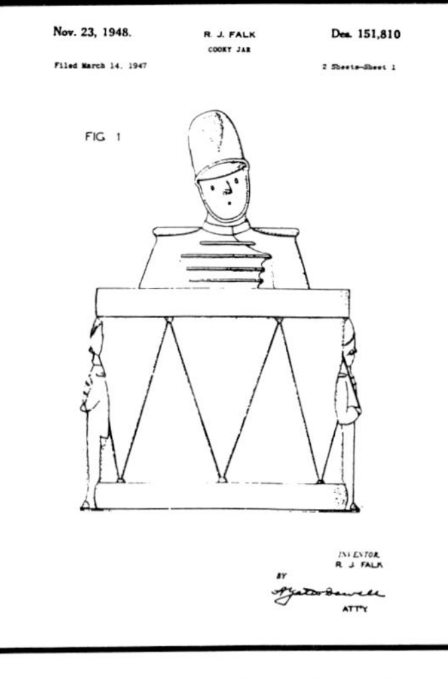
Nov. 23, 1948.
R. J. FALK
Des. 151,810
COOKY JAR
Filed March 14, 1947
2 Sheets-Sheet 1
FIG. 1
INVENTOR.
R. J. FALK
BY
ATT'Y

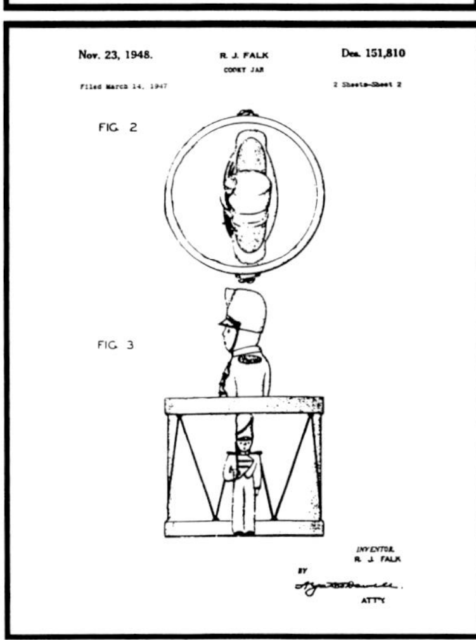
Nov. 23, 1948.
R. J. FALK
Des. 151,810
COOKY JAR
Filed March 14, 1947
2 Sheets-Sheet 2
FIG. 2
FIG. 3
INVENTOR.
R. J. FALK
BY
ATT'Y

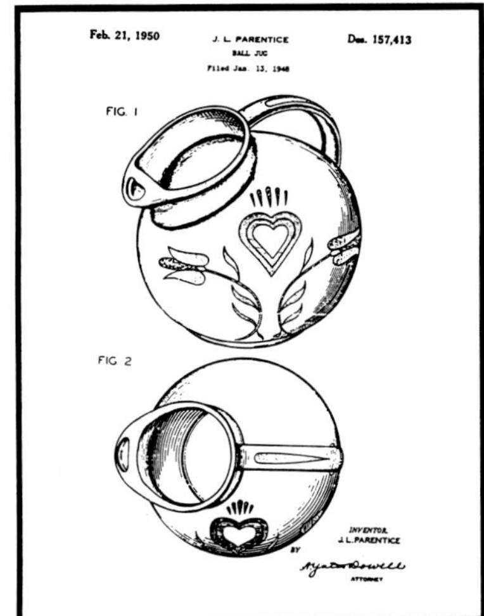
Feb. 21, 1950
J. L. PARENTICE
Des. 157,413
BALL JUG
Filed Jan. 13, 1948
FIG. 1
FIG. 2
INVENTOR.
J. L. PARENTICE
BY
ATTORNEY

Feb. 21, 1950
J. L. PARENTICE
Des. 157,414
JAR
Filed Jan. 13, 1948
FIG. 1
FIG. 2
INVENTOR.
J. L. PARENTICE
BY
ATTORNEY

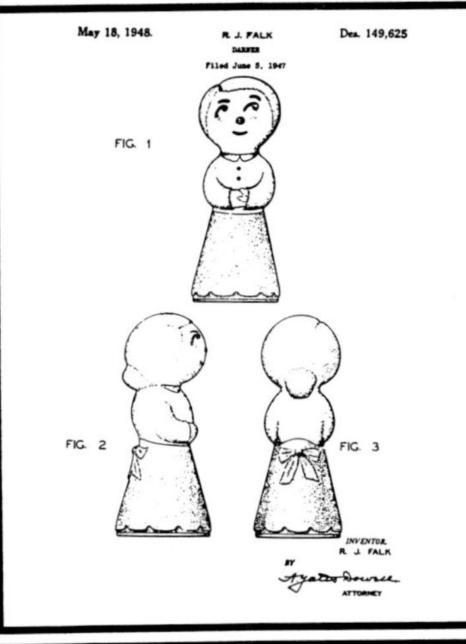
May 18, 1948.
R. J. FALK
Des. 149,625
DARNER
Filed June 5, 1947
FIG. 1
FIG. 2
FIG. 3
INVENTOR.
R. J. FALK
BY
ATTORNEY

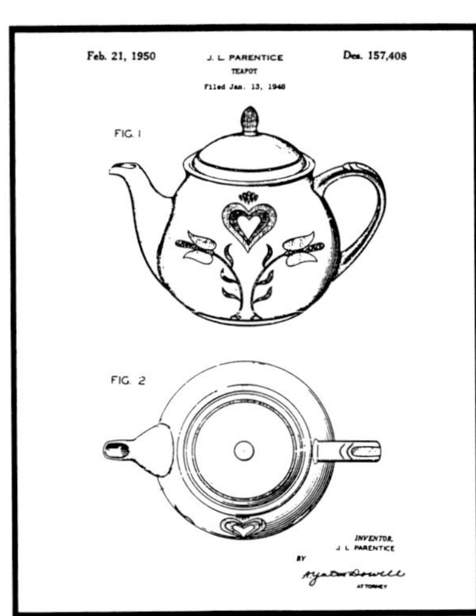
Feb. 21, 1950
J. L. PARENTICE
Des. 157,408
TEAPOT
Filed Jan. 13, 1948
FIG. 1
FIG. 2
INVENTOR.
J. L. PARENTICE
BY
ATTORNEY

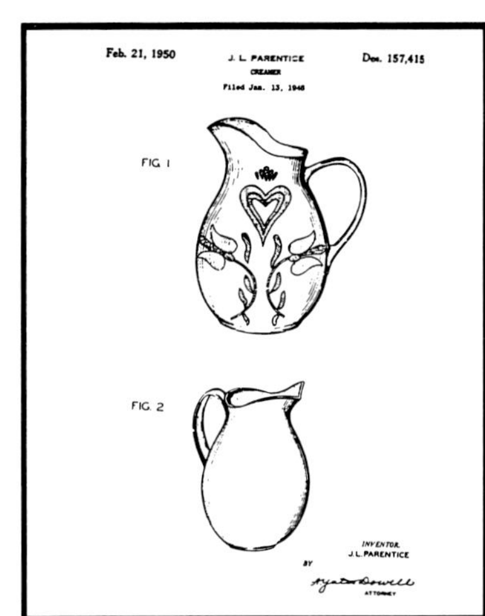
Feb. 21, 1950
J. L. PARENTICE
Des. 157,415
CREAMER
Filed Jan. 13, 1948
FIG. 1
FIG. 2
INVENTOR.
J. L. PARENTICE
BY
ATTORNEY

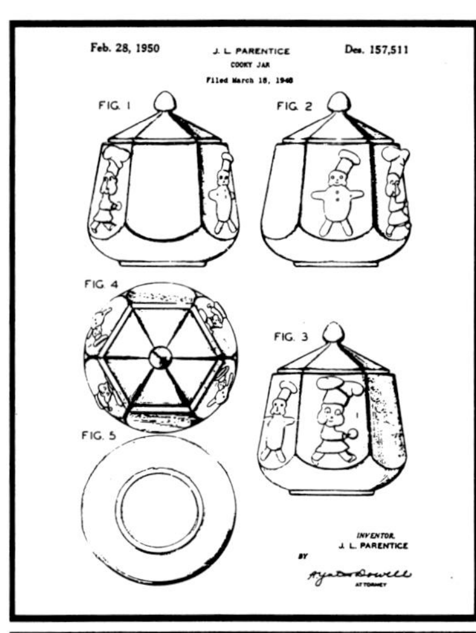
Feb. 28, 1950
J. L. PARENTICE
Des. 157,511
COOKY JAR
Filed March 18, 1948
FIG. 1
FIG. 2
FIG. 4
FIG. 3
FIG. 5
INVENTOR.
J. L. PARENTICE
BY
ATTORNEY

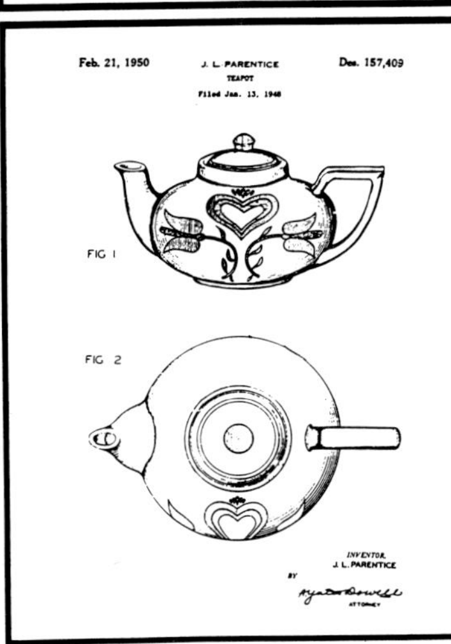
Feb. 21, 1950
J. L. PARENTICE
Des. 157,409
TEAPOT
Filed Jan. 13, 1948
FIG. 1
FIG. 2
INVENTOR.
J. L. PARENTICE
BY
ATTORNEY

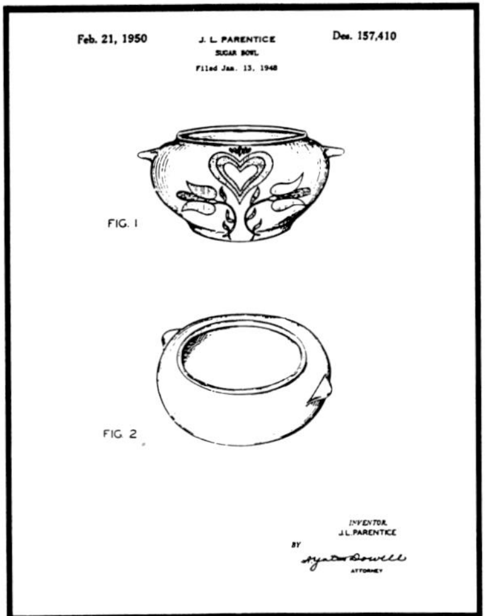
Feb. 21, 1950
J. L. PARENTICE
Des. 157,410
SUGAR BOWL
Filed Jan. 13, 1948
FIG. 1
FIG. 2
INVENTOR.
J. L. PARENTICE
BY
ATTORNEY

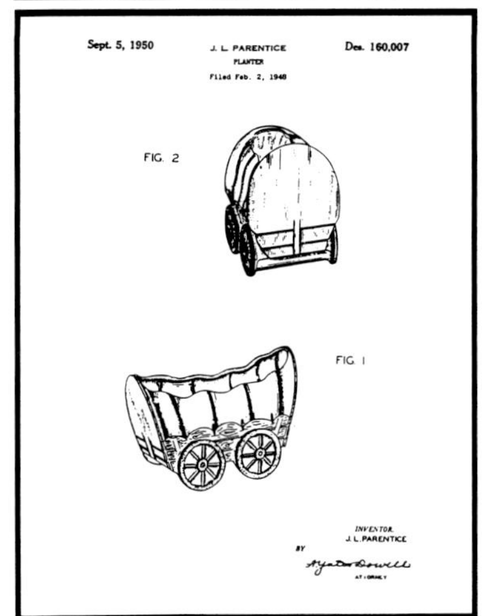
Sept. 5, 1950
J. L. PARENTICE
Des. 160,007
PLANTER
Filed Feb. 2, 1948
FIG. 2
FIG. 1
INVENTOR.
J. L. PARENTICE
BY

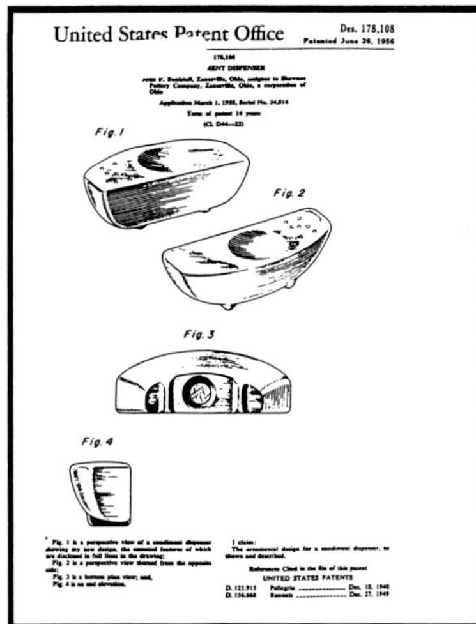
United States Patent Office
Des. 178,108
Patented June 26, 1956
Fig. 1
Fig. 2
Fig. 3
Fig. 4

Newsletters and Clubs

"EXCLUSIVELY SHAWNEE" Newsletter
Shawnee Pottery Collectors' Club
P. O. Box 713, New Smyrna Beach, FL 32170-0713
Pamela D. Curran, Founder & Publisher
Charter Year 1990 - Published Ten Times Per Year
Send Self-Addressed Stamped Envelope For Information

"Cookie Jarrin'" THE Cookie Jar Newsletter
Joyce & Fred Roerig, R.R. 2, Box 504, Walterboro, SC 29488
Charter Year 1991 - Bi-Monthly Newsletter
Send Self-Addressed Stamped Envelope For Information

Novelty Salt & Pepper Shakers Club
c/o Irene Thornburg, 581 Joy Rd, Battle Creek, MI 49017
Quarterly Newsletter - Annual Convention
Send Self-Addressed Stamped Envelope For Information

Bibliography

American Encaustic Tiling Company, Ltd. booklet, Zanesville, Ohio
Butler Brothers catalogs
Curran, Pamela D., personal collection of price listings, catalogs, photographs, and pottery
Dun & Bradstreet Inc., Analytical Report, October 2, 1959, Shawnee Pottery Company, Inc., Kenwood Ceramics Division
Exclusively Shawnee, The Shawnee Pottery Collectors Newsletter, copyright 1990, 1991, 1992, 1993, 1994, Pamela D. Curran
Financial Stock Guide Service Directory of Obsolete Securities, 1993 Edition, Financial Information, Inc.
General Information and Rules and Conditions, Shawnee Booklet No. 1, dated April 29, 1948
Gifford, David Edwin, *The Collector's Encyclopedia Of Niloak,* copyright 1993 Collector Books
Lehner, Lois, *Lehner's Encyclopedia of U.S. Marks on Pottery, Porcelain, & Clay*, copyright 1988 Collector Books
Martin, Jim and Cooper, Bette, *Monmouth-Western Stoneware*, copyright 1983 Wallace-Homestead Book Co.
Naval Ceremonies, Customs, and Traditions, Naval Institute Press, Annapolis, Maryland
Notes On A 50-Year Revolution, copyright 1973, private printing by American Olean Tile Company, Inc.
Ohio Historical Society, Columbus, Ohio
Personal Interviews and Correspondence by the author
RumRill Pottery Company catalogs
Schneider, Norris F., Zanesville, Ohio, researcher and historian
Shawnee Pottery Company Annual Reports, Zanesville, Ohio
Shawnee Pottery Company Catalogs, Zanesville, Ohio
Shawnee Pottery Company Prospectus dated May 6, 1937
Supnick, Mark E., *Collecting Shawnee Pottery*, copyright 1983, L-W Book Sales
United States Patent Office, Washington, D.C.
Wires, E. Stanley, Schneider, Norris F., Mesre, Moses, *Zanesville Decorative Tiles*, copyright 1972
Zaeske, Michael, Co-researcher of RumRill Pottery Company
Zanesville Times Recorder, Zanesville, Ohio, 1940s, 1950s, 1960s copyrighted material reprinted with permission

Additional References

Listed Are Additional References That May Be Of Interest To Shawnee Pottery Collectors:

Harvey Duke, **The Official Identification and Price guide to Pottery and Porcelain**, over 900 pages, copyright 1995, $18.00 plus $3.00 shipping. Elo Books, P.O. Box 020627, Brooklyn, NY 11202.

Lois Lehner, **Lehner's Encyclopedia of U.S. Marks on Pottery, Porcelain, & Clay**, copyright 1988, Collector Books.

Joyce & Fred Roerig, **The Collector's Encyclopedia of Cookie Jars, An Illustrated Value Guide**, copyright 1991, and **The Collector's Encyclopedia of Cookie Jars Book II**, copyright 1994, $24.95 each plus $3.00 shipping each. Joyce & Fred Roerig, Route 2, Box 504, Walterboro, SC 29488.

Mike Schneider, **The Complete Cookie Jar Book**, copyright 1991, $59.95 plus $2.95 shipping. Schiffer Publishing, Ltd., 77 Lower Valley Rd., Atglen, PA 19310.

Mike Schneider, **The Complete Salt and Pepper Shaker Book**, copyright 1993, $49.95 plus $2.95 shipping. Schiffer Publishing Ltd., 77 Lower Valley Rd., Atglen, PA 19310.

Mark Supnick, **Collecting Shawnee Pottery, A Pictorial Reference and Price Guide,** copyright 1993 L-W Book Sales (pocket-size book) $12.95 ppd to Mark Supnick, 2771 Oakbrook Manor, Ft. Lauderdale, FL 33332.

Mark & Ellen Supnick, **The Wonderful World of Cookie Jars**, copyright 1995, $34.95 plus $3.00 shipping, Mark & Ellen Supnick, 2771 Oakbrook Manor, Ft. Lauderdale, FL 33332.

Shawnee Pottery Price Guide

All prices are intended as guidelines only, with listed values placed only on items that are in excellent condition. This means that chips, hairlines, cracks, stains, or crazing on the pottery detract from the full values shown in this guide. For additional information refer to the *Condition and Value* chapter.

Prices in this guide may seem repetitious at times, but bear in mind that this book, more than any other published on the subject of Shawnee, often shows numerous variations of one particular jar or item. To this end, the minute variations shown from one item to another adds to our knowledge of what is available, but the price range for that item remains consistent. Perhaps the most noticeable of these is the yellow neckerchief Smiley Pig cookie jar, which may have many different combinations of decals and handpainted hair, flowers, patches, and bugs. But despite the numerous decorated combinations, many of the prices remain in a standard range. All salt & pepper shakers are priced as pairs, unless otherwise noted.

When laying out a book, the photos are often arranged in columns, starting on the left side of the page, and reading from top to bottom. When no positions are indicated, this is often the way to follow prices.

Abbreviations important to understanding this guide:

- **ND** = Not Determined, meaning no price can be fairly placed on this item due to rarity and/or uniqueness.
- **pl** = plain decorated, as it might have left the pottery, with no gold or decals
- **gt** = gold trim
- **dec** = decal(s)
- **g/d** = gold trim and decals
- **cp** = cold paint decorated, commonly found on pre-WWII items
- **hptd** = handpainted, such as in flowers, bugs, butterflies, etc.
- **neck** = neckerchief, such as on Smiley Pig
- **cllr** = collar, such as on Winnie Pig
- **ft** = feet
- **bl** = blue
- **wh** = white
- **yel** = yellow
- **blk** = black
- **grn** = green
- **brn** = brown
- **lt** = light
- **dk** = dark

Item	Price
36: Smiley, cp red neck	90-110
Smiley, repainted	75-80
Smiley, bl china, blk ft	225
Smiley, lt bl neck, brn ft	200
37: Smiley, bl neck, blk feet	225
Smiley, red neck, brn ft	200-225
Tulip Smiley, pl	250-275
Tulip Smiley, gt	450-500
Shamrock Smiley, pl	225-250
Shamrock Smiley, gt	400-425
38: Chrysan Smiley, pl	250-275
Chrysan Smiley, gt	425-450
Smiley, bl neck, pl	200
Smiley, bl neck, g/d	350-400
Roses Smiley, grn, g/d	600-650
Roses Smiley, red, g/d	600-650
39: Smiley, yel, g/d, red ft	325-350
Smiley, yel, g/d, wh ft	325-350
Smiley, bl, g/d, blk ft	350-400
Smiley, bl, g/d, brn ft	350-400
Smiley, yel, g/d, on left	325-350
Smiley, bl, g/d, brn ft	350-400
Daisy Smiley, g/d	650-700
Smil, yel, g/d, brn ft	325-350
40: Smil, yel g/d, block name	325-350
Smil, yel, hair, g/d, label	700-800
Smil, yel, hair, g/d, bug	700-800
Smil, hair, g/d, flwrs	700-800
Chrys Smil, red hair, gt	1000+
41: Smil, yel, g/d, spiky hair	700-800
Smil, yel g/d, bees/patch	500-525
Smil, bl, g/d, airbrushed	400-425
Smil, bl, g/d, hptd flwrs	450-475
42: Smil, g/d, ctr-part hair	700-800
Smil, g/d, hair, bee/nose	700-800
Smil, Lee Boy, g/d, hair	700-800
43: Sham Smil, gt, bug	600-650
Sham Smil, gt, btr-fly	600-650
Sham Smil, gt, bl neck	400-425
Smil, g/d, flwrs, 3 flies	500-525
44: Smil, bl, g/d, open eyes	450-500
Sham Smil, gt, btr-fly	600-650
Smil, g/d, blk patch	450-475
Smil, gt, flwrs/pants	475-500
Smil, g/d, hair, flwrs	700-800
45: Smiley, g/d, 2 bugs	500-525
Smiley, grn, g/d	350-400
Smiley, red, g/d	350-400
Smiley, g/d, poppy dec	600-650
46: Smiley, g/d, poppy dec	600-650
Chrys Smil, red neck gt	450-475
Apple Smiley, gt	700-800
Solid gold Smiley	1200+
Smiley, bl, g/d, label	350-400
Apple Smiley, gt	700-800
47: Smiley, bl g/d, Flat Head	350-400
Plum Smiley, no gold	500-550
Apple Smiley, no gold	550-600
Apple Smil, gt, lt app's	700-800
Apple Winn, gt, lt app's	750-850
Apple Smil, gt, dk app's	700-800
Apple Winn, gt, dk app's	750-850
48: Blue Winnie, pl	275-300
Blue Winnie, gt	500-525
Peach Winnie, pl	275-300
Peach Winnie, gt	500-525
Shamrock Winnie, pl	275-300
Blue Winnie, gt, red cllr	500-525
49: Blue Winnie, gt, red flwr	575-600
Pch Winnie, gt, red flwr	575-600
Blue Winnie, gt, red cllr	575-600
Blue Winnie, gt	500-525
Blue Winnie, gt, red flwr	575-600
Blue Winnie, gt	500-525
Pch Winn, gt, lime grn	ND
50: Pch Winn, gt, top1	575-600
Sham Winnie, gt, top 2	475-500
Sham Winnie, gt, top 3	575-600
Blue Winnie, gt, top 4	500-525
ClovB Winn, "Cookies"	350
ClovB Winnie, gt	650-750
Apple Winnie, pl	600-650
51: ClovB Winn, gt, top 1	650-750
Apple Winn, gt, top 2	750-850
Bl-berry Winn, gt, top 3	800-850
Apple Winnie, gt	750-850
Bl-berry Winn, gt, label	800-850
Bl-berry Winn, gt red cllr	750-800
52: B-sctch Winn bank, pl	375-425
B-sctch Smil bank, pl	350-400
Choc Winnie bank, pl	375-425
Choc Smiley bank, pl	350-400
B-sctch Smil bank, gt	500-525
Choc Smiley bank, gt	500-525
53: Choc Winnie bank, gt	525-550
Grn coat Winn bnk, gt	1000-1200
Platinum Winnie bank	ND
B-sctch Smiley c.jar, pl	600-650
54: Choc Smiley c.jar, pl	600-650
Choc Winnie c.jar, pl	650-700
55: Puss'nB, short tail, pl	150-175
Puss'nB, long tail, pl	175-200
Puss'nB, g/d	400-425
56: Puss'nB, g/d, wh bow	450-475
Puss'nB, g/d, top ctr	400-425
Puss'nB, g/d, top rt	400-425
Puss'nB, g/d, btm left	400-425
Puss'nB, g/d, long tail	450-475
57: Puss'nB, g/d, wh bow	450-475
Puss'nB, g/d, wh bow	450-475
Puss'nB, g/d, wedge ft	425-450
Puss'nB, solid gold	ND
58: Muggsy, pl	400-450
Muggsy, g/d	850
Muggsy, gold fur	1000+
Mussgy, gold wavy fur	1000+
Muggsy, Wh.Rose dec	1200+
59: Muggsy, grn scarf, g/d	2000+
Muggsy, blk fur, gt	1200+
Muggsy, g/d, left btm	850
Muggsy g/d, top rt pic, lf	850
Muggsy g/d, top rt pic, rt	850
Muggsy, g/d, right btm	850
60: Elephant, cp	90-100
Lucky Elephant, g/d	700-750
Lucky, g/d, label, flwrs	750-850
Lucky, g/d, bug on tusk	750-850
Lucky, g/d, bug & flwrs	750-850
61: Lucky, g/d, red cllr	850+
Lucky, gold, hptd flwrs	850+
Sailor Boy, blk hair, gt	700
Sailor Boy, pl, dotted tie	100-125
62: Sailor Boy, blond, gt	750
Sailor, g/d red/blnd hair	850
Sailor, g/d, blond hair	850
Sailor, blk hair, gt	700
Sailor, blond g/d bug/hat	1000+
Sailor, solid gold	ND
Sailor Boy, cp	100-125
63: Jack, yel, if w/orig cp	85-95
Jill, yel, if w/orig cp	85-95
Dutch Boy, stripes, pl	150-175
Dutch Girl, tulip, pl	175-200
Dutch Boy, stripes, g/d	300-325
Dutch Girl, g/d	275-325
64: Happy, g/d, flwrs/pants	275-300
Happy, gt, patches	300-325
Jack, bl pants, orig cp	85-95
Jill, bl skirt, orig cp	85-95
Happy, gt, patches	300-325
Happy, gt, patches	300-325
Happy, g/d	250-275
65: Happy, g/d	250-275
Happy, stripes, g/d	300-325
Happy, dbl stripes, pl	200-225
Cooky, g/d, top right	275-325
Cooky, g/d, btm right	275-325
66: Cooky, gt, flwrs/hand	325
Cooky, g/d, yel skirt	275-325
Cooky, g/d, bl skirt	275-325
Cooky, g/d, wh skirt	275-325
Jill, hptd flwrs on skirt	ND
67: Cooky, g/d, wh skirt	275-325
Cooky, g/d, flwrs/hand	325
Cooky, g/d	275-325
Cooky, g/d, tulip	300-325
Gr.North Dut Boy #1025	300-325
Gr.North Dut Girl #1026	350-375
68: Gr.North Dut Girl, beige	450+
Gr.North Dut Girl, white	275-300
Gr.North Dut Girl, Mimi	450+
Drum Major, pl	400-450
Drum Major, gt	700-725
Jo Jo Clown & Seal, pl	350-400
Jo Jo Clown & Seal, gt	650-700
69: Winking Owl, plain	125-140
Winking Owl gt, any shwn	275-300
Little Chef, green	100-110
Little Chef, white, gt	175-200
Little Chef, white, deco	125
Little Chef, cream, deco	125
70: Little Chef, caramel	100-110
Little Chef, yellow	100-110
Carousel, cp	100-110
Carousel, reptd	75
71: Corn King	225-250
Corn Queen	250-275
Jug, bl, grn, or yel	100-120
PennDutch	175
Jug, hptd pink flwrs	140-150
Jug, hptd yel flwrs	130-140
72: Fruit & Basket, gt	190-210
Fern	80-90
Snowflake	50-60
Lobster	250+
73: Basketweave, bl, pl	50-75
Basketweave, bl, g/d	100+
Basketweave, turq, dec	75-100
Basketweave, yel, dec	75-100
Basketweave, gt/flwrs	125
Basketweave, gt/flwrs	125
74: Canister, gt, saddle	125+
Canister, gt, leaves	125+
Canister, fruit dec, each	50-75
Canister, Dut B/G dec	50-75
Canister, yel, rose dec	50-75
75: Canister, gt, hat/cane	125+
Canister, gt, hat/cane	125+
76: Smiley, burg, pl	150-175
Smiley, burg, gt	275-300
Smiley, peach, pl	150-175
Smiley, peach, gt	275-300
Apple Smiley, pl	250
ClovB Smiley, gt	300-350
ClovB Smiley, gt	300-350
77: Smiley, solid platinum	600+
ClovB Smiley, solid plat	650+
Platinum goblet, each	80-100
ClovB Smiley, solid gold	600+
Gold goblet, each	75-95
78: Chanticleer, g/d	250
Chanticleer, pl	85-95
Chanticleer, g/d	250
Chanticleer, g/d	250
Chanti, gold spatter	275
79: Chanti, gt, poppy dec	250
Chanti, gt, airbrushed	270
Chanti, gt, airbrushed	270
Chanti, gt, airbrushed	270
Chanti, New Orleans	125
80: Chanti, g/d burg wings	295
Chanti, g/d, yel wings	250
Chanti, gold spatter	275
Chanticleer, gt	250
Chanticleer, solid gold	500+
Gold goblet, each	75-95
81: Left to right, top to btm:	
BoPeep, g/d red over pch	250
BoPeep, g/d bl over pch	250
BoPeep, bl hat, pl	100-110
BoPeep, bl hat, g/d	250
BoPeep, lav hat, pl	110-125
BoPeep, lav, pansy dec	250
BoPeep, g/d	250
BoPeep, g/d	250
BoPeep, gt, red ribbon	275
BoPeep, g/d	250
BoPeep, g/d	250
BoPeep, g/d	250
82: BoPeep, g/d	250
BoPeep, g/d	250
BoPeep, g/d	250
BoPeep, pl, grn bonnet	225+
BoPeep, gt, blue dress	350+
Top to bottom:	
BoPeep, red #47, gt	185-200
Boy Blue, #46, gt	200-225
BoPeep, red #47, pl	125
Boy Blue, #46, pl	135
BoPeep, red #47, gt	185-200
Boy Blue, #46, gt	200-225
83: Fruit, gt	90-100
Ribbed Utility	10-15
PennDutch	90-100
Space saver, left	15-18
Space saver, right	15-18
Sunflower	45-50
84: Flower & Fern	25-35
Valencia	35-45
Oval Ball Jug	22-25
White Corn	80-90
Corn King	80-90
Corn Queen	80-90
85: Fern	45-50
Snowflake	35-40
86: Smiley, pch flwr, pl	65-70
Child's Smiley	ND
ClovB Smiley, pl	90-95
Smiley, pch flwr, gt	150-160
Smiley #86, yel/bl, pl	70-75
Smiley #86, yel/bl, gt	150-160
ClovB Smiley, gt	175-200
ClovB Smiley, solid gold	300-325
87: Puss'nB, white, pl	35-50
Puss'nB, cream, pl	35-50
Puss'nB, gt, open eyes	175
Puss'nB, gt, closed eyes	175
Puss'nB, gt, roses dec	200-225
Puss'nB, #85, pl	35-40
Puss'nB, #85, pl	35-40
Puss'nB, #85, gt	125-135
Puss'nB, g/d	185-200
Puss'nB, all white	50+
88: Puss'nB, solid gold	300-325
Elephant, pl	25-30
Eleph, g/d, all shown, ea	175-200
89: Elephant solid gold	275-300
Elephant, g/d, ea shown	175-200
Elephant, white, gt	150
90: Spiral pitcher	15-18
Quill (Red Feather)	75-80
PD-style ball jug	25-30
PD-style tilt, hptd flwrs	45
PD-style tilt, bl/grn/yel	30
White Corn	35-40
Corn King	25-30
Corn Queen	25-30
91: Basket/ Smiley set, g/d	300
Ov Basket g/d, ea shown	95-110
Ov Basket pl, wh/blue	50-70
92: Oval Basket, g/d	110-120
Ov Basket g/d red on bl	125-150
Ov Basket, wh/grn, pl	50-70
Ov Basket, wh/grn, g/d	95-110
Basket/Smiley set, g/d	300
93: Rnd Basket, wh/grn, pl	70-90
Rnd Basket, wh/grn, g/d	100-125
Water Bucket, pl	45-50
Dutch Boy/Girl s&p, pl	50
Gr.N Bucket, pl	60-75
Gr.N Dut B&G s&p, pl	90-100
Water Bucket, g/d	100-110
Dutch B&G s&p, g/d	125
94: Bucket, g/d all shown, ea	100-110
PD-style jar, bl, grn, yel	35-40
Decorative sm shakers	20-25
Decorative grease jar	40-50
Decorative lg shakers	30-35
95: Sahara Range set, each	70-80
96: Pch Granny, pl	110-125
Pch Granny, g/d	225
Grn Granny, pl	135-150
Grn Granny, gt	260
Lav Granny, pl	110-125
Lav Granny, g/d	225
97: Pch Gran, g/d, ea shown	225
Lav Gran, matt finish, gt	300-325
Lav Gran, g/d, ea shown	225
98: Lav Granny, pl	110-125
Lav Granny, g/d	225
Pch Gran, g/d/& on apron	250
Lav Gran, red/hair g/d ea	325
Grn Gran, gt, matt finish	325-350
99: Grn Granny, pl	135-150
Pch Granny, g/d	225
Tom #44, red/bl, pl, ea	95-110
Far right, top to btm:	
Tom #44, bl/red, gt	225
Tom, wh body, label, pl	95-110
Tom #44, red/bl, gt	225
100: Tom #44, matt, gt	250+
Tom, gt, red patch	225+
Tom, gt, blue patch	225+
Elephant, yel, gt	300+
101: Elephant, yel, pl	175-195
Elephant, grn, pl	195-210
Elephant, bl, pl	175-195
Elephant, white deco	275
102: Rosette, half/full flwr	20-25
Drape	20-25
Criss Cross	20-25
103: Swirl	25-28
Rnd Conventional	25-28
Bell Flower	35-40
Flower & Fern paneled	35-40
104: Decorative Ribbed	25-30
Horizontal Ringed	22-25
Fern Embossed, gt	35-45
Elite, pl	30-35
Elite, g/d	45-50
Embossed Rose	30-35
105: Embossed Rose, pl	30-35
Conventional	30-35
Embossed Rose, gt	45-55
HorizRibbed Base, pl	30-35
HorizRib, gt, heart flwr	50-60
HorizRib, gt, bl flwr	50-60
106: Conventional, gt	45-50
Paneled, pl	30-35
Tulip, pl	40-45
Vertical Rib Base, gt	50-60
Ribbed Collar, pl	35-40
Ribbed Collar, gt	55-65
107: Clover Blossom, gt	150+
Sunflower, gt	100+
Sunflower, platinum	150+
White Corn, gt	150+
Corn King, 10-oz	200-225
Corn King, 30-oz	90-95
108: PennD (see pg 138 for prices)	
PD-style, 10-oz	30-35
PD-style, 14-oz	25-30
PD-style, 27-oz	30-35
PD-style, gt	45
109: Ribbed & Waves	45-50
Ribbed, yel or burg	40
Fern	75
Snowflake	75-95
110: Bell Flower, each	75-100
Flower/Fern Panel, ea	70-80
Flower/Fern	60-70
111: Fern, g/d	125
Penn Dutch	175
PD-style Jug	65-75
Sunflower	165
Patio Carafe w/stand	65-75
Embossed Flower, pl	85-95
Embossed Flower, gt	150-160
112: ClovB pigs, lg	135-145
ClovB pigs, sm	65-75
Heart pigs, lg	125

Item	Price
Heart pigs, sm	60
Heart pigs, lg, g/d	250+
Heart pigs, lg, g/d	250+
113: Heart pigs, lg, g/d	250+
Smiley, blue, g/d	190-200
Smiley, blue, pl	95-100
Smiley, blue, g/d	190-200
Smiley, red, g/d	190-200
114: Smiley, lg, red	95-100
Smil/Win, sm, red & bl	45-50
Smiley, lg, grn	95-100
Smil/Win, sm, grn	45-50
Right, top to bottom:	
Smiley, red, g/d	200-220
Smiley, grn, g/d	190-200
Smiley, fired-on red, g/d	190-200
Smiley, blue, g/d	190-200
115: Smiley, grn, g/d	190-200
Smiley mismtchd g/d, ea	85-90
Smiley, grn, g/d	190-200
Smiley, pch, g/d	200-220
Smiley, grn, g/d	190-200
Heart pigs, sm, gt	100-110
116: Left: Smiley, pch, sm	55-60
Ctr: Smiley, pch, lg	100-110
Right: Smil, pch, sm, gt	95-100
Left: Smil/Winn, sm, gt	95-100
Right: Smil/Winn, sm, gt	95-100
ClovB pigs, sm, gt	ND
Smil & Winn, sm, gt	95-100
Smiley, orig version, cp	35-40
Smiley, orig version, gt	75-85
117: Smil/Winn, gt, yel dots	95-100
ClovB pigs, gt, coats	ND
Smiley, grn neck, sm	75-85
Smiley, yel neck, sm	75-85
Smil, pch/red, gt, each	35-40
Farmer Pig, pl	25
Farmer Pig, gt	45
Muggsy, lg	110-125
Muggsy, sm	50-60
118: Muggsy, lg, gt	220-240
Muggsy, sm, gt	125
Muggsy, cropped ears	75
119: Puss'nB, pl	35
Puss'nB, gt, any shown	75-85
Grey-eyed Owls, pl	25
Grn-eyed Owls, pl	30
Owls, gt	45-50
120: Owls gt pch/yel feathers	55-65
Owls, gt, any shown	45-50
Ducks, pl	40
Chanticleer, lg, gt	100-125
121: Chanticleer, lg, pl	50-60
Chanti, sm, pl w/red	30-35
Left: Chanti, sm, pl	25-30
Right: Chanti, sm, gt	75-85
Dutch B&G, brn, pl	30-35
Dutch B&G, bl, pl	30-35
Dutch B&G, brn, gt	50-60
Dutch B&G, bl, gt	50-60
122: Dutch B&G, bl, gt	50-60
Swiss B&G, pl	30-35
Swiss B&G, gt	50-60
Sailor Boy & BoPeep	18-22
Dutch B&G, white, pl	50
Gr. N. Dutch B&G, pl	90-100
123: Dut B&G, g/d, any shown	125
Dut B&G, brown trim	ND
Dut B&G, rust color	60-70
124: Chef S&P, pl	20-25
Chef S&P, gt	35-40
Flower Pots, pl	20-25
Flower Pots, gt	35-40
Flwr Cluster, pl	35
Flwr Cluster, gt	65
Fruit, lg	30-35
Fruit, sm	22-25
Fruit, lg, gt	65-70
125: Lobster	125+
Lobster Claw	40-50
Water Can, pl	22-25
Water Can, g/d	60-65
Milk Can, pl	20-25
Milk Can, g/d	65-70
Wheelbarrow, pl	22-25
Wheelbarrow, g/d	65-70
Cottage	250-275
Deco, lg, gt	65-70
Susan shakers	25-35
126: Sahara	30-35
White Corn, pair	25-35
Corn King, pair	20-25
Corn Queen, pair	20-25
White Corn, lg, gt	125+
PD-style Jug	35
Stippled Birds	18-20

Item	Price
Modern Ribbed	20-25
127: Stippled Birds	18-20
Rabbit	20-25
Elephant	15-18
Stippled Fish	15-18
Stippled Trop Fish	15-18
Stippled Blow Fish	15-18
128: Grecian Pitcher	12-15
Ribbed Ewer	12-15
Jug w/Bug	15-18
Rib-Neck Pitcher	12-15
Pitcher	12-15
129: ClovBlos: Smiley c.jar	300-350
Winnie c.jar	350-375
Smiley pitcher	195
Smiley creamer	90-95
Teapot	95-100
Sugar w/lid	65-75
Winn/Smil range S&P	135-145
Winn/Smil table S&P	65-75
130: Cottage cookie jar	1000+
Cottage sugar bowl	325-350
Cottage S&P	250-275
Cottage teapot	400-425
Fern mixing bowl set	110-125
5" bowl	15-20
6" & 7" bowls, each	20-25
8" bowl	25-30
9" bowl	30
Fern ball jug	35-45
Fern creamer	20-25
Fern open sugar	20-25
131: Fern pitcher	45-50
Fern match box hldr	75-85
Fern salt box	95-100
Fern cookie jar	80-90
Fern canister	65-75
Fern grease jar	35-45
Fern teapot, 6-cup	35-45
Fern S&P	35-45
132: Fern teapot 2-cup	55-65
Flwr/Fern salt box	80-90
F/F open sugar	12-15
F/F creamer	12-15
F/F salt box, gt	110-125
F/F ball jug, g/d	50-55
F/F match box hldr	70-80
133: F/F grease jar	35-40
F/F Aladdin crmr	15-20
F/F Aladdin sugar	15-20
F/F range S&P	20-25
F/F ball jug	25-35
F/F table S&P	12-15
F/F ball crmr	15-20
134: F/F teapot 5-cup	20-25
F/F teapot 6-cup	25-30
F/F jardiniere	10-12
Fruit casserole	75-85
Fruit sm S&P	22-25
Fruit cookie jar	125-150
Fruit ball jug	55-65
Fruit lg S&P	30-35
Fruit sugar	30-35
135: Fruit lg S&P, 5-hole	ND
Fruit cookie jar, gt	190-210
Fruit casserole, gt	110-125
Fruit ball jug, gt	90-100
Fruit sugar, gt	65-70
Fruit lg S&P, gt	65-70
Fruit sm S&P, gt	35-40
Laurel pitcher	40-45
Laurel creamer	25-30
Laurel open sugar	25-30
136: Laurel grease jar	35-40
Laurel lg S&P	25-30
Laurel teapot	35-40
138: PennD listing of cat. pg 137:	
Jug #52, no insert	150
Cooky jar #75	175
Beater jug	ND
Teapot 10-oz	75-85
Teapot 14-oz	40-50
Teapot 18-oz	50-60
Teapot 27-oz	60-70
Teapot 30-oz	125
Ball jug #64	90-100
Utility jar	65-75
Range S&P	55-60
Ball jug crmr #12	40-50
Tilt creamer #10	50-60
Sugar bowl, open	55-65
139: Snowflake ball jug	35-40
Snowf mix bowl set	90-100
5" & 6" bowl, each	10-15
7" & 8" bowl, each	20
9" bowl	25
Snowf pitcher	40-45

Item	Price
Snowf cookie jar	50-60
Snowf grip top bowl, 7"	40
140: Snowf teapot 8-cup	45-50
Snowf teapot 2-cup	50-60
Snowf teapot 5-cup	35-40
Snowf creamer	15-18
Snowf open sugar	15-18
Snowf S&P	20-25
Snowf grease jar	30-35
141: Sunflower Ball jug	45-50
Sunf Range S&P	35
Sunf Coffee jug	135-145
Sunf Ball creamer	40-45
Sunf Teapot	50-60
Sunf Table S&P	25
Sunf Covered jar	35-40
Wave Range S&P	20-25
Wave Util ptchr #32	30-40
Wave Grease jar	30-35
Wave Open sugar	25-30
Wave Creamer #13	25-30
Wave Teapot	30-35
Wave ptchr #60, pg 142	40-50
142: White Corn sm S&P	25-35
WC Pitcher	80-90
WC Teapot	95-100
WC Creamer	35-40
WC Sugar shaker	50-60
WC Sugar bowl	45
WC Range S&P	35-40
WC Teapot, gt	150+
WC Pitcher, gt	125-150
WC Sugar shaker, gt	125
WC Sugar bowl, gt	85
WC Creamer, gt	75
WC Range S&P, gt	125+
WC Table S&P, gt	75
144: Valencia Dancers	250-300
Dinner plates, each	15-18
6-3/4 plates, each	8-10
145: Valencia: 13" chop pl	25+
15" chop plate	35+
Teacup	15-20
Saucer, each	8-10
Soup bowl	15-20
Bowl 9"	20-25
146: Tumblers, each	40-50
Relish tray	150-200
S&P	18-20
Teapot	50+
Carafe w/lid	50+
Sugar	15-20
Creamer	15-20
147: Batter jug w/lid	50+
Ice Pitcher, each	35-45
Mix bowl 9"	40+
Bud vase	20+
148: Ice Pitcher, each	35-45
Ash tray	15-20
Bowl, ftd	50+
Bowl, marmite	30+
Bowl, mix 5"	20+
Bowl, mix 6"	25+
Bowl, mix 7"	30+
Bowl, mix, 8,10,11,12"	40+
Bowl, 9-1/2"	25-30
Bowl, lug, lid	30+
Candle hldr, bulb pr	35+
Candle hldr, tripod, pr	45+
Casserole 7-1/2"	40
Casserole 8-1/2"	50
Casserole, ftd 8"	60
Casserole, lug	50
Coaster	15-20
Coffee pot	60+
Coffee pot, AD	60+
Compote ftd	50
Compote ped	50
Cookie jar	175+
Cup AD	15-20
Cup, cream soup	20-25
Cup tall	20-25
Dish 5"	10-15
Dish 6"	15-18
Egg cup	15-20
Jug, 32 oz ball	35
Jug, syrup	50
Marmalade	45
Mustard	45
Pie baker 9-1/4"	25
Pie baker 10-1/2"	25
Plate comptmt	25
Saucer AD	7-10
Saucer, off-ctr ring	7-10
Stack set, rnd	65+
Tray, for batter	50
Utensil fork	55

Item	Price
Utensil pie svr	35
Utensil spoon	45
Utility tray	30
Vase ftd 8"	25
Vase ftd 10"	35
Vase ftd 12"	45
149: Corn King: #5 mix bowl	30-35
#6 mix bowl	20-25
#8 mix bowl	30-40
#65 indv teapot	200-225
#66 cookie jar	225-250
#68 plate	35-40
#69 mug	45-50
#70 creamer	25-30
#71 pitcher	80-90
#72 butter	45-50
#73 indv cass	80-90
#74 casserole	60-70
#75 teapot	90-95
#76 S&P, sm	20-25
#77 S&P, lg	30-35
#78 sugar	35
#79 corn hldr	35
#90 teacup	35-40
#91 saucer	20-22
#92 fruit dish	40-45
#93 salad	35-40
#94 cereal	45-50
#95 veg dish	65-70
#96 platter	55
150: Polly Ann's Pop Corn set	300+
Sugar bowl, gt	75+
Teapot, gt	150+
Creamer, gt	75+
Indian Corn S&P	ND
Snack Set boxed	450+
151: Casserole, kernels on lid	ND
152: Lobster pin	75
Claw S&P	40-50
Snack jar	250+
Range Set, gt	125
153: Lobster S&P	125+
Hors d' hldr	125-150
Relish pot	75
Butter dish	65-75
Creamer	50+
Sugar bowl	25-30
Mug, each	100-125
154: Spoon hldr	150-175
Plate	25-30
Fr. cass 16-oz	25-30
Fr. cass 1-qt	30-35
155: Fr. cass 10-oz	12-15
Fr. cass 2-qt	40-45
Casserole & stand	40-50
Boxed cass set	175
Mix bowl #915	35
Mix bowl #917	40
Mix bowl #919	45
Salad bowl #921	25
Spaghetti #922	45-50
Batter #928	75+
156: Corn Queen: #5 mix bowl	30-35
#6 mix bowl	20-25
#8 mix bowl	30-40
#65 indv teapot	225
#66 cookie jar	250-275
#68 plate	35-40
#69 mug	45-50
#70 creamer	25-30
#71 pitcher	80-90
#72 butter	45-50
#73 indv cass	90
#74 casserole	60-70
#75 teapot	95
#76 S&P, sm	20-25
#77 S&P, lg	30-35
#78 sugar	35
#79 corn hldr	35
#90 teacup	35-40
#91 saucer	20-22
#92 fruit dish	40-45
#93 salad	35-40
#94 cereal	45-50
#95 veg dish	65-70
#96 platter	55
157: #100 Pop Corn set	250+
#101 Snack set	400+
#102 Table set	150+
#103 Mixing Bowl set	150+
#106 Place Setting	300+
#108 Corn-Roast set	350+
158: Brunch Bowl w/stand	45-55
3-pc Brunch bowl set	75-85
Sundial dish/stand, each	35-45
159: Salad Susan w/frame	90-100
Sundial casserole	25-30

Item	Price
160: Saucy Susan w/frame	85-90
Saucy Susan set w/box	110-125
Supper Susan on frame	50-60
161: Party Chafing Dish/stand	50-60
Toastee Susan w/frame	40-50
162: Two Birds & nest	22-25
Caricature Bird	8-10
Bird on shell	18-22
Top row: Carica Duck	8-10
Top row: Carica Bird	8-10
Btm row: Duckling	8-10
Btm row: Duckling	8-10
Btm row: Duck	12-15
163: Two Parakeets/stump	10-12
Bird on plant dish	20-22
Dove on plant dish	30-35
Duck and plant dish	25-30
Birds/dr-wood, gry, pl	45
Birds/dr-wood, brn, pl	45
Birds/dr-wood, brn, gt	75
164: Flying Mallard, pl	20
Flying Mallard, gt	30
Duckling #720, pl	18
Duckling #720, gt	25
Duckling/egg, pl	12-15
Flying goose #820	20-25
Duckling & egg, gt	20-22
165: Duck/cart, yel/wh	15-18
Chick & egg #730	30-35
Bird planter #508	10-12
Top row: Pig/basket	8-10
Top row: Duckling	8-10
Top row: Penguin	8-10
Ctr row: Rabbit/cabbage	8-10
Ctr row: Goose/hat	10-12
Ctr row: Kitten/yarn	8-10
Btm row: Rabbit/ basket	10-12
Btm row: Sitting pig	8-10
Btm row: Squirrel/stump	10-12
166: Top row: Parakeet	12-14
Top row: Rooster	22-25
Top row: Butterfly	12-14
Btm row: Ram	22-25
Btm row: Giraffe	25-30
Striped Kitten	25-30
Rooster Knwd #1503 ea	35-40
Kitty with bow	15-18
Cat & sax, #729	40-50
167: Pig #760	10-12
Hound/jug	10-12
Squirrel #664	10-12
Bird #502	10-12
Blackie the cat, pl	12-15
Blackie the cat, gt	20-22
Cat & sax, #729	40-50
Kitten/basket #2026	50-75
Fawn/stump #535	12-15
168: Fawn, P209	10-12
Fawn, P207	8-10
Fawn, P205	8-10
Lying Deer	18-20
Fawn/log #766, pl	25-30
Fawn/log #766, gt	35-45
Deer/shadowbox, pl	18-20
Deer/sh-box, gt, not shwn	25-30
Fawn/fern #737	20-22
Fawn/stump #624	14-16
Deer/fawn #669	14-16
169: Two fawns #721	20-22
Hound dog	8-10
Ibex #613	10-12
Dachshund, each	12-15
Gazelle/base #522, each	75-95
170: Puppy with bee	8-10
Crouching spaniel, ea	10-12
Puppy dog #662	15-18
Queenie, gt	20-22
Queenie, pl	12-15
Poodle/carriage, pl	20-25
Poodle/carriage, gt	30-35
171: Puppy dog, gt, #662	22-25
Sitting terrier	20
Hound/peke, pl	12-15
Hound/peke, gt	20-22
Dog in boat	20-22
Chihuahua/house, pl	25
Chihuahua/house, gt	35-40
Spaniel/house, pl	25
Spaniel/house, gt	35-40
172: Terrier/house, pl	25
Terrier/house, gt	35-40
Hound/jug, pl	10-12
Hound/jug, gt, "cider"	15-18
3-or-2 Button Shoe/dog	10-12
Frog/guitar	12-15
Panda/cradle, each	35-45
Poodle/bike	28-30

Item	Price
173: Cub bear/wagon, pl	75-85
Cub bear/wagon, gt	110-120
Cub bear, wagon & dog	ND
Elephant w/howdah	20-22
Elephant, P426, each	15-20
174: Elephant, leaf base	45-50
Bull, leaf base	40-45
Elephant #759, pl, ea	12-15
Elephant #759, gt	18-20
Frog	15-18
Bull, leaf base	40-45
Frog on lily pad	35-40
Bull #663	18-20
175: Dolphin, A674	8-12
Dolphin #845, ea	10-12
Blow fish, each	8-12
Tropical fish #717, pl	45-55
Tropical fish #717, gt	85-95
Angel fish	45-50
Turtle #661	15-18
176: Tropical fish #717, gt	85-95
Lamb w/flower, ea	10-15
Dancing lamb	25
177: Poodle #725, gt	22-25
Lamb #724, gt	22-25
Flowered pig	10-12
Mouse/cheese, pl	30-35
Mouse/cheese, gt	40-45
Circus horse	18-20
Pig/wheelbarrow	18-20
Melancholy donkey	15-18
178: Moon-eyed calf	15-18
Kentucky colt	15-18
Frisky colt	15-18
Donkey/basket #671	18-22
Colt/stump #2028	45-65
179: T-row: Red pony #506	25-30
T-row: Wh pony #506	25-30
B-row: Yel pony #1509	35-40
B-row: Brnze pony #506	65-75
Donkey/mex cart	10-12
Donkey/basket #671, gt	30-35
Sad-faced donkey	20-25
Sitting donkey #722	20-25
180: Donkey pulling cart	8-10
3 Pigs & fence	10-12
Fox & bag	40-45
Squirrel/nut, pl	25-30
Squirrel/nut, gt	40-45
181: Rabbit/turnip, pl	25-30
Rabbit/turnip, gt	40-45
Rabbit/wheelbarrow	22-25
Rabbit/stump	10-12
Baby skunk	35
182: Southern belle	18-22
Southern girl	15-20
Girl/wishing well	12-15
Dutch girl/flwrs	8-10
Children on shoe	15-18
183: Knomes/log	12-15
Girl/basket #534, gt	18-22
Girl/umbrella #560	18-22
184: Boy/low stump	15-18
Boy/high stump	12-15
T-row: Boy/w-barrow	18-22
T-row: Girl/umbrella	18-22
B-row: Fishing boy	12-15
B-row: Girl/basket, pl	12-15
Colonial lady #616	18-22
Boy/wheelbarrow, gt	25-30
185: Polynesian #896, pl	35-45
Polynesian #896, gt	55-65
Kerchief girl, pl	25-30
Kerchief girl, gt	35-45
Kneeling girl w/basket	22-25
Mexican boy, pl	18-20
Mexican girl, pl	18-20
186: Bicycle for two, pl	65
Bicycle for two, gt	100
T-row: Girl & gate	8-12
T-row: Boy & gate	8-12
B-row: Boy & dog	8-12
B-row: Pixie #562	8-12
Tony/Rum Carioca	45-55
Tony/peddler, pl	18-22
Tony/peddler, gt	25-30
187: Buddha #524	25
Elf/shoe #765, gt	20-22
Elf/shoe, pl, not shwn	15
Swan & elf	75-95
Elf & wheelbarrow	12-15
Elf & flower, pl	10-12
Elf & flower, gt	15-18
188: Wishing well, pl	15-20
Wish/well, gt, not shwn	25-28
Clown w/blocks	40-45
Clown w/pot	15-18

Jo Jo clown, pl	20-22
Jo Jo clown, gt	30
T-row: Girl/mandolin	20-25
T-row: Chin girl/urn	12-15
B-row: Chin boy/vase	10-12
B-row: Coolies/basket	8-10
Chinese boy/urn	12-15
189: T-row: Chin girl/book	10-12
T-row: Ancient chinese	12-15
T-row: Chin boy & girl	10-12
B-row: Coolie/cart, pl	8-10
B-row: Coolie/cart, gt	12-14
Coolie/rickshaw	18-22
Boy/chicken, all grn	25-30
Boy/chicken, pl	18-22
Boy/chicken, gt	30-35
190: Military boot	18-22
Italian boot	8-12
Button baby shoes/base	15-18
Button baby shoes, pair	15-20
Laced baby shoe	8-10
191: Elf shoe, gt	15-18
Elf shoe, pl	10-12
Shoe/flower, pl	8-12
Shoe/flower, gt	14-16
T-row: Double flower	8-10
T-row: Lady's slipper	12-15
B-row: Piano #528	22-25
B-row: Top hat	8-10
Piano #528, gt	35-40
Globe #635	25
192: Alarm clock #1262	12-15
Hobby horse #660	20-22
Double bowknot	18-20
Rocking horse #526	15-18
Sea shell #665	15-18
Leaf #509	10-12
Double bowknot, gt	20-22
193: Three pots/trellis	20-25
Canopy bed, pl	75-100
Canopy bed, gt	125+
Shadowbox w/rose	22-25
194: Basket cradle	14-16
High chair #727	50-60
Basket #640, each	15-20
Sprinkling can, 5-1/4"	12-14
Sprinkling can, 6"	14-16
195: Coal bucket	12-14
Wheelbarrows, cp	6-8
Wheelbarrow, undrglz	12-14
JP Picnic basket	25
JP Coal bucket	25
JP Cradle	25
JP House	25
JP Pushcart	30
JP Stagecoach	35
Watering can	12-14
196: Pump/trough, pl	12-15
Dutch windmill, pl	20-25
Dutch windmill, gt	35-40
Old mill/pond, pl	15-18
Old mill/pond, gt	25-30
Bridge, pl	15-18
Bridge, gt	25-30
197: 4-pc Train set, pl	115-125
Each pl piece separate	25
White caboose #553	30-35
4-pc Train set, gt	175
Each gt piece separate	40
4-pc White train, deco	225
Ea wh/deco pc separate	45-50
198: 19th Century Engine	50-60
Prairie schooner, pl	25-35
Prairie schooner, gt	45-55
Wood grain cart	8-10
Truck & trailer, 2-pc	70-75
199: Auto, 4-spoke	12-15
Auto, 8-spoke	12-15
Covered wagon	12-15
Circus wagon	45-55
Gondola	10-15
200: Oval plntr, plain	8-10
Oval plntr, undrglz deco	10-12
Oval plntr, shamrocks	8-10
Emb. flwrs & leaves	12-14
Emb. bulb bowl	8-10
Criss cross w-box	6-8
Paneled w-box	6-8
201: Wheat flwr bowl	15-18
Emb. flwr w-box	6-8

Planting dish #3002	6-8
Woven check	8-10
Ivy bulb bowl #3025	10-15
202: Shell bulb bowl	12-14
Lily of valley	6-8
Square pointed	6-8
Square planter	6-8
Wood grain bisque	8-10
Ribbed square bowl	8-10
Basket weave	8-10
203: Oval scalloped #2002	10-12
Square spatter	8-10
Shell planter	14-16
Basket weave	8-10
Leaf planter #442	16-18
204: Red leaf #440 or #441	12-14
Leaf dish #439	12-14
Emb Feather bowl	12-14
Flared leaf	10-12
Flower chain bowl	10-12
205: Oval leaf	14-16
Embossed daisy	8-10
Flower bowl w/stand	20-25
Planting dish w/stand	20-25
206: Calla lily, pl	12-14
Calla lily, gt	18-20
Wild rose, pl	12-14
Wild rose, gt	18-20
Blue flwr console, pl	18-22
Blue flwr console, gt	25-28
Blue flwr cornucopia	16-18
Blue flwr planter	16-18
207: All items shown, each	6-10
208: Pot & saucer	6-8
Emb diamond #453	8-10
Emb diamond #454	6-8
Emb diamond #455	8-10
Petal jardiniere	6-8
African violet #463	8-10
Diamond shape #416	10-12
Duotone #494	6-8
Two tone square #410	8-10
Swirled leaf	6-8
Ribbed vegetable	6-8
Leaf w/scallop top	8-10
Square jardiniere	6-8
209: Burlap	10-12
Flared petal #466	12-14
Woven checks #1501	10-12
Bamboo jardiniere	12-15
Classic jardiniere	12-15
African violet #533	10-12
Contiempo jard #438	10-12
Flower/fern jard	18-20
211: Tulip #1115	12-14
Swan #725	12-14
Lily #705	12-14
Flower #1135	12-14
Cornucopia #735	12-14
Flower #1135, gt, ea	16-18
Round cornucopia	12-14
Tilted flwr #1125, decal	16-18
Top: Clover bloom	12-14
Top: Fluted urn	8-10
Top: Chain of flwrs	6-8
Top: Asters	6-8
Top: Leaf	8-10
Btm: Daisy pitcher	8-10
Btm: Emb flwrs/stems	8-10
Btm: Dbl hndl vase	6-8
Btm: Rib/emb flwrs	8-10
212: Top photo: Panel 2-hndl	8-10
Emb feather	15-18
Swan #806, each	18-20
Square fluted	8-12
Dolphin	18-20
Hexagon swirl	8-12
Pedestal dbl hndl	8-10
Btm photo: Ribbed V	12-15
Flared swirl	12-15
Scalloped	12-15
Flared rib w/lugs	16-18
Paneled pitcher 9"	16-18
Paneled pitcher 8"	14-16
Emb. flwr w/loops	10-12
Bow knot #819	15-18
213: Top photo: Diag swirl	15-18
Pedestal base	18-20
Bulbous	15-18
Dove	18-20

Cat-o-nine-tails	18-20
Btm photo: Cornu's, oval	12-14
Cornu's, rectangle	14-16
214: Hand vases, 7"	12-14
Emb. iris vase	12-14
Iris fan vase	16-18
Hand vase 10"	14-16
Hand vase 7"	12-14
Rope vase	18-22
Burlap vase	16-18
Leather vase	16-18
Geometric	8-10
Tulip	10-12
Cornucopia	10-12
215: Pitcher bud vase	10-12
Dbl handle bud, pl	10-12
Dbl handle bud, gt	14-16
Scallop top panel	8-10
Scallop lug bud	12-14
Violet cornucopia	18-22
Philodendron, pl	18-20
Philodendron, gt	25-30
Diamond pitcher	18-20
216: Flared horn	18-20
Diagonal ribs/flwrs	16-18
Flwrs & ribs	16-18
Wicker w/chain flwrs	20-25
Emb. flwr & leaf	18-20
Flowers & bows	20-25
217: Diamond w/flwr, gt	25-30
Diamond w/flwr, pl	20-22
Bamboo 5"	10-12
Bamboo 7"	15-18
1200 Vase Series:	
Tulip 1269	20-22
Flwr bud 1201	12-14
Fan vase 1264	10-12
Cornucopia 1256	14-16
3-flwr lug 1205	16-18
Chain flwrs 1235	16-18
Short wheat 1215	12-14
Emb flwr 1257	18-20
Tall wheat 1259	20-22
218: Dbl wheat 1258	14-16
Trpl wheat 1267	18-20
Tall purple flwr 1268	20-22
Bl flwr bud 1202	12-14
Yel flwr bud 1203	12-14
Short purple 1225	16-18
Dbl pedestal 1266	16-18
Girl/cornu 1275	16-20
Boy/cornu 1265	16-20
Flower vase 865	12-15
Leaf 822, pl	20-25
Leaf 821, pl	14-18
Leaf 823, pl	25-30
219: Leaf 822, gt	30+
Leaf 821, gt	22-25
Leaf 823, gt	40+
Gazelle & baby	50-60
Giraffe & baby	50-60
Bud vase pitcher	12-15
8" vase #838	14-16
Flared vase #869	18-22
Cloth vase #880	18-22
220: Howdy Doody bank	450-550
Bulldog bank	175
Tumbling bear bank	175
221: Rondo experimental	ND
Simplex holders, each	8-10
222: Setter heads, ea pair	35-45
Potter's Wheel, dk grn	400-450
Potter's Wheel, brn	300-350
223: Flying geese, pl, pair	35-45
Flying geese, gt, pair	65-75
224: Pyramid clock	250+
Copper-clad clock	85-100
Trellis clock	50
225: Trellis, orig face	75-85
Grandaughter	125-150
226: 4-Cornu console set	30-40
4-Cornu console, g/d	75-80
Magnolia console set	50-55
Magnolia cand/hldrs	18-22
227: Magnolia bowl, pl	25-30
Magnolia cand/hldrs, gt	30-35
Blossom console set	30-40
Scallop emb petals bowl	18-22
228: Rib cornu console set	35-45
Emb rectangular set	35-45

Candle hldr #3026	25-30
Gold spatter console set	60-75
229: Candle hldr, platinum	40-50
Candle hldr FB222, pair	15-18
Cameo console set	30-35
230: Mini-mini animals, each	10-15
231: Stippled bird	8-12
Frog	12-15
Turtle	12-15
Bird in flight	10-12
Bird, head down	10-12
232: Sitting canary	10-12
Duck, A603	8-12
Duck 3"	8-10
Feeding duck	12-15
Crane	8-10
Spaniel	12-15
Swimming swan	12-15
233: Crane	10-12
Rabbit, ears up	12-15
Pekingese	15-18
Parrot	15-18
Standing bear	12-15
Swan preening	15-18
Dolphin	12-15
234: Elephant	10-12
Tropical fish 2-1/2"	12-15
Owl on book	15-18
Tropical fish	15-18
Stippled fish	12-15
Fish 2-1/4"	12-15
Fawn	10-12
235: Deer, facing front	10-12
Deer, facing left	10-12
Baby donkey	12-15
Terrier	18-22
Mumpy Kitty	25-35
Sealyham	25-35
Terrier, sore paw	25-35
236: Southern girl	12-15
Sailor boy	125-150
Dutch girl	12-15
Chinese girl, pl	10-12
Chinese boy, pl	10-12
Chinese girl, gt	18-20
Chinese boy, gt	18-20
Chinese girl, solid gold	30-35
Chinese boy, solid gold	30-35
237: Squirrel, pl	45-60
Squirrel, g/d	125
Squirrel, gt	100
Tumb bear, pl	45-60
Tumb bear, g/d	125
Tumb bear, gt	100
Puppy, pl	45-60
Puppy, g/d	125
Puppy, gt	100
Teddy bear, pl	45-60
Teddy bear, g/d	125
Pekingese, pl	45-60
Pekingese, g/d	125
Pekingese, g/d	125
Teddy bear, g/d	125
Squirrel, g/d	125
Rabbit, pl	50-60
Rabbit, gt	110
Deer, g/d	ND
238: Deer, pl	100
Lamb, pl	25-30
Lamb, gt	45-50
Terrier, pl	25-30
Terrier, gt	45-50
Gazelle, pl	45-50
Gazelle, gt	70-80
239: Swan	20-25
Sea horse	20-25
Dolphin	20-25
Snail, g/d	45-50
Snail, pl	30-35
240: Snail, pl	30-35
Turtle	30-35
Swan, high base	25-28
Dolphin, high base	25-28
Flower bouquet	25-30
241: Dolphin & rnd bowl	40-45
Dolphin & low bowl	40-45
Dolphin & flwr bowl	45-50
242: Elephant	55-65
Duck w/drum	55-65
243: Clown on drum	55-65

Mother Goose	65-75
Puppy	75-100
Rabbit eating corn	65-75
244: Deer, any but bl & pch	30-35
Deer, bl & pch	35-40
Black Moor, male	60-70
Black Moor, female	60-70
245: Native man	75-85
Native woman	75-85
Black native man	100+
Black native woman	100+
Harvest King	50-60
Ballerina	100+
246: Harvest King	50-60
Harvest Queen	50-60
Spanish dancers, ea	25-30
Emb. flwr wall lamp, ea	100-125
247: Ribbon & bow	30-35
Emb. flwrs	30-35
Bluebird	35-45
Victorian couple	40-50
Victorian man	25-30
Victorian woman	25-30
248: Oriental woman, each	45-50
Orient man/mandolin	30
Orient woman/mandolin	30
Oriental boy, sgl	18-20
Oriental girl, sgl	18-20
Oriental boy & girl, dbl	22-25
249: Oriental couple, dbl	30-35
Oriental man/mand	22-25
Oriental woman/mand	22-25
Stagecoach	40-45
Anchor, rope, stars	35-45
250: Snail mini	18-22
Grecian pitcher, flwrs	12-15
Star pitcher, flwrs	12-15
251: Photo, top left:	
All non-figural, each	8-12
Swan vase	12-15
Watering can, flwrs	12-15
Emb basket, flwrs	12-15
Tall leaf, label	12-15
Urn, label	12-15
Emb pitcher, flwrs	12-15
Jug w/bug, flwrs	12-15
252: Urn, flwrs	12-15
Vase, flwrs	12-15
Moon w/stars	12-15
Star pitcher	8-12
Emb loop hndl	8-12
Spinning wheel	12-15
Emb. flwrs/leaves	8-12
Feathered hndl	8-12
Scalloped top	8-12
Emb bud pitcher	8-12
Swirl bottom	8-12
253: Flat top dbl hndl	8-12
Fluted cornu	8-12
Ribbed ewer	8-12
Cornu, rect base	12-15
Short leaf	8-12
Tall leaf	8-12
Flower pot	12-15
254: Darn-Aide, ea	45-55
Incense burner, pl	60-70
Incense burner, gt	85-95
Kiln tester, each	15-18
Shaving mug	22-25
255: Pie bird, each	35-40
Toby mug, each	20-25
Emb. rib'd tumblers, ea	10-15
Medallion tankards, ea	40-50
256: Stars/stripes pitcher	30-40
Stars/strip goblet, ea	10-12
Jumbo ice server	125
Jumbo w/o gasket	90-100
257: Bird candy dish	25-30
Bon bon basket	15-18
Bon bon shell	15-18
Bon bon cornu	15-18
Oblong bon bon	8-10
Oval bon bon	8-10
258: Flying geese	20-25
Rib mixing bowl set	65-75
Spoon rest	15-20
Knwd brunch bowl	20-22
263: Tulip creamer	150+
Tulip ball jug	200+
Pauline's cannibal	ND

Little kerchief girl	ND
Rabbit eating corn	ND
265: Artique plaque, ea	8-10
Tile-blox, ea	10-15
266: Arrowhead ashtray	125-150
Arrowhead cig box, brn	250-275
Arrowhead cig box, wh	300-350
Cigarette box #682	30-40
Magnolia	15-20
267: Kashāni box/ashtrays	55-65
Confetti box/ashtrays	45-55
Squirrel, each	20-22
Fish #402, each	45-50
268: Maple leaf	8-12
Flying geese	20-25
Panther & paws set	75-85
Boomerang #300	10-12
Modern #301	10-12
Sombrero	20-25
269: All shown, each	8-12
270: Studio, set of 3, no box	20-25
Artique, set of 3, no box	20-25
Cameo	15-18
Riviera	20-25
Double #216	8-10
271: Coaster boxed set	65-75
Coaster ashtray only, ea	8-10
Flight #208	10-12
272: All shown (except listed):	8-12
Listed: Arrowhead #212	12-15
Shell #204	12-15
Decorator #206	12-15
273: Scottie	45-55
Cornucopia/bird	15-18
Cornu/butterfly	18-20
274: Star	25-30
Daffodil, each	25-30
Tropical fruit	25-30
Bird house	20-25
Sunflower	25-30
275: Red feather, each	35-40
Fluted, each	25-30
Wheat	25-30
Bow	15-20
Lovebirds/house	25-30
Grandfather clock	25-30
Mantel clock	25-30
Telephone	25-30
Mary & lamb	25-30
Jack Horner	25-30
Girl w/rag doll	25-30
276: Girl w/rag doll, gt	35-40
Lovebirds/house, gt	30-35
Mantel clock, gt	35-40
277: Cameo, each	10-15
278: Chantilly, each	10-20
279: Cherie, each	10-15
Confetti console set	35-45
Confetti Monte Carlo	35-45
Confetti cig box/ashtrays	45-55
Confetti remaining items	10-20
280: Diora, each	15-20
Elegance cone #1411	20-25
281: Elegance cone #1414	20-25
Elegance remaining pcs	10-15
Fairy Wood, each	10-15
282: Fernware, each	10-15
283: Kashāni, each	15-20
284: Kashāni vestal #3003, ea	35-45
Kashāni, any w/stand	35-45
Kashāni console set	35-45
Kashāni box/ashtrays	55-65
Kashāni remaining pcs	15-20
Liāna, each	10-15
285: Medallion rooster	75-95
Medallion pony	75-95
Medallion p-schooner	75-95
Medallion, non-figural	25-35
286: Medallion, non-figural	25-35
Pastel Medallion, each	15-20
287: Petit-Point, each	10-15
288: Stardust, each	10-20
Tiara, each	10-20
289: Touché, each	10-15

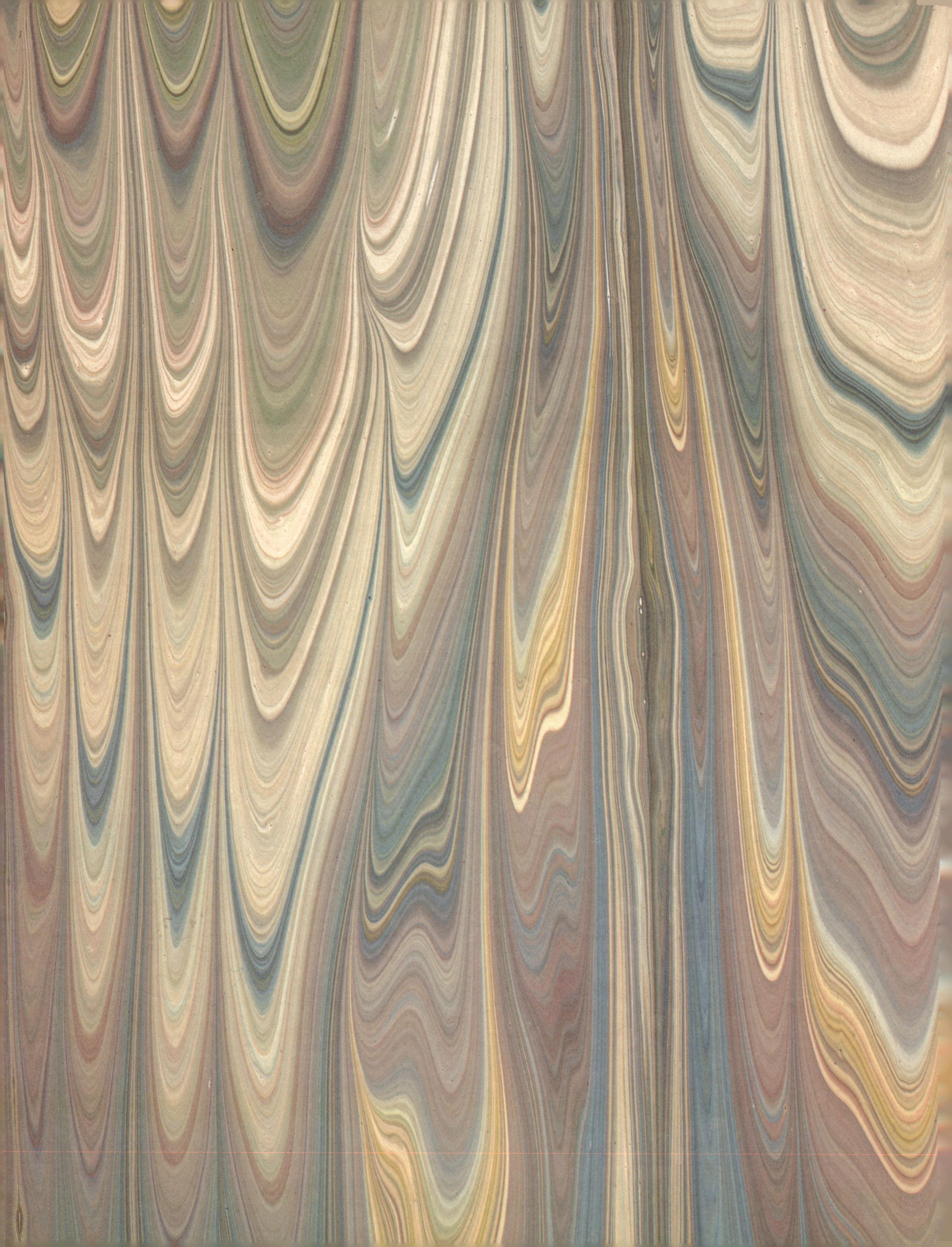